Looking towards a Church *fully reconciled*

The Final Report of the Anglican–Roman Catholic
International Commission 1983–2005 (ARCIC II)

Edited by Adelbert Denaux,
Nicholas Sagovsky &
Charles Sherlock

First published in Great Britain in 2016

Society for Promoting Christian Knowledge
36 Causton Street
London SW1P 4ST
www.spckpublishing.co.uk

British Library Cataloguing-in-Publication Data
A catalogue record for this book is available from the British Library

ISBN 978–028–107–779–3

Typeset by Graphicraft Ltd, Hong Kong
First printed in Great Britain by Ashford Colour Press
Subsequently digitally printed in Great Britain

Produced on paper from sustainable forests

Contents

Preface

By the Co-Chairs of ARCIC III

Looking towards a Church Fully Reconciled provides an accessible source for the five Agreed Statements of ARCIC II. It offers critical analyses of their contexts and of responses made, and resources 'to promote the reception of its previous work by presenting the previous work of ARCIC as a corpus' (from the mandate of ARCIC III). In fulfilling this task, ARCIC III has come to appreciate more fully its wider mandate, to explore 'the Church as Communion, local and universal, and how in communion the local and universal Church come to discern right ethical teaching'.

ARCIC I established a pattern of annual residential meetings for a week or more, with papers written in the interim, typically involving Sub-Commission meetings. This pattern continued with ARCIC II and III. At each meeting a daily eucharist is celebrated, Bible study is undertaken, and evening prayers are offered, alternating between the two traditions. The residential nature of the Commission's meetings makes for a high degree of understanding and trust being built up: this facilitates honesty and frank exchanges, as between friends unafraid to face differences. Further, alliances and faultlines often run across the Anglican–Roman Catholic boundary: a common bond exists between Scripture scholars, for example, while the joint pastoral insight of bishops on the Commission is significant.

The reality of our divisions since the Reformation remains a scandal, when we think of Christ's call to us to be one (*Ut unum sint*, Jn 17.21). We believe, however, that the redeeming grace of God is never withdrawn and that the reconciling movement of the Holy Spirit abounds all the more in the midst of our schism and woundedness.

As Anglicans and Roman Catholics we are called to witness to this grace-filled movement by reaching out to each other across the divide, by seeking increasing degrees of communion, and by creating partnerships in mission where we can. When this happens, there is a clear and strong witness to the world, which is itself riven with division and enmity.

Active Christian reconciliation can become a sign of hope in and for the world. This witnesses to the possibility of healing and bridge building, of the action of divine love in the conflicted realities of human life. We therefore pray that the work of ARCIC may be inspired by the

Spirit of God and so become a means of grace and a living parable of hope.

Continuing the journey which began with ARCIC I and continued to unfold in the work of ARCIC II, this book therefore seeks to look forward, anticipating what it will mean to live in a fully reconciled Church. Its authors trust that such reflection on the ARCIC heritage will serve the mission of God through the reconciled people of God, walking ever more closely together.

+ David Moxon
+ Bernard Longley
Pentecost 2016
The Sisterhood of St John the Divine, Toronto

The Status of this Volume

The book published here is the work of the Anglican–Roman Catholic International Commission (ARCIC). The authorities who appointed the Commission have allowed it to be published so that the Agreed Statements may be widely discussed. It is not an authoritative declaration by the Roman Catholic Church or by the Anglican Communion, who will study and evaluate the Agreed Statements in due course.

Three types of material are included, in fulfilment of ARCIC III's mandate 'to promote the reception of [the Commission's] previous work by presenting the work of ARCIC as a corpus, with appropriate introduction':

a. The five Agreed Statements issued by ARCIC II, presented in Part A. It is these which the Anglican Communion and the Roman Catholic Church are invited to receive.
b. Introductions for each Statement, together with a collation of responses (official, ecclesial, and scholarly) thus far made. ARCIC III has analysed these with a view to 'promote their reception' and identify further work that needs to be undertaken. This supplementary material in Part A, supported by bibliographies, is now presented for publication by the members of ARCIC III in fulfilment of its mandate.
c. Essays intended to support the reception of the work of ARCIC II 'as a corpus' (Parts B and C). The Commission asked the three members who had served on ARCIC II to prepare this material. Part B surveys theological themes which can be found throughout the corpus; Part C tells the ARCIC II story.

Abbreviations

ACC	Anglican Consultative Council
ARC Canada	Anglican–Roman Catholic Dialogue in Canada
ARCIC	Anglican–Roman Catholic International Commission
ARCUSA	Anglican–Roman Catholic Dialogue in the United States of America
AustARC	Australian Anglican–Roman Catholic Dialogue
CDF	Congregation for the Doctrine of the Faith
ECUSA	The Episcopal Church in the United States of America (now The Episcopal Church)
FOAG	Faith and Order Advisory Group of the Church of England
IARCCUM	International Anglican–Roman Catholic Commission on Unity and Mission
IASCER	Inter-Anglican Standing Commission on Ecumenical Relations
PCPCU	The Pontifical Council for Promoting Christian Unity (formerly SPCU)
SPCU	The Secretariat for Promoting Christian Unity (now PCPCU)
USCCB	United States Conference of Catholic Bishops
WCC	The World Council of Churches

Introduction

The Anglican–Roman Catholic International Commission (ARCIC) first met in January 1970. It was the outcome of the first official visit to Rome since the Reformation by an Archbishop of Canterbury. Pope Paul VI and Archbishop Michael Ramsey, in their Common Declaration of 24 March 1966, stated that they 'intend to inaugurate between the Roman Catholic Church and the Anglican Communion a serious dialogue which, founded on the Gospels and on the ancient common traditions, may lead to that unity in truth, for which Christ prayed'.[1] The Report of a Joint Preparatory Commission (*The Malta Report*), endorsed by the 1968 Lambeth Conference and by the Vatican Secretariat (now Pontifical Council) for Promoting Christian Unity (PCPCU), led to ARCIC's establishment a year later.

The Commission produced four Agreed Statements over twelve years of work: *Eucharistic Doctrine* (1971), *Ministry and Ordination* (1973), *Authority in the Church I* and *II* (1976, 1981), and *Elucidations on Eucharistic Doctrine* (1979) and *Elucidations on Ministry and Ordination* (1979). These were drawn together in *The Final Report*, issued in 1981, including an *Elucidation on Authority in the Church*. Official responses came from the Congregation for the Doctrine of the Faith (CDF) in 1982, the Lambeth Conference of 1988, and the Roman Catholic Church in 1991.[2]

ARCIC II was established in 1983, and continued until 2005. It was a particular fruit of the third Common Declaration, made in Canterbury on 29 May 1982 (the Eve of Pentecost) by Pope John Paul II and Archbishop Robert Runcie. Together they gave thanks to God for the work of the first ARCIC, and set out this mandate for ARCIC II:

> The new International Commission is to continue the work already begun; to examine, especially in the light of our respective judgements on The Final Report, the outstanding doctrinal differences which still separate us, with a view to their eventual resolution; to study all that hinders the mutual recognition of the ministries of our Communions, and to recommend what

---

[1] The texts of all the Common Declarations can be found in Appendix B.
[2] The text of *The Final Report* was republished, together with the responses listed, official comments, and expert opinion, in Christopher Hill and Edward Yarnold SJ (eds.), *Anglicans and Roman Catholics: The Search for Unity* (London: SPCK and CTS, 1994). Fr Yarnold was a Roman Catholic member of ARCIC I; Hill (now Bishop Hill) was the Anglican Co-Secretary of ARCIC I and II from 1974 to 1989, and is a member of ARCIC III.

practical steps will be necessary when, on the basis of our unity in faith, we are able to proceed to the restoration of full communion.

Archbishop Runcie and Pope John Paul II met again on 2 October 1989, and in a fourth Common Declaration committed the two traditions once more to 'the arduous journey to Christian unity', especially as represented in ARCIC's work. The difficult nature of this journey is recognized in the fifth Common Declaration, made on 5 December 1996 by Pope John Paul II and Archbishop George Carey, which notes 'the obstacle to reconciliation posed by the ordination of women'. Even so, this Declaration encouraged ARCIC II in its work, and led to a conference in 2000 at Mississauga, Toronto, of thirteen pairs of bishops from places across the globe where Anglican and Roman Catholic jurisdictions exist side by side. This conference led to the formation, a year later, of the International Anglican–Roman Catholic Commission on Unity and Mission (IARCCUM), whose aim is to facilitate the outcomes of ARCIC's work at the local level.

In 2007 IARCCUM issued an Agreed Statement, *Growing Together in Unity and Mission: Building on 40 Years of Anglican–Roman Catholic Dialogue* (London: SPCK). Its first part synthesizes the work of ARCIC I and ARCIC II under seven headings:

> Belief in God as Trinity;
> Church as Communion in Mission;
> The Living Word of God;
> Baptism, Eucharist, Ministry;
> Authority in the Church;
> Discipleship and Holiness; and
> the Blessed Virgin Mary.

The second part presents a series of practical proposals based upon this synthesis. The volume does not include ARCIC's Agreed Statements, however. The mandate of ARCIC III thus included the following request from Pope Benedict XVI and the Archbishop of Canterbury, Rowan Williams:

> We ask the Commission to promote the reception of its previous work by presenting the work of ARCIC as a corpus, with appropriate introduction.

To fulfil this request, ARCIC III established a working group of the three members who also served on ARCIC II—Adelbert Denaux, Nicholas Sagovsky, and Charles Sherlock—to have responsibility for this project. They have been assisted by other ARCIC III members in the task of gathering these Statements together, placing them in their context, assessing their reception, and setting out where further work needs to be undertaken. This volume represents the outcome of that task.

PART A

THE AGREED STATEMENTS
OF ARCIC II

Chapter 1

Salvation and the Church (1987)

Introducing the Statement

The Final Report brought to a close the first stage of ARCIC's work. The ecumenical optimism which accompanied its publication did not disguise, but rather amplified the recognition that more work needed to be done. In particular, significant numbers of Anglicans, not least from the evangelical tradition, argued that the agreements reached did not address the underlying theological issues on which the sixteenth-century breach of communion hinged. The 1981 Anglican Consultative Council meeting, noting the emerging agreement in Lutheran–Roman Catholic dialogue, thus requested that ARCIC take up 'justification by faith'. Conversely, several Roman Catholic responses asked for further exploration of the concept of Church as *koinonia* which undergirded *The Final Report*.

As noted earlier, ARCIC II was established as an outcome of the Third Common Declaration by the Archbishop of Canterbury (Robert Runcie) and Pope John Paul II.[1] The new Commission was mandated to explore remaining doctrinal differences, the mutual recognition of ministries, and practical steps towards unity. The new Commission's first meeting (1983) took as its theme 'The Church, Grace and Salvation': the doctrine of justification by faith was chosen as the focus of attention for a working group. The theme of the 1984 meeting was thus 'The Church, Salvation and the Doctrine of Justification'. Having reached agreement on the outline for a Statement, the drafting group prepared a text, 'The Church and Justification'. This would be the basis of the Agreed Statement, *Salvation and the Church*, adopted two years later.

In reading the text, it is important to appreciate that the inter-twining of ecclesiology and salvation around the presenting motif, 'justification by faith', was consciously intended from the beginning of ARCIC II's work. The choice of 'salvation' as the over-arching theme followed ARCIC's method of avoiding polemical language, and setting the dialogue in the

---

[1] For details of its meetings, see Part C below. Commission members are listed in Appendix A; the Common Declaration can be found in Appendix B3.

widest theological context. This theme is grounded in the name given by revelation to the Word incarnate, 'Jesus', meaning 'saviour' (Matthew 1.21, 25), and carries an 'all-embracing meaning' (§13). Further, ARCIC II situated its work in the context of ecclesiology in continuity with ARCIC I's focus on *koinonia*.

As regards justification itself, close attention was paid to the detailed work undertaken between Lutherans and Roman Catholics, especially in the USA. ARCIC II recognised from the beginning of its discussion that divergences between Anglicans and Roman Catholics on this issue were much less than between Roman Catholics and Lutherans: rather, the differences were in how justification is lived out—a further reason for taking 'salvation' as the core issue.[2]

---

[2] The focus of Articles XI–XIV and the Homilies listed in Article XXX is less on whether 'justification by faith only' is right, but that it is 'a most wholesome Doctrine, and very full of comfort' (i.e. strengthening). The focus is in what sense 'good works' are necessary—not as contributing to justification in any way, but as its proper fruit.

SALVATION AND THE CHURCH

An Agreed Statement by the Anglican–Roman
Catholic International Commission (ARCIC II)

CONTENTS

THE STATUS OF THE DOCUMENT

The document published here is the work of the Second Anglican–Roman Catholic International Commission (ARCIC II). It is simply a joint statement of the Commission. The authorities who appointed the Commission have allowed the statement to be published so that it may be discussed and improved by the suggestions received. It is not an authoritative declaration by the Roman Catholic Church or by the Anglican Communion, who will evaluate the document in order to take a position on it in due time.

The Commission will be glad to receive observations and criticisms made in a constructive and fraternal spirit. Its work is done to serve the progress of the two communions towards unity. It will give responsible attention to every serious comment which is likely to help in improving or completing the result so far achieved. This wider collaboration will make its work to a greater degree work in common, and by God's grace 'will lead us to the full unity to which he calls us' (*Common Declaration* of Pope John Paul II and the Archbishop of Canterbury, Pentecost 1982).

PREFACE

By the Co-Chairmen

The 29th of May 1982, the Eve of the Feast of Pentecost, was a day of great significance for the Anglican and Roman Catholic Churches on their path towards unity. In the footsteps of St Augustine of Canterbury whom his predecessor Pope Gregory the Great had sent from Rome to convert the English, Pope John Paul II visited Canterbury. There, in the church founded by Augustine, he and the present Archbishop of Canterbury, Dr Robert Runcie, along with representatives of the English churches and of the whole Anglican Communion, proclaimed and celebrated the one baptismal faith which we all share. The Pope and the Archbishop also gave thanks to God for the work of the first Anglican–Roman Catholic International Commission (ARCIC I) whose *The Final Report* had just been published, and agreed to the establishment of a new commission (ARCIC II) to continue its work.

The primary task of ARCIC II is to examine and try to resolve those doctrinal differences which still divide us. Accordingly, at the request of the Anglican Consultative Council (Newcastle, September 1981), we have addressed ourselves to the doctrine of justification, which at the time of the Reformation was a particular cause of contention. This request sprang out of a widespread view that the subject of justification and salvation is so central to the Christian faith that, unless there is assurance of agreement on this issue, there can be no full doctrinal agreement on this issue, there can be no full doctrinal agreement between our two Churches.

We have spent more than three years on this task. The doctrine of justification raises issues of great complexity and profound mystery. Furthermore it can be properly treated only within the wider context of the doctrine of salvation as a whole. This in turn has involved discussion of the role of the Church in Christ's saving work. Hence the title of our agreed statement: *Salvation and the Church*. We do not claim to have composed a complete treatment of the doctrine of the Church. Our discussion is limited to its role in salvation.

In our work, particularly on the doctrine of justification as such, we have been greatly helped by the statement *Justification by Faith* agreed in 1983 by the Lutheran–Roman Catholic Consultation in the USA (Augsburg

9

Publishing House, Minneapolis 1985). This illustrates the interdependence of all ecumenical dialogues—an interdependence which is an expression of the growing communion which already exists between the churches. For the search for unity is indivisible.

A question not discussed by the Commission, though of great contemporary importance, is that of the salvation of those who have no explicit faith in Christ. This has not been a matter of historical dispute between us. Our ancestors, though divided in Christian faith, shared a world in which the questions posed by people of other faiths, or none, could scarcely arise in their modern form. Today this is a matter for theological study in both our Communions.

Although our first concern has been to state our common faith on the issues in the doctrine of salvation which have proved problematic in the past, we believe that the world, now as much as ever, stands in need of the Gospel of God's free grace. Part of the challenge to Christians is this: how can we bear true witness to the good news of a God who accepts us, unless we can accept one another?

The purpose of our dialogue is the restoration of full ecclesial communion between us. Our work has recalled for us still wider perspectives—not only the unity of all Christian people but the fulfilment of all things in Christ.

We trust that God who has begun this good work in us will bring it to completion in Christ Jesus our Lord.

+ Cormac Murphy-O'Connor
+ Mark Santer

Llandaff, 3 September 1986
Feast of St Gregory the Great

SALVATION AND THE CHURCH

Introduction

1. The will of God, Father, Son and Holy Spirit, is to reconcile to himself all that he has created and sustains, to set free the creation from its bondage to decay, and to draw all humanity into communion with himself. Though we, his creatures, turn away from him through sin, God continues to call us and opens up for us the way to find him anew. To bring us to union with himself, the Father sent into the world Jesus Christ, his only Son, in whom all things were created. He is the image of the invisible God; he took flesh so that we in turn might share the divine nature and so reflect the glory of God. Through Christ's life, death and resurrection, the mystery of God's love is revealed, we are saved from the powers of evil, sin and death, and we receive a share in the life of God. All this is pure unmerited gift. The Spirit of God is poured into the hearts of believers—the Spirit of adoption, who makes us sons and daughters of God. The Spirit unites us with Christ and, in Christ, with all those who by faith are one with him. Through baptism we are united with Christ in his death and resurrection, we are by the power of the Spirit made members of one body, and together we participate in the life of God. This fellowship in one body, sustained through Word and Sacrament, is in the New Testament called *koinonia* (communion). '*Koinonia* with one another is entailed by our *koinonia* with God in Christ. This is the mystery of the Church' (ARCIC I *The Final Report*, Introduction 5). The community of believers, united with Christ, gives praise and thanksgiving to God, celebrating the grace of Christ as they await his return in glory, when he will be all in all and will deliver to the Father a holy people. In the present age the Church is called to be a sign to the world of God's will for the healing and re-creation of the whole human race in Jesus Christ. As the Church proclaims the good news which it has received, the heart of its message must be salvation through the grace of God in Christ.

2. The doctrine of salvation has in the past been a cause of some contention between Anglicans and Roman Catholics. Disagreements, focusing on the doctrine of justification, were already apparent in the

Church of the later Middle Ages. In the sixteenth century these became a central matter of dispute between Roman Catholics and continental Reformers. Though the matter played a less crucial role in the English Reformation, the Church of England substantially adopted the principles expressed in the moderate Lutheran formulations of the Augsburg and Württemberg Confessions. The Decree on Justification of the Council of Trent was not directed against the Anglican formularies, which had not yet been compiled. Anglican theologians reacted to the decree in a variety of ways, some sympathetic, others critical at least on particular points.[1] Nevertheless in the course of time Anglicans have widely come to understand that decree as a repudiation of their position. Since the sixteenth century, various debates on the doctrine of justification and on related issues (such as predestination, original sin, good works, sanctification) have been pursued within each of our Communions.

3. In the area of the doctrine of salvation, including justification, there was much agreement. Above all it was agreed that the act of God in bringing salvation to the human race and summoning individuals into a community to serve him is due solely to the mercy and grace of God, mediated and manifested through Jesus Christ in his ministry, atoning death and rising again. It was also no matter of dispute that God's grace evokes an authentic human response of faith which takes effect not only in the life of the individual but also in the corporate life of the Church. The difficulties arose in explaining how divine grace related to human response, and these difficulties were compounded by a framework of discussion that concentrated too narrowly upon the individual.

4. *One* difficulty concerned the understanding of the *faith* through which we are justified, in so far as this included the individual's confidence

---

[1] The Council of Trent's Decree on Justification was issued after seven months' work on 13 January 1547 and should be read as a whole. It is printed in Denzinger-Schönmetzer, *Enchiridion Symbolorum Definitionum et Declarationum* (=DS) (Herder, Freiburg 1965), DS 1520–1583. English translation in H. Schroeder (ed.), *The Canons and Decrees of the Council of Trent* (Tan Books and Publishers, USA, 1978); extracts in J. Neuner and J. Dupuis (edd.), *The Christian Faith in the Doctrinal Documents of the Catholic Church* (Collins, 1983) Nos. 1924–83. The principal documents and authors for Anglican consideration of the subject in the period before 1661 are the Thirty-nine Articles (1571); Cranmer's Homily '*Of Salvation*' (1547), to which Article 11 refers; Richard Hooker's *Learned Discourse of Justification* (1586); Richard Field, *Of the Church*, III Appendix, chapter 11 (1606); John Davenant, *Disputatio de Iustitia habituali et actuali* (1631, translated by Allport, 1844 as *Treatise on Justification*); William Forbes, *Considerationes Modestae et Pacificae* I (posthumously published 1658, translated 1850 as *Calm Considerations*).

in his or her own final salvation. Everyone agreed that confidence in God was a mark of Christian hope, but some feared that too extreme an emphasis on assurance, when linked with an absolute doctrine of divine predestination, encouraged a neglect of the need for justification to issue in holiness of life. Catholics thought that this Protestant understanding of assurance confused faith with a subjective state and would actually have the effect of undermining hope in God. Protestants suspected that Catholics, lacking confidence in the sufficiency of Christ's work and relying overmuch on human efforts, had lapsed either into a kind of scrupulosity or into a mere legalism and so lost Christian hope and assurance.

5. A *second* difficulty concerned the understanding of *justification* and the associated concepts, righteousness and justice. Fearing that justification might seem to depend upon entitlement arising from good works, Reformation theologians laid great emphasis on the imputation to human beings of the righteousness of Christ. By this they meant that God declared the unrighteous to be accepted by him on account of the obedience of Christ and the merits of his passion. Catholics took them to be implying that imputed righteousness was a legal fiction, that is, a merely nominal righteousness that remained only external to the believer. They objected that this left the essential sinfulness of the individual unchanged, and excluded the imparted, or habitual and actual, righteousness created in the inner being of the regenerate person by the indwelling Spirit. Anglican theologians of the sixteenth and seventeenth centuries saw imputed and imparted righteousness as distinct to the mind, but indissoluble in worship and life. They also believed that, while we are made truly righteous because we are forgiven, we know ourselves to be in continuing need of forgiveness.

6. A *third* difficulty concerned the bearing of *good works* on salvation. Reformation theologians understood the Catholic emphasis on the value of good works and religious practices and ceremonies to imply that justification in some degree depended upon them in such a way as to compromise the sovereignty and unconditional freedom of God's grace. Catholics, on the other hand, saw the Reformation's understanding of justification as implying that human actions were of no worth in the sight of God. This, in their judgement, led to the negation of human freedom and responsibility, and to the denial that works, even when supernaturally inspired, deserved any reward. The Anglican theologians of the Reformation age, taking 'by faith alone'

to mean 'only for the merit of Christ', also held good works to be not irrelevant to salvation, but imperfect and therefore inadequate. They saw good works as a necessary demonstration of faith, and faith itself as inseparable from hope and love.

7. Although the sixteenth century disagreements centred mainly on the relationship of faith, righteousness and good works to the salvation of the individual, the role of the Church in the process of salvation constituted a fourth difficulty. As well as believing that Catholics did not acknowledge the true authority of Scripture over the Church, Protestants also felt that Catholic teaching and practice had interpreted the mediatorial *role of the Church* in such a way as to derogate from the place of Christ as 'sole mediator between God and man' (1 Tim 2.5). Catholics believed that Protestants were abandoning or at least devaluing the Church's ministry and sacraments, which were divinely appointed means of grace; also that they were rejecting its divinely given authority as guardian and interpreter of the revealed Word of God.

8. The break in communion between Anglicans and Roman Catholics encouraged each side to produce caricatures of the other's beliefs. There were also extremists on both sides whose words and actions seemed to confirm the anxieties of their opponents.

   The renewal of biblical scholarship, the development of historical and theological studies, new insights gained in mission, and the growth of mutual understanding within the ecumenical movement enable us to see our divisions in a new perspective. We have explored our common faith in the light of these shared experiences and are able in what follows to affirm that the four areas of difficulty outlined above need not be matters of dispute between us.

Salvation and Faith

9. When we confess that Jesus Christ is Lord, we praise and glorify God the Father, whose purpose for creation and salvation is realised in the Son, whom he sent to redeem us and to prepare a people for himself by the indwelling of the Holy Spirit. This wholly unmerited love of God for his creatures is expressed in the language of grace, which embraces not only the once-for-all death and resurrection of Christ, but also God's continuing work on our behalf. The Holy Spirit makes the fruits of Christ's sacrifice actual within the Church through Word and Sacrament: our sins are forgiven, we are enabled to

respond to God's love, and we are conformed to the image of Christ. The human response to God's initiative is itself a gift of grace, and is at the same time a truly human, personal response. It is through grace that God's new creation is realised. Salvation is the gift of grace; it is by faith that it is appropriated.

10. The gracious action of God in Christ is revealed to us in the Gospel. The Gospel, by proclaiming Christ's definitive atoning work, the gift and pledge of the Holy Spirit to every believer, and the certainty of God's promise of eternal life, calls Christians to faith in the mercy of God and brings them assurance of salvation. It is God's gracious will that we, as his children, called through the Gospel and sharing in the means of grace, should be confident that the gift of eternal life is assured to each of us. Our response to this gift must come from our whole being. Faith, therefore, not only includes an assent to the truth of the Gospel but also involves commitment of our will to God in repentance and obedience to his call; otherwise faith is dead (Jas 2.17). Living faith is inseparable from love, issues in good works, and grows deeper in the course of a life of holiness. Christian assurance does not in any way remove from Christians the responsibility of working out their salvation with fear and trembling (Phil 2.12–13).

11. Christian assurance is not presumptuous. It is always founded upon God's unfailing faithfulness and not upon the measure of our response. God gives to the faithful all that is needed for their salvation. This is to believers a matter of absolute certitude. The word of Christ and his sacraments give us this assurance. Throughout the Christian tradition there runs the certainty of the infinite mercy of God, who gave his Son for us. However grave our sins may be, we are sure that God is always ready to forgive those who truly repent. For the baptized and justified may still sin. The New Testament contains warnings against presumption (e.g. Col 1.22 ff; Heb 10.36 ff). Christians may never presume on their perseverance but should live their lives with a sure confidence in God's grace. Because of what God has revealed of his ultimate purpose in Christ Jesus, living faith is inseparable from hope.

Salvation and Justification

12. In baptism, the 'sacrament of faith' (cf. Augustine *Ep.* 98, 9), together with the whole Church, we confess Christ, enter into communion

15

with him in his death and resurrection, and through the gift of the Holy Spirit are delivered from our sinfulness and raised to new life. The Scriptures speak of this salvation in many ways. They tell of God's eternal will fulfilled in Christ's sacrifice on the cross, his decisive act in overcoming the power of evil and reconciling sinners who believe. They also speak of the abiding presence and action of the Holy Spirit in the Church, of his present gifts of grace, and of our continuing life and growth in this grace as we are transformed into the likeness of Christ. They also speak of our entry with all the saints into our eternal inheritance, of our vision of God face to face, and of our participation in the joy of the final resurrection.

13. In order to describe salvation in all its fullness, the New Testament employs a wide variety of language. Some terms are of more fundamental importance than others: but there is no controlling term or concept; they complement one another. The concept of salvation has the all-embracing meaning of the deliverance of human beings from evil and their establishment in that fullness of life which is God's will for them (e.g. Lk 1.77; John 3.16–17; cf. John 10.10). The idea of reconciliation and forgiveness stresses the restoration of broken relationships (e.g. 2 Cor 5.18 ff; Eph 2.13–18). The language of expiation or propitiation (*hilasterion* etc.), drawn from the context of sacrifice, denotes the putting away of sin and the reestablishment of right relationship with God (e.g. Rm 3.25; Heb 2.17; 1 John 2.2, 4.10). To speak of redemption or liberation is to talk of rescue from bondage so as to become God's own possession, and of freedom bought for a price (e.g. Mk 10.45; Eph 1.7; 1 Pet 1.18 ff). The notion of adoption refers to our new identity as children of God (e.g. Rm 8.15–17, 23; Gal 4.4 ff). Terms like regeneration, rebirth and new creation speak of God's work of re-creation and the beginning of new life (e.g. John 3.3; 2 Cor 5.17; 1 Pet 1.23). The theme of sanctification underlines the fact that God has made us his own and calls us to holiness of life (e.g. John 17.15ff; Eph 4.25 ff; 1 Pet 1.15 ff). The concept of justification relates to the removal of condemnation and to a new standing in the eyes of God (e.g. Rm 3.22 ff, 4.5, 5.1 ff; Acts 13.39). Salvation in all these aspects comes to each believer as he or she is incorporated into the believing community.

14. Roman Catholic interpreters of Trent and Anglican theologians alike have insisted that justification and sanctification are neither wholly distinct from nor unrelated to one another. The discussion, however,

has been confused by differing understandings of the word justification and its associated words. The theologians of the Reformation tended to follow the predominant usage of the New Testament, in which the verb *dikaioun* usually means 'to pronounce righteous'. The Catholic theologians, and notably the Council of Trent, tended to follow the usage of patristic and medieval Latin writers, for whom *justificare* (the traditional translation of *dikaioun*) signified 'to make righteous'. Thus the Catholic understanding of the process of justification, following Latin usage, tended to include elements of salvation which the Reformers would describe as belonging to sanctification rather than justification. As a consequence, Protestants took Catholics to be emphasising sanctification in such a way that absolute gratuitousness of salvation was threatened. On the other side, Catholics feared that Protestants were so stressing the justifying action of God that sanctification and human responsibility were gravely depreciated.

15. Justification and sanctification are two aspects of the same divine act (1 Cor 6.11). This does not mean that justification is a reward for faith or works: rather, when God promises the removal of our condemnation and gives us a new standing before him, this justification is indissolubly linked with his sanctifying recreation of us in grace. This transformation is being worked out in the course of our pilgrimage, despite the imperfections and ambiguities of our lives. God's grace effects what he declares: his creative word imparts what it imputes. By pronouncing us righteous, God also makes us righteous. He imparts a righteousness which is his and becomes ours.[2]

16. God's declaration that we are accepted because of Christ together with his gift of continual renewal by the indwelling Spirit is the pledge and first instalment of the final consummation and the ground of the believer's hope. In the life of the Church, the finality of God's declaration and the continuing movement towards our ultimate goal are reflected in the relation between baptism and the eucharist. Baptism is the unrepeatable sacrament of justification and incorporation into Christ (1 Cor 6.11; 12.12–13; Gal 3.27). The eucharist is the

---

[2] For Richard Hooker, 'we participate Christ partly by imputation, as when those things which he did and suffered for us are imputed unto us for righteousness; partly by habitual and real infusion, as when grace is inwardly bestowed while we are on earth, and afterwards more fully both our souls and bodies made like unto his in glory'. *Laws of Ecclesiastical Polity*, V. lvi. 11.

repeated sacrament by which the life of Christ's body is constituted and renewed, when the death of Christ is proclaimed until he comes again (1 Cor 11.26).

17. Sanctification is that work of God which actualises in believers the righteousness and holiness without which no one may see the Lord. It involves the restoring and perfecting in humanity of the likeness of God marred by sin. We grow into conformity with Christ, the perfect image of God, until he appears and we shall be like him. The law of Christ has become the pattern of our life. We are enabled to produce works which are the fruit of the Holy Spirit. Thus the righteousness of God our Saviour is not only declared in a judgement made by God in favour of sinners, but is also bestowed as a gift to make them righteous. Even though our acceptance of this gift will be imperfect in this life, Scripture speaks of the righteousness of believers as already effected by God through Christ: 'he raised us up with him and seated us with him in the heavenly realms in Christ Jesus' (Eph 2.6).

18. The term justification speaks of a divine declaration of acquittal, of the love of God manifested to an alienated and lost humanity prior to any entitlement on our part. Through the life, death and resurrection of Christ, God declares that we are forgiven, accepted and reconciled to him. Instead of our own strivings to make ourselves acceptable to God, Christ's perfect righteousness is reckoned to our account. God's declaration is sometimes expressed in the New Testament in the language of law, as a verdict of acquittal of the sinner. The divine court, where the verdict is given, is the court of the judge who is also Father and Saviour of those whom he judges. While in a human law court an acquittal is an external, even impersonal act, God's declaration of forgiveness and reconciliation does not leave repentant believers unchanged but establishes with them an intimate and personal relationship. The remission of sins is accompanied by a present renewal, the rebirth to newness of life. Thus the juridical aspect of justification, while expressing an important facet of the truth, is not the exclusive notion in the light of which all other biblical ideas and images of salvation must be interpreted. For God sanctifies as well as acquits us. He is not only the judge who passes a verdict in our favour, but also the Father who gave his only Son to do for us what we could not do for ourselves. By virtue of Christ's life and self-oblation on the cross we are able with him to say through the Holy Spirit, 'Abba, Father' (Rom 8.15; Gal 4.6).

Salvation and Good Works

19. As justification and sanctification are aspects of the same divine act, so also living faith and love are inseparable in the believer. Faith is no merely private and interior disposition, but by its very nature is acted out: good works necessarily spring from a living faith (Jas 2.17 ff). They are truly good because, as the fruit of the Spirit, they are done in God, in dependence on God's grace.

   The person and work of Christ are central to any understanding of the relation between salvation and good works. God has brought into being in the person of his Son a renewed humanity, the humanity of Jesus Christ himself, the 'last Adam' or 'second man' (cf. 1 Cor 15.45, 47). He is the firstborn of all creation, the prototype and source of our new humanity. Salvation involves participating in that humanity, so as to live the human life now as God has refashioned it in Christ (cf. Col 3.10). This understanding of our humanity as made new in Christ by God's transforming power throws light on the New Testament affirmation that, while we are not saved because of works, we are created in Christ for good works (Eph 2.8 ff). 'Not because of works': nothing even of our best achievement or good will can give us any claim to God's gift of renewed humanity. God's recreating deed originates in himself and nowhere else. 'For good works': good works are the fruit of the freedom God has given us in his Son. In restoring us to his likeness, God confers freedom on fallen humanity. This is not the natural freedom to choose between alternatives, but the freedom to do his will: 'the law of the Spirit of life in Christ Jesus has set me free from the law of sin and death . . . in order that the just requirement of the law might be fulfilled in us' (Rom 8.2, 4). We are freed and enabled to keep the commandments of God by the power of the Holy Spirit, to live faithfully as God's people and to grow in love within the discipline of the community, bringing forth the fruit of the Spirit.[3]

   Inasmuch as we are recreated in his 'own image and likeness', God involves us in what he freely does to realise our salvation (Phil 2.12 ff). In the words of Augustine: 'The God who made you without you, without you does not make you just' (Sermons 169,13). Thus

---

[3] Cf. Article 10 of the Thirty-nine Articles: 'we have no power to do good works pleasant and acceptable to God, without the grace of God by Christ preventing us, that we may have a good will, and working with us (*cooperante*), when we have that good will'. This echoes Augustine's language about 'prevenient' and 'co-operating' grace (*De Gratia et libero arbitrio* 17, 33).

from the divine work follows the human work: it is we who live and act in a fully human way, yet never on our own or in a self-sufficient independence. This fully human life is possible if we live in the freedom and activity of Christ who, in the words of St Paul, 'lives in me' (Gal 2.20).

20. To speak thus of freedom in Christ is to stress that it is in Jesus Christ that the shape of human life lived in total liberty before God is decisively disclosed. Our liberation commits us to an order of social existence in which the individual finds fulfilment in relationship with others. Thus freedom in Christ does not imply an isolated life, but rather one lived in a community governed by mutual obligations. Life in Christ sets us free from the demonic forces manifested not only in individual but also in social egotism.

21. The growth of believers to maturity, and indeed the common life of the Church, are impaired by repeated lapses into sin. Even good works, done in God and under the grace of the Spirit, can be flawed by human weakness and self-centredness, and therefore it is by daily repentance and faith that we reappropriate our freedom from sin. This insight has sometimes been expressed by the paradox that we are at once just and sinners.[4]

22. The believer's pilgrimage of faith is lived out with the mutual support of all the people of God. In Christ all the faithful, both living and departed, are bound together in a communion of prayer. The Church is entrusted by the Lord with authority to pronounce forgiveness in his name to those who have fallen into sin and repent. The Church may also help them to a deeper realisation of the mercy of God by asking for practical amends for what has been done amiss. Such penitential disciplines, and other devotional practices, are not in any way intended to put God under obligation. Rather, they provide a form in which one may more fully embrace the free mercy of God.

23. The works of the righteous performed in Christian freedom and in the love of God which the Holy Spirit gives us are the object of God's commendation and receive his reward (Mt 6.4; 2 Tim 4.8; Heb 10.35, 11.6). In accordance with God's promise, those who have responded to the grace of God and consequently borne fruit for the kingdom

---

[4] *Simul iustus et peccator* is a Lutheran not a characteristically Anglican expression. It does not appear in Trent's Decree on Justification. The Second Vatican Council (*Lumen Gentium* 8) speaks of the Church as 'holy and at the same time always in need of purification' (*sancta simul et semper purificanda*). The paradox is ultimately of Augustinian inspiration (cf. *En. in Ps.* 140, 14f and *Ep.* 185, 40).

will be granted a place in that kingdom when it comes at Christ's appearing. They will be one with the society of the redeemed in rejoicing in the vision of God. This reward is a gift depending wholly on divine grace. It is in this perspective that the language of 'merit'[5] must be understood, so that we can say with Augustine: 'When God crowns our merits it is his own gifts that he crowns' (*Ep.* 194, 5.19). Christians rest their confidence for salvation on the power, mercy and loving-kindness of God and pray that the good work which God has begun he will in grace complete. They do not trust in their own merits but in Christ's. God is true to his promise to 'render to everyone according to his works' (Rom 2.6); yet when we have done all that is commanded we must still say: 'We are unprofitable servants, we have only done our duty' (Luke 17.10).

24. The language of merit and good works, therefore, when properly understood, in no way implies that human beings, once justified, are able to put God in their debt. Still less does it imply that justification itself is anything but a totally unmerited gift. Even the very first movements which lead to justification, such as repentance, the desire for forgiveness and even faith itself, are the work of God as he touches our hearts by the illumination of the Holy Spirit.

The Church and Salvation

25. The doctrine of salvation is intimately associated with the doctrine of the Church, which 'is the community of those reconciled with God and with each other because it is the community of those who believe in Jesus Christ and are justified through God's grace' (ARCIC I, *The Final Report*, Introduction 8). The Church proclaims the good news of our justification and salvation by God in Christ Jesus. Those who respond in faith to the Gospel come to the way of salvation through incorporation by baptism into the Church. They are called to witness to the Gospel as members of the Church.

26. The Church is itself a *sign* of the Gospel, for its vocation is to embody and reveal the redemptive power contained within the Gospel. What Christ achieved through his cross and resurrection is communicated

---

[5] Misunderstanding has been caused by the fact that the Latin *mereor* has a range of meanings, from 'deserve' to 'be granted' and 'obtain'. This range is reflected in patristic and mediaeval Christian Latin usage. By 'merit' the Council of Trent (DS 1545) did not mean the exact equality between achievement and reward, except in the case of Christ, but the value of goodness, as being, in the divine liberality, pleasing to God who is not so unjust as to overlook this work and love of the justified (Heb 6.10).

by the Holy Spirit in the life of the Church. In its life the Church signifies God's gracious purpose for his creation and his power to realise this purpose for sinful humanity. It is thus a sign and foretaste of God's kingdom. In fulfilling this vocation the Church is called to follow the way of Jesus Christ, who being the image of the Father took the form of a servant and was made perfect by suffering. When for Christ's sake the Church encounters opposition and persecution, it is then a sign of God's choice of the way of the cross to save the world.

27. This once-for-all atoning work of Christ, realised and experienced in the life of the Church and celebrated in the eucharist, constitutes the free gift of God which is proclaimed in the Gospel. In the service of this mystery the Church is entrusted with a responsibility of *stewardship*. The Church is called to fulfil this stewardship by proclaiming the Gospel and by its sacramental and pastoral life. The Church is required to carry out this task in such a way that the Gospel may be heard as good news in differing ages and cultures, while at the same time seeking neither to alter its content nor minimise its demands. For the Church is servant and not master of what it has received. Indeed, its power to affect the hearer comes not from our unaided efforts but entirely from the Holy Spirit, who is the source of the Church's life and who enables it to be truly the steward of God's design.

28. The Church is also an *instrument* for the realisation of God's eternal design, the salvation of humanity. While we recognise that the Holy Spirit acts outside the community of Christians, nevertheless it is within the Church, where the Holy Spirit gives and nurtures the new life of the kingdom, that the Gospel becomes a manifest reality. As this instrument, the Church is called to be a living expression of the Gospel, evangelised and evangelising, reconciled and reconciling, gathered together and gathering others. In its ministry to the world the Church seeks to share with all people the grace by which its own life is created and sustained.

29. The Church is therefore called to be, and by the power of the Spirit actually is, a *sign*, *steward* and *instrument* of God's design. For this reason it can be described as sacrament of God's saving work. However, the credibility of the Church's witness is undermined by the sins of its members, the shortcomings of its human institutions, and not least by the scandal of division. The Church is in constant need of repentance and renewal so that it can be more clearly seen for what it is: the one, holy body of Christ. Nevertheless the Gospel

contains the promise that despite all failures the Church will be used by God in the achievement of his purpose: to draw humanity into communion with himself and with one another, so as to share his life, the life of the Holy Trinity.

30. The Church which in this world is always in need of renewal and purification, is already here and now a foretaste of God's kingdom in a world still awaiting its consummation—a world full of suffering and injustice, division and strife. Thus Paul speaks of a fellowship which is called to transcend the seemingly insuperable divisions of the world; where all, because of their equal standing before the Lord, must be equally accepted by one another; a fellowship where, since all are justified by the grace of God, all may learn to do justice to one another; where racial, ethnic, social, sexual and other distinctions no longer cause discrimination and alienation (Gal 3.28). Those who are justified by grace, and who are sustained in the life of Christ through Word and Sacrament, are liberated from self-centredness and thus empowered to act freely and live at peace with God and with one another. The Church, as the community of the justified, is called to embody the good news that forgiveness is a gift to be received from God and shared with others (Matt 6.14–15). Thus the message of the Church is not a private pietism irrelevant to contemporary society, nor can it be reduced to a political or social programme. Only a reconciled and reconciling community, faithful to its Lord, in which human divisions are being overcome, can speak with full integrity to an alienated, divided world, and so be a credible witness to God's saving action in Christ and a foretaste of God's kingdom. Yet, until the kingdom is realised in its fullness, the Church is marked by human limitation and imperfection. It is the beginning and not yet the end, the firstfruits and not yet the final harvest.

31. The source of the Church's hope for the world is God, who has never abandoned the created order and has never ceased to work within it. It is called, empowered, and sent by God to proclaim this hope and to communicate to the world the conviction on which this hope is founded. Thus the Church participates in Christ's mission to the world through the proclamation of the Gospel of salvation by its words and deeds. It is called to affirm the sacredness and dignity of the person, the value of natural and political communities and the divine purpose for the human race as a whole; to witness against the structures of sin in society, addressing humanity with the Gospel of repentance and forgiveness and making intercession for the world,

it is called to be an agent of justice and compassion, challenging and assisting society's attempts to achieve just judgement, never forgetting that in the light of God's justice all human solutions are provisional. While the Church pursues its mission and pilgrimage in the world, it looks forward to 'the end, when Christ delivers the kingdom to God the Father after destroying every rule and every authority and power' (1 Cor 15.24).

Conclusion

32. The balance and coherence of the constitutive elements of the Christian doctrine of salvation had become partially obscured in the course of history and controversy. In our work we have tried to rediscover that balance and coherence and to express it together. We are agreed that this is not an area where any remaining differences of theological interpretation or ecclesiological emphasis, either within or between our Communions, can justify our continuing separation. We believe that our two Communions are agreed on the essential aspects of the doctrine of salvation and on the Church's role within it. We have also realised the central meaning and profound significance which the message of justification and sanctification, within the whole doctrine of salvation, continues to have for us today. We offer our agreement to our two Communions as a contribution to reconciliation between us, so that together we may witness to God's salvation in the midst of the anxieties, struggles and hopes of our world.

Responses

Responses have come in a variety of forms, from both Anglican and Roman Catholic sources. In the wake of ARCIC's *The Final Report*, Roman Catholic authorities decided that for future Agreed Statements, an official commentary would be issued at the same time. The first of these, by Donato Valentini SDB, was included immediately following the Statement in the *Information Service* bulletin of the Pontifical Council for Promoting Christian Unity (PCPCU).[1]

Official Roman Catholic Commentary

Valentini's 'Contribution' thus constitutes the first response to *Salvation and the Church*. Having introduced its preparation, scope, and contents, he assesses the Statement as 'balanced and coherent'. In a detailed Evaluation, he pays particular attention to the Commission's method, noting that it focuses on essentials, uses a deductive rather than inductive approach (in contrast with ARCIC I), shows a 'critical distancing' from the past while taking historic formulations seriously, is sensitive to the new contexts arising from biblical and theological study, and is logical in form. Three aspects of the Statement are seen as particularly positive: the use of language ('the statement is wideawake to [its] methodological value'); the grounding of ecclesiology in the model of Trinitarian communion; and the emphasis on the missionary dimension of the Church, understood as sign, instrument, steward, and foretaste of the kingdom of God. Valentini concludes by writing,

> With this text another great step has been taken towards the union of the two Churches ... Some further clarifications would improve the statement and make it even more reliable and transparent. I am persuaded none the less that, from a Roman Catholic point of view, an 'agreement' has been reached on the chief essential aspects of the subject. What has been achieved in this statement leaves no further ground for division on this topic between the Anglican Communion ... and the Roman Catholic Church.[2]

This initial response, however, and many others, was made prior to the publication of the *Joint Declaration on the Doctrine of Justification*

---

[1] Donato Valentini SDB, 'A Contribution to the Reading of the ARCIC II Statement on *Salvation and the Church*', *Information Service*, 63 (1987), 41–53. This and other Commentaries on ARCIC II Statements were not included in the Statements published jointly as booklets by the ACC and the Secretariat for Promoting Christian Unity (SPCU) and its successor the PCPCU.

[2] Valentini, 'Contribution', 53.

of 1999 by the Lutheran World Federation and the PCPCU.[3] This, with its acknowledgement that the sixteenth-century excommunications and condemnations relating to the doctrine of justification no longer apply,[4] has changed the context for the reception of *Salvation and the Church*. The *Joint Declaration* broadly corroborates ARCIC in both method and content, especially in placing the discussion about justification in the context of membership of the body of Christ, the Church, and in holding imputed and imparted righteousness together, on account of a retrieval of the dimension of Luther's theology that deals with participation in Christ.[5]

Other responses from Anglican and Roman Catholic sources are taken in turn.[6] Analyses which appear to misunderstand the Statement are addressed as they are discussed.

Anglican Responses: Ecclesial

The 1988 Lambeth Conference, in Resolution 8, overwhelmingly supported *The Final Report*. The Resolution concluded by stating that the Conference

> warmly welcomes the first Report of ARCIC II, Salvation and the Church (1987), as a timely and significant contribution to the understanding of the Churches' doctrine of salvation, and commends this Agreed Statement about the heart of Christian faith to the Provinces for study and reflection.[7]

---

[3] The Co-Chairmen's Preface acknowledges the assistance given to ARCIC II's discussion by the Lutheran–Roman Catholic Consultation in the USA. The international Lutheran–Roman Catholic *Joint Declaration on the Doctrine of Justification* was adopted on 31 October 1999. On 18 July 2006 it was also adopted by the World Methodist Council. It is available at www.vatican.va/roman_curia/pontifical_councils/chrstuni/documents/rc_pc_chrstuni_doc_31101999_cath-luth-joint-declaration_en.html.

[4] *Official Common Statement by the Lutheran World Federation and the Catholic Church*, §1 (citing the *Joint Declaration*, §41), www.vatican.va/roman_curia/pontifical_councils/chrstuni/documents/rc_pc_chrstuni_doc_31101999_cath-luth-official-statement_en.html.

[5] Among other influences, the *Joint Declaration* was indebted to the Finnish school of Mannermaa: see Tuomo Mannermaa, *Christ Present in Faith: Luther's View of Justification*, trans. Kirsi I. Stjerna (Philadelphia: Fortress, 2005), and *Two Kinds of Love: Martin Luther's Religious World*, trans. Kirsi I. Stjerna (Philadelphia: Fortress, 2010). Both volumes were originally published in the early 1980s.

[6] Responses from ecclesial sources are given priority. Though the work of individual scholars in analysing each Agreed Statement was taken into account, individuals are named only where their work is closely related to ecclesial response, for example essays from the Faith and Order Advisory Group of the Church of England (FOAG).

[7] *The Truth Shall Make You Free: The Lambeth Conference 1988. The Reports, Resolutions & Pastoral Letters from the Bishops* (London: Church House, 1988), Resolution 8.5, which enlarges on one passed by the Anglican Consultative Council's Seventh Meeting (1987). Resolution IV.23 of the 1998 Lambeth Conference extended the 1988 Resolution to *Church as Communion* and *Life in Christ*, asking the Communion for feedback so that the 2008 Lambeth Conference could assess ARCIC's work as a whole. As events transpired, the 2008 Conference did not pass Resolutions: see Chapters 11 and 12 below.

Discussion subsequently took place across the Anglican Communion, mostly through local study groups.[8] Mary Tanner lists official responses having been made by 2000 from four provinces: Ireland, England, South Africa, and Canada. All were warmly positive.[9]

The Church of England General Synod debated the Statement in January 1989, and invited dioceses and deaneries to send comments to its Board for Mission and Unity (BMU). The Board's report notes that the Synod 'was generally very affirmative of the text [and] a number of points were raised which were considered to need elucidation including: good works, indulgences, purgatory, masses for the dead'.[10] It summarized responses received, from all but two of forty-three dioceses, as follows:

a. The language used was seen as too technical for some, and too imprecise for others, especially Anglican evangelicals: see further below.
b. The 'ecclesiological model' assumed was questioned by some, especially the relation of the individual to the Church as regards salvation. The Report recognizes that *Church as Communion* addresses this.
c. 'Elucidation' (of the sort provided by ARCIC I) was asked for on a number of points, and 'expansion' or 'further consideration' on others'.[11] Those listed are the relation of baptism to saving faith; 'penitential and devotional teaching and practices', notably praying for the departed, purgatory, penance, and indulgences; faith, justification, and sanctification; and the relationship of grace to free will. All are viewed, however, as having their real significance in 'the implications of the theology of the Statement for current church practice. Theology must be "earthed" if it is truly to live.'[12]

This summary is representative of concerns raised across the Anglican Communion, notably by evangelicals.[13] *Church as Communion* takes up issues of ecclesiology, while *Mary: Grace and Hope in Christ* Section A explores the relationship of grace to the human will, and Section D is relevant to 'praying for the departed'.

---

[8] For example, M. Cecily Boulding OP and Timothy Bradshaw (eds.), *Salvation and the Church: ARCIC II, with Commentary and Study Guide*, published for ARC England (London: Catholic Truth Society/Church House, 1989).

[9] Mary Tanner, *Provincial Responses to the Work of the Second Anglican–Roman Catholic International Commission: An Interim Report for IASCER* (London: ACC, 2000).

[10] Board for Mission and Unity of the Church of England, *The Response of the Dioceses to Salvation and the Church: An Agreed Statement from ARCIC II*, GS Misc 400 (London: Church House, 1991), §4.

[11] Ibid., §19.

[12] Ibid., §30.

[13] The request for ARCIC II to address 'justification by faith' came in part from evangelical Anglicans, and detailed responses came from this quarter, notably Alister McGrath, *ARCIC II and Justification: An Evangelical Anglican Assessment of 'Salvation and the Church'* (Oxford: Latimer House, 1987).

Anglican Responses: The 1988 Anglican Evangelical Assembly

A response expressing the view of Anglican evangelicals was made at the Church of England's 1988 Anglican Evangelical Assembly (AEA),[14] whose theme was 'Justification'. The following resolutions were passed 'overwhelmingly':[15]

> That this AEA, thankful for the renewed attention directed to the Biblical doctrine of Justification by the publication of the ARCIC II statement, urges bishops, clergy and all who preach and teach, to restore to its rightful place in the pulpits of our Church the truth that the justification of sinners in God's sight by grace through faith alone on the basis of the atoning work of Christ, is the one way into salvation and thus the God-given basis for reconciling people to himself and to one another.
>
> That this Assembly asks ARCIC II
> 1. to examine the Marian doctrines and dogmas, and whether acceptance of them is to be held as necessary to salvation;
> 2. for an elucidation of Salvation and the Church, paragraph 22, explaining the relationship between the Roman Catholic teaching on indulgences and prayers for the dead.[16]

The first request—which implies a high degree of acceptance of *Salvation and the Church*—is addressed in *Mary: Grace and Hope in Christ*.

A wider Evangelical concern was the question of appropriate Christian assurance.[17] When 'justification' is seen as already completed, while 'salvation' is understood as awaiting fulfilment, one can have assurance that one has been justified, but not that one will be saved. It has been argued that the Statement should focus on the question 'How is the Christian life begun?', not also on 'How is it lived and completed?'[18] Yet, as ARCIC II would later argue in *The Gift of Authority* §§11–13, the beginning of Christian life is inseparable from the believer becoming 'a member of Christ', so that personal faith is integrated into the faith of the Church. How Christian life

---

[14] The Assembly is not an official body of the Church of England, but is widely representative of its Evangelical clergy and lay people.

[15] George Locke, *'Just before God?' Justification and ARCIC II: A Study Guide to the Debate, on Behalf of the Church of England Evangelical Council* (Nottingham: Grove Books, 1989), Appendix 2. This booklet was written on behalf of the Church of England Evangelical Council, which sponsored the Assembly. This motion was also passed: 'That this Assembly notes with concern the fact that the membership of ARCIC II includes no representative from Latin America and requests those who are responsible for deciding the membership of ARCIC to seek to rectify this in the future.' In 1991 the Revd Dr Jaci Maraschin (Brazil) was appointed as an Anglican member.

[16] Invocation of the saints is addressed in *Mary: Grace and Hope in Christ*, Section D.

[17] McGrath, *ARCIC II and Justification*, 39–41.

[18] Ibid., 42.

begins in temporal terms is particular to each individual. Justification and regeneration, and their sacramental expression in once-for-all baptism, are not so much experiences at particular points in time, as theological models of the reality of God's grace taking hold of a person.[19] In the New Testament, we are taught that the people of God have been, are being, and will be saved.

Roman Catholic Response

As noted earlier, *Salvation and the Church* was issued in 1987, with the accompanying Roman Catholic official commentary offering a positive evaluation. A year later, however, the Congregation for the Doctrine of the Faith (CDF) published brief *Observations on Salvation and the Church*, together with a fuller Commentary, on 18 November 1988 (a decade prior to the *Joint Declaration*). As 'an authoritative doctrinal judgement', the 'substantially positive' stance of *Observations* on the Agreed Statement is significant:

> Taken as a whole, even though it does not present a complete teaching on this question and even though it contains several ambiguous formulations, [it] can be interpreted in a way that conforms with Catholic faith.

The CDF nevertheless judges that things have not yet sufficiently progressed to 'the point of being able to ratify the final affirmation (No. 32)', which claims that the 'Catholic Church and the Anglican Communion "are agreed on the essential aspects of the doctrine of salvation and on the Church's role within it"'.

Four specific areas are identified in relation to which, for the CDF, the teaching of *Salvation and the Church* needs to be completed or clarified if it is to provide the basis for 'a definitive declaration of agreement'.

a. The Statement's language is described as 'symbolic', so that it is 'difficult to interpret univocally'. The Commentary thus asks for 'more rigorous doctrinal formulations, though not necessarily scholastic ones'. This is taken up below.

b. As regards 'Salvation and Faith', further precision on 'the relationship between grace and faith as *initium salutis* (cf. §9)' is seen to be desirable, as would 'more be extended discussion of the "controversial point" with Protestants, *sola fides*' ('faith alone'). This term, which runs the danger of faith being seen in isolation from grace and Christian life, is not used by Anglicans, but rather *sola fide*, 'by faith', reflecting the conviction that faith is initiated and sustained by divine grace. The only

---

[19] McGrath appears to see justification and regeneration as temporally locatable: thus he asks, 'Is regeneration prior or posterior to baptism?' (ibid., 49).

reference to 'faith' in *Salvation and the Church* §9 is at its conclusion, 'Salvation is the gift of grace; it is by faith that it is appropriated.'[20]

c. With respect to 'Salvation and Good Works', more precision was requested 'on the doctrine of grace and merit in relation to the distinction between justification and sanctification'. Merit is considered in *Salvation and the Church* §24; as regards the distinct yet interwoven relationship between justification and sanctification, both Anglican and Roman Catholic theology, spirituality, and liturgy postulate real change in the justified believer, through ongoing participation in the grace of Christ.[21]

The CDF also looked for more on the formula '*simul iustus et peccator*', alluded to in §21: but, as *Salvation and the Church* footnote 4 indicates, this is a Lutheran expression, not found in Anglican formularies, and is now to be interpreted in the light of the Lutheran–Roman Catholic *Joint Declaration*, which affirms that justification by faith in Christ is for good works (see *Salvation and the Church*, §19).

d. In relation to 'The Church and Salvation', the CDF states as an 'essential point' that 'the role of Church in salvation is not only to bear witness to it, but also and above all, to be the effective instrument . . . of justification and salvation'. Further, a clearer 'distinction between the holiness of the Church . . . and its members, who in some measure are still given to sin', is sought.

ARCIC II affirmed that Christian existence is not merely the collective living of one's personal story of transformation in the company of others: it is the corporate participation in the life of the Church. 'The Church is both the sign of salvation in Christ, for to be saved is to be brought into communion with God through Him, and at the same time the instrument of salvation' (*Church as Communion*, §19).

In conclusion, the CDF sees that 'The vision of the Church as sacrament of salvation and the specifically sacramental dimension of man's justification and sanctification are too vague and too weak to allow us to affirm that ARCIC II has arrived at substantial agreement.' These significant

---

[20] The relationship between grace and faith is further developed in *Mary: Grace and Hope in Christ*, §§5, 8–11, 15–16, 30, 53–57.

[21] For the Anglican tradition, the Post-Communion Prayers in the Book of Common Prayer speak of communicants' true incorporation in 'the mystical Body of Christ', and request that, by Christ's merit, members of the Church may continue in its communion 'and do all such good works as [God] has prepared for [them] to walk in' (see Ephesians 2.10). Similarly, the Ash Wednesday Collect asks that God not only forgive penitent sinners, but would also 'create and make in [the faithful] new and contrite hearts', with a view to their obtaining 'perfect remission and forgiveness'.

questions about ecclesiology are taken up in *Church as Communion*, especially Section II, 'Communion: Sacramentality and the Church' (§§16–24). Further, since the CDF played a significant part in the adoption of the Lutheran–Roman Catholic *Joint Declaration on the Doctrine of Justification*, the Statement *Salvation and the Church* should be read in the light of this agreement.

Salvation and the Church: The Language Employed

As noted in Chapter 8, ARCIC's linguistic method was commended by Pope John Paul II in 1980, at an audience for ARCIC I in Castel Gandolfo. The Pope observed that the method of ARCIC is 'to go behind the habit of thought and expression born and nourished in enmity and controversy, to clothe it in a language at once traditional and expressive of the insights of an age which no longer glories in strife'. Further, as noted above, the 1999 Lutheran–Roman Catholic *Joint Declaration* sets the issue of terminology around justification in a new light. As the processes around the reception of this agreement show, while it is essential that any such new formula not allow for incompatible interpretations, it can properly allow for legitimate differences of emphasis and theological expression. Such a strategy of 'differentiated consensus' is properly to be seen as expressing the kind of diversity in unity, or internal pluralism in communion, that is appropriate and healthy, indeed necessary, within the dynamically integrated catholicity of the Church.

More widely, it is important to recognize that, since it deals with the mystery of God and God's dealings with creation, all theological language is symbolic, and necessarily employs categories such as metaphor and analogy. As *Salvation and the Church* §13 puts it, 'In order to describe salvation in all its fullness, the New Testament employs a wide variety of language', listing half a dozen examples. ARCIC II's approach to its mandate to explore remaining doctrinal differences took matters such as these into account. As Bishop Richard Harries said in addressing the General Synod of the Church of England,

> One of the reasons for the convergence recorded in the ARCIC process is the attempt to get behind scholastic formulations to more biblical categories. And closely linked with this, biblical categories are primarily personal. One of the reasons why the old debates have been transcended is the realisation that in all the debates on justification and salvation we have, above all, to do with a personal relationship between God and human beings. Past Christian thinkers sometimes went astray in thinking of grace in impersonal terms or salvation in only legal ones. What we have to do with is the metaphor of personal relationship, according to the Bible the controlling image in our

thought about God and man ... [T]he valuable emphasis present in Salvation and the Church is on this as the controlling image or metaphor.[22]

Conclusion

Some Anglican responses to *Salvation and the Church* ask for elucidation of Roman Catholic teaching on penance, purgatory, and indulgences.[23] These are alluded to in §22 as 'penitential disciplines, and other devotional practices', items which ARCIC II 'did consider discussing ... explicitly and in greater detail, but [they] finally decided to leave the fuller treatment of them for a separate document, if this should be requested'.[24] Further work is likely to be needed in these areas, though several related aspects are taken up in the later Agreed Statements of ARCIC II, notably *Church as Communion* and *Mary: Grace and Hope in Christ*. The most significant development in ecumenical reflection on the doctrine of salvation since the publication of *Salvation and the Church* is the Lutheran–Roman Catholic *Joint Declaration*, which puts it in a welcome new context.

Bibliography

Lutheran World Federation and the Roman Catholic Church, *Joint Declaration on the Doctrine of Justification* (Grand Rapids: Eerdmans, 2000, and London: CTS, 2001), www.vatican.va/roman_curia/pontifical_councils/chrstuni/documents/rc_pc_chrstuni_doc_31101999_cath-luth-joint-declaration_en.html

Ecclesial Responses: Official Roman Catholic Commentaries

CDF, 'Observations on ARCIC II's *Salvation and the Church*' and 'Commentary on the Observations' (18 November 1988), *Origins*, 18/27 (15 December 1988), 429–34, www.vatican.va/roman_curia/congregations/cfaith/documents/rc_con_cfaith_doc_19881118_chiesa-salvezza_en.html

Donato, Valentini, SDB, 'A Contribution to the Reading of the ARCIC II Statement on *Salvation and the Church*', *Information Service*, 63 (1987), 41–53

Ecclesial Responses: Anglican Resolutions

Many Gifts, One Spirit: Report of the Anglican Consultative Council Seventh Meeting 1987 (London: ACC, 1988):

---

[22] During the 1989 Church of England General Synod debate over *Salvation and the Church*, cited in Council for Christian Unity of the Church of England, 'The Response of the Dioceses to Salvation and the Church: An Agreed Statement by the Second Anglican–Roman Catholic International Commission (ARCIC II)', GS Misc 400 (London: Church House, 1992), 18.

[23] See AEA Resolution 2 (see p. 28 above), and McGrath, *ARCIC II and Justification*, 47–9.

[24] Boulding and Bradshaw (eds.), *Study Guide*, 30: Sr Boulding was a member of ARCIC II.

'warmly welcomed' Salvation and the Church and commended it to the Churches of the Communion for study and evaluation, in the hope that that there would be some provisional response at Lambeth 1988.

Transformation and Renewal: The Official Report of the Lambeth Conference 1998 (Harrisburg, PA: Morehouse, 1999), Resolution IV.23 (pp. 415–16; see Section IV: 'The Roman Catholic Church', pp. 255–6):

encourages the referral of Salvation and the Church (1987), Church as Communion (1991), Life in Christ (1994), and the anticipated completion of ARCIC's work on authority in the Church to the Provinces for study and response back to the proposed Inter-Anglican Standing Commission on Ecumenical Relations and (through the Primates' Meeting and the Anglican Consultative Council) to the next Lambeth Conference.

The Truth Shall Make You Free: The Lambeth Conference 1988. The Reports, Resolutions & Pastoral Letters from the Bishops (London: Church House, 1988), Resolution 8.5:

warmly welcomes the first Report of ARCIC II, Salvation and the Church (1987), as a timely and significant contribution to the understanding of the Church's doctrine of salvation and commends this Agreed Statement about the heart of Christian faith to the Provinces for study and reflection.

Ecclesial Responses: Assessments

ARC Canada, 'Comments on the Observations of the CDF on Salvation and the Church', in Jeffrey Gros, E. Rozanne Elder, and Ellen K. Wondra (eds.), *Common Witness to the Gospel. Documents on Anglican–Roman Catholic Relations 1983–1995* (Washington DC: US Catholic Conference, 1997), 52–62

Board of Mission and Unity of the Church of England, 'Salvation and the Church: An Agreed Statement by ARCIC II. Preliminary Consideration by the General Synod: A Report', GS Misc 865 (London: Church House, 1989)

Boulding, M. Cecily, and Bradshaw, Timothy (eds.), *Salvation and the Church: ARCIC II, with Commentary and Study Guide*, published for ARC England (London: Catholic Truth Society and Church House, 1989)

Council for Christian Unity of the Church of England, 'The Response of the Dioceses to Salvation and the Church: An Agreed Statement by the Second Anglican–Roman Catholic International Commission (ARCIC II)', GS Misc 400 (London: Church House, 1992)

Executive Committee of the Evangelical Fellowship in the Anglican Communion, *ARCIC: An Open Letter to the Anglican Episcopate* (Nottingham: Grove Booklets, 1988)

International Anglican–Roman Catholic Communion on Unity and Mission (IARCCUM) and PCPCU, 'Ecclesiological Reflections on the Current Situation in the Anglican Communion in the Light of ARCIC' (2004), https://iarccum.org/archive/IARCCUM_2000-2010/2004_iarccum_ecclesiological_reflections.pdf; *Information Service*, 119/3 (2005), 102–5

Tanner, Mary, *Provincial Responses to the Work of the Second Anglican–Roman Catholic International Commission: An Interim Report for IASCER* (London: ACC, 2000)

Significant Publications

Boulding, M. Cecily, 'The ARCIC Agreement on Salvation and the Church', *Doctrine and Life*, 39 (1989), 452–8

Bradshaw, Timothy, 'ARCIC 2: Salvation and the Church—Pastoral and Spiritual Implications', *The Evangelical Quarterly*, 63 (1991), 331–40

Celsor, Scott, '"God's Grace Effects what he Declares": Scriptural Support for the Agreement on Justification in the *Joint Declaration on the Doctrine of Justification* and *Salvation and the Church*', *Journal of Ecumenical* Studies, 39 (2002), 289–304

Chadwick, Henry, 'Some Occasional Remarks on Dr A. McGrath's Pamphlet, "ARCIC II and Justification"', unpublished paper (1988)

Curry, George, '*Salvation and the Church*: An Agreed Statement by the Second Anglican–Roman Catholic International Commission ARCIC II. A Response', *Churchman*, 101/2 (1987), 146–56

England, Robert, *Justification Today: The Roman Catholic and Anglican Debate*, Latimer Studies, 4 (Oxford: Latimer House, 1979)

England, Robert, '*Salvation and the Church*: A Review Article', *Churchman*, 101/1 (1987), 49–57

Lane, Anthony N. S., *Justification by Faith in Catholic–Protestant Dialogue: An Evangelical Assessment* (London and New York: T & T Clark, 2002)

Locke, George, '*Just before God?' Justification and ARCIC II: A Study Guide to the Debate, on Behalf of the Church of England Evangelical Council* (Nottingham: Grove Books, 1989)

Lüning, P., 'Das Dialogdokument *Das Heil und die Kirche* (1990)', in *Offenbarung und Rechtfertigung: Eine Studie zu ihrer Verhältnisbestimmung anhand des anglikanisch/römisch-katholischen Dialogs*, Konfessionskundliche und kontroverstheologische Studien, 70 (Paderborn: Bonifatius, 1999), 266–331

McGrath, Alister, *ARCIC II and Justification: An Evangelical Anglican Assessment of 'Salvation and the Church'* (Oxford: Latimer House, 1987)

McGrath, Alister, *Iustitia Dei: The History of the Christian Doctrine of Justification* (2nd edn, Cambridge: Cambridge University Press, 1998)

Murray, Paul D., 'St Paul and Ecumenism: Justification and All That', *New Blackfriars* (March 2010), 142–70

Sagovsky, Nicholas, *Ecumenism, Christian Origins and the Practice of Communion* (Cambridge: Cambridge University Press, 2000)

Scott, David A, '*Salvation and the Church* and Theological Truth-Claims', *Journal of Ecumenical Studies*, 25 (1988), 428–36

Simons, John, 'Anglicans, Lutherans, and Roman Catholics on Justification: Is there a Real Consensus?', *Ecumenism*, 36 (2001), 29–33

Wright, J. Robert, '*Salvation and the Church*: A Response to David Scott', *Journal of Ecumenical Studies*, 25 (1988), 437–44

Chapter 2

Church as Communion (1991)

Introducing the Statement

ARCIC II completed its second Agreed Statement, *Church as Communion*, in 1990: it was published in the following year. In this the Commission reflected more explicitly upon the *koinonia* ecclesiology which formed the background of its previous work. In 1982, when looking back on the Statements collected in *The Final Report*, ARCIC I retrospectively recognized that the subjects it had considered all related to the nature of the Church. In particular, the concept of *koinonia* (communion, participation, fellowship) was 'fundamental to all our Statements' (*The Final Report*, §4). 'In them we present the eucharist as the effectual sign of *koinonia*, *episcope* as serving the *koinonia*, and primacy as a visible link and focus of *koinonia*' (§6); '*Koinonia* with one another is entailed by our *koinonia* with God in Christ. This is the mystery of the Church' (§5).

This retrospective by ARCIC I is not without analogy to the way in which the 1985 Extraordinary Synod of Roman Catholic Bishops reinterpreted the work of the Second Vatican Council in saying: 'The ecclesiology of communion is the central and fundamental idea of the Council's documents.'[1] These two forms of re-appraisal show how the notion of *koinonia* as an ecclesiological category was simultaneously pervading both the theology and the authoritative statements of churches individually, and of the ecumenical movement as a whole.

While ARCIC II's first Agreed Statement, *Salvation and the Church*, pointed to the soteriological dimension of *koinonia*, *Church as Communion* explored its ecclesiological dimensions. The Commission thereby explicitly unfolded what *The Final Report* had initiated in its retrospective on its work. In drafting *Church as Communion*, Commission members were aware of its distinctive nature, in that, diverging from previous ARCIC Statements, 'it does not focus specifically on doctrinal questions that have been historically divisive. Nor does it seek to treat all the issues pertaining

---

[1] Final Report of the 1985 Extraordinary Synod, II, C, 1, www.ewtn.com/library/CURIA/SYNFINAL. HTM.

to the doctrine of the Church' (*Church as Communion*, §2) It surveys how communion is unfolded in Scripture (§§6–15); how a communion ecclesiology expresses the sacramentality of the Church as 'sign, instrument and foretaste of communion' (§§16–24), and how communion relates to the creedal marks of the Church—its apostolicity, catholicity, and holiness (§§25–41); considers the necessary 'constitutive elements' required for unity and ecclesial communion (§§42–48); and finally affirms 'that certain yet imperfect communion [which Anglicans and Roman Catholics] already share',[2] while outlining some of the issues which continue to divide them (§§49–58).

Church as Communion is not only a retrospective survey, however, but also has a prospective character. The Commission stresses the usefulness of communion ecclesiology for its future work:

> we believe that within the perspective of communion the outstanding diffi-
> culties that remain between us will be more clearly understood and are more
> likely to be resolved; thus we shall be helped to grow into a more profound
> communion.   (*Church as Communion*, §2)

---

[2] Pope John Paul II and Archbishop Robert Runcie, Common Declaration, 2 October 1989: see Appendix B4 below.

CHURCH AS COMMUNION

An Agreed Statement by the Second
Anglican–Roman Catholic International
Commission (ARCIC II)

CONTENTS

THE STATUS OF THE DOCUMENT

The Document published here is the work of the Second Anglican–Roman Catholic International Commission (ARCIC II). It is a joint statement of the Commission. The authorities who appointed the Commission have allowed the statement to be published so that it may be widely discussed. It is not an authoritative declaration by the Roman Catholic Church or by the Anglican Communion, who will evaluate the document in order to take a position on it in due time.

PREFACE

By the Co-Chairmen

During the past four years the members of the Anglican–Roman Catholic International Commission have considered the mystery of communion which is given and made visible in the Church. This has not been an easy task, because of the inherent complexity and depth of the mystery. For the same reason, our study cannot be complete or perfect. We have paid particular attention to the sacramentality of the Church; that is to the Church as a divine gift, grounded in Christ himself and embodied in human history, through which the grace of Christ is mediated for the salvation of humankind. In doing this, we believe that we have laid a necessary foundation for further work on vital topics which were broached by our predecessors in the first Anglican–Roman Catholic International Commission. In particular we look forward to deeper study of the nature of the authority of Christ, the living Word of God, over his Church, and of the means through which he exercises that authority and his people respond to it.

In considering the Church as communion we have drawn upon thinking in both our churches and in the dialogues with other Christian bodies in which both are engaged. It is important always to understand that each dialogue is part of a larger whole: all are part of a long process of doctrinal and spiritual reconciliation. Accordingly we offer the outcome of our labours not only to our own respective churches, but to all who are concerned with the common search for that full ecclesial unity which we believe to be God's will for all his people. We do this in the hope of study and response.

The members of the Commission have not only been engaged in theological dialogue. Their work and study have been rooted in shared prayer and common life. This in itself has given them a profound experience of communion in Christ: not indeed that full sacramental communion which is our goal, but nevertheless a true foretaste of that fullness of communion for which we pray and strive.

We are painfully aware of the difficulties which still lie in our way. Nevertheless, we are heartened and encouraged by the words of Pope John Paul II and Archbishop Robert Runcie in their Common Declaration of 2 October 1989:

Against the background of human disunity the arduous journey to Christian unity must be pursued with determination and vigour, whatever obstacles are perceived to block the path. We here solemnly recommit ourselves and those we represent to the restoration of visible unity and full ecclesial communion in the confidence that to seek anything less would be to betray our Lord's intention for the unity of his people.

The Pope and the Archbishop also declared: 'The ecumenical journey is not only about the removal of obstacles but also about the sharing of gifts.' That indeed has been the experience of the members of the Commission. In giving we receive. That is of the essence of communion in Christ.

+ CORMAC MURPHY-O'CONNOR
+ MARK SANTER

Dublin, 6 September 1990

CHURCH AS COMMUNION

Introduction

1. Together with other Christians, Anglicans and Roman Catholics are committed to the search for that unity in truth and love for which Christ prayed. Within this context, the purpose of the Anglican–Roman Catholic International Commission is to examine and try to resolve those doctrinal differences which stand in the way of ecclesial communion between Anglicans and Roman Catholics. *The Final Report* of ARCIC I and the publication of ARCIC II's statement on *Salvation and the Church* have contributed to progress in mutual understanding and growing awareness of the need for ecclesial communion. We believe it is time now to reflect more explicitly upon the nature of communion and its constitutive elements. This will enable us to meet the requests that have been made for further clarification of the ecclesiological basis of our work.

2. This statement on communion differs from previous ARCIC reports in that it does not focus specifically on doctrinal questions that have been historically divisive. Nor does it seek to treat all the issues pertaining to the doctrine of the Church. Its purpose is to give substance to the affirmation that Anglicans and Roman Catholics are already in a real though as yet imperfect communion and to enable us to recognise the degree of communion that exists both within and between us.[1] Moreover, we believe that within the perspective of communion the outstanding difficulties that remain between us will be more clearly understood and are more likely to be resolved; thus we shall be helped to grow into a more profound communion.

3. There are advantages in adopting the theme of communion in an exploration of the nature of the Church. Communion implies that the Church is a dynamic reality moving towards its fulfilment. Communion embraces both the visible gathering of God's people and its divine life-giving source. We are thus directed to the life of God, Father, Son and Holy Spirit, the life God wills to share with all people. There is held before us the vision of God's reign over the whole of creation, and of the

---

[1] Cf. *Common Declaration*, Pope John Paul II and the Archbishop of Canterbury, Robert Runcie, 2 October 1989.

43

Church as the firstfruits of humankind which is drawn into that divine life through acceptance of the redemption given in Jesus Christ. Moreover this focus on communion enables us to affirm that which is already realised in the Church, the eucharistic community. It enables us also to acknowledge as a gift of God the good that is present in community life in the world: communion involves rejoicing with those who rejoice and being in solidarity with those who suffer and those who search for meaning in life. To explore the meaning of communion is not only to speak of the Church but also to address the world at the heart of its deepest need, for human beings long for true community in freedom, justice and peace and for the respect of human dignity.

4. Furthermore to understand the Church in terms of communion confronts Christians with the scandal of our divisions. Christian disunity obscures God's invitation to communion for all humankind and makes the Gospel we proclaim harder to hear. But the consideration of communion also enables Christians to recognise that certain yet imperfect communion they already share. Christians of many traditions are coming to acknowledge the central place of communion in their understanding of the nature of the Church and its unity and mission. This is the communion to the study of which our paper is devoted.

5. After a survey of how communion is unfolded in Scripture, we explore the way in which the Church as communion is sacrament of the merciful grace of God for all humankind. Then follows a treatment of the relationship of communion to the apostolicity, catholicity and holiness of the Church and a consideration of the necessary elements required for unity and ecclesial communion. Finally, we affirm the existing communion between our two churches and outline some of the remaining issues which continue to divide us.

I Communion Unfolded in Scripture

6. The relationship between God and his creation is the fundamental theme of Holy Scripture. The drama of human existence, as expounded in Scripture, consists in the formation, breakdown and renewal of this relationship. The biblical story opens with God establishing this relationship by creating human beings in his image and likeness; God blesses and honours them by inviting them to live in communion both with him and with one another as stewards of his creation. In the unfolding saga of Genesis the disobedience of Adam and Eve undermines both their relation with God and their relation with each

other: they hide from God; Adam blames Eve; they are expelled from the garden; their relationship with the rest of creation is distorted. What ensues in Genesis illustrates this recurrent pattern in human history.

7. In the variety of literary styles and theological traditions coming from every period of the long history of the people of Abraham, the books of the Old Testament bear witness to the fact that God wants his people to be in communion with him and with each other. God's purpose is re-affirmed in covenant with his people. Through Abraham God gives the promise of blessing to all the nations (Gen 12.1–3). Through Moses God establishes a people as his own possession, a community in a covenant relationship with him (Ex 19.5ff). In the Promised Land the Temple becomes the place where God chooses to set his name, where he dwells with his people (Deut 12.5). The prophets consistently denounce the community's faithlessness as threatening this relationship. Nevertheless, God's fidelity remains constant and he promises through the prophets that his promise will be accomplished. Although division and exile follow upon the sins of the chosen people, reconciliation of the scattered people of God will spring from a radical transformation within a new covenant (Jer 31.31). God will raise up a servant to fulfil his purpose of communion and peace for his chosen people and also for all the nations (Is 49.6; cf. also Mic 4.1–4).

8. In the fullness of time, God sends his Son, born of a woman, to redeem his people and bring them into a new relationship as his adopted children (cf. Gal 4.4). When Jesus begins his ministry he calls together a band of disciples with whom he shares his mission (Mk 3.14; cf. Jn 20.21). After Easter they are to be witnesses to his life, teaching, death and resurrection. In the power of the Spirit given at Pentecost they proclaim that God's promises have been fulfilled in Christ. For the apostolic community the baptism of repentance and faith bestowed in this new covenant does more than restore that which was lost: by the Spirit believers enter Christ's own communion with the Father (cf. Rom 8.15; Gal 4.6). In the eucharist, the memorial of the New Covenant, believers participate in the body and blood of Christ and are made one body in him (1 Cor 10.16–17; 11.23–27). It is communion with the Father, through the Son, in the Holy Spirit which constitutes the people of the New Covenant as the Church, 'a people still linked by spiritual ties to the stock of Abraham'.[2]

---

[2] Second Vatican Council, *Nostra Aetate*, 4.

9. On Calvary the hideous nature of sin and evil is clearly exposed. In the cross are found God's judgement upon the world and his gift of reconciliation (2 Cor 5.19). Through the Paschal victory all estrangement occasioned by differences of culture, class, privilege and sex is overcome. All those who are united with the death and resurrection of Christ have equal standing before God. Moreover, because Christ is the one in whom and through whom all things are created and reconciled, the proper relationship between humanity and the rest of creation is restored and renewed in him (Col 1.15–20; Gal 3.27–29; Col 3.11).

10. However, the life of communion is still impaired by human sin (1 Cor 1.10ff). The failure of Christians to respond to the demands of the Gospel gives rise to divisions among Christians which obscure the Church's witness. The New Testament affirms that there is a constant need for recourse to the repentance and reconciliation offered by Christ through the Church (Mt 18.15–20; cf. 1 Jn 1.5–10).

11. In the writings of the New Testament the failures of the disciples and the divisions among them are fully recognised. Nevertheless the reign of God is already described as a feast, 'the wedding supper of the Lamb' (Rev 19.9), a vivid image of communion deeply rooted in human experience. This feast is spoken of by Jesus in the parables and foreshadowed in the feeding of the multitudes (Mt 22.1–10; Jn 6). The celebration of the eucharist prefigures and provides a foretaste of this messianic banquet (Lk 22.30). In the world to come, such signs will cease since the sacramental order will no longer be needed, for God will be immediately present to his people. They will see him face to face and join in endless praise (Rev 22.3–4). This will be the perfection of communion.

12. In the New Testament the word *koinonia* (often translated 'communion' or 'fellowship') ties together a number of basic concepts such as unity, life together, sharing and partaking. The basic verbal form means 'to share', 'to participate', 'to have part in', 'to have something in common' or 'to act together'. The noun can signify fellowship or community. It usually signifies a relationship based on participation in a shared reality (e.g. 1 Cor 10.16). This usage is most explicit in the Johannine writings: 'We proclaim to you what we have seen and heard, so that you also may have fellowship with us. And our fellowship is with the Father and with his Son, Jesus Christ' (1 Jn 1.3; cf. 1 Jn 1.7).[3]

---

[3] 'Communion' has been treated in many ecumenical documents including *The Final Report* of ARCIC I (Introduction). Cf. also *Communion-Koinonia: A Study* by the Institute for Ecumenical Research, Strasbourg, 1990.

13. In the New Testament the idea of communion is conveyed in many ways. A variety of words, expressions and images points to its reality; the people of God (1 Pt 2.9–10); flock (Jn 10.14; Acts 20.28–29; 1 Pt 5.3, 4); vine (Jn 15.5); temple (1 Cor 3.16–17); bride (Rev 21.2); body of Christ (1 Cor 12.27; 1 Cor 10.16–17; Rom 12.4–5; Eph 1.22–23). All these express a relationship with God and also imply a relationship among the members of the community. The reality to which this variety of images refers is communion, a shared life in Christ (1 Cor 10.16–17; cf. Jn 17) which no one image exhaustively describes. This communion is participation in the life of God through Christ in the Holy Spirit, making Christians one with each other.

14. It is characteristic of the Apostle Paul to speak of the relationship of believers to their Lord as being 'in Christ' and of Christ being in the believer through the indwelling of the Holy Spirit (Rom 8.1–11; 2 Cor 5.17; Col 1.27–28; Gal 2.20; cf. also Jn 15.1–11). This relationship Paul also affirms in his description of the Church as the one body of Christ. This description is integrally linked with the presence of Christ in the eucharist. Those who share in the supper of the Lord are one body in Christ because they all partake of the one bread (1 Cor 10.16–17 and 12.23–30). This description underlines the intimate, organic relationship which exists between the Risen Lord and all those who receive new life through communion with him. Equally it emphasises the organic relationship thus established among the members of the one body, the Church. All who share in the 'holy things' of the sacramental life are made holy through them: because they share in them together they are in communion with each other.

15. The New Testament reflects different dimensions of communion as experienced in the life of the Church in apostolic times.

    At the centre of this communion is life with the Father, through Christ, in the Spirit. Through the sending of his Son the living God has revealed that love is at the heart of the divine life. Those who abide in love abide in God and God in them; if we, in communion with him, love one another, he abides in us and his love is perfected in us (cf. 1 Jn 4.7–21). Through love God communicates his life. He causes those who accept the light of the truth revealed in Christ rather than the darkness of this world to become his children. This is the most profound communion possible for any of his creatures.

Visibly, this communion is entered through baptism and nourished and expressed in the celebration of the eucharist. All who are baptized in the one Spirit into one body are united in the eucharist by this sacramental participation in this same one body (1 Cor 10.16–17; 12.13). This community of the baptized, devoted to the apostolic teaching, fellowship, breaking of bread and prayer (Acts 2.42), finds its necessary expression in a visible human community. It is a community which suffers with Christ in anticipation of the revelation of his glory (Phil 3.10; Col 1.24; 1 Pt 4.13; Rom 8.17). Those who are in communion participate in one another's joys and sorrows (Heb 10.33; 2 Cor 1.6, 7); they serve one another in love (Gal 5.13) and share together to meet the needs of one another and of the community as a whole. There is a mutual giving and receiving of spiritual and material gifts, not only between individuals but also between communities, on the basis of a fellowship that already exists in Christ (Rom 15.26–27; 2 Cor 8.1–15). The integrity and building up of that fellowship requires appropriate structure, order and discipline (cf. 1 Cor 11.17–34; and the Pastoral Epistles).

Communion will reach its fulfilment when God will be all in all (1 Cor 15.28). It is the will of God for the whole creation that all things should be brought to ultimate unity and communion in Christ (Eph 1.10; Col 1.19–20).

Already in the New Testament these different dimensions of communion are discernible, together with a striving towards their ever more faithful realisation.

II Communion: Sacramentality and the Church

16. God's purpose is to bring all people into communion with himself within a transformed creation (cf. Rom 8.19–22). To accomplish this the eternal Word became incarnate. The life and ministry of Jesus Christ definitively manifested the restored humanity God intends. By who he was, by what he taught, and by what he accomplished through the Cross and resurrection, he became the sign, the instrument and the firstfruits of God's purpose for the whole of creation (Col 1.15–17). As the new Adam, the Risen Lord is the beginning and guarantor of this transformation. Through this transformation alienation is overcome by communion, both between human beings and above all between them and God. These two dimensions

of communion are inseparable. This is the mystery of Christ (Eph 2.11–3.12).

17. Communion with God through Christ is constantly established and renewed through the power of the Holy Spirit. By the power of the Spirit, the incomparable riches of God's grace are made present for all time through the Church. Those who are reconciled to God form 'one body in Christ and are individually members one of another' (Rom 12.5). By the action of the same Spirit, believers are baptized into the one body (1 Cor 12.13) and in the breaking of the bread they also participate in that one body (1 Cor 10.16–17; 11.23–29). Thus the Church 'which is Christ's body, the fullness of him who fills all in all', reveals and embodies 'the mystery of Christ' (cf. Eph 1.23; 3.4, 8–11). It is therefore itself rightly described as a visible sign which both points to and embodies our communion with God and with one another; as an instrument through which God effects this communion; and as a foretaste of the fullness of communion to be consummated when Christ is all in all. It is a 'mystery' or 'sacrament'.

18. The Church as communion of believers with God and with each other is a sign of the new humanity God is creating and a pledge of the continuing work of the Holy Spirit. Its vocation is to embody and reveal the redemptive power of the Gospel, signifying reconciliation received through faith and participation in the new life in Christ. The Church is the sign of what God has done in Christ, is continuing to do in those who serve him, and wills to do for all humanity. It is the sign of God's abiding presence, and of his eternal faithfulness to his promises, for in it Christ is ever present and active through the Spirit. It is the community where the redemptive work of Jesus Christ has been recognised and received, and is therefore being made known to the world. Because Christ has overcome all the barriers of division created by human sin, it is the mission of the Church as God's servant to enter into the struggle to end those divisions (cf. Eph 2.14–18; 5.1–2).

19. The Holy Spirit uses the Church as the means through which the Word of God is proclaimed afresh, the sacraments are celebrated, and the people of God receive pastoral oversight, so that the life of the Gospel is manifested in the life of its members. The Church is both the sign of salvation in Christ, for to be saved is to be brought into communion with God through Him, and at the same time the instrument of salvation, as the community through which this salvation is offered and received. This is what is meant when the Church

49

is described as an 'effective sign', given by God in the face of human sinfulness, division and alienation .[4]

20. Human sinfulness and Christian division obscure this sign. However, Christ's promise of his abiding presence in the midst of his people (Mt 18.20; 28.19–20) gives the assurance that the Church will not cease to be this effective sign. In spite of the frailty and sinfulness of its members, Christ promises that the powers of destruction will never prevail against it (Mt 16.18).

21. Paradoxically it is pre-eminently in its weakness, suffering and poverty that the Church becomes the sign of the efficacy of God's grace (cf. 2 Cor 12.9; 4.7–12). It is also paradoxical that the quality of holiness is rightly attributed to the Church, a community of sinners. The power of God to sanctify the Church is revealed in the scandal of the Cross where Christ in his love gave himself for the Church so that it might be presented to him without spot or wrinkle, holy and without blemish (Eph 5.26–27). 'God was in Christ reconciling the world to himself' . . . 'making him who knew no sin to be sin for us so that in him we might become the righteousness of God' (2 Cor 5.19; 8.21).

22. The communion of the Church demonstrates that Christ has broken down the dividing wall of hostility, so as to create a single new humanity reconciled to God in one body by the cross (cf. Eph 2.14–16). Confessing that their communion signifies God's purpose for the whole human race the members of the Church are called to give themselves in loving witness and service to their fellow human beings.

   This service is focused principally in the proclaiming of the Gospel in obedience to the command of Christ. Having received this call, the Church has been entrusted with the stewardship of the means of grace and with the message of salvation. In the power of Christ's

---

[4] The language of 'effective sign' and 'instrument' is known to Anglicans in the Catechism of the *Book of Common Prayer* and in the Articles of Religion, in which baptism and the eucharist are said to be 'not only a sign . . . but rather . . . a sacrament', 'sure witnesses, and effectual signs of grace' whereby we receive grace 'as a means' or 'as by an instrument', and which 'be effectual because of Christ's institution and promise' (The Catechism; Articles 25, 26, 27, 28). For the Roman Catholic Church, similarly, instrumental language was largely developed in relation to the sacraments rather than the Church. But reflection on the mystery of Christ and the Church led to the development of its self-understanding in terms of itself being, 'in Christ . . . in the nature of sacrament–a sign and instrument, that is, of communion with God and of unity among all people', and 'as the universal sacrament of salvation' (*Lumen Gentium* 1 and 48).

presence through the Spirit it is caught up in the saving mission of Christ. The mandate given to the Church to bring salvation to all the nations constitutes its unique mission. In this way the Church not only signifies the new humanity willed by God and inaugurated by Christ. It is itself an instrument of the Holy Spirit in the extension of salvation to all human beings in all their needs and circumstances to the end of time. To speak of the Church as sacrament is to affirm that in and through the communion of all those who confess Jesus Christ and who live according to their confession, God realises his plan of salvation for all the world. This is not to say that God's saving work is limited to those who confess Christ explicitly. By God's gift of the same Spirit who was at work in the earthly ministry of Christ Jesus, the Church plays its part in bringing his work to its fulfilment.

23. To be united with Christ in the fulfilment of his ministry for the salvation of the world is to share his will that the Church be one, not only for the credibility of the Church's witness and for the effectiveness of its mission, but supremely for the glorification of the Father. God will be truly glorified when all peoples with their rich diversity will be fully united in one communion of love. Our present communion with God and with each other in the Holy Spirit is a pledge and foretaste here and now of the ultimate fulfilment of God's purpose for all, as proclaimed in the vision of 'a great multitude which none could number, from every nation, from all tribes and peoples and tongues . . . crying out with a loud voice "salvation belongs to our God who sits upon the throne, and to the Lamb!"' (Rev 7.9–10).

24. The sacramental nature of the Church as sign, instrument and foretaste of communion is especially manifest in the common celebration of the eucharist. Here, celebrating the memorial of the Lord and partaking of his body and blood, the Church points to the origin of its communion in Christ, himself in communion with the Father; it experiences that communion in a visible fellowship; it anticipates the fullness of the communion in the kingdom; it is sent out to realise, manifest and extend that communion in the world.

III Communion: Apostolicity, Catholicity and Holiness

25. The Church points to its source and mission when it confesses in the Creed, 'We believe in one holy catholic and apostolic Church'. It is because the Church is built up by the Spirit upon the foundation

of the life, death and resurrection of Christ as these have been witnessed and transmitted by the apostles that the Church is called *apostolic*. It is also called apostolic because it is equipped for its mission by sharing in the apostolic mandate.

26. The content of the faith is the truth of Christ Jesus as it has been transmitted through the apostles. This God-given deposit of faith cannot be dissociated from the gift of the Holy Spirit. Central to the mission of the Spirit is the safeguarding and quickening of the memory of the teaching and work of Christ and of his exaltation, of which the apostolic community was the first witness. To safeguard the authenticity of its memory the Church was led to acknowledge the canon of Scripture as both test and norm. But the quickening of its memory requires more than the repetition of the words of Scripture. It is achieved under the guidance of the Holy Spirit by the unfolding of revealed truth as it is in Jesus Christ. According to the Johannine gospel the mission of the Holy Spirit is intimately linked with all that Christ Jesus said, did and accomplished. Christ promised that the Father will send the Holy Spirit in his name to teach the disciples all things and to bring to remembrance all that he has said (cf. Jn 14.26). To keep alive the memory of Christ means to remain faithful to all that we know of him through the apostolic community.

27. Such faithfulness must be realised in daily life. Consequently in every age and culture authentic faithfulness is expressed in new ways and by fresh insights through which the understanding of the apostolic preaching is enriched. Thus the gospel is not transmitted solely as a text. The living Word of God, together with the Spirit, communicates God's invitation to communion to the whole of his world in every age. This dynamic process *constitutes* what is called the living Tradition, the living memory of the Church. Without this the faithful transmission of the Gospel is impossible.

28. The living memory of the mystery of Christ is present and active within the Church as a whole; it is at work in the constant confession and celebration of the apostolic faith and in the insights, emphases and perspectives of faithful members of the Church. And since faith seeks understanding, this includes an examination of the very foundations of faith. As the social setting of the Christian community changes, so the questions and challenges posed both from within and from without the Church are never entirely the same. Even within the period covered by the New Testament this process is evident when

new images and fresh language are used to express the faith as it is handed on in changing cultural contexts.

29. If the Church is to remain faithfully rooted and grounded in the living truth and is to confess it with relevance, then it will need to develop new expressions of the faith. Diversity of cultures may often elicit a diversity, in the expression of the one Gospel; within the same community distinct perceptions and practices arise. Nevertheless these must remain faithful to the tradition received from the apostles (cf. Jude 3). Since the Holy Spirit is given to all the people of God, it is within the Church as a whole, individuals as well as communities, that the living memory of the faith is active. All authentic insights and perceptions, therefore, have their place within the life and faith of the whole Church, the temple of the Holy Spirit.

30. Tensions inevitably appear. Some are creative of healthy development. Some may cause a loss of continuity with apostolic Tradition, disruption within the community, estrangement from other parts of the Church. Within the history of Christianity, some diversities have become differences that have led to such conflict that ecclesial communion has been severed. Whenever differences become embodied in separated ecclesial communities, so that Christians are no longer able to receive and pass on the truth within the one community of faith, communion is impoverished and the living memory of the Church is affected. As Christians grow apart, complementary aspects of the one truth are sometimes perceived as mutually incompatible. Nevertheless the Church is sustained by Christ's promise of its perseverance in the truth (cf. Mt 16.18), even though its unity and peace are constantly vulnerable. The ultimate God-given safeguard for this assurance is the action of the Spirit in preserving the living memory of Christ.

31. This memory, realised and freshly expressed in every age and culture, constitutes the apostolic tradition of the Church. In recognizing the canon of Scripture as the normative record of the revelation of God, the Church sealed as authoritative its acceptance of the transmitted memory of the apostolic community. This is summarised and embodied in the creeds. The Holy Spirit makes this tradition a living reality which is perpetually celebrated and proclaimed by word and sacrament, pre-eminently in the eucharistic memorial of the once-for-all sacrifice of Christ, in which the Scriptures have always been read. Thus the apostolic tradition is fundamental to the Church's communion which spans time and space, linking the present to past and future generations of Christians.

32. Responsibility for the maintenance of the apostolic faith is shared by the whole people of God. Every Christian has a part in this responsibility. The task of those entrusted with oversight, acting in the name of Christ, is to foster the promptings of the Spirit and to keep the community within the bounds of the apostolic faith, to sustain and promote the Church's mission, by preaching, explaining and applying its truth. In responding to the insights of the community, and of the individual Christian, whose conscience is also moulded by the same Spirit, those exercising oversight seek to discern what is the mind of Christ. Discernment involves both heeding and sifting in order to assist the people of God in understanding, articulating and applying their faith. Sometimes an authoritative expression has to be given to the insights and convictions of the faithful. The community actively responds to the teaching of the ordained ministry, and when, under the guidance of the Spirit, it recognises the apostolic faith, it assimilates its content into its life.

33. Succession in the episcopal ministry is intended to assure each community that its faith is indeed the apostolic faith, received and transmitted from apostolic times. Further, by means of the communion among those entrusted with the episcopal ministry, the whole Church is made aware of the perceptions and concerns of the local churches: at the same time the local churches are enabled to maintain their place and particular character within the communion of all the churches.

34. In the creeds the Church has always confessed its *catholicity*: 'I believe in . . . the holy catholic Church'. It gets this title from the fact that by its nature it is to be scattered throughout the world, from one end of the earth to the other, from one age to the next. The Church is also catholic because its mission is to teach universally and without omission all that has been revealed by God for the salvation and fulfilment of humankind; and also because its vocation is to unite in one eucharistic fellowship men and women of every race, culture and social condition in every generation. Because it is the fruit of the work of Christ upon the cross, destroying all barriers of division, making Jews and Gentiles one holy people, both having access to the one Father by the one Spirit (cf. Eph 2.14–18), the Church is catholic.

35. In the mystery of his will God intends the Church to be the re-creation in Christ Jesus of all the richness of human diversity that sin turns into division and strife (cf. Eph 1.9, 10). Insofar as this re-creation is authentically demonstrated in its life, the Church is a sign of hope

to a divided world that longs for peace and harmony. It is the grace and Gospel of God that brings together this human diversity without stifling or destroying it; the Church's catholicity expresses the depth of the wisdom of the Creator. Human beings were created by God in his love with such diversity in order that they might participate in that love by sharing with one another both what they have and what they are, thus enriching each other in their mutual communion.

36. Throughout its history the Church has been called to demonstrate that salvation is not restricted to particular cultures. This is evident in the variety of liturgies and forms of spirituality, in the variety of disciplines and ways of exercising authority, in the variety of theological approaches, and even in the variety of theological expressions of the same doctrine. These varieties complement one another, showing that, as the result of communion with God in Christ, diversity does not lead to division; on the contrary, it serves to bring glory to God for the munificence of his gifts. Thus the Church in its catholicity is the place where God brings glory to his name through the communion of those he created in his own image and likeness, so diverse yet profoundly one. At every eucharistic celebration of Christian communities dispersed throughout the world, in their variety of cultures, languages, social and political contexts, it is the same, one and indivisible body of Christ reconciling divided humanity that is offered to believers. In this way the eucharist is the sacrament of the Church's catholicity in which God is glorified.

37. In the eucharist the Church also manifests its solidarity with the whole of humanity. This is given expression in intercession and thanksgiving, and in the sending out of the people of God to serve and to proclaim the message of salvation to the world. The Church's concern for the poor and oppressed is not peripheral but belongs to the very heart of its mission (cf. 2 Cor 8.1–9).

Moreover, for the Church effectively to carry out its ministry of reconciliation, it is necessary that its members and communities display in their common life the fruits of Christ's reconciling work. As long as Christians are divided, they do not fully manifest the catholic nature of the Church.

38. Catholicity is inseparable from holiness, as is evident from the early liturgical traditions which often speak of 'the holy catholic church' and from early forms of the creed which include the words 'We believe in the Holy Spirit in the holy Catholic Church'. The Church is *holy* because it is 'God's special possession', endowed with his

Spirit (cf. 1 Pt 2.9–10; Eph 2.21–22), and it is his special possession since it is there that 'the mystery of his will, according to his good pleasure' is realised, 'to bring all things in heaven and on earth together under one head, Christ' (Eph 1.9, 10).

Being set apart as God's special possession means that the Church is the communion of those who seek to be perfect as their Heavenly Father is perfect (Mt 5.48). This implies a life in communion with Christ, a life of compassion, love and righteousness. The holiness of the Church does not mean that it is to be cut off from the world (Jn 17.14ff). Its vocation is to be, through its holiness, salt of the earth, light to the world (Mt 5.13 and 16). In this way the Church declares the praises of him who called his people out of darkness into his marvellous light (cf. 1 Pt 2.9).

39. The catholicity of God's purpose requires that all the diverse gifts and graces given by God to sanctify his people should find their proper place in the Church. Every Christian is called to be consecrated to the life and service of the communion (Acts 2.42; 1 Pt 4.10ff; 1 Cor 12.4ff). And what is true of the individual is equally true of the local churches. Communion with other local churches is essential to the integrity of the self-understanding of each local church, precisely because of its catholicity. Life in self-sufficient isolation, which rejects the enrichment coming from other local churches as well as the sharing with them of gifts and resources, spiritual as well as material, is the denial of its very being. It is the particular ministry of oversight to affirm and order the diverse gifts and graces of individuals and communities; to effect and embody the unity of the local church and its unity with the wider communion of the churches. By the example of their lives those who bear oversight are to witness to the holiness of the Church and in their ministry foster holiness amongst its members.

Amid all the diversity that the catholicity intended by God implies, the Church's unity and coherence are maintained by the common confession of the one apostolic faith, a shared sacramental life, a common ministry of oversight and joint ways of reaching decisions and giving authoritative teaching.

40. The catholicity of the Church is threatened, in the first place, when the apostolic faith is distorted or denied within the community. It is also threatened whenever the faith is obscured by attitudes and behaviour in the Church which are not in accord with its calling to be the holy people of God, drawn together by the Spirit to live in

communion. Just as the Church has to distinguish between tolerable and intolerable diversity in the expression of the apostolic faith, so in the area of life and practice the Church has to discover what is constructive and what is disruptive of its own communion. Catholicity and holiness are also impaired when the Church fails to confront the causes of injustice and oppression which tear humanity apart or when it fails to hear the cries of those calling for sustenance, respect, peace and freedom.

41. When the Creed speaks of the Church as holy, catholic and apostolic, it does not mean that these attributes are distinct and unrelated. On the contrary, they are so interwoven that there cannot be one without the others. The holiness of the Church reflects the mission of the Spirit of God in Christ, the Holy One of God, made known to all the world through the apostolic teaching. Catholicity is the realisation of the Church's proclamation of the fullness of the Gospel to every nation throughout the ages. Apostolicity unites the Church of all generations and in every place with the once-for-all sacrifice and resurrection of Christ, where God's holy love was supremely demonstrated.

IV Unity and Ecclesial Communion

42. The Church, since apostolic times, has always included belief in its unity among the articles of faith (e.g. 1 Cor 12.12ff; Eph 4—6). Because there is only one Lord, with whom we are called to have communion in the one Spirit, God has given his Church one gospel, one faith, one baptism, one eucharist, and one apostolic ministry through which Christ continues to feed and guide his flock.

43. For a Christian the life of *communion* means sharing in the divine life, being united with the Father, through his Son, in the Holy Spirit, and consequently to be in fellowship with all those who share in the same gift of eternal life. This is a spiritual communion in which the reality of the life of the world to come is already present. But it is inadequate to speak only of an invisible spiritual unity as the fulfilment of Christ's will for the Church; the profound communion fashioned by the Spirit requires visible expression. The purpose of the visible ecclesial community is to embody and promote this spiritual communion with God (cf. paras 16–24).

For a local community to be a *communion* means that it is a gathering of the baptized brought together by the apostolic preaching,

57

confessing the one faith, celebrating the one eucharist, and led by an apostolic ministry. This implies that this local church is in communion with all Christian communities in which the essential constitutive elements of ecclesial life are present.

For all the local churches to be together in *communion*, the one visible communion God wills, it is required that all the essential constitutive elements of ecclesial communion are present and mutually recognised in each of them. Thus the visible communion between these churches is complete and their ministers are in communion with each other. This does not necessitate precisely the same canonical ordering: diversity of canonical structure is part of the acceptable diversity which enriches the one communion of all the churches.

44. The *constitutive elements* essential for the visible communion of the Church are derived from and subordinate to the common confession of Jesus Christ as Lord. In the picture of the Jerusalem church in the Acts of the Apostles we can already see in nascent form certain necessary elements of ecclesial communion which must be present in the Church in every age (cf. para 15).

45. In the light of all that we have said about communion it is now possible to describe what constitutes ecclesial communion. It is rooted in the confession of the one apostolic faith, revealed in the Scriptures, and set forth in the Creeds. It is founded upon one baptism. The one celebration of the eucharist is its pre-eminent expression and focus. It necessarily finds expression in shared commitment to the mission entrusted by Christ to his Church. It is a life of shared concern for one another in mutual forbearance, submission, gentleness and love; in the placing of the interests of others above the interests of self; in making room for each other in the body of Christ; in solidarity with the poor and the powerless; and in the sharing of gifts both material and spiritual (cf. Acts 2.44). Also constitutive of life in communion is acceptance of the same basic moral values, the sharing of the same vision of humanity created in the image of God and recreated in Christ and the common confession of the one hope in the final consummation of the kingdom of God.

For the nurture and growth of this communion, Christ the Lord has provided a ministry of oversight, the fullness of which is entrusted to the episcopate, which has the responsibility of maintaining and expressing the unity of the churches (cf. paras 33 & 39; *The Final Report*, Ministry and Ordination). By shepherding, teaching and the celebration of the sacraments, especially the eucharist, this ministry holds believers together in the communion of the local church and in the wider communion of all the churches (cf. para 39). This ministry of oversight has both collegial and primatial dimensions. It is grounded in the life of the community and is open to the community's participation in the discovery of God's will. It is exercised so that unity and communion are expressed, preserved and fostered at every level—locally, regionally and universally. In the context of the communion of all the churches the episcopal ministry of a universal primate finds its role as the visible focus of unity.

Throughout history different means have been used to express, preserve and foster this communion between bishops: the participation of bishops of neighbouring sees in episcopal ordinations; prayer for bishops of other dioceses in the liturgy; exchanges of episcopal letters. Local churches recognised the necessity of maintaining communion with the principal sees, particularly with the See of Rome. The practice of holding synods or councils, local, provincial, ecumenical, arose from the need to maintain unity in the one apostolic faith (cf. ARCIC I, *The Final Report*, Authority in the Church 19–23 II.12).

46. All these inter-related elements and facets belong to the visible communion of the universal Church. Although their possession cannot guarantee the constant fidelity of Christians, neither can the Church dispense with them. They need to be present in order for one local church to recognise another canonically. This does not mean that a community in which they are present expresses them fully in its life.

47. Christians can never acquiesce with complacency in disunity without impairing further their communion with God. As separated churches grow towards ecclesial communion it is essential to recognise the profound measure of communion they already share through participation in spiritual communion with God and through those elements of a visible communion of shared faith and sacramental life they can already recognise in one another. If some element or important facet of visible communion is judged to be lacking, the communion between them, though it may be real, is incomplete.

48. Within the pilgrim Church on earth, even when it enjoys complete ecclesial communion, Christians will be obliged to seek even deeper communion with God and one another. This is also expressed through faith in the 'Communion of Saints', whereby the Church declares its conviction that the eucharistic community on earth is itself a participation in a larger communion which includes the martyrs and confessors and all who have fallen asleep in Christ throughout the

ages. The perfection of full communion will only be reached in the fullness of the kingdom of God.

V   Communion Between Anglicans and Roman Catholics

49. The convictions which this Commission believes that Anglicans and Roman Catholics share concerning the nature of communion challenge both our churches to move forward together towards visible unity and ecclesial communion. Progress in mutual understanding has been achieved. There exists a significant degree of doctrinal agreement between our two Communions even upon subjects which previously divided us. In spite of past estrangements, Anglicans and Roman Catholics now enjoy a better understanding of their longstanding shared inheritance. This new understanding enables them to recognise in each other's churches a true affinity.

50. Thus we already share in the communion founded upon the saving life and work of Christ and his continuing presence through the Holy Spirit. This was acknowledged jointly in the Common Declaration of Pope John Paul II and Archbishop Robert Runcie of 2 October 1989.

> We also urge our clergy and faithful not to neglect or undervalue that certain yet imperfect communion we already share. This communion already shared is grounded in faith in God our Father, in our Lord Jesus Christ, and in the Holy Spirit; our common baptism into Christ; our sharing of the Holy Scriptures, of the Apostles' and Nicene Creeds; the Chalcedonian definition and the teaching of the Fathers; our common Christian inheritance for many centuries. This communion should be cherished and guarded as we seek to grow into the fuller communion Christ wills. Even in the years of our separation we have been able to recognise gifts of the Spirit in each other. The ecumenical journey is not only about removal of obstacles but also about the sharing of gifts.

51. One of the most important ways in which there has already been a sharing of gifts is in spirituality and worship. Roman Catholics and Anglicans now frequently pray together. Alongside common participation in public worship and in private prayer, members of both churches draw from a common treasury of spiritual writing and direction. There has been a notable convergence in our patterns of liturgy, especially in that of the eucharist. The same lectionary is used by both churches in many countries. We now agree on the use

of the vernacular language in public worship. We agree also that communion in both kinds is the appropriate mode of administration of the eucharist. In some circumstances, buildings are shared.

52. In some areas there is collaboration in Christian education and in service to local communities. For a number of years, Roman Catholic and Anglican scholars have worked together in universities and other academic institutions. There is closer cooperation in ministerial formation and between parochial clergy and religious communities. The responsibility for the pastoral care of inter-church families is now increasingly entrusted to both churches. Meetings of Roman Catholic and Anglican bishops are becoming customary, engendering mutual understanding and confidence. This often results in joint witness, practical action and common statements on social and moral issues. The growing measure of ecclesial communion experienced in these ways is the fruit of the communion we share with the Father, through the Son, in the Holy Spirit.

53. We cannot, however, ignore the effects of our centuries of separation. Such separation has inevitably led to the growth of divergent patterns of authority accompanied by changes in perceptions and practices. The differences between us are not only theological. Anglicans and Roman Catholics have now inherited different cultural traditions. Such differences in communities which have become isolated from one another have sometimes led to distortions in the popular perceptions which members of one church have of the other. As a result visible unity may be viewed as undesirable or even unattainable. However, a closer examination of the developments which have taken place in our different communities shows that these developments when held in complementarity can contribute to a fuller understanding of communion.

54. In recent years each communion has learnt from its own and each other's experiences, as well as through contact with other churches. Since the Second Vatican Council, the principle of collegiality and the need to adapt to local cultural conditions have been more clearly recognised by the Roman Catholic Church than before. Developing liturgical diversity, the increasing exercise of provincial autonomy and the growing appreciation of the universal nature of the Church have led Anglicans to develop organs of consultation and unity within their own communion. These developments remind us of the significance of mutual support and criticism, as together we seek to understand ecclesial communion and to achieve it.

55. Developments in the understanding of the theology of communion in each of our churches have provided the background for the Commission's reflections on the nature of communion. This Statement intends to be faithful to the doctrinal formulations to which Anglicans and Roman Catholics are each committed without providing an exhaustive treatment of the doctrine of the Church.

56. Grave obstacles from the past and of recent origin must not lead us into thinking that there is no further room for growth towards fuller communion. It is clear to the Commission as we conclude this document, that, despite continuing obstacles, our two Communions agree in their understanding of the Church as communion. Despite our distinct historical experiences, this firm basis should encourage us to proceed to examine our continuing differences.

57. Our approach to the unresolved matters we must now face together will be shaped by the agreed understanding of communion we have elaborated.

  An appreciation both of the existing degree of communion between Anglicans and Roman Catholics as well as the complete ecclesial communion to which we are called will provide a context for the discussion of the longstanding problem of the reconciliation of ministries which forms part of ARCIC II's mandate. This will build upon ARCIC I's work on Ministry and Ordination, which provides a new context for discussion of the consequences of the Bull *Apostolicae Curae* (1896).

  In the light of our agreement we must also address the present and future implications of the ordination of women to the priesthood and episcopate in those Anglican provinces which consider this to be a legitimate development within the catholic and apostolic tradition. The Lambeth Conference of 1988, while resolving that 'each Province respect the decision and attitudes of other Provinces in the ordination or consecration of women to the episcopate', also stressed the importance of 'maintaining the highest possible degree of communion with the Provinces that differ' (Resolution 1,1).

  Writing to the Archbishop of Canterbury shortly after the Lambeth Conference, Pope John Paul II said of the ordination of women that 'The Catholic Church, like the Orthodox Church and the Ancient Oriental Churches is firmly opposed to this development, viewing it as a break with Tradition of a kind we have no competence to authorise'. Referring to ARCIC's work in the reconciliation of ministries the Pope said 'the ordination of women to the episcopacy appears to pre-empt this study and effectively block the path to the mutual recognition of ministries' (Letter of Pope John Paul II to the Archbishop of Canterbury, 8th December 1988).

Another area which the Commission is currently engaged in studying is that of moral issues. Our distinct cultural inheritances have sometimes led us to treat of moral questions in different ways. Our study will explore the moral dimension of Christian life and seek to explain and assess its significance for communion as well as the importance of agreement or difference on particular moral questions.

It is evident that the above issues are closely connected with the question of authority. We continue to believe that an agreed understanding of the Church as communion is the appropriate context in which to continue the study of authority in the Church begun by ARCIC I. Further study will be needed of episcopal authority, particularly of universal primacy, and of the office of the Bishop of Rome; of the question of provincial autonomy in the Anglican Communion; and the role of the laity in decision-making within the Church. This work will take into account the response of the Lambeth Conference 1988 and the response of the Roman Catholic Church to *The Final Report* of ARCIC I.

58. Serious as these remaining obstacles may seem, we should not overlook the extent of the communion already existing between our two churches, which we have described in the last part of this Statement. Indeed, awareness of this fact will help us to bear the pain of our differences without complacency or despair. It should encourage Anglicans and Roman Catholics locally to search for further steps by which concrete expression can be given to this communion which we share. Paradoxically the closer we draw together the more acutely we feel those differences which remain. The forbearance and generosity with which we seek to resolve these remaining differences will testify to the character of the fuller communion for which we strive. Together with all Christians, Anglicans and Roman Catholics are called by God to continue to pursue the goal of complete communion of faith and sacramental life. This call we must obey until all come into the fullness of that Divine Presence, to whom Father, Son and Holy Spirit be ascribed all honour, thanksgiving and praise to the ages of ages. Amen.

Responses

Church as Communion has drawn little attention from officials, theologians, and ecumenists (as can be seen in the Bibliography on p. 69). This may be due to the nature of the Statement, since it does not deal with divisive issues, or to the fact that it reflects the development of wider ecumenical thinking about the nature of the Church. Other publications in the same period, such as the WCC's Statement *The Unity of the Church: Gift and Calling* (Canberra, 1991),[1] with its focus on *koinonia*, or the Letter of the Vatican Congregation for the Doctrine of the Faith (CDF) on 'Some Aspects of the Church Understood as Communion' (1992),[2] have attracted more attention.

Official Roman Catholic Responses: The Extent of Ecclesial Communion

The Roman Catholic official Commentary on *Church as Communion*, prepared by Francis Sullivan SJ, assessed the Statement's contribution as 'a rather modest one', 'not something new, but a more extensive and systematic treatment of the idea of ecclesial communion'.[3] Its 'principal merit' is that 'it demonstrates the very considerable extent to which Anglicans and Roman Catholics share a common ecclesiology'. Further, the Commission has 'taken the trouble to work out the implications of the notion of communion for some fundamental aspects of the nature of the Church'.

But questions are raised, notably concern about the way the terms 'Church' (with capital) and 'church(es)' (lower case) are used. The Agreed Statement adopts the convention that 'church' refers to a local or particular ecclesial body, whereas by 'Church' is meant both the universal Church of Christ, and also the communion of local churches, or of particular churches, Anglican or Roman Catholic. The question then arises as to whether the presently imperfect communion (of the churches of the Anglican Communion, for example) justifies describing this communion as 'Church'. A related question is how the use of 'Church'/'churches' in *Church as Communion* corresponds to Vatican II's distinction between 'churches' and 'ecclesial communities', and to the claim that the Church of Christ 'subsists'

[1] www.oikoumene.org/en/resources/documents/commissions/faith-and-order/i-unity-the-church-and-its-mission/the-unity-of-the-church-gift-and-calling-the-canberra-statement.

[2] CDF, Letter to the Bishops of the Catholic Church on 'Some Aspects of the Church Understood as Communion' (1992), www.vatican.va/roman_curia/congregations/cfaith/documents/rc_con_cfaith_doc_28051992_communionis-notio_en.html.

[3] F. A. Sullivan SJ, 'Comment on *Church as Communion*', *Information Service*, 77 (1991–2), 97–102.

in the Roman Catholic Church.[4] Moreover, it is not clear whether 'the Church' refers to the Church as it actually exists, or to the ideal, eschatological Church. Given the acknowledgement that 'diversity of canonical structures is part of the acceptable diversity which enriches the one communion of all the churches' (*Church as Communion*, §43), Sullivan asks, 'how great a diversity of canonical structures would be acceptable?' The Statement thus leaves 'the "hard questions" still be to answered.' These matters are relevant to the mandate of ARCIC III, to consider 'Church as Communion, local and universal'.

Another question has to do with the notion of 'communion'. The purpose of *Church as Communion* is 'to give substance to the affirmation that Anglicans and Roman Catholics are already in a real though imperfect communion' (§2). Lying behind this is the fundamental question as to whether both traditions really do agree about what 'full communion' means and involves. *Church as Communion* speaks of the 'essential constitutive elements of ecclesial communion', and seeks to describe them (§§42–45).[5] But how the precise content of these elements is to be understood is left open.

The Letter of the CDF on 'Some Aspects of the Church Understood as Communion' (1992) is addressed to the bishops of the Catholic Church, and as such cannot be seen as a direct response to *Church as Communion*. It rather deals with what it considers to be inadequate interpretations of the ecclesiology of communion within the Roman Catholic Church, without citing names. The Letter notes several aspects of this ecclesiology which are in line with *Church as Communion* and are to be welcomed in ecumenical circles:[6]

- communion has to be understood both vertically and horizontally;
- communion is inseparable from the sacramentality of the Church;
- the eucharist as the source of communion within the Church;
- communion includes the larger communion of saints;
- the unity of the Church is also rooted in the episcopate;
- forms of primacy, including the universal primacy of the Bishop of Rome, are genuinely episcopal ministries; and
- fostering unity does not contradict diversity.

---

[4] *Lumen Gentium*, §8. Cf. *Unitatis Redintegratio*, §§19–23.
[5] The use of the term 'elements' in an ecclesial context is indebted to *Unitatis Redintegratio*, §3.
[6] See Christopher Hill, '*Church as Communion*: An Anglican Response', *One in Christ*, 28/4 (1992), 323–30. Hill was the Anglican Co-Secretary for ARCIC from 1974 to 1981.

The main emphasis of the Letter, however, falls on two areas:

i. the relationship of mutual interiority between the particular churches and the universal Church: compare the CDF formula 'Churches in and from the Church' (*Ecclesiae in et ex Ecclesia*) and the Vatican II formula 'the Church in and from the Churches' (*Ecclesia in et ex Ecclesiis: Lumen Gentium*, §23); and

ii. the ontological and temporal priority of the universal Church on the one hand, and the indispensability of the Petrine office of the Bishop of Rome in an authentically catholic ecclesiology of communion on the other.

In the Letter, two approaches regarding the way 'communion' is understood and used as an ecclesial category have been identified. One begins with the concrete, historical manifestation of the Church at the local level; another starts from the universal Church as an ideal, spiritual reality.[7] The way in which these positions may be understood as not mutually exclusive, but rather as complementary, goes to the heart of the mandate for ARCIC III, 'Church as Communion, local and universal'.

Faith and Order Advisory Group of the Church of England: Communion as an Ecclesial Concept

The Faith and Order Advisory Group of the Church of England (FOAG) briefed the 2008 General Synod regarding *Church as Communion*.[8] After a comprehensive summary of the Agreed Statement, noting some 'particularly important' aspects, Section 4 states some apparent difficulties. These warn against simplistic use of 'communion' in the analysis of biblical material; against relating the doctrine of the Church simplistically to the doctrine of the Trinity; against undervaluing 'the way in which participation in the life of God involves sharing in the sufferings of Christ (Philippians 3.10)'; and against undervaluing the 'equally important role of the preaching of the word in creating and sustaining communion' alongside baptism and eucharist.

FOAG recognized that since the 1970s 'communion' has become a predominant ecclesiological concept into which other ecclesial images or

---

[7] See Edward Hahnenberg, 'The Mystical Body of Christ and Communion Ecclesiology: Historical Parallels', *Irish Theological Quarterly*, 70 (2005), 3–30, especially 20–1. He attributes the distinction to Cardinal Walter Kasper, who suggests that 'The conflict is between theological opinions and underlying philosophical assumptions': 'On the Church: A Friendly Reply to Cardinal Ratzinger', *America*, 184 (23–30 April 2001), 8–14, at p. 13.

[8] FOAG, '*Church as Communion*: Briefing for the General Synod' (2008), GS Misc 1713, www.churchofengland.org/media/1236810/gs1713.pdf.

categories are integrated. It has become an elastic and encompassing category, suggesting that the whole reality of the Church is aptly described and understood in this way. It affirmed that a 'communion ecclesiology' offers a framework for dealing with issues such as the importance of the local church, the eucharist as its central mystery, and the participation of all believers in the divine life and in ecclesial life. It has shown rich ecumenical potentialities, in giving Christian traditions a common language and motif to express their mutual relationships, by using qualifiers such as 'real but imperfect' to describe the actual situation, and 'full and perfect' communion as the final goal of the ecumenical movement.

Nevertheless a note of caution is in place:

> Is [the term koinonia] becoming an umbrella term in ecclesiology generally, and in ecumenical dialogues in particular, with the result that in coming to refer to everything, in the end it will refer to nothing?[9]

No one ecclesiological concept is self-sufficient, FOAG argues: 'communion' should be seen in relation to other images or categories—people of God, body of Christ, temple of the Holy Spirit, and so on (see *Church as Communion*, §13).

In response, it is instructive to reflect on the extent to which recent Anglican documents have embraced an ecclesiology of *koinonia* that is demonstrably congruent with *Church as Communion*. This has been most noticeable in the continuing and painful debates about authority within the Anglican Communion. Successive reports of the Eames Commission (on the ordination of women to the episcopate) expounded a *koinonia* ecclesiology with explicit reference to *Church as Communion*, amongst other ecumenical documents.[10] *The Virginia Report* of the Inter-Anglican Theological and Doctrinal Commission, following through on the Eames Commission's work as stipulated in Resolution 18.1 of the 1988 Lambeth Conference, likewise begins its exploration of ecclesial communion with the *koinonia* of the Trinity and the life of the Church.[11] Significantly from the perspective of ARCIC, *Growing Together in Unity and Mission* (the

---

[9] Susan Wood, 'Ecclesial *Koinonia* in Ecumenical Dialogues', *One in Christ*, 30 (1994), 124–45, at 124. See further 'Communion Ecclesiology: Critique' in Chapter 10 below.

[10] The Eames Commission, *The Official Reports of the Archbishop of Canterbury's Commission on Communion and Women in the Episcopate* (Toronto: Anglican Book Centre, 1994). The three reports were produced in March 1989, October 1989, and December 1993.

[11] *The Virginia Report*, in James M. Rosenthal and Nicola Currie (eds.), *Being Anglican in the Third Millennium: The Official Report of the 10th Meeting of the Anglican Consultative Council* (Harrisburg: Morehouse, 1997), 211–81. Resolution 18 concerned 'The Anglican Communion: Identity and Authority' (pp. 283–5).

2007 report of IARCCUM) also begins with an exposition of communion ecclesiology.[12]

At the provincial level in the Anglican Communion, it is also evident that *Church as Communion* and other ecumenical agreements, together with the understanding of *koinonia* emerging from the Second Vatican Council, have influenced important teaching documents. In the Church of England, for example, teaching documents of the House of Bishops such as *Apostolicity and Succession* (1994) and *Bishops in Communion* (2000) have been influenced by the work of ARCIC on *koinonia*—the former document with five direct references. Several Anglican–Roman Catholic national dialogues prepared study guides to *Church as Communion*—AustARC in Australia for example.[13]

Conclusion

All this is indicative of a positive, actual reception of ARCIC and other ecumenical thinking about the Church as communion, participating in the *koinonia* of God. The full implications of these developments in ecclesiology are still to be considered and worked through by the churches. Since the emergence of this communion ecclesiology in the second half of the twentieth century, new questions have arisen: questions relating to secularism and religious indifference, religious pluralism, violence and religion, human sexuality and relationships, churches stressing their confessional identity and accepting the status quo of division, inter-religious dialogue, new forms of mission, inculturation, evangelization and ministry, and structures of clericalism and power. Unless these questions are addressed, the model of communion ecclesiology which has undergirded much of ARCIC's work will be seen to be irrelevant.[14]

Aspects of these issues were taken up by ARCIC II in its subsequent Agreed Statement, *The Gift of Authority: Authority in the Church III* (1999).

---

[12] IARCCUM, *Growing Together in Unity and Mission: Building on 40 Years of Anglican–Roman Catholic Dialogue. An Agreed Statement of the International Anglican-Roman Catholic Commission for Unity and Mission* (London: SPCK, 2007), www.vatican.va/roman_curia/pontifical_councils/chrstuni/angl-comm-docs/rc_pc_chrstuni_doc_20070914_growing-together_en.html.

[13] AustARC, *Church as Communion: A Discussion Resource for Anglicans and Roman Catholics* (Brisbane: Faith Education Services, 2004) is an attractively produced book including meeting guides, prayers, and stories as well as commentary on the text. The Anglican–Roman Catholic Commission in Aotearoa New Zealand adapted this for use by Anglicans and Roman Catholics in Aotearoa, New Zealand, releasing it as an online PDF.

[14] Hahnenberg, 'The Mystical Body of Christ and Communion Ecclesiology', 28–9, and some contributors to the Church of England General Synod debate on *Church as Communion*, suggest that communion ecclesiology be supplemented by a *missio* ecclesiology and a *baptismal* ecclesiology—the approach taken by IARCCUM.

It is the mandate of ARCIC III to address 'Church as Communion, local and universal, and how in communion the local and universal Church come to discern right ethical teaching'. The responses made to *Church as Communion*, limited in number though they may be, underline the importance of this task.

Bibliography

Official Responses

CDF, Letter to the Bishops of the Catholic Church on 'Some Aspects of the Church Understood as Communion' (1992), www.vatican.va/roman_curia/congregations/cfaith/documents/rc_con_cfaith_doc_28051992_communionis-notio_en.html

FOAG, '*Church as Communion*: Briefing for the General Synod' (2008), GS Misc 1713, www.churchofengland.org/media/1236810/gs1713.pdf

Sullivan, F. A., SJ, 'Comment on *Church as Communion*', *Information Service*, 77 (1991–2), 97–102

Significant Publications

Anglican–Roman Catholic Commission in Aotearoa New Zealand, *Church as Communion: A Discussion Resource for Anglicans and Roman Catholics in Aotearoa New Zealand* (Auckland, 2005), based on:

AustARC, *Church as Communion: A Discussion Resource for Anglicans and Roman Catholics* (Brisbane: Faith Education, 2004)

Hill, Christopher, 'Church as Communion: An Anglican Response', *One in Christ*, 28/4 (1992), 323–30

Lüning, P., 'Das Dialogdokument *Kirche als Gemeinschaft* (1990)', in *Offenbarung und Rechtfertigung: Eine Studie zu ihrer Verhältnisbestimmung anhand des anglikanisch/römisch-katholischen Dialogs*, Konfessionskundliche und kontroverstheologische Studien, 70 (Paderborn: Bonifatius, 1999), 332–67

Yarnold, E., 'The Church as Communion', *The Tablet*, 245 (1991), 117–18

Chapter 3

Life in Christ: Morals, Communion and the Church (1994)

Introducing the Statement

Although *Life in Christ*, the first Agreed Statement on morals arising from ecumenical dialogue, was not issued until 1994, the need for work on this area was recognized in the 1968 *Malta Report*. As well as noting the work of the Joint Commission on Marriage (§16), it recommended 'joint study of moral theology to determine similarities and differences in our teaching and practice in this field' (§23). Nonetheless, ARCIC I gave priority to the tasks set down in the *Malta Report* §22, namely 'inter-communion, and the related matters of Church and Ministry' and 'author-ity, its nature, exercise and implications', as reflected in *The Final Report*.

ARCIC II in its first phase (1983–90) focused on matters which arose from responses to *The Final Report* of ARCIC I, and consolidated its *koinonia* approach to ecclesiology. Work on morals was initiated at the 1990 meeting, and a subcommittee was asked to draft material. In 1991, however, the Commission's membership changed significantly: a new start was made, assisted by several specialists in moral theology as consultants (see Chapter 13 below). It was soon realized that significant differences had arisen in the centuries of separation between Rome and the Church of England, as diverse approaches were taken, in separation, to new issues such as marriage following divorce. In contrast with earlier ARCIC Statements, *Life in Christ* gives much more space to the exploration of historical factors. It also notes changes in moral theology which have taken place in recent decades, such as the shift towards more personal and rela-tional approaches.

A New Context

The conclusions reached in *Life in Christ*, as stated in its opening paragraph, are based on agreement about a 'shared vision' of moral life. The Statement maintains that both Anglican and Roman Catholic traditions acknowledge a set of underlying values as necessary elements of Christian life, in response to 'the patterning power of the kingdom'. The conviction that the two traditions share a common vision of human fulfilment in Christ gave hope that differences between Anglican and Roman Catholic teaching on moral issues could either be resolved or be accepted as legitimate, differentiated responses, thus promoting common witness and cooperation.

In the two decades since the Statement was published, however, the ecclesial and wider social situation regarding moral life has changed. ARCIC II faced a situation in 1991 where the documented differences between Anglican and Roman Catholic moral positions were twofold, namely teaching on contraception and divorce: this is why *Life in Christ* gives much space to these issues. Potential differences over abortion and homosexuality were noted, but viewed as less serious, though sharp divergences have since emerged in the latter area. As the Anglican–Roman Catholic Dialogue in the USA (ARCUSA) in its 1995 analysis of *Life in Christ* stated,

> The experience of our two Churches in the United States indicates further that the specific moral issues highlighted in Life in Christ are considerably more conflictual—both within each of our Churches and between us—than ARCIC appears to have recognised ... The sometimes sharply divergent specific teachings and practices of our Churches regarding divorce, contraception, abortion, and homosexuality are actually a frequently given reason why Roman Catholic and Episcopalian Christians leave one Church and enter the other.[1]

Since then, debate about the treatment accorded to Christians who experience same-sex attraction has become a divisive issue in the Anglican Communion, focused on the consecration in 2003 of a bishop in a non-celibate same-sex relationship. The magisterium of the Roman Catholic Church continues to teach that same-sex sexual acts are immoral and same-sex marriages are impossible, and that, while the inclination to same-sex behaviour is not sinful, it is nonetheless a disorder. These teachings on same-sex issues are widely accepted in some parts of the world, and resisted more and more in other parts. Considerable questions are thus raised as to whether the agreements in *Life in Christ* can be sustained.[2]

---

[1] ARCUSA, 'Christian Ethics in the Ecumenical Dialogue: Anglican–Roman Catholic International Commission II and Recent Papal Teachings' (June 1995), Conclusion, www.usccb.org/beliefs-and-teachings/ecumenical-and-interreligious/ecumenical/anglican/ethics-in-ecumenical-dialogue.cfm.

[2] See further ARCUSA, *Ecclesiology and Moral Discernment: Seeking a Unified Moral Witness* (April 2014), §§43–59, www.episcopalchurch.org/library/document/ecclesiology-and-moral-discernment-statement-anglican-roman-catholic-theological.

Also on the Roman Catholic side, a new context for assessing ARCIC's work on morals is provided in a number of significant documents. John Paul II issued *Veritatis Splendor* in 1993, just before *Life in Christ* was published.[3] This was followed by *Evangelium Vitae* (1995) and Part III of the *Catechism of the Catholic Church*, 'Life in Christ' (1997). The English publication in 2006 of John Paul II's *Man and Woman He Created Them: A Theology of the Body* provided a more biblically based defence of the Roman Catholic Church's teaching on sexuality: this has shaped other magisterial documents such as *Mulieris Dignitatem* (1988), *The Truth and Meaning of Human Sexuality* (Congregation for the Doctrine of the Faith (CDF), 1995), and Pope Benedict XVI's *Deus Caritas Est* (2005). It is important to acknowledge that these documents place *Life in Christ* in a new context which must be respected as ecumenical dialogue on Christian morality progresses.

Life in Christ: What is Not Said

A significant omission from *Life in Christ* is the large and increasing degree of agreement between the Anglican Communion and Roman Catholic Church on issues of social and environmental ethics. ARCIC II was mandated to consider matters which divide the two traditions: in the case of moral life, these clearly concerned personal much more than social ethics. Hence the concentration in *Life in Christ* on divorce, abortion, contraception, and same-sex relationships. Had ARCIC II been asked to express areas of moral consensus, much more might have been said about shared social teaching.

The need for ethical reflection and common action by Anglicans, Roman Catholics, and others is evident and urgent. In *Life in Christ* it is recognized that 'no arbitrary boundaries may be set between the good of the individual, the common good of humanity, and the good of the whole created order' (§93).

---

[3] In the same year, the CDF issued its 'Letter to the Bishops of the Catholic Church concerning the Reception of Holy Communion by the Divorced and Remarried Members of the Faithful'.

LIFE IN CHRIST

Morals, Communion and the Church

An Agreed Statement by the
Second Anglican–Roman Catholic
International Commission (ARCIC II)

CONTENTS

THE STATUS OF THE DOCUMENT

The Document published here is the work of the Second Anglican–Roman Catholic International Commission (ARCIC II). It is a joint statement of the Commission. The authorities who appointed the Commission have allowed the statement to be published so that it may be widely discussed. It is not an authoritative declaration by the Roman Catholic Church or by the Anglican Communion, who will evaluate the document in order to take a position on it in due time.

Citations from Scripture are mostly from the Revised Standard Version. However, use has also been made of the Jerusalem Bible and the Revised English Bible.

PREFACE

By the Co-Chairmen

As we reach the end of ten years in the life of ARCIC II it may be opportune to recall the words of Pope John Paul II and Archbishop Robert Runcie in their *Common Declaration* at Canterbury in May, 1982:

> The new International Commission is to continue the work already begun; to examine, especially in the light of our respective judgements on *The Final Report*, the outstanding doctrinal differences which still separate us, with a view to their eventual resolution; to study all that hinders the mutual recognition of the ministries of our Communions, and to recommend what practical steps will be necessary when, on the basis of our unity in faith, we are able to proceed to the restoration of full communion. We are well aware that this new Commission's task will not be easy but we are encouraged by our reliance on the grace of God and by all that we have seen of the power of that grace in the ecumenical movement of our time.

We repeat these words in order to assure both our Communions that the work of the Commission, however long or difficult it may be, must continue and is continuing. Among the many international dialogues, bilateral and multilateral, between divided Christians, the Anglican–Roman Catholic International Commission is the first to have directly attempted the subject of morals. We have prepared this statement in response to requests from the authorities of both our Communions. These requests have given voice to a widespread belief that Anglicans and Roman Catholics are as much, if not more, divided on questions of morals as of doctrine. This belief in turn reflects the profound and true conviction that authentic Christian unity is as much a matter of life as of faith. Those who share one faith in Christ will share one life in Christ. Hence the title of this statement: Life in Christ: Morals, Communion and the Church.

The theme of this statement was already adumbrated in our previous work on Church as Communion. In describing 'the constitutive elements essential for the visible communion of the Church', we wrote: 'Also constitutive of life in communion is acceptance of the same basic moral values, the sharing of the same vision of humanity created in the image of God and recreated in Christ, and the common confession of the one hope in the final consummation of the kingdom of God' (44, 45).

As Christians we seek a common life not for our own sakes only, but for the glory of God and the good of humankind. In the face of the world around us, the name of God is profaned whenever those who call themselves Christians show themselves divided in their witness to the objective moral demands which arise from our life in Christ. Our search for communion and unity in morals as in faith is therefore a form of the Lord's own prayer to this Father:

> Hallowed be thy name, thy kingdom come,
> thy will be done, on earth as it is in heaven.

+ Cormac Murphy-O'Connor
+ Mark Santer

Venice, 5 September 1993

LIFE IN CHRIST

A INTRODUCTION

1. There is a popular and widespread belief that the Anglican and Roman Catholic Communions are divided most sharply by their moral teaching. Careful consideration has persuaded the Commission that, despite existing disagreement in certain areas of practical and pastoral judgement, Anglicans and Roman Catholics derive from the Scriptures and Tradition the same controlling vision of the nature and destiny of humanity and share the same fundamental moral values. This substantial area of common conviction calls for shared witness, since both Communions proclaim the same Gospel and acknowledge the same injunction to mission and service. A disproportionate emphasis on particular disagreements blurs this important truth and can provoke a sense of alienation. There is already a notable convergence between the two Communions in the witness they give, for example, on war and peace, euthanasia, freedom and justice, but exaggeration of outstanding differences makes this shared witness— a witness which could give direction to a world in danger of losing its way—more difficult to sustain and at the same time hinders its further development. Such a shared witness is, in today's society, urgent. It is also, we believe, possible. The widespread assumption, therefore, that differences of teaching on certain particular moral issues signify an irreconcilable divergence of understanding, and therefore present an insurmountable obstacle to shared witness, needs to be countered. Even on those particular issues where disagreement exists, Anglicans and Roman Catholics, we shall argue, share a common perspective and acknowledge the same underlying values. This being so, we question whether the limited disagreement, serious as it is, is itself sufficient to justify a continuing breach of communion.

2. In presenting this statement on morals, we are responding, not simply to popular concern, but also to requests from the authorities of both Communions. In the past, ecumenical dialogue has concentrated on matters of doctrine. These are of primary importance and work here still remains to be done. However, the Gospel we proclaim cannot be divorced from the life we live. Questions of

doctrine and of morals are closely inter-connected, and differences in the one area may reflect differences in the other. Common to both is the matter of authority and the manner of its exercise. Although we shall not here be addressing the issue of authority directly, nevertheless we hope that an understanding of the relationship between freedom and authority in the moral life may contribute to our understanding of their relationship in the life of the Church.

3. In what follows we shall attempt to display the basis and shape of Christian moral teaching and to show that both our Communions apprehend it in the same light. We begin by re-affirming our common faith that the life to which God, through Jesus Christ, calls women and men is nothing less than participation in the divine life, and we spell out some of the characteristics and implications of our shared vision of life in Christ. We go on to remind ourselves of our common heritage and of the living tradition through which both Communions have sought to develop a faithful and appropriate response to the good news of the Gospel. Next we review the ways in which this tradition has diverged since the break in communion, at the same time drawing attention to signs of a new convergence, not least in our emphasis on the common good. We fasten upon the two particular issues of marriage after divorce and contraception— issues upon which the two Communions have expressed their disagreement in official documents and pastoral practice—in order to determine as precisely as we can the nature and extent of our moral disagreement and to relate it to our continuing agreement on fundamental values. In our last section we return to the theme of communion and, in the light of what has gone before, show how communion determines both the structure of the moral order and the method of the Church's discernment and response. Finally, we re-affirm our belief that differences and disagreements are exacerbated by a continuing breach of communion, and that integrity of moral response itself requires a movement towards full communion. We conclude by suggesting steps by which we may move forward together along this path to the greater glory of God and the wellbeing of God's world.

B SHARED VISION

4. The Christian life is a response in the Holy Spirit to God's selfgiving in Jesus Christ. To this gift of himself in incarnation, and to

this participation in the divine life, the Scriptures bear witness (cf. 1 Jn 1.1–3; 2 Pt 1.3–4). Made in the image of God (cf. Gen 1.27), and part of God's good creation (cf. Gen 1.31), women and men are called to grow into the likeness of God, in communion with Christ and with one another. What has been entrusted to us through the incarnation and the Christian tradition is a vision of God. This vision of God in the face of Jesus Christ (cf. 2 Cor 4.6; compare Gen 1.3) is at the same time a vision of humanity renewed and fulfilled. Life in Christ is the gift and promise of new creation (cf. 2 Cor 5.17), the ground of community, and the pattern of social relations. It is the shared inheritance of the Church and the hope of every believer.

5. God creates human beings with the dignity of persons in community, calls them to a life of responsibility and freedom, and endows them with the hope of happiness. As children of God, our true freedom is to be found in God's service, and our true happiness in faithful and loving response to God's love and grace. We are created to glorify and enjoy God, and our hearts continue to be restless until they find in God their rest and fulfilment.

6. The true goal of the moral life is the flourishing and fulfilment of that humanity for which all men and women have been created. The fundamental moral question, therefore, is not 'What ought we to do?', but 'What kind of persons are we called to become?' For children of God, moral obedience is nourished by the hope of becoming like God (cf. 1 Jn 3.1–3).

7. True personhood has its origins and roots in the life and love of God. The mystery of the divine life cannot be captured by human thought and language, but in speaking of God as Trinity in Unity, Father, Son and Holy Spirit, we are affirming that the Being of God is a unity of self-communicating and interdependent relationships. Human persons, therefore, made in this image, and called to participate in the life of God, may not exercise a freedom that claims to be independent, wilful and self-seeking. Such a use of freedom is a distortion of their God-given humanity. It is sin. The freedom that is properly theirs is a freedom of responsiveness and interdependence. They are created for communion, and communion involves responsibility, in relation to society and nature as well as to God.

8. Ignorance and sin have led to the misuse and corruption of human freedom and to delusive ideas of human fulfilment. But God has been faithful to his eternal purposes of love and, through the redemption

of the world by Jesus Christ, offers to human beings participation in a new creation, recalling them to their true freedom and fulfilment. As God remains faithful and free, so those who are in Christ are called to be faithful and free, and to share in God's creative and redemptive work for the whole of creation.

9. The new life in Christ is for the glorification of God. Living in communion with Christ, the Church is called to make Christ's words its own: 'I have glorified you on earth' (cf. Jn 17.4). The new life has also been entrusted to the Church for the good of the whole world (cf. Church as Communion, 18). This life is for everyone and embraces everyone. In seeking the common good, therefore, the Church listens and speaks, not only to the faithful, but also to women and men of good will everywhere. Despite the ambiguities and evils in the world, and despite the sin that has distorted human life, the Church affirms the original goodness of creation and discerns signs and contours of an order that continues to reflect the wisdom and goodness of the Creator. Nor has sin deprived human beings of all perception of this order. It is generally recognised, for example, that torture is intrinsically wrong, and that the integration of sexual instincts and affections into a lifelong relationship of married love and loyalty constitutes a uniquely significant form of human flourishing and fulfilment. Reflection on experience of what makes human beings, singly and together, truly human gives rise to a natural morality, sometimes interpreted in terms of natural justice or natural law, to which a general appeal for guidance can be made. In Jesus Christ this natural morality is not denied. Rather, it is renewed, transfigured and perfected, since Christ is the true and perfect image of God.

10. Christian morality is one aspect of the life in Christ which shapes the tradition of the Church, a tradition which is also shaped by the community which carries it. Christian morality is the fruit of faith in God's Word, the grace of the sacraments, and the appropriation, in a life of forgiveness, of the gifts of the Spirit for work in God's service. It manifests itself in the practical teaching and pastoral care of the Church and is the outward expression of that continual turning to God whereby forgiven sinners grow up together into Christ and into the mature humanity of which Christ is the measure and fullness (cf. Eph 4.13). At its deepest level, the response of the Church to the offer of new life in Christ possesses an unchanging identity from age to age and place to place. In its particular teachings, however, it takes account of changing circumstances

and needs, and in situations of unusual ambiguity and perplexity it seeks to combine new insight and discernment with an underlying continuity and consistency.

11. Approached in this light the fundamental questions with which a Christian morality engages are such as these:

> What are persons called to be, as individuals and as members one of another in the human family?
>
> What constitutes human dignity, and what are the social as well as the individual dimensions of human dignity and responsibility?
>
> How does divine forgiveness and grace engage with human finitude, fragility and sin in the realisation of human happiness?
>
> How are the conditions and structures of human life related to the goal of human fulfilment?
>
> What are the implications of the creatureliness which human beings share with the rest of the natural world?

At this fundamental level of inquiry and concern, we believe, our two Communions share a common vision and understanding. To affirm our agreement here will prove a significant step forward towards the recovery of full communion. It will put in proper perspective any disagreement that may continue to exist in official teaching and pastoral practice on particular issues, such as divorce and contraception. The crisis of the modern world is more than a crisis of sexual ethics. At stake is our humanity itself.

C COMMON HERITAGE

1 A Shared Tradition

12. Anglicans and Roman Catholics are conscious that their respective traditions, rooted in a shared vision, stem from a common heritage, which in spite of stress and strain, within and without, shaped the Church's life for some 1500 years. Drawing upon the faith of Israel, this common heritage springs from the conversion of the disciples to faith in Jesus Christ and their mission to share that faith with others. Fullness of life in Christ in the kingdom of God is its goal. It is also the norm by which the tradition in all its varied manifestations is to be judged. Any manifestation that no longer has the power to nurture and sustain the new life in Christ is thereby shown to be corrupt. Anglicans and Roman Catholics firmly believe that their respective traditions continue to nourish and support them in

their daily discipleship, but they are aware of the impairment to their common heritage caused by the breach in their communion, and they look forward to the time when both traditions will again flow together for their mutual enrichment and for their common witness and service to the world.

13. The shared tradition was richly woven from many strands. These include faith in God, Father, Son and Holy Spirit, publicly professed in baptism; a common life, founded on love, centred in eucharistic prayer and worship, expressed in service; the teaching and nourishment of the Scriptures; an ordered leadership, entrusted with guarding and guiding the tradition through the conflicts of history; a sense of discipleship, manifested in the lives of the saints and acknowledged by devotion and piety; the proscription of deeds that undermine the values of the Gospel and threaten to destroy the new life in Christ; ways of reconciliation, by which sinners may be brought back into communion with God and with one another. At the same time the tradition drew upon the inherited wisdom and culture of the world in which it was embedded.

14. This common tradition carried with it a 'missionary imperative'— a call to preach the Gospel, to live the life of the Gospel in the world, and to work out a faithful and fruitful response to the Gospel in encounter with different cultures. Both Anglicans and Roman Catholics have understood the missionary task in this way, and both have been eager to fulfil the claims of their earthly citizenship (cf. Rom 13.4–5), while remembering that they are citizens of heaven (cf. Phil 3.20). They have attempted to carry out Christ's missionary injunction accordingly, though sometimes they have interpreted their involvement in the cultural life of the world in very different ways. In their engagement with culture they have been led to give careful thought to the practical expression of the new life in Christ and to provide specific teaching on some of its moral and social aspects.

15. This openness to the world, which has characterised both our traditions, has shaped the pattern of life which these traditions have sustained. It is not the life of an inwardly pious and self-regarding group, withdrawn from the world and its conflicts. It is, rather, a life to be lived out amidst the ambiguities of the world. Yet it is also a pilgrim life which, while seeking the welfare of the world, has a destiny which transcends the present age. Admittedly, this involvement with the world has from time to time led the Church into compromise and alliance with corrupt principalities and powers. At

other times, however, cooperation with secular authorities has borne good fruit, and the conviction that the Church is called to live in the world and to work for the salvation of the world has remained strong. Thus, while both our Communions retain painful memories of occasions of betrayal and sin, both put their trust, not in human strength, but in the saving power of God.

16. Both our traditions draw their vision from the Scriptures. To the Scriptures, therefore, we now turn, to discover the origins of our common heritage in the Gospel of Jesus Christ and the faithful response of the Christian community.

2 The Pattern of Our Life in Christ

17. The good news of the Gospel is the coming of the kingdom of God (cf. Mk 1. 15), the redemption of the world by our Lord Jesus Christ (cf. Gal 4.4–5), the forgiveness of sins and new life in the Spirit (cf. Acts 2.38), and the hope of glory (cf. Col 1.27).

18. The redemption won by Jesus Christ carries with it the promise of a new life of freedom from the domination of sin (cf. Rom 6.18). Through his dying on the cross Christ has overcome the powers of darkness and death, and through his rising again from the dead he has opened the gates of eternal life (cf. Heb 10.19–22). No longer are men and women alienated from God and from one another, enslaved by sin, abandoned to despair and destined to destruction (cf. Eph 2.1–12). The entail of sin has been broken and humanity set free—free to enter upon the liberty and splendour of the children of God (cf. Rom 6.23; 8.21).

19. The liberty promised to the children of God is nothing less than participation, with Christ and through the Holy Spirit, in the life of God. The gift of the Spirit is the pledge and first instalment of the coming kingdom (cf. 2 Cor 1.21–22). Patterned according to Christ, the Wisdom of God, and empowered by the Holy Spirit of God, the Church is called, not only to proclaim God's kingdom, but also to be the sign and first-fruits of its coming. The unity, holiness, catholicity and apostolicity of the Church derive their meaning and reality from the meaning and reality of God's kingdom. They reflect the fullness of the life of God. They are signs of the universal love of God, Father, Son and Holy Spirit, the love poured out upon the whole creation. Hence the life of the Church, the body of Christ, the community of the Holy Spirit, is rooted and grounded in the eternal life and love of God.

20. It is this patterning power of the kingdom that gives the Church its distinctive character (cf. Rom 14.17). The new humanity, which the Gospel makes possible, is present in the community of those who already belonging to the new world inaugurated by the resurrection, live according to the law of the Spirit written in their hearts (cf. Jer 31.33). However, the Church has always to become more fully what its title-deeds proclaim it to be. It exists in the 'between-time', between the coming of Christ in history and his coming again as the Christ of glory. In so far as it remains in the world, it too has to learn obedience to its living Lord, and to work out in its own life in community the matter and manner of its discipleship.

21. The earliest disciples devoted themselves to the 'apostles' teaching and fellowship, the breaking of bread and the prayers' (Acts 2.42). In the portrayal of this communion the disciples were said to have had all things 'in common', selling their possessions and sharing their goods 'as any had need' (Acts 2.44–45). This striking example of community care and concern has, down the ages, prompted a critique of every form of society based on the unbridled pursuit of wealth and power. It has challenged Christians to use their gifts and resources to equip God's people for the work of service (cf. Eph 4.12). Its deep significance is disclosed in the claim that the whole company of believers was 'of one heart and soul . . . and everything they owned was held in common' (Acts 4.32).

22. This communion in heart and soul is inspired by the Holy Spirit and manifested in a life patterned according to the mind of Christ. As Paul puts it, 'if there is any encouragement in Christ, any incentive of love, any participation in the Spirit, any affection and sympathy, complete my joy by being of the same mind, having the same love, being in full accord and of one mind . . . that same mind which was in Christ Jesus' (Phil 2.1–2. 5). The distinctive mark of the mind of Christ, Paul goes on to explain, is humble obedience and self-emptying love (cf. Phil 2.7–8).

3 The Mind of Christ

23. The mind of Christ remains in the Church through the presence of the Paraclete/Spirit (cf. Jn 14.26). It is mediated through the remembered teaching of Jesus and the prayerful discernment of the body of Christ and its members, and gives shape and direction to the practical life of the Christian community. This teaching is expressed in Jesus' summary of the Law in the twofold command-

ment of love (cf. Mt 22.37–40), and spelled out in the Sermon on the Mount, especially the Beatitudes and the reinterpretation of the Commandments (cf. Mt 5.3–12, 21–48). It has a dual focus in the radical command 'Love your enemies' (cf. Mt 5.43) and the new commandment 'Love one another as I have loved you' (cf. Jn 13.34). The mind of Christ, so disclosed, determines the character of renewed humanity, forms the pattern of Christian obedience, and establishes the universe of shared moral values. In this important sense there is a givenness within the Christian response, which the changes of history and culture cannot impair.

24. The mind of Christ, who is the Way as well as the Truth and the Life (cf. Jn 14.6; Mt 7.14), also shapes the process by which Christians approach the challenge of new and complex moral and pastoral problems. Because they worship the same God and follow the same Lord, with the guidance of the Holy Spirit they approach these problems with similar resources and concerns. The method of arriving at practical decisions may vary, but underlying any differences of method there is a shared understanding of the need to use practical reason in interpreting the witness of the Scriptures, tradition and experience.

25. The mind of Christ also exposes the continuing threat of sin—sins of ignorance and neglect as well as deliberate sins. A knowing and willing disregard of the pattern of life which Christ sets before us is deliberate sin. But people can also drift into sin without any clear perception of what they are doing. Distorted structures of common life prompt a sinful response. Habits of sin then dull the conscience, until sinners come to prefer darkness to light. So solidarity in sin threatens to disrupt the fellowship of the Holy Spirit.

26. In Christ freedom and order are mutually supportive. The obedience of Christian discipleship is neither the mechanical application of regulation and rule, nor the wilful decision of arbitrary choice. In the freedom of a faithful and obedient response the disciples of Christ seek to discern Christ's mind rather than express their own. In exercising its authority to remit and retain sins (cf. Jn 20.23), the Church has a twofold task: of guarding against the power of sin to destroy the life of the community, and of fostering the freedom of its members to discern what is 'good and acceptable and perfect' (Rom 12.2).

4   Growing up into Christ

27. The salvation which God has secured for us once and for all, through the death and resurrection of Jesus Christ, he has now to secure

in us and with us through the power of the Holy Spirit. We have to become what, in Christ, we already are. We have to 'grow up in every way into him who is the head, into Christ' (Eph 4.15). We have to 'work out (our) own salvation with fear and trembling; for God is at work in (us), both to will and to work for his good pleasure' (Phil 2.12–13).

28. The lived response of the Church to the grace of God develops its own shape and character. The pattern of this response is fashioned according to the mind of Christ; the raw material is the stuff of our everyday world. In Johannine language, believers are still 'in' the world, but are not 'of' the world (cf. Jn 17.13–14). In Pauline language, they continue to live 'in the body' (2 Cor 5.6), but no longer 'in the flesh' (Rm 8.9). Christians are to continue in their secular roles and relationships according to the accepted social codes of behaviour, but are to do so as 'in the Lord' (cf. Eph 5.21—6.11; Col 3.18—4.1). Their new intention and motivation, while affirming the need for these social structures, contain the seeds of radical critique and reappraisal.

29. The fidelity of the Church to the mind of Christ involves a continuing process of listening, learning, reflecting and teaching. In this process every member of the community has a part to play. Each person learns to reflect and act according to conscience. Conscience is informed by, and informs, the tradition and teaching of the community. Learning and teaching are a shared discipline, in which the faithful seek to discover together what obedience to the gospel of grace and the law of love entails amidst the moral perplexities of the world. It is this task of discovering the moral implications of the Gospel which calls for continuing discernment, constant repentance and 'renewal of the mind' (Rm 12.2), so that through discernment and response men and women may become what in Christ they already are.

30. As part of its missionary imperative and pastoral care, the Church has not only to hand on from generation to generation its understanding of life in Christ, but also from time to time to determine how best to reconcile and support those members of the community who have, for whatever reason, failed to live up to its moral demands. Its aim is twofold: on the one hand, both to minimise the harm done by their falling away and to maintain the integrity of the community; and on the other, to restore the sinner to the life of grace in the fellowship of the Church.

5 Discerning the Mind of Christ

31. Christian morality is an authentic expression of the new life lived in the power of the Holy Spirit and fashioned according to the mind of Christ. In the tradition common to both our Communions, discerning the mind of Christ is a patient and continuing process of prayer and reflection. At its heart is the turning of the sinner to God, sacramentally enacted in baptism and renewed through participation in the sacramental life of the Church, meditation on the scriptures, and a life of daily discipleship. The process unfolds through the formation of a character, individual and communal, that reflects the likeness of Christ and embodies the virtues of a true humanity (cf. Gal 5.19–24). At the same time shared values are formulated in terms of principles and rules defining duties and protecting rights. All this finds expression in the common life of the Church as well as in its practical teaching and pastoral care.

32. The teaching developed in this way is an essential element in the process by which individuals and communities exercise their discernment on particular moral issues. Holding in mind the teaching they have received, drawing upon their own experience, and exploring the particularities of the issue that confronts them, they have then to decide what action to take in these circumstances and on this occasion. Such a decision is not only a matter of deduction. Nor can it be taken in isolation. It also calls for detailed and accurate assessment of the facts of the case, careful and consistent reflection and, above all, sensitivity of insight inspired by the Holy Spirit.

6 Continuity and Change

33. Guided by the Holy Spirit, believer and believing community seek to discern the mind of Christ amidst the changing circumstances of their own histories. Fidelity to the Gospel, obedience to the mind of Christ, openness to the Holy Spirit—these remain the source and strength of continuity. Where communities have separated, traditions diverge; and it is only to be expected that a difference of emphasis in moral judgement will also occur. Where there has been an actual break in communion, this difference cannot but be the more pronounced, giving rise to the impression, often mistaken, that there is some fundamental disagreement of understanding and approach.

34. Moral discernment is a demanding task both for the community and for the individual Christian. The more complex the particular issue, the greater the room for disagreement. Christians of different Communions are more likely to agree on the character of the Christian life and the fundamental Christian virtues and values. They are more likely to disagree on the consequent rules of practice, particular moral judgements and pastoral counsel.

35. In this chapter we have been concerned to re-affirm the heritage which Anglicans and Roman Catholics share together. We believe that the elements of this heritage provide the basis for a common witness to the world. But since the Reformation the traditions of our two Communions have diverged, and there are now differences between them which we must acknowledge and face with honesty and patience. Left unacknowledged, they remain a threat to any common task we might undertake. Faced together with honesty and integrity, they will, we believe, be seen at a deeper level to reflect different aspects of a living whole.

D PATHS DIVERGE

36. For some fifteen centuries the Church in the West struggled to maintain a single, living tradition of communion in worship, faith and practice. In the sixteenth century, however, this web of shared experience was violently broken. Movements for reform could no longer be contained within the one Communion. The Roman Catholic Church and the Churches of the Reformation went their different ways and fruits of shared communion were lost. It is in this context of broken communion and diverging histories that the existing differences between Anglicans and Roman Catholics on matters of morality must be located if they are to be rightly understood.

37. These differences, we believe, do not derive from disagreement on the sources of moral authority or on fundamental moral values. Rather, they have arisen from the different emphases which our two Communions have given to different elements of the moral life. In particular, differences have occurred in the ways in which each, in isolation from the other, has developed its structures of authority and has come to exercise that authority in the formation of moral judgement. These factors, we believe, have contributed significantly to the differences that have arisen in a limited number of important moral issues. We cannot, of course, hope to do justice

to the complex histories that have shaped our two Communions and given to each its distinctive ethos. However, we wish to draw attention to two strands in our histories which, for present purposes, are of special significance: first, structures of government and the voice of the laity; and secondly, processes of moral formation and individual judgement.

1 Structures of Government and the Voice of the Laity

38. At the Reformation the Church of England abjured papal supremacy, acknowledged the Sovereign as its Supreme Governor (cf. Article 37), and adopted English as the language of its liturgy (cf. Article 24). Thus the life of the church, the culture of the nation and the law of the land were inextricably combined. In particular, the lay voice was given, through Parliament, a substantial measure of authority in the affairs of the church. With the growth of the Anglican Communion as a world-wide body, patterns of synodical government developed in which laity, clergy and bishops shared the authority of government, the bishops retaining a special voice and responsibility in safeguarding matters of doctrine and worship.

39. As the Anglican Communion has spread, provinces independent of the Church of England have come into being, each with its own history and culture. English culture has become less and less of a common bond as other cultures have exercised an increasing influence. Each province is responsible for the ordering of its own life and has independent legislative and juridical authority; yet each continues in communion with the Church of England and with one another. Every ten years since 1867 the bishops of the Anglican Communion have met together at Lambeth at the invitation of the Archbishop of Canterbury, to whom they continue to ascribe a primacy of honour. The resolutions of their conferences have a high degree of authority, but they do not become the official teaching of the individual provinces until these have formally ratified them. In recent times regular meetings of the Primates of the Anglican Communion, as well as of the Anglican Consultative Council, in which laity, clergy and bishops are all represented, have contributed to this network of dispersed authority. Whether existing instruments of unity in the Anglican Communion will prove adequate to the task of preserving full communion between the provinces, as they develop their moral teaching in a rapidly changing and deeply perplexing world, remains to be seen.

40. The Reformation and its aftermath also had repercussions in the government of the Roman Catholic Church. Some of the European rulers who maintained allegiance to Rome found this relationship strained and frustrating, especially since, in certain areas, the papacy also exercised temporal power. The church reacted strongly, however, to any attempt by a secular power to arrogate to itself prerogatives that it believed were rightfully its own. This concern of the church to uphold its independence from the state, together with its need to re-affirm and strengthen its unity in the face of divisive forces, lent to the papal office a renewed significance, and provided the context for the solemn definition of the first Vatican Council which clarified the universal jurisdiction of the Bishop of Rome and his infallibility.

41. A further development in the Roman Catholic Church since Vatican I has clarified the teaching role of the college of bishops in communion with its head, the Bishop of Rome. Bishops are not only the chief teachers in their own dioceses, but they also share responsibility for the teaching of the whole church. For Roman Catholics, government and teaching continue to be the prerogative of the episcopal office. Their experience has been that these structures of authority have served the church well in maintaining a fundamental unity of moral teaching.

42. There has also been a significant development in the Roman Catholic Church in the ways by which the laity participate in the discernment and articulation of the church's faith. Lay persons have taken on new roles in liturgy, catechesis and pastoral work, and have come to be involved with their pastors in a variety of consultative and advisory bodies at parochial, diocesan and national levels. This collaboration has been enhanced by their involvement in theological education.

2 Processes of Moral Formation and Individual Judgement

43. After the breakdown in communion, Anglicans and Roman Catholics continued to develop, in related but distinctive ways, their common tradition of moral theology and its application by a process of casuistry to specific moral problems. This process has its roots in the New Testament and the writings of the Church Fathers. In the late Middle Ages, however, certain widespread philosophical views diverted attention from the controlling moral vision and concentrated on the obligations of the individual will and the legality of particular acts.

What was intended to be a painstaking search for the will of God in the complex circumstances of daily life ran the danger of becoming either meticulous moralism or a means of minimizing the challenge of the Gospel.

44. Developments in Roman Catholic moral theology after the Council of Trent were not altogether free from this danger. In the 17th century papal authority countermanded both rigorism and laxity. It sought to re-establish a vision of the moral life which respected the demands of the Gospel while, at the same time, acknowledging the costliness of discipleship and the frailties of the human condition. During this and subsequent periods, moral theology and spiritual theology were treated as two distinct disciplines, the former tending to restrict itself to the minimal requirements of Christian obedience. In the second half of the present century the Roman Catholic Church, in its desire to set the moral life within a comprehensive vision of life in the Spirit, has witnessed a renewal of moral theology. There has been a return to the Scriptures as the central source of moral insight. Older discussions, based on the natural law, with the Scriptures cited solely for confirmation, have been integrated into a more personalistic account of the moral life, which itself has been grounded in the vocation of all human persons to participate in the life of God. An emphasis on the community of persons has led to significant developments, not only in the Church's teaching on personal relationships, but also in its teaching on the economic and social implications of the common good.

45. The Anglican tradition of moral theology has been varied and heterogeneous. In the 17th century Anglican theologians of both catholic and puritan persuasion produced comprehensive works of 'practical divinity'. Drawing on the scholastic tradition, and determined to hold together the moral and spiritual life, they developed this tradition within a context of the Christian vocation to personal holiness. Thus they rejected any approach to the moral life that smacked of moral laxity, and mistrusted any casuistry that, in the details of its analysis of the moral act, threatened to destroy an integral spirit of genuine repentance and renewal. In subsequent centuries the practice of casuistry fell largely into disuse, to be replaced by teaching on 'Christian ethics'. The aim of this discipline was to set forth the ideal character and pattern of the Christian life and so to prepare Christians for making their own decisions how best to realise that ideal in their own circumstances. The present

century has seen a renewal among Anglicans of the discipline of moral theology, sustained by a growing recognition of the need for systematic reflection on the difficult moral issues raised by new technologies, the limits of natural resources and the claims of the natural environment. In recent times, in response to widespread appeals for guidance on issues of public and social morality, representatives of Christian bodies and other persons of good will have been brought together to study these issues and to suggest how society might best respond to them for the sake of the common good.

46. Anglicans and Roman Catholics have both used a variety of means to strengthen Christian discipleship in its moral dimension. These have included preaching, regular use of catechisms, and public recitation of the Commandments. In one matter of special significance, however, the Reformation and the consequent Counter Reformation moved the Church of England and the Roman Catholic Church in different directions. The Reformers' emphasis on the direct access of the sinner to the forgiving and sustaining Word of God led Anglicans to reject the view that private confession before a priest was obligatory, although they continued to maintain that it was a wholesome means of grace, and made provision for it in the Book of Common Prayer for those with an unquiet and sorely troubled conscience. While many Anglicans value highly the practice of private confession of sins, others believe with equal sincerity that it is for them unhelpful and unnecessary. It is sufficient for themselves, they say, that the Word of God, expressed in the Scriptures and appropriated in the power of the Holy Spirit, speaks authoritatively to their conscience, offering both assurance of forgiveness and practical guidance. For both those who do, and for those who do not, confess their sins privately, general confession and absolution by the priest remains an integral part of the regular Anglican liturgy, a ministry designed to cover both individual and corporate sin. Furthermore, Anglicans often turn to their pastors and advisers, lay and ordained, for moral and spiritual counsel.

47. The Roman Catholic Church, on the other hand, has continued to emphasise the sacrament of penance and the obligation, for those conscious of serious sin, of confessing their sins privately before a priest. Indeed, the renewal of private confession was a major concern of the Council of Trent. Since Vatican II the development of the ministry of forgiveness and healing has led to new forms of

sacramental reconciliation, both individual and communal. For centuries the discipline of the confession of sins before a priest has provided an important means of communicating the church's moral teaching and nurturing the spiritual lives of penitents.

3   Moral Judgement and the Exercise of Authority

48.   Reflection on the divergent histories of our two Communions has shown that their shared concern to respond obediently to God's Word and to foster the common good has nevertheless resulted in differing emphases in the ways in which they have nurtured Christian liberty and exercised Christian authority. Both Communions recognise that liberty and authority are essentially interdependent, and that the exercise of authority is for the protection and nurture of liberty. It cannot be denied, however, that there is a continuing temptation—a temptation which the continued separation of our two Communions serves only to accentuate—to allow the exercise of authority to lapse into authoritarianism and the exercise of liberty to lapse into individualism.

49.   All moral authority is grounded in the goodness and will of God. Our two Communions are agreed on this principle and on its implications. Both our Communions, moreover, have developed their own structures and institutions for the teaching ministry of the Church, by which the will of God is discerned and its implications for the common good declared. Our Communions have diverged, however, in their views of the ways in which authority is most fruitfully exercised and the common good best promoted. Anglicans affirm that authority needs to be dispersed rather than centralised, that the common good is better served by allowing to individual Christians the greatest possible liberty of informed moral judgement, and that therefore official moral teaching should as far as possible be commendatory rather than prescriptive and binding. Roman Catholics, on the other hand, have, for the sake of the common good, emphasised the need for a central authority to preserve unity and to give clear and binding teaching.

4   Differing Emphases, Shared Perspectives

50.   In our conversations together we have made two discoveries: first, that many of the preconceptions that we brought with us concerning each other's understanding of moral teaching and discipline were often little more than caricatures; and secondly, that the differences

which actually exist between us appear in a new light when we consider them in their origin and context.

51. Some of these differences lend themselves to misperception and caricature. It is not true, for instance, that Anglicans concern themselves solely with liberty, while Roman Catholics concern themselves solely with law. It is not true that the Roman Catholic Church has predetermined answers to every moral question, while the Anglican Church has no answers at all. It is not true that Roman Catholics always agree on moral issues, nor that Anglicans never agree. It is not true that Anglican ethics is pragmatic and unprincipled, while Roman Catholic moral theology is principled but abstract. It is not true that Roman Catholics are always more careful of the institution in their concern for the common good, while Anglicans disregard the common good in their concern for the individual. It is not true that Roman Catholic moral teaching is legalistic, while Anglican moral teaching is utilitarian. Caricature, we may grant, is never totally contrived; but caricature it remains. In fact, there is good reason to hope that, if they can pray, think and act together, Anglicans and Roman Catholics, by emphasizing different aspects of the moral life, may come to complement and enrich each other's understanding and practice of it.

52. Nevertheless, differences there are and differences they remain. Both Anglicans and Roman Catholics are accustomed to using the concept of law to give character and form to the claims of morality. However, this concept is open to more than one interpretation and use, so causing real and apparent differences between our two traditions. For example, a notable feature of established Roman Catholic moral teaching is its emphasis on the absoluteness of some demands of the moral law and the existence of certain prohibitions to which there are no exceptions. In these instances, what is prohibited is intrinsically disordered and therefore objectively wrong. Anglicans, on the other hand, while acknowledging the same ultimate values, are not persuaded that the laws as we apprehend them are necessarily absolute. In certain circumstances, they would argue, it might be right to incorporate contextual and pastoral considerations in the formulation of a moral law, on the grounds that fundamental moral values are better served if the law sometimes takes into account certain contingencies of nature and history and certain disorders of the human condition. In so doing, they do not make the clear-cut distinction, which Roman Catholics make, between

canon law, with its incorporation of contingent and prudential considerations, and the moral law, which in its principles is absolute and universal. In both our Communions, however, there are now signs of a shift away from a reliance on the concept of law as the central category for providing moral teaching. Its place is being taken by the concept of 'persons in community'. An ethic of response is preferred to an ethic of obedience. In the desire to respond as fully as possible to the new law of Christ, the primacy of persons is emphasised above the impersonalism of a system of law, thus avoiding the distortions of both individualism and utilitarianism. The full significance of this shift of emphasis is not yet clear, and its detailed implications have still to be worked out. It should be emphasised, however, that whatever differences there may be in the way in which they express the moral law, both our traditions respect the consciences of persons in good faith.

53. We hope we have said enough in this chapter to explain how a deeper understanding of our separated histories has enabled us to appreciate better the real character of our divergences, and has persuaded us that it has been our broken communion, more than anything else, that has exacerbated our disagreements. In recent times there has been a large measure of cross-fertilisation between our two traditions. Both our Communions, for example, have shared in the renewal of biblical, historical and liturgical studies, and both have participated in the ecumenical movement. Our separated paths have once again begun to converge. It is in the conviction that we also possess a shared vision of Christian discipleship and a common approach to the moral life, that we take courage now to look directly at our painful disagreement on two particular moral issues.

E AGREEMENT AND DISAGREEMENT

54. The two moral issues on which the Anglican and Roman Catholic Communions have expressed official disagreement are: the marriage of a divorced person during the lifetime of a former partner; and the permissible methods of controlling conception. There are other issues concerning sexuality on which Anglican and Roman Catholic attitudes and opinions appear to conflict, especially abortion and the exercise of homosexual relations. These we shall consider briefly at the end of this section; but because of the official nature of the disagreement on the former two issues, we shall concentrate on them.

1 Human Sexuality

55. Before considering the points of disagreement, we need to emphasise the extent of our agreement. Both our traditions affirm with Scripture that human sexuality is part of God's good creation (cf. Gen 1.27; see further Gen 24; Ruth 4; the Song of Songs; Eph 5.21–32; etc.). Sexual differentiation within the one human nature gives bodily expression to the vocation of God's children to inter-personal communion. Human sexuality embraces the whole range of bodily, imaginative, affective and spiritual experience. It enters into a person's deepest character and relationships, individual and social, and constitutes a fundamental mode of human communication. It is ordered towards the gift of self and the creation of life.

56. Sexual experience, isolated from the vision of the full humanity to which God calls us, is ambivalent. It can be as disruptive as it can be unitive, as destructive as it can be creative. Christians have always known this to be so (cf. Mt 5.28). They have therefore recognised the need to integrate sexuality into an ordered pattern of life, which will nurture a person's spiritual relationships both with other persons and with God. Such integration calls for the exercise of the virtue traditionally termed chastity, a virtue rooted in the spiritual significance of bodily existence (cf. 1 Thess 4.1–8; Gal 5.23; 1 Cor 6.9, 12–20).

57. Both our traditions offer comparable accounts of chastity, which involves the ordering of the sexual drive either towards marriage or in a life of celibacy. Chastity does not signify the repression of sexual instincts and energies, but their integration into a pattern of relationships in which a person may find true happiness, fulfilment and salvation. Anglicans and Roman Catholics agree that the new life in Christ calls for a radical break with the sin of sexual self-centredness, which leads inevitably to individual and social disintegration. The New Testament is unequivocal in its witness that the right ordering and use of sexual energy is an essential aspect of life in Christ (cf. Mk 10.9; Jn 8.11; 1 Cor 7; 1 Pt 3.1–7; Heb 13.4), and this is reiterated throughout the common Christian tradition, including the time since our two Communions diverged.

58. Human beings, male and female, flourish as persons in community. Personal relationships have a social as well as a private dimension. Sexual relationships are no exception. They are bound up with issues of poverty and justice, the equality and dignity of women

and men, and the protection of children. Both our traditions treat of human sexuality in the context of the common good, and regard marriage and family life as institutions divinely appointed for human well-being and happiness. It is in the covenanted relationship between husband and wife that the physical expression of sexuality finds its true fulfilment (cf. Gen 2.18–25), and in the procreation and nurturing of children that the two persons together share in the life-giving generosity of God (cf. Gen 1.27–29).

2 Marriage and Family

59. Neither of our two traditions regards marriage as a human invention. On the contrary, both see it as grounded by God in human nature and as a source of community, social order and stability. Nevertheless, the institution of marriage has found different expression in different cultures and at different times. In our own time, for instance, we are becoming increasingly aware that some forms, far from nurturing the dignity of persons, foster oppression and domination, especially of women. However, despite the distortions that have affected it, both our traditions continue to discern and uphold in marriage a God-given pattern and significance.

60. Marriage gives rise to enduring obligations. Personal integrity and social witness both require a life-long and exclusive commitment, and the 'goods' which marriage embodies include the reciprocal love of husband and wife, and the procreation and raising of children. When these realities are disregarded, a breakdown of family life may ensue, carrying with it a heavy burden of misery and social disintegration. The word 'obligation', however, is inadequate to express the profound personal call inherent in the Christian understanding of marriage. Both our traditions speak of marriage as a vocation: as a 'vocation to holiness' (Lambeth 1968, Resolution 22), as involving an 'integral vision of . . . vocation' (*Familiaris Consortio*, 32). When God calls women and men to the married estate, and supports them in it, God's love for them is creative, redemptive and sanctifying (cf. Lambeth, ibid.).

61. The mutual pact, or covenant, made between the spouses (cf. *Gaudium et Spes*, 47–52, and *Final Report on the Theology of Marriage and its Application to Mixed Marriages*, 1975, 21) bears the mark of God's own abundant love (cf. Hos 2.19–21). Covenanted human love points beyond itself to the covenantal love and fidelity of God and to God's will that marriage should be a means of universal

blessing and grace. Marriage, in the order of creation, is both sign and reality of God's faithful love, and thus it has a naturally sacramental dimension. Since it also points to the saving love of God, embodied in Christ's love for the Church (cf. Eph 5.25), it is open to a still deeper sacramentality within the life and communion of Christ's own Body.

62. So far, we believe, our traditions agree. Further discussion, however, is needed on the ways in which they interpret this sacramentality of marriage. The Roman Catholic tradition, following the common tradition of the West, which was officially promulgated by the Council of Florence in 1439, affirms that Christian marriage is a sacrament in the order of redemption, the natural sign of the human covenant having been raised by Christ to become a sign of the irrevocable covenant between himself and his Church. What was sacramental in the order of creation becomes a sacrament of the Church in the order of redemption. When solemnized between two baptized persons, marriage is an effective sign of redeeming grace. Anglicans, while affirming the special significance of marriage within the body of Christ, emphasise a sacramentality of marriage that transcends the boundaries of the Church. For many years in England after the Reformation, marriages could be solemnized only in church. When civil marriage became possible, Anglicans recognised such marriages, too, as sacramental and graced by God, since the state of matrimony had itself been sanctified by Christ by his presence at the marriage at Cana of Galilee (cf. BCP Introduction to the Solemnization of Holy Matrimony, 1662). From these considerations it would appear that, in this context, Anglicans tend to emphasise the breadth of God's grace in creation, while Roman Catholics tend to emphasise the depth of God's grace in Christ. These emphases should be seen as complementary. Ideally, they belong together. They have, however, given rise to differing understandings of the conditions under which the sacramentality of a marriage is fulfilled.

63. The vision of marriage as a fruitful, life-long covenant, full of the grace of God, is not always sustained in the realities of life. Its very goodness, when corrupted by human frailty, self-centredness and sin, gives rise to pain, despair and tragedy, not only for the couple immediately involved in marital difficulty or breakdown, but also for their children, the wider family and the social order. Faced with such situations, the Church endeavours to minister the grace and

discipline of Christ himself. Anglicans and Roman Catholics have both sought to act in obedience to the teaching of Christ. However, in their separation their practice and pastoral discipline came to differ and diverge. In order to elucidate the significance of such differences and divergences we shall now turn to the two issues on which disagreement has been officially voiced, namely, marriage after divorce, and contraception.

3   Marriage After Divorce

64.   Before the break in communion in the 16th century, the Church in the West had come to derive a doctrine of indissolubility from its interpretation of the teaching of Jesus concerning marriage. The official Church teaching included two affirmations: not only was it the case that the marriage bond ought not to be dissolved; but it was also the case that it could not be dissolved. At the Reformation, continental Protestant Reformers interpreted the teaching of Jesus (cf. Mt 5.32; 19.9) differently, and argued that divorce was permissible on grounds of adultery or desertion. The Council of Trent, on the other hand, re-affirmed the teaching, first, that the marriage bond could not be dissolved, even by adultery, and secondly, that neither partner, not even the innocent one, could contract a second marriage during the lifetime of the other.

(a)   *The Anglican Communion*

65.   The development of a distinctive marriage discipline within Anglicanism can be understood only in the context of the development of diverse civil jurisdictions. This is true both of the Church of England and of other Anglican provinces. At the time of the Reformation the Church of England passed no formal resolution on marriage and divorce. It never officially accepted the teaching of the continental Reformers but, despite attempts to introduce an alternative discipline, held to the older belief and practice. Revisions of Canon Law in 1597 and 1604 established no change in teaching or discipline, although, in the centuries that followed, theological opinion varied and even practice was not completely uniform. Up to the middle of the 19th century, divorce, with the consequent freedom to marry again, was available only to the rich and influential few by Act of Parliament. In 1857, when matrimonial matters were transferred from ecclesiastical to civil jurisdiction, divorce on grounds of adultery was legalised. Although clergy were given the right to refuse to solemnize

the marriage of a divorced person in the lifetime of a former partner, the Church of England as a whole came to accept de facto the new state of affairs: marriages after divorce occurred, but the church refused to give official approval to their solemnization.

66. As Anglican provinces were inaugurated outside England, each had to formulate its own pastoral marriage discipline in the light of local civil law and marriage customs. In an attempt to secure a coherent policy among the provinces, the Lambeth Conference of 1888 re-affirmed the life-long intention of the marriage covenant, but recognised that some marriages dissolved by the state had in fact ceased to exist. It left open the question whether or not the innocent party was free to enter a second marriage. Since then, theological opinion has varied. Some Anglicans have continued to hold the traditional view of indissolubility. Others have argued that, once the married relationship has been destroyed beyond repair, the marriage itself is as if dead, the vows have been frustrated and the bond has been broken. The Lambeth Conference of 1978 re-affirmed the 'first-order principle' of life-long union, but it also acknowledged a responsibility for those for whom 'no course absolutely consonant with the first-order principle of marriage as a life-long union may be available' (Resolution 34). Subsequent practice has varied. Different provinces of the Anglican Communion have devised different marriage disciplines. Among some of them permission is granted, on carefully considered pastoral grounds, for a marriage after divorce to be solemnized in church, although even in these cases practice varies concerning the precise form the complete service takes. In other cases, after a civil ceremony, a service of prayer and dedication may be offered instead. The practical decision normally lies with the bishop and the bishop's advisers.

(b) The Roman Catholic Church

67. In the period following the breach of communion, the Roman Catholic Church continued to uphold the doctrine of indissolubility re-affirmed at Trent. At the same time it developed a complex system of jurisprudence and discipline to meet its diverse practical and pastoral needs and to provide a supportive role for those whose faith was threatened by a destructive marital relationship.

68. A distinction is made between marriages that are sacraments—those in which both partners are baptized—and marriages that are not sacraments (natural marriages)—those in which one or both partners

are unbaptized. In Roman Catholic teaching both forms of marriage are in principle indissoluble. A sacramental marriage which has been duly consummated cannot be dissolved by any human power, civil or ecclesiastical. Where such a marriage, however, has not been consummated, it can be dissolved. On the other hand, it has come to be accepted that a non-sacramental marriage, whether consummated or not, can in certain cases be dissolved.

69. The history of these matters is long and complex. In his first letter to the Corinthians St Paul deals with the case of a married couple, one of whom is a believer, the other a non-believer. If the non-believer refuses to stay with the believer, then, he says, 'the brother or sister is not bound' (1 Cor 7.15; cf. 12—15). This was later interpreted in Canon Law to mean that the partner who had become a Christian was free to leave an unbelieving spouse who was unwilling to continue married life 'in peace', and to marry again. There are several references to this 'Pauline text' in the writings of the early Church Fathers dealing with the dissolution of marriage. It became part of church legislation in 1199, but was fully clarified only in the *Code of Canon Law* of 1917. It is still part of Roman Catholic practice (cf. CIC, Can. 1143).

70. The exercise of the 'Pauline privilege' is not the only occasion when the power to dissolve a marriage is invoked. In the course of the missionary expansion of the Church other situations have prompted similar action. From 1537 Popes used their powers to dissolve the natural marriages of inhabitants of Africa and the Indies who wished to convert to the Catholic faith. In 1917 this practice 'in favour of the faith' (or, as it is sometimes called, the 'Petrine privilege') was extended to other parts of the world and applied to similar situations. The 'privilege of the faith' is still recognised today, and subject to certain conditions, a dissolution of a non-sacramental marriage may, by way of exception, be granted on these grounds by the Holy See.

71. Other elements in Roman Catholic doctrine and practice have been prompted by particular practical problems. For example, it was the problem of clandestine marriages, valid but not proved to be so, that prompted the Council of Trent to promulgate the decree *Tametsi* (1563). This required that marriages be celebrated before the pastor (or another priest delegated by him or the ordinary) and two or three witnesses. With certain modifications, this 'form' is still binding, and failure to observe it, without due dispensation, renders

a marriage null and void (cf. CIC, Can. 1108). A partner to such a union, therefore, is not considered in Canon Law to be held by a marital bond and is free to contract a valid marriage. In the case of an intended marriage between a Roman Catholic and a person who is not a Roman Catholic, the church today often grants a dispensation from the 'form', out of respect for the beliefs, conscience and family ties of the person concerned.

72. Another development in Roman Catholic jurisprudence concerns the practice of annulment, that is, the declaration of the fact that a true marriage never existed. The marriage contract requires full and free consent. If this is lacking, there can be no marriage. It has always been recognised that there can be no marriage if a person is forced to enter it against his or her own will. More recent reflection has analysed in greater depth the nature of consent. It is now recognised that there may be serious psychological as well as physical defects. If such defects can be demonstrated to have existed when verbal consent was exchanged, it can be declared, according to Roman Catholic teaching, that there was never a marriage at all (cf. CIC, Can. 1095). Serious defect is also present if, at the time of exchanging consent, there is a deliberate rejection of some element essential to marriage (cf. CIC, Can. 1056; 1101, 2).

(c) The Situation Today

73. Clearly there are differences of discipline and pastoral practice between Anglicans and Roman Catholics. Some of the factors in our traditions are the result of responses to contingent historical circumstances: for example, the Roman Catholic Church's requirement of the 'form' for valid marriage. However, other elements have deeper roots. When we explore our differences it is to these, in particular, that we must direct our attention. Before doing so, however, it is important to note that both Communions make provision for marital separation, without excluding the persons concerned, even after civil divorce, from the eucharist.

74. In accord with the western tradition, Anglicans and Roman Catholics believe that the ministers of the marriage are the man and woman themselves, who bring the marriage into being by making a solemn vow and promise of life-long fidelity to each other. Anglicans and Roman Catholics both regard this vow as solemn and binding. Anglicans and Roman Catholics both believe that marriage points to the love of Christ, who bound himself in an irrevocable covenant

to his Church, and that therefore marriage is in principle indissoluble. Roman Catholics go on to affirm that the unbreakable bond
between Christ and his Church, signified in the union of two baptized
persons, in its turn strengthens the marriage bond between husband
and wife and renders it absolutely unbreakable, except by death.
Other marriages can, in exceptional circumstances, be dissolved.
Anglicans, on the other hand, do not make an absolute distinction
between marriages of the baptized and other marriages, regarding
all marriages as in some sense sacramental. Some Anglicans hold
that all marriages are therefore indissoluble. Others, while holding
that all marriages are indeed sacramental and are in principle indissoluble, are not persuaded that the marriage bond, even in the case
of marriage of the baptized, can never in fact be dissolved.

75. Roman Catholic teaching that, when a sacramental marriage has
been consummated, the covenant is irrevocable, is grounded in
its understanding of sacramentality, as already outlined. Further, its
firm legal framework is judged to be the best protection for the
institution of marriage, and thus best to serve the common good of
the community, which itself redounds to the true good of the persons
concerned. Thus Roman Catholic teaching and law uphold the
indissolubility of the marriage covenant, even when the human
relationship of love and trust has ceased to exist and there is no
practical possibility of recreating it. The Anglican position, though
equally concerned with the sacramentality of marriage and the
common good of the community, does not necessarily understand
these in the same way. Some Anglicans attend more closely to the
actual character of the relationship between husband and wife.
Where a relationship of mutual love and trust has clearly ceased
to exist, and there is no practical possibility of remaking it, the bond
itself, they argue, has also ceased to exist. When the past has been
forgiven and healed, a new covenant and bond may in good faith
be made.

76. Our reflections have brought to the fore an issue of considerable
importance. What is the right balance between regard for the person and regard for the institution? The answer must be found
within the context of our theology of communion and our understanding of the common good. For the reasons which have been
explained, in the Roman Catholic Church the institution of marriage
has enjoyed the favour of the law. Marriages are presumed to
be valid unless the contrary case can be clearly established. Since

Vatican II renewed emphasis has been placed upon the rights and welfare of the individual person, but tensions still remain. A similar tension is felt by Anglicans, although pastoral concern has sometimes inclined them to give priority to the welfare of the individual person over the claims of the institution. History has shown how difficult it is to achieve the right balance.

77. Our shared reflections have made us see more clearly that Anglicans and Roman Catholics are at one in their commitment to following the teaching of Christ on marriage; at one in their understanding of the nature and meaning of marriage; and at one in their concern to reach out to those who suffer as a result of the breakdown of marriage. We agree that marriage is sacramental, although we do not fully agree on how, and this affects our sacramental discipline. Thus, Roman Catholics recognise a special kind of sacramentality in a marriage between baptized persons, which they do not see in other marriages. Anglicans, on the other hand, recognise a sacramentality in all valid marriages. On the level of law and policy, neither the Roman Catholic nor the Anglican practice regarding divorce is free from real or apparent anomalies and ambiguities. While, therefore, there are differences between us concerning marriage after divorce, to isolate those differences from this context of far-reaching agreement and to make them into an insuperable barrier would be a serious and sorry misrepresentation of the true situation.

4 Contraception

78. Both our traditions agree that procreation is one of the divinely intended 'goods' of the institution of marriage. A deliberate decision, therefore, without justifiable reason, to exclude procreation from a marriage is a rejection of this good and a contradiction of the nature of marriage itself. On this also we agree. We are likewise at one in opposing what has been called a 'contraceptive mentality', that is, a selfish preference for immediate satisfaction over the more demanding good of having and raising a family.

79. Both Roman Catholics and Anglicans agree, too, that God calls married couples to 'responsible parenthood'. This refers to a range of moral concerns, which begins with the decision to accept parenthood and goes on to include the nurture, education, support and guidance of children. Decisions about the size of a family raise many questions for both Anglicans and Roman Catholics. Broader

questions concerning the pressure of population, poverty, the social and ecological environment, as well as more directly personal questions concerning the couple's material, physical and psychological resources, may arise. Situations exist in which a couple would be morally justified in avoiding bringing children into being. Indeed, there are some circumstances in which it would be morally irresponsible to do so. On this our two Communions are also agreed. We are not agreed, however, on the methods by which this responsibility may be exercised.

80. The disagreement may be summed up as follows. Anglicans understand the good of procreation to be a norm governing the married relationship as a whole. Roman Catholic teaching, on the other hand, requires that each and every act of intercourse should be 'open to procreation' (cf. *Humanae Vitae*, 11). This difference of understanding received official expression in 1930. Before this, both churches would have counselled abstinence for couples who had a justifiable reason to avoid conception. The Lambeth Conference of Anglican bishops, however, resolved in 1930 that 'where there is a clearly felt moral obligation to limit or avoid parenthood, and where there is a morally sound reason for avoiding complete abstinence . . . other methods may be used'. The encyclical of Pope Pius XI (*Casti Connubii*, 1930), which was intended among other things as a response to the Lambeth resolution, renewed the traditional Roman Catholic position. In 1968 the teaching was further developed and clarified in Pope Paul VI's encyclical, *Humanae Vitae*. This was itself subjected to adverse criticism by the Lambeth Conference later the same year. The Roman Catholic position has been frequently re-affirmed since: for example, in the documents *Familiaris Consortio* 1981, and Catechism of the Catholic Church 1992. This teaching belongs to the ordinary magisterium calling for 'religious assent'.

81. The immediate point at issue in this controversy would seem to concern the moral integrity of the act of marital intercourse. Both our traditions agree that this involves the two basic 'goods' of marriage, loving union and procreation. Moral integrity requires that husband and wife respect both these goods together. For Anglicans, it is sufficient that this respect should characterise the married relationship as a whole; whereas for Roman Catholics, it must characterise each act of sexual intercourse. Anglicans understand the moral principle to be that procreation should not arbitrarily be excluded from the continuing relationship; whereas Roman Catholics

hold that there is an unbreakable connexion, willed by God, between the two 'goods' of marriage and the corresponding meanings of marital intercourse, and that therefore they may not be sundered by any direct and deliberate act (cf. *Humanae Vitae*, 12).

82. The Roman Catholic doctrine is not simply an authoritative state- ment of the nature of the integrity of the marital act. The whole teaching on human love and sexuality, continued and developed in *Humanae Vitae*, must be taken into account when considering the Roman Catholic position on this issue. The definition of integrity is founded upon a number of considerations: a way of understanding human persons; the meaning of marital love; the unique dignity of an act which can engender new life; the relationship between human fruitfulness and divine creativity; the special vocation of the married couple; and the requirements of the virtue of marital chastity. Anglicans accept all of these considerations as relevant to determining the integrity of the marital relationship and act. Thus they share the same spectrum of moral and theological considera- tions. However, they do not accept the arguments Roman Catholics derive from them, nor the conclusions they draw from them regard- ing the morality of contraception.

5 Other Issues

83. So far in this section we have argued that our disagreements in the areas of marriage, procreation and contraception, areas in which our two Communions have made official but conflicting pro- nouncements, are on the level of derived conclusions rather than fundamental values. However, as we observed earlier, there are other important issues in the area of sexuality where no official disagreement has been expressed between our two Communions, but where disagreement is nonetheless perceived to exist. Although Anglicans and Roman Catholics may often achieve a common mind and witness on many issues of peace and social justice, never- theless, it is said, their teaching is irreconcilable on such matters as abortion and homosexual relations. What is more, there are other difficult and potentially divisive issues in the offing, as scientific and technological expertise develops the unprecedented power to manipulate the basic material, not only of the environment, but also of human life itself.

84. This is not the time or place to discuss such further issues in detail. However, confining ourselves to the two issues of abortion

and homosexual relations, we would argue that, in these instances too, the disagreements between us are not on the level of fundamental moral values, but on their implementation in practical judgements.

85. Anglicans have no agreed teaching concerning the precise moment from which the new human life developing in the womb is to be given the full protection due to a human person. Only some Anglicans insist that in all circumstances, and without exception, such protection must extend back to the time of conception. Roman Catholic teaching, on the other hand, is that the human embryo must be treated as a human person from the moment of conception (cf. *Donum Vitae*, 1987 and *Declaration on Procured Abortion* 1974). Difference of teaching on this matter cannot but give rise to difference of judgement on what is morally permissible when a tragic conflict occurs between the rights of the mother and the rights of the foetus. Roman Catholic teaching rejects all direct abortion. Among Anglicans the view is to be found that in certain cases direct abortion is morally justifiable. Anglicans and Roman Catholics, however, are at one in their recognition of the sanctity, and right to life, of all human persons, and they share an abhorrence of the growing practice in many countries of abortion on grounds of mere convenience. This agreement on fundamentals is reflected both in pronouncements of bishops and in official documents issued by both Communions (cf. *Catechism of the Catholic Church*, 1992, 2270, and *Lambeth Conference Report*, 1930, 16; 1978, 10).

86. We cannot enter here more fully into this debate, and we do not wish to underestimate the consequences of our disagreement. We wish, however, to affirm once again that Anglicans and Roman Catholics share the same fundamental teaching concerning the mystery of human life and the sanctity of the human person. They also share the same sense of awe and humility in making practical judgements in this area of profound moral complexity. Their differences arise in the way in which they develop and apply fundamental moral teaching. What we have said earlier about our different formulations of the moral law is here relevant (see §52). For Roman Catholics, the rejection of abortion is an example of an absolute prohibition. For Anglicans, however, such an absolute and categorical prohibition would not be typical of their moral reasoning. That is why it is important to set such differences in context. Only then shall we be able to assess their wider implications.

87. In the matter of homosexual relationships a similar situation obtains. Both our Communions affirm the importance and significance of human friendship and affection among men and women, whether married or single. Both affirm that all persons, including those of homosexual orientation, are made in the divine image and share the full dignity of human creatureliness. Both affirm that a faithful and lifelong marriage between a man and a woman provides the normative context for a fully sexual relationship. Both appeal to Scripture and the natural order as the sources of their teaching on this issue. Both reject, therefore, the claim, sometimes made, that homosexual relationships and married relationships are morally equivalent, and equally capable of expressing the right ordering and use of the sexual drive. Such ordering and use, we believe, are an essential aspect of life in Christ. Here again our different approaches to the formulation of law are relevant (cf. §52). Roman Catholic teaching holds that homosexual activity is 'intrinsically disordered', and concludes that it is always objectively wrong. This affects the kind of pastoral advice that is given to homosexual persons. Anglicans could agree that such activity is disordered; but there may well be differences among them in the consequent moral and pastoral advice they would think it right to offer to those seeking their counsel and direction.

88. Our two Communions have in the past developed their moral teaching and practical and pastoral disciplines in isolation from each other. The differences that have arisen between them are serious, but careful study and consideration has shown us that they are not fundamental. The urgency of the times and the perplexity of the human condition demand that they now do all they can to come together to provide a common witness and guidance for the well-being of humankind and the good of the whole creation.

F TOWARDS SHARED WITNESS

89. We have already seen how divergence between Anglicans and Roman Catholics on matters of practice and official moral teaching has been aggravated, if not caused, by the historic breach of communion and the consequent breakdown in communication. Separation has led to estrangement, and estrangement has fostered misperception, misunderstanding and suspicion. Only in recent times has this process been reversed and the first determined steps taken along the way to renewed and full communion.

90. The theme of communion illumines, we believe, not only the reality of the Church as a worshipping community, but also the form and fullness of Christian life in the world. Indeed, since the Church is called in Christ to be a sign and sacrament of a renewed humanity, it also illumines the nature and destiny of human life as such. As ARCIC has affirmed in *Church as Communion*:

> to explore the meaning of communion is not only to speak of the church but also to address the world at the heart of its deepest need, for human beings long for true community in freedom, justice and peace and for respect of human dignity   (para. 3)

In this final section, therefore, we return once again to the theme of communion and consider the light it sheds both on the moral order and on the Church's moral response.

1 Communion and the Moral Order

91. Communion, we have argued, is a constitutive characteristic of a fully human life, signifying 'a relationship based on participation in a shared reality' (cf. *Church as Communion*, §12). From this perspective the moral dimension of human life is itself perceived to be fundamentally relational, determined both by the nature of the reality in which it participates and by the form appropriate to such participation.

92. Participation of human beings in the life of God, in whom they live and move and have their being (cf. Acts 17.28), is grounded in their creation in God's image (cf. *Church as Communion*, §6). The fundamental relationship in which they stand, therefore, is their relationship to God, Creator and goal of all that is, seen and unseen. Created and sustained in this relationship, they are drawn towards God's absolute goodness, which they experience as both gift and call. Moral responsibility is a gift of divine grace; the moral imperative is an expression of divine love. When Jesus bids his disciples before all else to seek the kingdom of God (cf. Mt 6.33), he tells them also that they are to reflect in their own lives the 'perfection' which belongs to the divine life (cf. Mt 5.48). This call to 'perfection' echoes the Lord's call to the people of Israel to participate in his holiness (cf. Lev 19.2). As such, it does not ignore human fragility, failure and sin; but it does lay bare the full dimensions of a response that reflects the height and breadth and depth of the divine righteousness and love (cf. Rom 8.1–4).

93. Human beings are not purely spiritual beings; they are fashioned out of the dust (cf. Gen 2.7). Created in the image of God, they are shaped by nature and culture, and participate in both the glory and the shame of the human story. Their responsibility to God issues in a responsibility for God's world, and their transformation into the likeness of God embraces their relationships both to the natural world and to one another. Hence no arbitrary boundaries may be set between the good of the individual, the common good of humanity, and the good of the whole created order. The context of the truly human life is the universal and all-embracing rule of God.

94. The world in which human beings participate is a changing world. Science and technology have given them the power, to a degree unforeseen in earlier centuries, to impress their own designs on the natural environment, by adapting the environment to their own needs, by exploiting it and even by destroying it. However, there are ultimate limits to what is possible. Nature is not infinitely malleable. Moreover, not everything that is humanly possible is humanly desirable, or morally right. In many situations, what is sometimes called progress is, as a consequence of human ignorance and arrogance, degrading and destructive. The moral task is to discern how fundamental and eternal values may be expressed and embodied in a world that is subject to continuing change.

95. The world in which human beings participate is not only a changing world; it is also a broken and imperfect world. It is subject to futility and sin, and stands under the judgement of God. Its human structures are distorted by violence and greed. Inevitably, conflicts of value and clashes of interest arise, and situations occur in which the requirements of the moral order are uncertain. Law is enacted and enforced to preserve order and to protect and serve the common good. Admittedly, it can perpetuate inequalities of wealth and power, but its true end is to ensure justice and peace. At a deeper level, the moral order looks for its fulfilment to a renewal of personal freedom and dignity within a forgiving, healing and caring community.

2 Communion and the Church

96. Life in Christ is a life of communion, to be manifested for the salvation of the world and for the glorification of God the Father. In the fellowship of the Holy Spirit the Church participates in the Son's loving and obedient response to the Father. But even if, in

the resurrection of Christ, the new world has already begun, the end is not yet. So the Church continues to pray and prepare for the day when Christ will deliver the kingdom to the Father (cf. 1 Cor 15.24–28) and God will be all in all. In the course of history Anglicans and Roman Catholics have disagreed on certain specific matters of moral teaching and practice, but they continue to hold to the same vision of human nature and destiny fulfilled in Christ. Furthermore, their deep desire to find an honest and faithful resolution of their disagreements is itself evidence of a continuing communion at a more profound level than that on which disagreement has occurred.

97. The Church as communion reflects the communion of the triune God, Father, Son and Holy Spirit (cf. Jn 17, 20—22; Jn 14.16f; 2 Cor 13.13), and anticipates the fullness of communion in the kingdom of God. Consequently, communion means that members of the Church share a responsibility for discerning the action of the Spirit in the contemporary world, for shaping a truly human response, and for resolving the ensuing moral perplexities with integrity and fidelity to the Gospel. Within this shared responsibility, those who exercise the office of pastor and teacher have the special task of equipping the Church and its members for life in the world, and for guiding and confirming their free and faithful response to the Gospel. The exercise of this authority will itself bear the marks of communion, in so far as a sustained attentiveness to the experience and reflection of the faithful becomes part of the process of making an informed and authoritative judgement. One such example of this understanding of the interaction of communion and authority, we suggest, is the careful and sustained process of listening and public consultation which has preceded the publication of some of the pastoral letters of Bishops' Conferences of the Roman Catholic Church in different parts of the world.

98. Communion also means that, where there has been a failure to meet the claims of the moral order to which the Church bears witness, there will be a determined attempt to restore the sinner to the life of grace in the community, thereby allowing the gospel of forgiveness to be proclaimed even to the greatest of sinners. Anglicans and Roman Catholics share the conviction that God's righteousness and God's love and mercy are inseparable (cf. *Salvation and the Church*, §§17 and 18), and both Communions continue to exercise a ministry of healing, forgiveness and reconciliation.

3 Towards Moral Integrity and Full Communion

99.   Anglicans and Roman Catholics share a deep desire, not only for full communion, but also for a resolution of the disagreement that exists between them on certain specific moral issues. The two are related. On the one hand, seeking a resolution of our disagreements is part of the process of growing together towards full communion. On the other hand, only as closer communion leads to deeper understanding and trust can we hope for a resolution of our disagreements.

100.   In order to make an informed and faithful response to the moral perplexities facing humanity today, Christians must promote a global and ecumenical perception of fundamental human relationships and values. Our common vision of humanity in Christ places before us this responsibility, while at the same time requiring us to develop a greater sensitivity to the different experiences, insights and approaches that are appropriate to different cultures and contexts. The separation that still exists between our two Communions is a serious obstacle to the Church's mission and a darkening of the moral wisdom it may hope to share with the world.

101.   Our work together within this Commission has shown us that the discernment of the precise nature of the moral agreement and disagreement between Anglicans and Roman Catholics is not always an easy task. One problem we faced was the fact that we often found ourselves comparing the variety of moral judgements present and permissible among Anglicans with the official, authoritative teachings of the Roman Catholic Church. This feature of our discussions was inevitable, given the differences between our two Communions in the way they understand and exercise authority. Working together, however, has convinced us that the disagreements on moral matters, which at present exist between us, need not constitute an insuperable barrier to progress towards fuller communion. Painful and perplexing as they are, they do not reveal a fundamental divergence in our understanding of the moral implications of the Gospel.

102.   Continuing study is needed of the differences between us, real or apparent, especially in our understanding and use of the notion of 'law'. A clearer understanding is required of the relation of the concept of law to the concepts of moral order and the common good, and the relation of all these concepts to the vision of human

happiness and fulfilment as 'persons in community' that we have been given in and through Jesus Christ. However, Anglicans and Roman Catholics do not talk to each other as moral strangers. They both appeal to a shared tradition, and they recognise the same Scriptures as normative of that tradition. They both respect the role of reason in moral discernment. They both give due place to the classic virtue of prudence. We are convinced, therefore, that further exchange between our two traditions on moral questions will serve both the cause of Christian unity and the good of that larger society of which we are all part.

103. We end our document with a specific practical recommendation. We propose that steps should be taken to establish further instruments of cooperation between our two Communions at all levels of church life (especially national and regional), to engage with the serious moral issues confronting humanity today. In view of our common approach to moral reflection, and in the light of the agreements we have already discovered to exist between us, we believe that bilateral discussions between Anglicans and Roman Catholics would be especially valuable.

We make this proposal for the following reasons:

> Working together on moral issues would be a practical way of expressing the communion we already enjoy, of moving towards full communion, and of understanding more clearly what it entails; without such collaboration we run the risk of increasing divergence.
>
> Moving towards shared witness would contribute significantly to the mission of the Church and allow the light of the Gospel to shine more fully upon the moral perplexities of human existence in today's world.
>
> Having a shared vision of a humanity created in the image of God, we share a common responsibility to challenge society in places where that image is being marred or defaced.

104. We do not underestimate the difficulties that such collaboration would involve. Nevertheless, we dare not continue along our separated ways. Our working and witnessing together to the world is in itself a form of communion. Such deepening communion will enable us to handle our remaining disagreements in a faithful and more creative way. 'He who calls you is faithful, and he will do it' (1 Thess 5.24).

Responses and Directions for Further Work

Official Roman Catholic Commentary

As with other ARCIC II Statements, the first response was the official Roman Catholic Commentary, prepared by Thomas Kopfensteiner.[1] This engages with the Statement from the perspective of 'the newness of Christ [which] has put into motion a new history of insight', and endeavours to contribute to the dialogue rather than entering into detailed critique. 'The four issues on which the Anglican and Roman Catholic Communions diverge' (see *Life in Christ*, Section E) form the basis of assessment: in each case the agreements reached are noted, but it is 'fundamental moral concerns' that are the focus of this Commentary. Thus in relation to divorce, it is 'the meaning of an irrevocable life-choice', especially one 'into which the newness of Jesus enters'. Likewise, 'behind the discussion of contraception is the relationship of person and nature . . . [and] the metaphysics of the moral act'. As regards abortion, 'two issues whose clarification will contribute to future dialogue between the churches, and between the churches and society' are 'the moral status of the embryo' and 'reflection on a social context'. The latter includes both 'a theological critique of the language of rights' and that 'the sacrifice that is required of the woman . . . will require a commensurate sacrifice on the part of the community as a whole'. Finally, in considering homosexuality, some positive suggestions are made and specifically that 'the dialogue between morality and the empirical sciences' could use homosexuality as a test case, in which moral theology is both 'in the position of being an *apprentice* . . . and being a *tutor*.'

Kopfensteiner's Conclusion begins by acknowledging that '*Life in Christ* does not resolve any of the outstanding differences between the Anglican Communion and the Roman Catholic Church: that is clearly beyond the goals of the Commission.' While 'Anglicans and Roman Catholics are not moral strangers', he argues that there are 'differing conceptions of the relationships between metaphysic and history, person and act, person and nature, and norms and conflict situations.' These are 'tacit' in the Statement, yet offer 'fertile ground for future dialogue', which 'not only anticipates but is the means for achieving full communion'. It is hard to think of a better way of encouraging ARCIC III to pursue its mandate to explore 'how in communion the local and universal Church come to discern right ethical teaching'.

---

[1] Thomas Kopfensteiner, 'Commentary on *Life in Christ: Morals, Communion, and the Church*', *Information Service*, 85/1 (1994), www.vatican.va/roman_curia/pontifical_councils/chrstuni/information_service/pdf/information_service_85_en.pdf.

Other Responses

Responses to *Life in Christ* since this Commentary was issued have been few, especially from ecclesial bodies.[2] Those made by ARCUSA and IARCCUM note the changes in the Anglican and Roman Catholic traditions which have shifted the context in relation to morals (see the Introduction). Further, *Life in Christ* was published after John Paul II's encyclical *Veritatis Splendor*. ARCUSA concludes that

> The optimistic thesis of Life in Christ appears to be significantly challenged, in its turn, by the papal encyclical *Veritatis Splendor* (VS), which was published only months earlier (5 Oct. 1993). We note with regret that these two documents were prepared independently of each other, and we find our Churches challenged to be more collaborative in the future. Still, now we must take account of important contrasts in outlook between the two documents and the likely implication of these contrasts for the eventual assessment of Life in Christ by the papal magisterium.[3]

This assessment undergirds other areas where further dialogue is needed. ARCUSA went on to note the need for further reflection on 'the contemporary influence of theological, geographical, and cultural diversity—on the formulation of Anglican doctrines concerning moral questions, by contrast with the universal teaching that characterises the Roman Catholic magisterium in such matters'.

The Archbishop of Canterbury, Rowan Williams, in his briefing document to the Church of England General Synod in 2009 on *Life in Christ*, said that 'the introductory material on the biblical understanding of the human person is of key significance to reading the whole of the report'. While regretting the lack of explicit mention of Anglican moral theologians such as Richard Hooker, Jeremy Taylor, and Joseph Butler, he also noted what he called the fierce debate inside the Roman Catholic Church about issues of personal morality.[4]

---

[2] Most notably, the 1995 ARCUSA Statement, 'Christian Ethics in the Ecumenical Dialogue', and more recently, IARCCUM and PCPCU, 'Ecclesiological Reflections on the Current Situation in the Anglican Communion in the Light of ARCIC' (2004), https://iarccum.org/archive/IARCCUM_2000-2010/2004_iarccum_ecclesiological_reflections.pdf; *Information Service*, 119/3 (2005), 102–15. Significant scholarly articles include Jon Nilson, 'Must Disagreements Divide? The Achievements and Challenges of ARCIC-II's *Life in Christ*', *One in Christ*, 31/3 (1995), 222–36, and Julie Clague, 'On Agreeing to Differ: Some Reflections on the ARCIC Statement on Morals in Light of *Veritatis Splendor*', *Irish Theological Quarterly*, 62/1 (1996), 70–4.

[3] ARCUSA, 'Christian Ethics in the Ecumenical Dialogue', §3.

[4] Abp Rowan Williams, '*Life in Christ*: Considerations for Synod Group Discussion' (24 June 2009), GS 1736-01, www.churchofengland.org/media/39700/gs17360901.rtf. See further FOAG, Briefing Paper, 'Anglican–Roman Catholic International Commission: *Life in Christ: Morals, Communion and the Church*', GS 1736, www.churchofengland.org/media/39696/gs1736.doc.

'Law' and Absolute Values

An underlying issue in the responses concerns whether differences over the ways in which 'law' is understood are adequately examined—an area which *Life in Christ* itself suggests needs more study (§102). It argues that the central question shaping a Christian moral vision is not so much 'What ought we to do?' as 'what kind of persons are we called to become?' (§6), and that in both traditions a shift is taking place away from an emphasis on the demands of positive law to an emphasis on the dignity of the person and on the demands of conscience. *Veritatis Splendor*, on the other hand, reflects the shift from a morality of obligation (such as in Ockham and Paley) to one of virtue (as exemplified in Aquinas and Hooker). Some argue, however, that this encyclical marries an ethic of virtue ('what I am called to become') with one of law (seen as an expression of truths beneficial to the person: 'what I ought to do').[5]

Put simply, do the Anglican and Roman Catholic traditions have sufficient commonality over whether some actions are always wrong, that is, that there are absolute values, moral norms that do not allow of exceptions? *Life in Christ* §52 maintains that both Anglicans and Roman Catholic typically include prudential factors in moral judgement, but in different ways:

> While acknowledging the same ultimate values, [Anglicans] are not per-suaded that the laws as we apprehend them are necessarily absolute. In certain circumstances, they would argue, it might be right to incorporate contextual and pastoral considerations in the formulation of a moral law, on the grounds that fundamental moral values are better served if the law sometimes takes into account certain contingencies of nature and history and certain disorders of the human condition. In so doing, they do not make the clear-cut distinction, which Roman Catholics make, between canon law, with its incorporation of contingent and prudential considerations, and the moral law, which in its principles is absolute and universal.

Successive Statements by the Lambeth Conference support the notion of universal moral norms, but always with a discussion of how these work

---

[5] So Livio Melina, *Sharing in Christ's Virtues: For the Renewal of Moral Theology in Light of Veritatis Splendor*, trans. William E. May (Washington DC: The Catholic University of America Press, 2001); Servais Pinckaers, 'Conscience and the Virtue of Prudence', in John Beckman and Craig Stevens (eds.), *The Pinckaers Reader: Renewing Thomistic Moral Theology* (Washington DC: The Catholic University of America Press, 2002); Janet E. Smith, 'Natural Law and Personalism in *Veritatis Splendor*', in Charles E. Curran and Richard A. McCormick SJ (eds.), *John Paul II and Moral Theology*, Readings in Moral Theology, 10 (Mahwah, NJ: Paulist Press, 1998), 67–84.

out in particular areas. Thus the 1930 Conference spoke of 'axiomatic moral principles', seeing abortion as 'contrary to the law of God and man', while allowing the use of (non-abortive) contraception as a means of family planning within marriage (and while holding procreation as its primary good).[6] On the other hand, the magisterium of the Roman Catholic Church continues to teach that those acts are always wrong, while permitting Natural Family Planning to control family size.

Conscience and Particular Matters

Life in Christ recognizes the shared respect that both traditions have for the role of personal conscience in moral decision-making (see §§29–31), and how this relates to the authority of the Church as institution giving moral teaching (§49). The question has been raised as to the Statement gives little attention to the phenomenon of dissent: nothing is said about the widespread lack of acceptance of and adherence to some official teaching among Roman Catholics, a problem which Anglicans recognize in themselves from their own experience. Moreover, although the role of *sensus fidei* and the place of conscience in the discernment of ecclesial teaching is addressed in *The Gift of Authority*, more work is needed in this area.

There are also particular matters about which questions have been raised regarding claims made in *Life in Christ*:

- that both Anglican and Roman Catholic traditions consider marriage to be sacramental, though in different ways (§62);
- that differences over the acceptability of divorce are because the Anglican Communion has a predominant concern for the people involved, whereas the Roman Catholic Church has a predominant concern for the institution of marriage (§76).

Conclusion: The Path Ahead

The significant changes in the moral, ecclesial, and cultural contexts since *Life in Christ* was issued mean that no simple response is adequate to fulfil ARCIC's calling to work towards 'that unity in truth, for which Christ prayed'. This reality has been recognized by the decision of the authorities in both traditions to establish a third phase of ARCIC, whose mandate

---

[6] *Lambeth Conference 1930. Encyclical Letter from the Bishops with the Resolutions and Reports* (New York: SPCK and Macmillan, 1930), 89–90. ARCUSA, *Ecclesiology and Moral Discernment*, §§22–33 sets out clearly the different approaches to official moral teaching in the Anglican Communion and the Roman Catholic Church.

includes exploration of 'how in communion the local and universal Church come to discern right ethical teaching'.

As well as the issues identified above, ARCIC III should consider the discernment of right ethical teaching in the social sphere, where there are large areas of agreement between Anglicans and Roman Catholics. Pressing issues have emerged since 1994—the ecological crisis, new volumes of migration, increasing levels of modern slavery and human trafficking, the growing gap between rich and poor, the rapidly changing disciplines of bioethics, the effect of new technologies on work practices, the development of social media, for example—and this in the context of Western cultures which are losing their Christian identity and heritage. As Archbishop Rowan Williams concluded his remarks on *Life in Christ* to the Church of England's General Synod,

> If the Church's 'moral principles' are inseparable from its character as Christ's Body, as a community existing essentially in relation to the gift and grace of Jesus and his Spirit, we all need to think harder about how the distinctiveness of the Church is articulated in respect of society in general—not so as to dig some great gulf between Church and society but so as to clarify how and why the Church claims to offer human society a promise that it could not achieve out of its own resources. For this generation, the issues of ethics are bound up more profoundly with the need to understand secularisation in an adequately theological way.[7]

Life in Christ thus stands as a significant achievement, but the Commission was restricted by its mandate, and the context within which its agreement was reached has changed: the baton has been passed to ARCIC III. Ecumenical consensus on moral life is vital not only for Anglicans and Roman Catholics looking towards a Church fully reconciled, but for the well-being of the modern world, whose crisis 'is more than a crisis of sexual ethics. At stake is our humanity itself' (*Life in Christ*, §11).

Bibliography

Ecclesial Responses

Official Roman Catholic Commentary

Kopfensteiner, Thomas R., 'Commentary on *Life in Christ: Morals, Communion, and the Church*', *Information Service*, 85/1 (1994/), www.vatican.va/roman_curia/pontifical_councils/chrstuni/information_service/pdf/information_service_85_en.pdf.

---

[7] Williams, '*Life in Christ*: Considerations for Synod Group Discussion'.

Significant Ecclesial Documents

ARCUSA, 'Christian Ethics in the Ecumenical Dialogue: Anglican–Roman Catholic International Commission II and Recent Papal Teachings' (June 1995), www.usccb.org/beliefs-and-teachings/ecumenical-and-interreligious/ecumenical/anglican/ethics-in-ecumenical-dialogue.cfm

ARCUSA, *Ecclesiology and Moral Discernment: Seeking a Unified Moral Witness* (April 2014), www.episcopalchurch.org/library/document/ecclesiology-and-moral-discernment-statement-anglican-roman-catholic-theological

Benedict XVI, *Caritas in Veritate* (London: CTS, 2009), www.vatican.va/holy_father/benedict_xvi/encyclicals/documents/hf_ben-xvi_enc_20090629_caritas-in-veritate_en.html

Benedict XIV, *Deus est Caritas* (London: CTS, 2005), www.vatican.va/holy_father/benedict_xvi/encyclicals/documents/hf_ben-xvi_enc_20051225_deus-caritas-est_en.html

CDF, 'Doctrinal Commentary on the Concluding Formula of the *Professio Fidei*' (1998), www.vatican.va/roman_curia/congregations/cfaith/documents/rc_con_cfaith_doc_1998_professio-fidei_en.html

Church of England General Synod, *Report of Proceedings* (July 2009), 27–31, www.churchofengland.org/media/41001/ropjuly2009.pdf

FOAG, General Synod Briefing Paper, 'Anglican–Roman Catholic International Commission: *Life in Christ: Morals, Communion and the Church*', GS 1736, www.churchofengland.org/media/39696/gs1736.doc

IARCCUM and PCPCU, 'Ecclesiological Reflections on the Current Situation in the Anglican Communion in the Light of ARCIC' (2004), https://iarccum.org/archive/IARCCUM_2000-2010/2004_iarccum_ecclesiological_reflections.pdf; *Information Service*, 119/3 (2005), 102–15

John Paul II, *Evangelium Vitae* (London: CTS, 1995), www.vatican.va/holy_father/john_paul_ii/encyclicals/documents/hf_jp-ii_enc_25031995_evangelium-vitae_en.html

John Paul II, *Veritatis Splendor* (London: CTS, 1993), www.vatican.va/holy_father/john_paul_ii/encyclicals/documents/hf_jp-ii_enc_06081993_veritatis-splendor_en.html

Transformation and Renewal: The Official Report of the Lambeth Conference 1998 (Harrisburg: Morehouse, 1999), Resolution I.10, pp. 381–2, 436–8,http://www.anglicancommunion.org/resources/document-library/lambeth-conference/1998/section-i-called-to-full-humanity/section-i10-human-sexuality?author=Lambeth+Conference&year=1998

Significant Publications

Clague, Julie, 'On Agreeing to Differ: Some Reflections on the ARCIC Statement on Morals in Light of *Veritatis Splendor*', *Irish Theological Quarterly*, 62/1 (1996), 70–4

Hutter, Reinhard, and Dieter, Theodor (eds.), *Ecumenical Ventures in Ethics: Protestants Engage Pope John Paul II's Moral Encyclicals* (Grand Rapids: Eerdmans, 1998)

Lüning, P., 'Das Dialogdokument "*Life in Christ: Morals, Communion and the Church*" (1994)', in *Offenbarung und Rechtfertigung: eine Studie zu ihrer Verhältnisbestimmung anhand des anglikanisch/römisch-katholischen Dialogs*, Konfessionskundliche und kontroverstheologische Studien, 70 (Paderborn: Bonifatius, 1999), 368–97

Marko, Robert, 'Early Protestant Readings of *Veritatis Splendor*: Implications for Christian Ethics', *Josephinum Journal of Theology*, 3/1 (Winter–Spring 1996), 22–7

Meilaender, Gilbert, '*Veritatis Splendor*: Reopening Some Questions of the Reformation', *The Journal of Religious Ethics*, 23/2 (Fall 1995), 225–38

Meyer, Harding, 'Ecumenical Consensus: Our Quest for and the Emerging Structures of Consensus', *Gregorianum*, 77/2 (1996), 213–25

Murray, Donal, 'Is Ecumenical Consensus Possible on Moral Questions?', *Doctrine and Life*, 50 (March 2000), 132–43

Nilson, John, 'Must Disagreements Divide? The Achievements and Challenges of ARCIC-II's *Life in Christ*', *One in Christ*, 31/3 (1995), 222–36

O'Donovan, Oliver, '*Life in Christ*', *The Tablet* (2 July 1994), 826–8

Phillips, David, 'ARCIC—*Life in Christ*', Church Society 'Ecumenical' web page, www.churchsociety.org/issues_new/ecum/iss_ecum_arcic-lifechrist.asp

Rasmusson, Arne, 'Ecclesiology and Ethics: The Difficulties of Ecclesial Moral Reflection', *Ecumenical Review*, 52 (April 2000), 180–94

Root, Michael, 'Ethics in Ecumenical Dialogues: A Survey and Analysis', *Journal of Ecumenical Studies* (22 June 2010)

Sedgwick, Timothy F., 'Exploring the Great Divide: Sex, Ethics, and Ecumenism', *Journal of Ecumenical Studies* (22 June 2010)

Sherlock, Charles, 'Anglican–Roman Catholic Dialogue on Ethics and Moral Theology: An Anglican Perspective', *One in Christ*, 46/1 (2012), 89–107

Sherrington, John, and Faley, Andrew, 'Foundations of Catholic Moral Teaching', GS 1736-02, www.churchofengland.org/about-us/structure/general-synod/agendas-and-papers/july-2009-group-of-sessions.aspx

Smith, Janet E., 'The *Sensus Fidelium* and *Humanae Vitae*', *Angelicum*, 83 (2006), 271–97; also published in Stephen Boguslawski and Robert Fastiggi (eds.), *Called to Holiness and Communion* (Washington DC: Catholic University of America, 2009)

Tillard, Jean-Marie, 'The Call to Goodness', *The Tablet* (16 October 1993), 1365

Veliko, Lydia, and Gros, Jeffrey (eds.), *Growing Consensus II: Church Dialogues in the United States, 1992–2004* (Washington DC: USCCB, 2005)

Williams, Rowan, '*Life in Christ*: Considerations for Synod Group Discussion' (24 June 2009), GS 1736-01, www.churchofengland.org/media/39700/gs17360901.rtf

Chapter 4

The Gift of Authority: Authority in the Church III (1999)

Introducing the Statement

The Gift of Authority (1999) is the third ARCIC Statement on authority, the first two being included in *The Final Report* of ARCIC I (1981).

Authority I set the discussion within an understanding of Church as a *koinonia* in Christ, and goes on to identify four areas where Anglicans and Roman Catholics do not agree: the interpretation of the New Testament texts about Peter; the language of *ius divinum* (divine right) used by the First Vatican Council (1870) about succession in papal office; the Roman Catholic claim for the dogmatic teaching of the Pope, under certain specific conditions, to be infallible; and the universal, immediate jurisdiction also claimed for the Pope. The *Elucidation to Authority I* answers some objections to the agreement claimed, while *Authority II* probes these four controversial areas in greater depth.

The official Roman Catholic response to *The Final Report* was issued by the Vatican in late 1990. While generally affirmative of the texts on eucharist and ministry,[1] it was critical of those on authority, especially in their treatment of infallibility and reception, where it found a 'different understanding' from that of Vatican I. This response, along with Anglican requests for further work, set the agenda for a third Statement on authority.

Gift opens with a summary of the agreements reached in *Authority in the Church I* and *II*, a convergence already welcomed by the authorities of the Anglican Communion and the Roman Catholic Church. *Gift* then outlines the specific areas which the Commission was requested to explore further:

---

[1] These were built on by ARCIC II in *Clarifications of Certain Aspects of the Agreed Statements on Eucharist and Ministry of the First Anglican–Roman Catholic International Commission* (London: Church House and CTS, 1994). This Statement was positively received by the PCPCU, as indicated in the included Letter from Cardinal Cassidy, then PCPCU President.

- the relationship between Scripture, Tradition, and the exercise of teaching authority;
- collegiality, conciliarity, and the role of laity in decision-making;
- the Petrine ministry of universal primacy in relation to Scripture and Tradition.

ARCIC II also noted that new questions concerning the exercise of authority had been raised by current issues, particularly the ordination of Anglican women as priests.[2]

Approaching *The Gift of Authority*

The title—*The Gift of Authority*—already suggests a distinctive approach to authority and its exercise, one grounded in God's initiative and grace. It follows the broad method of *koinonia* ecclesiology, but develops it in a new way, around the motif of God's 'Yes' to humanity in Jesus Christ which draws out our responsive 'Amen' (see 2 Cor 1.18–20). This 'Yes/Amen' motif becomes the key to the Statement's exposition of authority in the Church (§8). Jesus Christ spoke and acted with authority because of his perfect communion (*koinonia*) with the Father; by the Spirit, the 'Amen' of believers who accept the authority of Christ is incorporated in the 'Amen' of Christ to the Father. This motif recurs through *Gift*, relating the 'Amen' of believers to baptism (§10) and the eucharist (§§13, 33, 36). The Statement thus has a strongly liturgical and doxological character: it sets Christian authority, and its exercise, in these contexts.

Part III, 'The Exercise of Authority', notes points of divergence between Anglicans and Roman Catholics, although within a common framework. Two key sections are 'Perseverance in the Truth: The Exercise of Authority in Teaching', and 'Primacy: The Exercise of Authority in Collegiality and Conciliarity'. These include a significant discussion of the possibility that 'the Church may teach *infallibly*' (§42). It is important to note that the word 'infallible' is used in the Statement only here and in the following paragraph: 'The truth and authority of its Head is the source of infallible teaching in the body of Christ' (§43). This precedes the discussion of universal primacy and the Bishop of Rome's 'specific ministry concerning the discernment of truth', which has been a 'source of difficulties and misunderstandings among the churches' (§47).

In short, what *Gift* offers is an understanding of the ministry of the Bishop of Rome which, so far as it goes, could be acceptable to both

---

[2] ARCIC II's considerations of this development are outlined in Chapters 11 and 13 below.

Anglicans and Roman Catholics: it concludes, 'We believe that this is a gift to be received by all the churches' (§47). Having made such a bold statement, the Commission notes that 'This authority is exercised by fragile Christians for the sake of other fragile Christians' (§48). It is also emphasized that the exercise of authority must always respect freedom of conscience, 'because the divine work of salvation affirms human freedom' (§49).

In Part IV, the advances made by the Commission are brought together. The most striking is agreement on 'a universal primacy, exercised collegially in the context of synodality, as integral to *episcope* at the service of universal communion; such a primacy having always been associated with the Bishop and See of Rome' (§52). The Statement goes on to identify 'Issues Facing Anglicans' (§56) and 'Issues Facing Roman Catholics' (§57), by posing sharp questions to each tradition. In finding universal primacy 'a gift to be shared' (§§60–62), it suggests that 'such a primacy could be offered and received even before our churches are in full communion' (§60). *Gift* ends with challenges: for Anglicans, to 'be open to and desire a recovery and re-reception under certain clear conditions of the exercise of universal primacy by the Bishop of Rome'; for Roman Catholics, to 'be open to and desire a re-reception of the exercise of the primacy by the Bishop of Rome and the offering of such a ministry to the whole Church of God' (§62).

At first sight this conclusion seems to ask more of Anglicans than of Roman Catholics. While ARCIC II was studying the exercise of authority in the Church, Pope John Paul II published his Encyclical Letter on Christian unity, *Ut Unum Sint* (1995). In this he invited leaders and theologians of other churches to engage with him in a 'patient and fraternal dialogue' as to how the particular ministry of unity of the Bishop of Rome might be exercised in a new ecumenical situation (*Ut Unum Sint*, §96; cf. *Gift*, §4). By this timely invitation, Roman Catholics as well as Anglicans were encouraged to engage in new thinking about the office of the Bishop of Rome. The conclusion of *Gift* is thus challenging for both Roman Catholics and Anglicans.

New Contexts for Reading *The Gift of Authority*

The Joint International Commission for the Theological Dialogue between the Roman Catholic Church and the Orthodox Church covered much of the same ground as *Gift*, though more briefly, in its 2007 Statement *Ecclesiological and Canonical Consequences of the Sacramental Nature of the Church* ('The Ravenna Statement').[3] Authority is discussed as it pertains to the local, regional, and universal levels of the Church. It is acknowledged that 'Conciliarity at the universal level, exercised in the ecumenical councils, implies an active role of the Bishop of Rome, as *protos* of the bishops of the major sees, in the consensus of the assembled bishops' (§42). In a significant paragraph, areas for future study concerning the role of the Bishop of Rome are indicated:

> What is the specific function of the bishop of the 'first see' in an ecclesiology of koinonia and in view of what we have said on conciliarity and authority in the present text? How should the teaching of the first and second Vatican Councils on the universal primacy be understood and lived in the light of the ecclesial practice of the first millennium? These are crucial questions for our dialogue and for our hopes of restoring full communion between us. (§45)

It is also important to take note of the report by the (Roman Catholic) International Theological Commission, '*The Sensus Fidei* in the Life of the Church' (2014), which makes explicit reference to *Gift* and, although it does not deal with the question of universal primacy, demonstrates a convergence of method, notably in the areas of *sensus fidei* and *sensus fidelium* (see *Gift*, §§29–30). It explores an understanding of these terms embedded within a post-Vatican II ecclesiology in greater depth than was possible for ARCIC II. In this way, aspects of *Gift's* method have been affirmed at high levels by Roman Catholic authorities.

The reception of *Gift* has also been aided by the remarkable ministry of Pope Francis, who often speaks of himself as 'Bishop of Rome', emphasizing the collegial nature of his authority, which is shared with other bishops. The Extraordinary Synod on the Family (2014), which included lay and ecumenical participation, demonstrated his commitment to synodality within the Church. The emphasis on the preaching of the Gospel in his Apostolic Exhortation *Evangelii Gaudium* (2013), the repeated references to the documents of episcopal conferences throughout his encyclical *Laudato Si'* (2015), showing their teaching authority, the simplicity of his personal lifestyle, his stress on ministry to the poor and marginalized, and the positive role he has played in international reconciliation, have all played their part in commending the ministry of the Bishop of Rome to Christians throughout the world.

---

[3] The Joint Commission is engaged on a study of 'The Role of the Bishop of Rome in the Communion of the Church in the First Millennium', which will be of direct relevance to the reception of *Gift*.

THE GIFT OF AUTHORITY

Authority in the Church III

An Agreed Statement by
the Anglican–Roman Catholic
International Commission (ARCIC II)

CONTENTS

THE STATUS OF THE DOCUMENT

The Document published here is the work of the Anglican–Roman Catholic International Commission (ARCIC). It is a joint statement of the Commission. The authorities who appointed the Commission have allowed the statement to be published so that it may be widely discussed. It is not an authoritative declaration by the Roman Catholic Church or by the Anglican Communion, who will evaluate the document in order to take a position on it in due time.

Citations from Scripture are from the New Revised Standard Version.

PREFACE

By the Co-Chairmen

An earnest search for full visible unity between the Anglican Communion and the Roman Catholic Church was initiated over thirty years ago by the historic meeting in Rome of Archbishop Michael Ramsey and Pope Paul VI. The Commission set up to prepare for the dialogue recognised, in its 1968 *Malta Report*, that one of the 'urgent and important tasks' would be to examine the question of authority. In a sense, this question is at the heart of our sad divisions.

When *The Final Report* of ARCIC was published in 1981 half of it was devoted to the dialogue about authority in the Church, with two agreed statements and an elucidation. This was important groundwork, preparing the way for further convergence. The official responses, by the 1988 Lambeth Conference of the Anglican Communion and by the Catholic Church in 1991, encouraged the Commission to carry forward the 'remarkable progress' that had been made. Accordingly ARCIC now offers this further agreed statement, *The Gift of Authority*.

A scriptural image is the key to this statement. In chapter one of his second letter to the Corinthians, Paul writes of God's 'Yes' to humanity and our answering 'Amen' to God, both given in Jesus Christ (cf. 2 Cor 1.19–20). God's gift of authority to his Church is at the service of God's 'Yes' to his people and their 'Amen'.

The reader is invited to follow the path that led the Commission to its conclusions. They are the fruit of five years of dialogue, of patient listening, study, and prayer together. The statement will, we hope, prompt further theological reflection; its conclusions present a challenge to our two Churches, not least in regard to the crucial issue of universal primacy. Authority is about how the Church teaches, acts and reaches doctrinal decisions in faithfulness to the Gospel, so real agreement about authority cannot be theoretical. If this statement is to contribute to the reconciliation of the Anglican Communion and the Catholic Church and is accepted, it will require a response in life and in deed.

Much has happened over these years to deepen our awareness of each other as brothers and sisters in Christ. Yet our journey towards full, visible unity is proving longer than some expected and many hoped.

We have encountered serious obstacles which make progress difficult. At such a stage, the persevering, painstaking work of dialogue is all the more vital. The present Archbishop of Canterbury, Dr George Carey, and Pope John Paul II stated very frankly the need for this work on authority when they met in 1996: 'Without agreement in this area we shall not reach the full, visible unity to which we are both committed'.

We pray that God will enable the Commission's work to contribute to the end we all desire, the healing of our divisions so that together we may say a united '"Amen" to the glory of God' (2 Cor 1.20).

+ Cormac Murphy-O'Connor
+ Mark Santer

Palazzola
3 September 1998
The Feast of St Gregory the Great

THE GIFT OF AUTHORITY
(Authority in the Church III)

I INTRODUCTION

1. The dialogue between Anglicans and Roman Catholics has shown significant signs of progress on the question of authority in the Church. This progress can already be seen in the convergence in understanding of authority achieved by previous ARCIC Statements, notably:

    *   acknowledgement that the Spirit of the Risen Lord maintains the people of God in obedience to the Father's will. By this action of the Holy Spirit, the authority of the Lord is active in the Church (cf. *The Final Report, Authority in the Church I*, 3);
    *   a recognition that because of their baptism and their participation in the *sensus fidelium* the laity play an integral part in decision-making in the Church (cf. *Authority in the Church: Elucidation*, 4);
    *   the complementarity of primacy and conciliarity as elements of *episcope* within the Church (cf. *Authority in the Church I*, 22);
    *   the need for a universal primacy exercised by the Bishop of Rome as a sign and safeguard of unity within a reunited Church (cf. *Authority in the Church II*, 9);
    *   the need for the universal primate to exercise his ministry in collegial association with the other bishops (cf. *Authority in the Church II*, 19);
    *   an understanding of universal primacy and conciliarity which complements and does not supplant the exercise of *episcope* in local churches (cf. *Authority in the Church I*, 21–23; *Authority in the Church II*, 19).

2. This convergence has been officially noted by the authorities of the Anglican Communion and the Roman Catholic Church. The Lambeth Conference, meeting in 1988, not only saw the ARCIC agreements on eucharistic doctrine and on ministry and ordination as consonant in substance with the faith of Anglicans (*Resolution 8.1*) but affirmed that the agreed statements on authority in the church provided a

basis for further dialogue (*Resolution 8.3*). Similarly, the Holy See, in its official response of 1991, recognising areas of agreement on questions of very great importance for the faith of the Roman Catholic Church, such as the eucharist and the Church's ministry, noted the signs of convergence between our two communions on the question of authority in the Church, indicating that this opened the way to further progress.

3. However, the authorities of our two communions have asked for further exploration of areas where, although there has been convergence, they believe that a necessary consensus has not yet been achieved. These areas include:

- the relationship between Scripture, Tradition and the exercise of teaching authority;
- collegiality, conciliarity, and the role of laity in decision-making;
- the Petrine ministry of universal primacy in relation to Scripture and Tradition.

Even though progress has been made, some serious difficulties have emerged on the way to unity. Issues concerning authority have been raised acutely for each of our communions. For example, debates and decisions about the ordination of women have led to questions about the sources and structures of authority and how they function for Anglicans and Roman Catholics.

4. In both communions the exploration of how authority should be exercised at different levels has been open to the perspectives of other churches on these issues. For example, *The Virginia Report* of the Inter-Anglican Theological and Doctrinal Commission (prepared for the Lambeth Conference of 1998) declares:

> The long history of ecumenical involvement, both locally and internationally, has shown us that Anglican discernment and decision-making must take account of the insights into truth and the Spirit-led wisdom of our ecumenical partners. Moreover, any decisions we take must be offered for the discernment of the universal Church.
>
> (*The Virginia Report*, 6.37)

Pope John Paul II also, in his Encyclical Letter *Ut Unum Sint*, invited leaders and theologians of other churches to engage with him in a fraternal dialogue on how the particular ministry of unity of the Bishop of Rome might be exercised in a new situation (cf. *Ut Unum Sint*, 95–96).

5. There is an extensive debate about the nature and exercise of authority both in the churches and in wider society. Anglicans and Roman Catholics want to witness, both to the churches and to the world, that authority rightly exercised is a gift of God to bring reconciliation and peace to humankind. The exercise of authority can be oppressive and destructive. It may, indeed, often be so in human societies and even in churches when they uncritically adopt certain patterns of authority. The exercise of authority in the ministry of Jesus shows a different way. It is in conformity with the mind and example of Christ that the Church is called to exercise authority (cf. Lk 22.24–27; Jn 13.14–15; Phil 2.1–11). For the exercise of this authority the Church is endowed by the Holy Spirit with a variety of gifts and ministries (cf. 1 Cor 12.4–11; Eph 4.11–12).

6. From the beginning of its work, ARCIC has considered questions of Church teaching or practice in the context of our real but imperfect communion in Christ and the visible unity to which we are called. The Commission has always sought to get behind opposed and entrenched positions to discover and develop our common inheritance. Building on the previous work of ARCIC, the Commission offers a further statement on how the gift of authority, rightly exercised, enables the Church to continue in obedience to the Holy Spirit, who keeps it faithful in the service of the Gospel for the salvation of the world. We wish further to clarify how the exercise and acceptance of authority in the Church is inseparable from the response of believers to the Gospel, how it is related to the dynamic interaction of Scripture and Tradition, and how it is expressed and experienced in the communion of the churches and the collegiality of their bishops. In the light of these insights we have come to a deepened understanding of a universal primacy which serves the unity of all the local churches.

II AUTHORITY IN THE CHURCH

Jesus Christ: God's 'Yes' to Us and our 'Amen' to God

7. God is the author of life. By his Word and Spirit, in perfect freedom, God calls life into being. In spite of human sin, God in perfect faithfulness remains the author of the hope of new life for all. In Jesus Christ's work of redemption God renews his promise to his creation, for 'God's purpose is to bring all people into communion with himself

within a transformed creation' (ARCIC, *Church as Communion*, 16). The Spirit of God continues to work in creation and redemption to bring this purpose of reconciliation and unity to completion. The root of all true authority is thus the activity of the triune God, who authors life in all its fullness.

8. The authority of Jesus Christ is that of the 'faithful witness', the 'Amen' (cf. Rev 1.5; 3.14) in whom all the promises of God find their 'Yes'. When Paul had to defend the authority of his teaching he did so by pointing to the trustworthy authority of God: 'As surely as God is faithful, our word to you has not been Yes and No. For the Son of God, Jesus Christ, whom we preached among you . . . was not Yes and No; but in him it is always Yes. For all the promises of God find their Yes in him. That is why we utter the Amen through him, to the glory of God' (2 Cor 1.18–20). Paul speaks of the 'Yes' of God to us and the 'Amen' of the Church to God. In Jesus Christ, Son of God and born of a woman, the 'Yes' of God to humanity and the 'Amen' of humanity to God become a concrete human reality. This theme of God's 'Yes' and humanity's 'Amen' in Jesus Christ is the key to the exposition of authority in this statement.

9. In the life and ministry of Jesus, who came to do his Father's will (cf. Heb 10.5–10) even unto death (cf. Phil 2.8; Jn 10.18), God provided the perfect human 'Amen' to his purpose of reconciliation. In his life, Jesus expressed his total dedication to the Father (cf. Jn 5.19). The way Jesus exercised authority in his earthly ministry was perceived by his contemporaries as something new. It was recognised in his powerful teaching and in his healing and liberating word (cf. Mt 7.28–29; Mk 1.22, 27). Most of all, his authority was demonstrated by his self-giving service in sacrificial love (cf. Mk 10.45). Jesus spoke and acted with authority because of his perfect communion with the Father. His authority came from the Father (cf. Mt 11.27; Jn 14.10–12). It is to the Risen Lord that all authority is given in heaven and on earth (cf. Mt 28.18). Jesus Christ now lives and reigns with the Father, in the unity of the Holy Spirit; he is the Head of his Body, the Church, and Lord of all Creation (cf. Eph 1.18–23).

10. The life-giving obedience of Jesus Christ calls forth through the Spirit our 'Amen' to God the Father. In this 'Amen' through Christ we glorify God, who gives the Spirit in our hearts as a pledge of his faithfulness (cf. 2 Cor 1.20–22). We are called in Christ to witness to God's

purpose (cf. Lk 24.46–49), a witness that may for us too, include obedience to the point of death. In Christ obedience is not a burden (cf. 1 Jn 5.3). It springs from the liberation given by the Spirit of God. The divine 'Yes' and our 'Amen' are clearly seen in baptism, when in the company of the faithful we say 'Amen' to God's work in Christ. By the Spirit, our 'Amen' as believers is incorporated in the 'Amen' of Christ, through whom, with whom, and in whom we worship the Father.

The Believer's 'Amen' in the 'Amen' of the Local Church

11. The Gospel comes to people in a variety of ways: the witness and life of a parent or other Christian, the reading of the Scriptures, participation in the liturgy, or some other spiritual experience. Acceptance of the Gospel is also enacted in many ways: in being baptized, in renewal of commitment, in a decision to remain faithful, or in acts of self-giving to those in need. In these actions the person says, 'Indeed, Jesus Christ is *my* God: he is *for me* salvation, the source of hope, the true face of the living God.'

12. When a believer says 'Amen' to Christ individually, a further dimension is always involved: an 'Amen' to the faith of the Christian community. The person who receives baptism must come to know the full implication of participating in divine life within the body of Christ. The believer's 'Amen' to Christ becomes yet more complete as that person receives all that the Church, in faithfulness to the Word of God, affirms to be the authentic content of divine revelation. In that way, the 'Amen' said to what Christ is *for each believer* is incorporated within the 'Amen' the Church says to what Christ is *for his Body*. Growing into this faith may be for some an experience of questioning and struggle. For all it is one in which the integrity of the believer's conscience has a vital part to play. The believer's 'Amen' to Christ is so fundamental that individual Christians throughout their life are called to say 'Amen' to all that the whole company of Christians receives and teaches as the authentic meaning of the Gospel and the way to follow Christ.

13. Believers follow Christ in communion with other Christians in their local church (cf. *Authority in the Church I*, 8, where it is explained that 'the unity of local communities under one bishop constitutes what is commonly meant in our two communions by 'a local church''). In the local church they share Christian life, together finding guidance for the formation of their conscience and strength

to face their difficulties. They are sustained by the means of grace which God provides for his people: the Holy Scriptures, expounded in preaching, catechesis and creeds; the sacraments; the service of the ordained ministry; the life of prayer and common worship; the witness of holy persons. The believer is incorporated into an 'Amen' of faith, older, deeper, broader, richer than the individual's 'Amen' to the Gospel. So the relation between the faith of the individual and the faith of the Church is more complex than may sometimes appear. Every baptized person shares the rich experience of the Church which, even when it struggles with contemporary questions, continues to proclaim what Christ is *for his Body*. Each believer, by the grace of the Spirit, together with all believers of all times and all places, inherits this faith of the Church in the communion of saints. Believers then live out a twofold 'Amen' within the continuity of worship, teaching and practice of their local church. This local church is a eucharistic community. At the centre of its life is the celebration of the Holy Eucharist in which all believers hear and receive God's 'Yes' in Christ to them. In the Great Thanksgiving, when the memorial of God's gift in the saving work of Christ crucified and risen is celebrated, the community is at one with all Christians of all the churches who, since the beginning and until the end, pronounce humanity's 'Amen' to God—the 'Amen' which the Apocalypse affirms is at the heart of the great liturgy of heaven (cf. Rev 5.14; 7.12).

Tradition and Apostolicity: The Local Church's 'Amen' in the Communion of the Churches

14. The 'Yes' of God commands and invites the 'Amen' of believers. The revealed Word, to which the apostolic community originally bore witness, is received and communicated through the life of the whole Christian community. Tradition (*paradosis*) refers to this process.[1]

---

[1] In accord with ecumenical usage, the capitalised word Tradition here refers to 'the Gospel itself, transmitted from generation to generation in and by the Church', while the uncapitalised word tradition refers to 'the traditionary process', the handing-on of the revealed truth (The Fourth World Conference on Faith and Order, Montreal, 1963, Section II, para. 39). The plural traditions refers to the peculiar features of liturgy, theology, canonical and ecclesiastical life in the various cultures and faith communities. These uses, however, often cannot be sharply distinguished. When 'tradition' is capitalised at the beginning of a sentence, context must determine sense. The phrase apostolic Tradition refers to the content of what has been transmitted from apostolic times and continues to be foundation of Christian life and theology.

The Gospel of Christ crucified and risen is continually handed on and received (cf. 1 Cor 15.3) in the Christian churches. This tradition, or handing on, of the Gospel is the work of the Spirit, especially through the ministry of Word and Sacrament and in the common life of the people of God. Tradition is a dynamic process, communicating to each generation what was delivered once-for-all to the apostolic community. Tradition is far more than the transmission of true propositions concerning salvation. A minimalist understanding of Tradition that would limit it to a storehouse of doctrine and ecclesial decisions is insufficient. The Church receives, and must hand on, all those elements that are constitutive of ecclesial communion: baptism, confession of the apostolic faith, celebration of the Eucharist, leadership by an apostolic ministry (cf. *Church as Communion*, 15, 43). In the economy (*oikonomia*) of God's love for humanity, the Word who became flesh and dwelt among us is at the centre of what was transmitted from the beginning and what will be transmitted until the end.

15. Tradition is a channel of the love of God, making it accessible in the Church and in the world today. Through it, from one generation to another, and from one place to another, humanity shares communion in the Holy Trinity. By the process of tradition, the Church ministers the grace of the Lord Jesus Christ and the *koinonia* of the Holy Spirit (cf. 2 Cor 13.14). Therefore Tradition is integral to the economy of grace, love and communion. For those whose ears have not heard and eyes have not seen, the moment of receiving the saving Gospel is an experience of enlightenment, forgiveness, healing, liberation. Those who participate in the communion of the Gospel cannot refrain from transmitting it to others, even if this means martyrdom. Tradition is both a treasure to be received by the people of God and a gift to be shared with all humanity.

16. Apostolic Tradition is a gift of God which must be constantly received anew. By means of it, the Holy Spirit forms, maintains and sustains the communion of the local churches from one generation to the next. The handing on and reception of apostolic Tradition is an act of communion whereby the Spirit unites the local churches of our day with those that preceded them in the one apostolic faith. The process of tradition entails the constant and perpetual reception and communication of the revealed Word of God in many varied circumstances and continually changing times. The Church's 'Amen'

to apostolic Tradition is a fruit of the Spirit who constantly guides the disciples into all the truth; that is, into Christ who is the way, the truth and the life (cf. Jn 16.13; 14.6).

17. Tradition expresses the apostolicity of the Church. What the apostles received and proclaimed is now found in the Tradition of the Church where the Word of God is preached and the sacraments of Christ celebrated in the power of the Holy Spirit. The churches today are committed to receiving the one living apostolic Tradition, to ordering their life according to it, and to transmitting it in such a way that the Christ who comes in glory will find the people of God confessing and living the faith once-for-all entrusted to the saints (cf. Jude 3).

18. Tradition makes the witness of the apostolic community present in the Church today through its corporate *memory*. Through the proclamation of the Word and the celebration of the sacraments the Holy Spirit opens the hearts of believers and manifests the Risen Lord to them. The Spirit, active in the once-for-all events of the ministry of Jesus, continues to teach the Church, bringing to remembrance what Christ did and said, making present the fruits of his redemptive work and the foretaste of the kingdom (cf. Jn 2.22; 14.26). The purpose of Tradition is fulfilled when, through the Spirit, the Word is received and lived out in faith and hope. The witness of proclamation, sacraments and life in communion is at one and the same time the content of Tradition and its result. Thus memory bears fruit in the faithful life of believers within the communion of their local church.

The Holy Scriptures: The 'Yes' of God and the 'Amen' of God's People

19. Within Tradition the Scriptures occupy a unique and normative place and belong to what has been given once-for-all. As the written witness to God's 'Yes' they require the Church constantly to measure its teaching, preaching and action against them. 'Since the Scriptures are the uniquely inspired witness to divine revelation, the Church's expression of that revelation must be tested by its consonance with Scripture' (*Authority in the Church: Elucidation*, 2). Through the Scriptures God's revelation is made present and transmitted in the life of the Church. The 'Yes' of God is recognised in and through the 'Amen' of the Church which receives the authentic revelation of God. By receiving certain texts as true witnesses to divine revelation,

the Church identified its Holy Scriptures. It regards this corpus alone as the inspired Word of God written and, as such, uniquely authoritative.

20.   The Scriptures bring together diverse streams of Jewish and Christian traditions. These traditions reveal the way God's Word has been received, interpreted and passed on in specific contexts according to the needs, the culture, and the circumstances of the people of God. They contain God's revelation of his salvific design, which was realised in Jesus Christ and experienced in the earliest Christian communities. In these communities God's 'Yes' was received in a new way. Within the New Testament we can see how the Scriptures of the First Testament were both received as revelation of the one true God and also reinterpreted and re-received as revelation of his final Word in Christ.

21.   All the writers of the New Testament were influenced by the experience of their own local communities. What they transmitted, with their own skill and theological insights, records those elements of the Gospel which the churches of their time and in their various situations kept in their memory. Paul's teaching about the body of Christ, for instance, owes much to the problems and divisions of the local church in Corinth. When Paul speaks about 'our authority which the Lord gave for building you up and not for destroying you' (2 Cor 10.8), he does so in the context of his turbulent relationship with the church of Corinth. Even in the central affirmations of our faith there is often a clear echo of the concrete and sometimes dramatic situation of a local church or of a group of local churches, to which we are indebted for the faithful transmission of apostolic Tradition. The emphasis in the Johannine literature on the presence of the Lord in the flesh of a human body that could be seen and touched both before and after the resurrection (cf. Jn 20.27; 1 Jn 4.2) is linked to the conflict in the Johannine communities on this issue. It is through the struggle of particular communities at particular times to discern God's Word for them that we have in Scripture an authoritative record of the apostolic Tradition which is to be passed from one generation to another and from one church to another, and to which the faithful say 'Amen'.

22.   The formation of the canon of the Scriptures was an integral part of the process of tradition. The Church's recognition of these Scriptures as canonical, after a long period of critical discernment, was at the same time an act of *obedience* and of authority. It was an act of

obedience in that the Church discerned and received God's life-giving 'Yes' through the Scriptures, accepting them as the norm of faith. It was an act of *authority* in that the Church, under the guidance of the Holy Spirit, received and handed on these texts, declaring that they were inspired and that others were not to be included in the canon.

23. The meaning of the revealed Gospel of God is fully understood only within the Church. God's revelation has been entrusted to a community. The Church cannot properly be described as an aggregate of individual believers, nor can its faith be considered the sum of the beliefs held by individuals. Believers are together the people of faith because they are incorporated by baptism into a community which receives the canonical Scriptures as the authentic Word of God; they receive faith within this community. The faith of the community precedes the faith of the individual. So, though one person's journey of faith may begin with individual reading of Scripture, it cannot remain there. Individualistic interpretation of the Scriptures is not attuned to the reading of the text within the life of the Church and is incompatible with the nature of the authority of the revealed Word of God (cf. 2 Pet 1.20–21). Word of God and Church of God cannot be put asunder.

Reception and Re-Reception: The Church's 'Amen' to the Word of God

24. Throughout the centuries, the Church receives and acknowledges as a gracious gift from God all that it recognises as a true expression of the Tradition which has been once-for-all delivered to the apostles. This reception is at one and the same time an act of faithfulness and of freedom. The Church must continue faithful so that the Christ who comes in glory will recognise in the Church the community he founded; it must continue to be free to receive the apostolic Tradition in new ways according to the situations by which it is confronted. The Church has the responsibility to hand on the whole apostolic Tradition, even though there may be parts which it finds hard to integrate in its life and worship. It may be that what was of great significance for an earlier generation will again be important in the future, though its importance is not clear in the present.

25. Within the Church the memory of the people of God may be affected or even distorted by human finitude and sin. Even though promised

the assistance of the Holy Spirit, the churches from time to time lose sight of aspects of the apostolic Tradition, failing to discern the full vision of the kingdom of God in the light of which we seek to follow Christ. The churches suffer when some element of ecclesial communion has been forgotten, neglected or abused. Fresh recourse to Tradition in a new situation is the means by which God's revelation in Christ is recalled. This is assisted by the insights of biblical scholars and theologians and the wisdom of holy persons. Thus, there may be a rediscovery of elements that were neglected and a fresh remembrance of the promises of God, leading to renewal of the Church's 'Amen'. There may also be a sifting of what has been received because some of the formulations of the Tradition are seen to be inadequate or even misleading in a new context. This whole process may be termed *re-reception*.

Catholicity: The 'Amen' of the Whole Church

26. There are two dimensions to communion in the apostolic Tradition: diachronic and synchronic. The process of tradition clearly entails the transmission of the Gospel from one generation to another (diachronic). If the Church is to remain united in the truth, it must also entail the communion of the churches in all places in that one Gospel (synchronic). Both are necessary for the catholicity of the Church. Christ promises that the Holy Spirit will keep the essential and saving truth in the memory of the Church, empowering it for mission (cf. Jn 14.26; 15.26–27). This truth has to be transmitted and received anew by the faithful in all ages and in all places throughout the world, in response to the diversity and complexity of human experience. There is no part of humanity, no race, no social condition, no generation, for whom this salvation, communicated in the handing on of the Word of God, is not intended (cf. *Church as Communion*, 34).

27. In the rich diversity of human life, encounter with the living Tradition produces a variety of expressions of the Gospel. Where diverse expressions are faithful to the Word revealed in Jesus Christ and transmitted by the apostolic community, the churches in which they are found are truly in communion. Indeed, this diversity of traditions is the practical manifestation of catholicity and confirms rather than contradicts the vigour of Tradition. As God has created diversity among humans, so the Church's fidelity and identity require not uniformity of expression and formulation at all levels in all situations,

143

but rather catholic diversity within the unity of communion. This richness of traditions is a vital resource for a reconciled humanity. 'Human beings were created by God in his love with such diversity in order that they might participate in that love by sharing with one another both what they have and what they are, thus enriching each other in their mutual communion' (*Church as Communion*, 35).

28. The people of God as a whole is the bearer of the living Tradition. In changing situations producing fresh challenges to the Gospel, the discernment, actualisation and communication of the Word of God is the responsibility of the whole people of God. The Holy Spirit works through all members of the community, using the gifts he gives to each for the good of all. Theologians in particular serve the communion of the whole Church by exploring whether and how new insights should be integrated into the ongoing stream of Tradition. In each community there is an exchange, a mutual give-and-take, in which bishops, clergy and lay people receive from as well as give to others within the whole body.

29. In every Christian who is seeking to be faithful to Christ and is fully incorporated into the life of the Church, there is a *sensus fidei*. This *sensus fidei* may be described as an active capacity for spiritual discernment, an intuition that is formed by worshipping and living in communion as a faithful member of the Church. When this capacity is exercised in concert by the body of the faithful we may speak of the exercise of the *sensus fidelium* (cf. *Authority in the Church: Elucidation*, 3–4). The exercise of the *sensus fidei* by each member of the Church contributes to the formation of the *sensus fidelium* through which the Church as a whole remains faithful to Christ. By the *sensus fidelium*, the whole body contributes to, receives from and treasures the ministry of those within the community who exercise *episcope*, watching over the living memory of the Church (cf. *Authority in the Church I*, 5–6). In diverse ways the 'Amen' of the individual believer is thus incorporated within the 'Amen' of the whole Church.

30. Those who exercise *episcope* in the body of Christ must not be separated from the 'symphony' of the whole people of God in which they have their part to play. They need to be alert to the *sensus fidelium*, in which they share, if they are to be made aware when something is needed for the well-being and mission of the community, or when some element of the Tradition needs to be received in a fresh way. The charism and function of *episcope* are specifically

connected to the *ministry of memory*, which constantly renews the Church in hope. Through such ministry the Holy Spirit keeps alive in the Church the memory of what God did and revealed, and the hope of what God will do to bring all things into unity in Christ. In this way, not only from generation to generation, but also from place to place, the one faith is communicated and lived out. This is the ministry exercised by the bishop, and by ordained persons under the bishop's care, as they proclaim the Word, minister the sacraments, and take their part in administering discipline for the common good. The bishops, the clergy and the other faithful must all recognise and receive what is mediated from God through each other. Thus the *sensus fidelium* of the people of God and the ministry of memory exist together in reciprocal relationship.

31. Anglicans and Roman Catholics can agree in principle on all of the above, but need to make a deliberate effort to retrieve this shared understanding. When Christian communities are in real but imperfect communion they are called to recognise in each other elements of the apostolic Tradition which they may have rejected, forgotten or not yet fully understood. Consequently, they have to receive or reappropriate these elements, and reconsider the ways in which they have separately interpreted the Scriptures. Their life in Christ is enriched when they give to, and receive from, each other. They grow in understanding and experience of their catholicity as the *sensus fidelium* and the ministry of memory interact in the communion of believers. In this economy of giving and receiving within real but imperfect communion, they move closer to an undivided sharing in Christ's one 'Amen' to the glory of God.

III THE EXERCISE OF AUTHORITY IN THE CHURCH

Proclaiming the Gospel: The Exercise of Authority for Mission and Unity

32. The authority which Jesus bestowed on his disciples was, above all, the authority for mission, to preach and to heal (cf. Lk 9.1–2, 10.1). The Risen Christ empowered them to spread the Gospel to the whole world (cf. Mt 28.18–20). In the early Church, the preaching of the Word of God in the power of the Spirit was seen as the defining characteristic of apostolic authority (cf. 1 Cor 1.17, 2.4–5). In the proclamation of Christ crucified, the 'Yes' of God to humanity is made a present reality and all are invited to respond with their 'Amen'.

Thus, the exercise of ministerial authority within the Church, not least by those entrusted with the ministry of *episcope*, has a radically missionary dimension. Authority is exercised within the Church for the sake of those outside it, that the Gospel may be proclaimed 'in power and in the Holy Spirit and with full conviction' (1 Thess 1.5). This authority enables the whole Church to embody the Gospel and become the missionary and prophetic servant of the Lord.

33. Jesus prayed to the Father that his followers might be one 'so that the world may know that you have sent me and have loved them even as you have loved me' (Jn 17.23). When Christians do not agree about the Gospel itself, the preaching of it in power is impaired. When they are not one in faith they cannot be one in life, and so cannot demonstrate fully that they are faithful to the will of God, which is the reconciliation through Christ of all things to the Father (cf. Col 1.20). As long as the Church does not live as the community of reconciliation God calls it to be, it cannot adequately preach this Gospel or credibly proclaim God's plan to gather his scattered people into unity under Christ as Lord and Saviour (cf. Jn 11.52). Only when all believers are united in the common celebration of the Eucharist (cf. *Church as Communion*, 24) will the God whose purpose it is to bring all things into unity in Christ (cf. Eph 1.10) be truly glorified by the people of God. The challenge and responsibility for those with authority within the Church is so to exercise their ministry that they promote the unity of the whole Church in faith and life in a way that enriches rather than diminishes the legitimate diversity of local churches.

Synodality: The Exercise of Authority in Communion

34. In each local church all the faithful are called to walk together in Christ. The term *synodality* (derived from *syn-hodos* meaning 'common way') indicates the manner in which believers and churches are held together in communion as they do this. It expresses their vocation as people of the Way (cf. Acts 9.2) to live, work and journey together in Christ who is the Way (cf. Jn 14.6). They, like their predecessors, follow Jesus on the way (cf. Mk 10.52) until he comes again.

35. Within the communion of local churches the Spirit is at work to shape each church through the grace of reconciliation and communion in Christ. It is only through the activity of the Spirit that the local church can be faithful to the 'Amen' of Christ and can be sent into the world

146

to draw all people to participate in this 'Amen'. Through this presence of the Spirit the local church is maintained in the Tradition. It receives and shares the fullness of the apostolic faith and the means of grace. The Spirit confirms the local church in the truth in such a way that its life embodies the saving truth revealed in Christ. From generation to generation the authority of the living Word should be made present in the local church through all aspects of its life in the world. The way in which authority is exercised in the structures and corporate life of the Church must be conformed to the mind of Christ (cf. Phil 2.5).

36. The Spirit of Christ endows each bishop with the pastoral authority needed for the effective exercise of *episcope* within a local church. This authority necessarily includes responsibility for making and implementing the decisions that are required to fulfil the office of a bishop for the sake of *koinonia*. Its binding nature is implicit in the bishop's task of teaching the faith through the proclamation and explanation of the Word of God, of providing for the celebration of the sacraments, and of maintaining the Church in holiness and truth. Decisions taken by the bishop in performing this task have an authority which the faithful have a duty to receive and accept (cf. *Authority in the Church II*, 17). By their *sensus fidei* the faithful are able in conscience both to recognise God at work in the bishop's exercise of authority, and also to respond to it as believers. This is what motivates their obedience, an obedience of freedom and not slavery. The jurisdiction of bishops is one consequence of the call they have received to lead their churches in an authentic 'Amen'; it is not arbitrary power given to one person over the freedom of others. Within the working of the *sensus fidelium* there is a complementary relationship between the bishop and the rest of the community. In the local church the Eucharist is the fundamental expression of the walking together (synodality) of the people of God. In prayerful dialogue, the president leads the people to make their 'Amen' to the eucharistic prayer. In unity of faith with their local bishop, their 'Amen' is a living memorial of the Lord's great 'Amen' to the will of the Father.

37. The mutual interdependence of all the churches is integral to the reality of the Church as God wills it to be. No local church that participates in the living Tradition can regard itself as self-sufficient. Forms of synodality, then, are needed to manifest the communion of the local churches and to sustain each of them in fidelity to the

Gospel. The ministry of the bishop is crucial, for this ministry serves communion within and among local churches. Their communion with each other is expressed through the incorporation of each bishop into a college of bishops. Bishops are, both personally and collegially, at the service of communion and are concerned for synodality in all its expressions. These expressions have included a wide variety of organs, instruments and institutions, notably synods or councils, local, provincial, world-wide, ecumenical. The maintenance of communion requires that at every level there is a capacity to take decisions appropriate to that level. When those decisions raise serious questions for the wider communion of churches, synodality must find a wider expression.

38. In both our communions, the bishops meet together collegially, not as individuals but as those who have authority within and for the synodal life of the local churches. Consulting the faithful is an aspect of episcopal oversight. Each bishop is both a voice for the local church and one through whom the local church learns from other churches. When bishops take counsel together they seek both to discern and to articulate the *sensus fidelium* as it is present in the local church and in the wider communion of churches. Their role is magisterial: that is, in this communion of the churches, they are to determine what is to be taught as faithful to the apostolic Tradition. Roman Catholics and Anglicans share this understanding of synodality, but express it in different ways.

39. In the Church of England at the time of the English Reformation the tradition of synodality was expressed through the use both of synods (of bishops and clergy) and of Parliament (including bishops and lay people) for the settlement of liturgy, doctrine and church order. The authority of General Councils was also recognised. In the Anglican Communion, new forms of synods came into being during the nineteenth century and the role of the laity in decision-making has increased since that time. Although bishops, clergy, and lay persons consult with each other and legislate together, the responsibility of the bishops remains distinct and crucial. In every part of the Anglican Communion, the bishops bear a unique responsibility of oversight. For example, a diocesan synod can be called only by the bishop, and its decisions can stand only with the bishop's consent. At provincial or national levels, Houses of Bishops exercise a distinctive and unique ministry in relation to matters of doctrine, worship and moral life. Further, though Anglican synods largely use

parliamentary procedures, their nature is eucharistic. This is why the bishop as president of the Eucharist appropriately presides at the diocesan synod, which assembles to bring God's redemptive work into the present through the life and activity of the local church. Furthermore, each bishop has not only the *episcope* of the local church but participates in the care of all the churches. This is exercised within each province of the Anglican Communion with the help of organs such as Houses of Bishops and the Provincial and General Synods. In the Anglican Communion as a whole the Primates' Meeting, the Anglican Consultative Council, the Lambeth Conference and the Archbishop of Canterbury serve as instruments of synodality.

40.   In the Roman Catholic Church the tradition of synodality has not ceased. After the Reformation, synods of bishops and clergy continued to be held from time to time in different dioceses and regions, and on the universal level three Councils have been held. By the turn of the twentieth century specific meetings of bishops and episcopal conferences emerged as means of consultation to enable local churches of a given region to face together the demands of their mission and to deal with new pastoral situations. Since the Second Vatican Council these have become a regular structure in nations and regions. In a decision which received the support of the bishops at that Council, Pope Paul VI instituted the Synod of Bishops to deal with issues concerning the Church's mission throughout the world. The ancient custom of *ad limina* visits to the tombs of the apostles Peter and Paul and to the Bishop of Rome has been renewed by their visiting not singly but in regional groups. The more recent custom of visits by the Bishop of Rome to local churches has attempted to foster a deeper sense of their belonging to the communion of churches, and to help them be more aware of the situation of others. All these synodal institutions provide the possibility of a growing awareness by both local bishops and the Bishop of Rome of ways of working together in a stronger communion. Complementing this collegial synodality, a growth in synodality at the local level is promoting the active participation of lay persons in the life and mission of the local church.

Perseverance in the Truth: The Exercise of Authority in Teaching

41.   In every age Christians have said 'Amen' to Christ's promise that the Spirit will guide his Church into all truth. The New Testament

frequently echoes this promise by referring to the boldness, assurance and certainty to which Christians can lay claim (cf. Lk 1.4; 1 Thess 2.2; Eph 3.2; Heb 11.1). In their concern to make the Gospel accessible to all who are open to receive it, those charged with the ministry of memory and teaching have accepted new and hitherto unfamiliar expressions of faith. Some of these formulations have initially generated doubt and disagreement about their fidelity to the apostolic Tradition. In the process of testing such formulations, the Church has moved cautiously, but with confidence in the promise of Christ that it will persevere and be maintained in the truth (cf. Mt 16.18; Jn 16.13). This is what is meant by the *indefectibility* of the Church (cf. *Authority in the Church I*, 18; *Authority in the Church II*, 23).

42. In its continuing life, the Church seeks and receives the guidance from the Holy Spirit that keeps its teaching faithful to apostolic Tradition. Within the whole body, the college of bishops is to exercise the ministry of memory to this end. They are to discern and give teaching which may be trusted because it expresses the truth of God surely. In some situations, there will be an urgent need to test new formulations of faith. In specific circumstances, those with this ministry of oversight (*episcope*), assisted by the Holy Spirit, may together come to a judgement which, being faithful to Scripture and consistent with apostolic Tradition, is preserved from error. By such a judgement, which is a renewed expression of God's one 'Yes' in Jesus Christ, the Church is maintained in the truth so that it may continue to offer its 'Amen' to the glory of God. This is what is meant when it is affirmed that the Church may teach *infallibly* (see *Authority in the Church II*, 24–28, 32). Such infallible teaching is at the service of the Church's indefectibility.

43. The exercise of teaching authority in the Church, especially in situations of challenge, requires the participation, in their distinctive ways, of the whole body of believers, not only those charged with the ministry of memory. In this participation the *sensus fidelium* is at work. Since it is the faithfulness of the whole people of God which is at stake, reception of teaching is integral to the process. Doctrinal definitions are received as authoritative in virtue of the divine truth they proclaim as well as because of the specific office of the person or persons who proclaim them within the *sensus fidei* of the whole people of God. When the people of God respond by faith and say 'Amen' to authoritative teaching it is because they

recognise that this teaching expresses the apostolic faith and operates within the authority and truth of Christ, the Head of the Church.[2] The truth and authority of its Head is the source of infallible teaching in the body of Christ. God's 'Yes' revealed in Christ is the standard by which such authoritative teaching is judged. Such teaching is to be welcomed by the people of God as a gift of the Holy Spirit to maintain the Church in the truth of Christ, our 'Amen' to God.

44. The duty of maintaining the Church in the truth is one of the essential functions of the episcopal college. It has the power to exercise this ministry because it is bound in succession to the apostles, who were the body authorised and sent by Christ to preach the Gospel to all the nations. The authenticity of the teaching of individual bishops is evident when this teaching is in solidarity with that of the whole episcopal college. The exercise of this teaching authority requires that what it teaches be faithful to Holy Scripture and consistent with apostolic Tradition. This is expressed by the teaching of the Second Vatican Council, 'This teaching office is not above the Word of God, but serves it' (Dogmatic Constitution on Divine Revelation, *Dei Verbum*, 10).

Primacy: The Exercise of Authority in Collegiality and Conciliarity

45. In the course of history the synodality of the Church has been served through conciliar, collegial and primatial authority. Forms of primacy exist in both the Anglican Communion and in the churches in communion with the Bishop of Rome. Among the latter, the offices of Metropolitan Archbishop or Patriarch of an Eastern Catholic Church are primatial in nature. Each Anglican province has its Primate and the Primates' Meeting serves the whole Communion. The Archbishop of Canterbury exercises a primatial ministry in the whole Anglican Communion.

46. ARCIC has already recognised that the 'pattern of complementary primatial and conciliar aspects of *episcope* serving the *koinonia* of the churches needs to be realised at the universal level' (*Authority*

---

[2] This has been stated by the Second Vatican Council: 'The whole body of the faithful who have an anointing that comes from the Holy One (cf. 1 Jn. 2.20, 2.27) cannot err in matters of belief. This characteristic is shown in the supernatural appreciation of the faith (*sensus fidei*) of the whole people, when, "from the Bishops down to the last of the faithful" they manifest a universal consent in matters of faith and morals' (Dogmatic Constitution on the Church, *Lumen Gentium*, 12).

in the Church I, 23). The exigencies of church life call for a specific exercise of *episcope* at the service of the whole Church. In the pattern found in the New Testament one of the twelve is chosen by Jesus Christ to strengthen the others so that they will remain faithful to their mission and in harmony with each other (see the discussion of the Petrine texts in *Authority in the Church II*, 2–5). Augustine of Hippo expressed well the relationship among Peter, the other apostles and the whole Church, when he said:

> After all, it is not just one man that received these keys, but the Church in its unity. So this is the reason for Peter's acknowledged pre-eminence, that he stood for the Church's universality and unity, when he was told, *To you I am entrusting*, what has in fact been entrusted to all. I mean to show you that it is the Church which has received the keys of the kingdom of heaven. Listen to what the Lord says in another place to all his apostles: *Receive the Holy Spirit*; and straight away, *whose sins you forgive, they will be forgiven them*; *whose sins you retain, they will be retained* (Jn 20.22–23). This refers to the keys, about which is said, *whatever you bind on earth shall be bound in heaven* (Mt 16.19). But that was said to Peter . . . Peter at that time stood for the universal Church.
>
> *(Sermon 295, On the Feast of the Martyrdom*
> *of the Apostles Peter and Paul)*

ARCIC has also previously explored the transmission of the primatial ministry exercised by the Bishop of Rome (see *Authority in the Church II*, 6–9). Historically, the Bishop of Rome has exercised such a ministry either for the benefit of the whole Church, as when Leo contributed to the Council of Chalcedon, or for the benefit of a local church, as when Gregory the Great supported Augustine of Canterbury's mission and ordering of the English church. This gift has been welcomed and the ministry of these Bishops of Rome continues to be celebrated liturgically by Anglicans as well as Roman Catholics.

47. Within his wider ministry, the Bishop of Rome offers a specific ministry concerning the discernment of truth, as an expression of universal primacy. This particular service has been the source of difficulties and misunderstandings among the churches. Every solemn definition pronounced from the chair of Peter in the church of Peter and Paul may, however, express only the faith of the Church. Any such definition is pronounced *within* the college of those who exercise *episcope* and not outside that college. Such authoritative teaching is a particular exercise of the calling and responsibility of the body of bishops to teach

and affirm the faith. When the faith is articulated in this way, the Bishop of Rome proclaims the faith of the local churches. It is thus the wholly reliable teaching of the whole Church that is operative in the judgement of the universal primate. In solemnly formulating such teaching, the universal primate must discern and declare, with the assured assistance and guidance of the Holy Spirit, in fidelity to Scripture and Tradition, the authentic faith of the whole Church, that is, the faith proclaimed from the beginning. It is this faith, the faith of all the baptized in communion, and this only, that each bishop utters with the body of bishops in council. It is this faith which the Bishop of Rome in certain circumstances has a duty to discern and make explicit. This form of authoritative teaching has no stronger guarantee from the Spirit than have the solemn definitions of ecumenical councils. The reception of the primacy of the Bishop of Rome entails the recognition of this specific ministry of the universal primate. We believe that this is a gift to be received by all the churches.

48. The ministers God gives the Church to sustain her life are marked by fragility:

> Therefore, since it is by God's mercy that we are engaged in this ministry, we do not lose heart . . . but we have this treasure in clay jars, so that it may be made clear that this extraordinary power belongs to God and does not come from us (2 Cor 4.1; 4.7).

It is clear that only by the grace of God does the exercise of authority in the communion of the Church bear the marks of Christ's own authority. This authority is exercised by fragile Christians for the sake of other fragile Christians. This is no less true of the ministry of Peter:

> Simon, Simon, behold Satan demanded to have you, that he might sift you like wheat, but I have prayed for you that your faith may not fail; and when you have turned again, strengthen your brethren.
> (Lk 22.31–32; cf. Jn 21.15–19)

Pope John Paul II makes this clear in *Ut Unum Sint*:

> I carry out this duty with the profound conviction that I am obeying the Lord, and with a clear sense of my own human frailty. Indeed, if Christ himself gave Peter this special mission in the Church and exhorted him to strengthen his brethren, he also made clear to him his human weakness and his special need of conversion.   (*Ut Unum Sint*, 4)

Human weakness and sin do not only affect individual ministers: they can distort the human structuring of authority (cf. Mt 23). Therefore, loyal criticism and reforms are sometimes needed, following the example of Paul (cf. Gal 2.11–14). The consciousness of human frailty in the exercise of authority ensures that Christian ministers remain open to criticism and renewal and above all to exercising authority according to the example and mind of Christ.

Discipline: The Exercise of Authority and the Freedom of Conscience

49. The exercise of authority in the Church is to be recognised and accepted as an instrument of the Spirit of God for the healing of humanity. The exercise of authority must always respect conscience, because the divine work of salvation affirms human freedom. In freely accepting the way of salvation offered through baptism, the Christian disciple also freely takes on the discipline of being a member of the body of Christ. Because the Church of God is recognised as the community where the divine means of salvation are at work, the demands of discipleship for the well-being of the entire Christian community cannot be refused. There is also a discipline required in the exercise of authority. Those called to such a ministry must themselves submit to the discipline of Christ, observe the requirements of collegiality and the common good, and duly respect the consciences of those they are called to serve.

The Church's 'Amen' to God's 'Yes' in the Gospel

50. We have come to a shared understanding of authority by seeing it, in faith, as a manifestation of God's 'Yes' to his creation, calling forth the 'Amen' of his creatures. God is the source of authority, and the proper exercise of authority is always ordered towards the common good and the good of the person. In a broken world, and to a divided Church, God's 'Yes' in Jesus Christ brings the reality of reconciliation, the call to discipleship, and a foretaste of humanity's final goal when through the Spirit all in Christ utter their 'Amen' to the glory of God. The 'Yes' of God, embodied in Christ, is received in the proclamation and Tradition of the Gospel, in the sacramental life of the Church and in the ways that *episcope* is exercised. When the churches, through their exercise of authority, display the healing and reconciling power of the Gospel, then the wider world is offered a vision of what God intends for all creation. The aim of the exercise of authority and of its reception is to enable the Church to say 'Amen' to God's 'Yes' in the Gospel.

IV AGREEMENT IN THE EXERCISE OF AUTHORITY: STEPS TOWARDS VISIBLE UNITY

51. We submit to our respective authorities this agreed statement on authority in the Church. We believe that if this statement about the nature of authority and the manner of its exercise is accepted and acted upon, this issue will no longer be a cause for continued breach of communion between our two churches. Accordingly, we set out below some of the features of this agreement, recent significant developments in each of our communions, and some issues which they still have to face. As we move towards full ecclesial communion, we suggest ways in which our existing communion, albeit imperfect, may be made more visible through the exercise of a renewed collegiality among the bishops and a renewed exercise and reception of universal primacy.

Advances in Agreement

52. The Commission is of the view that we have deepened and extended our agreement on:

   - how the authority of Christ is present and active in the Church when the proclamation of God's 'Yes' calls forth the 'Amen' of all believers (paragraphs 7–18);
   - the dynamic interdependence of Scripture and apostolic Tradition and the normative place of Scripture within Tradition (paragraphs 19–23);
   - the necessity of constant reception of Scripture and Tradition, and of re-reception in particular circumstances (paragraphs 24–26);
   - how the exercise of authority is at the service of personal faith within the life of the Church (paragraphs 23, 29, 49);
   - the role of the whole people of God, within which, as teachers of the faith, the bishops have a distinctive voice in forming and expressing the mind of the Church (paragraphs 29–30);
   - synodality and its implications for the communion of the whole people of God and of all the local churches as together they seek to follow Christ who is the Way (paragraphs 34–40);
   - the essential cooperation of the ministry of *episcope* and the *sensus fidei* of the whole Church in the reception of the Word of God (paragraphs 29, 36, 43);
   - the possibility, in certain circumstances, of the Church teaching infallibly at the service of the Church's indefectibility (paragraphs 41–44);

- a universal primacy, exercised collegially in the context of synodality, as integral to *episcope* at the service of universal communion; such a primacy having always been associated with the Bishop and See of Rome (paragraphs 46–48);
- how the ministry of the Bishop of Rome assists the ministry of the whole episcopal body in the context of synodality, promoting the communion of the local churches in their life in Christ and the proclamation of the Gospel (paragraphs 46–48);
- how the Bishop of Rome offers a specific ministry concerning the discernment of truth (paragraph 47).

Significant Developments in Both Communions

53. The Lambeth Conference of 1988 recognised a need to reflect on how the Anglican Communion makes authoritative decisions. At the international level, Anglican instruments of synodality have considerable authority to influence and support provinces, yet none of these instruments has power to overrule a provincial decision, even if it threatens the unity of the Communion. Accordingly, the Lambeth Conference of 1998, in the light of *The Virginia Report* of the Inter-Anglican Theological and Doctrinal Commission, resolved to strengthen these instruments in various ways, particularly the role of the Archbishop of Canterbury and of the Primates' Meeting. The Conference also requested the Primates' Meeting to initiate a study in each province 'on whether effective communion, at all levels, does not require appropriate instruments, with due safeguards, not only for legislation, but also for oversight . . . as well as on the issue of a universal ministry in the service of Christian unity' (*Resolution III, 8(h)*). Alongside the autonomy of provinces, Anglicans are coming to see that interdependence among local churches and among provinces is also necessary for fostering communion.

54. The Roman Catholic Church, especially since the Second Vatican Council, has been gradually developing synodal structures for sustaining *koinonia* more effectively. The developing role of national and regional episcopal conferences and the regular holding of General Assemblies of the Synod of Bishops demonstrate this evolution. There has also been renewal in the exercise of synodality at the local level, although this varies from place to place. Canonical legislation now requires lay men and women, persons in the religious life, deacons and priests to play a part in parochial and diocesan pastoral councils, diocesan synods and a variety of other bodies, whenever these are convened.

55. In the Anglican Communion there is a reaching towards universal structures which promote *koinonia*, and in the Roman Catholic Church a strengthening of local and intermediate structures. In our view these developments reflect a shared and growing awareness that authority in the Church needs to be properly exercised at all levels. Even so there are still issues to be faced by Anglicans and Roman Catholics on important aspects of the exercise of authority in the service of *koinonia*. The Commission poses some questions frankly but in the conviction that we need the support of one another in responding to them. We believe that in the dynamic and fluid situation in which they are posed, seeking to answer them must go together with developing further steps towards a shared exercise of authority.

Issues Facing Anglicans

56. We have seen that instruments for oversight and decision-making are necessary at all levels to support communion. With this in view the Anglican Communion is exploring the development of structures of authority among its provinces. Is the Communion also open to the acceptance of instruments of oversight which would allow decisions to be reached that, in certain circumstances, would bind the whole Church? When major new questions arise which, in fidelity to Scripture and Tradition, require a united response, will these structures assist Anglicans to participate in the *sensus fidelium* with all Christians? To what extent does unilateral action by provinces or dioceses in matters concerning the whole Church, even after consultation has taken place, weaken *koinonia*? Anglicans have shown themselves to be willing to tolerate anomalies for the sake of maintaining communion. Yet this has led to the impairment of communion manifesting itself at the Eucharist, in the exercise of *episcope* and in the inter-changeability of ministry. What consequences flow from this? Above all, how will Anglicans address the question of universal primacy as it is emerging from their life together and from ecumenical dialogue?

Issues Facing Roman Catholics

57. The Second Vatican Council has reminded Roman Catholics of how the gifts of God are present in all the people of God. It has also taught the collegiality of the episcopate in its communion with the Bishop of Rome, head of the college. However, is there at all levels effective participation of clergy as well as lay people in emerging

synodal bodies? Has the teaching of the Second Vatican Council regarding the collegiality of bishops been implemented sufficiently? Do the actions of bishops reflect sufficient awareness of the extent of the authority they receive through ordination for governing the local church? Has enough provision been made to ensure consultation between the Bishop of Rome and the local churches prior to the making of important decisions affecting either a local church or the whole Church? How is the variety of theological opinion taken into account when such decisions are made? In supporting the Bishop of Rome in his work of promoting communion among the churches, do the structures and procedures of the Roman Curia adequately respect the exercise of *episcope* at other levels? Above all, how will the Roman Catholic Church address the question of universal primacy as it emerges from 'the patient and fraternal dialogue' about the exercise of the office of the Bishop of Rome to which John Paul II has invited 'church leaders and their theologians'?

Renewed Collegiality: Making Visible our Existing Communion

58. Anglicans and Roman Catholics are already facing these issues but their resolution may well take some time. However, there is no turning back in our journey towards full ecclesial communion. In the light of our agreement the Commission believes our two communions should make more visible the *koinonia* we already have. Theological dialogue must continue at all levels in the churches, but is not of itself sufficient. For the sake of *koinonia* and a united Christian witness to the world, Anglican and Roman Catholic bishops should find ways of cooperating and developing relationships of mutual accountability in their exercise of oversight. At this new stage we have not only to do together whatever we can, but also to be together all that our existing *koinonia* allows.

59. Such cooperation in the exercise of *episcope* would involve bishops meeting regularly together at regional and local levels and the participation of bishops from one communion in the international meetings of bishops of the other. Serious consideration could also be given to the association of Anglican bishops with Roman Catholic bishops in their *ad limina* visits to Rome. Wherever possible, bishops should take the opportunity of teaching and acting together in matters of faith and morals. They should also witness together in the public sphere on issues affecting the common good. Specific practical aspects of sharing *episcope* will emerge from local initiatives.

Universal Primacy: A Gift to be Shared

60. The Commission's work has resulted in sufficient agreement on universal primacy as a gift to be shared, for us to propose that such a primacy could be offered and received even before our churches are in full communion. Both Roman Catholics and Anglicans look to this ministry being exercised in collegiality and synodality—a ministry of *servus servorum Dei* (Gregory the Great, cited in *Ut Unum Sint*, 88). We envisage a primacy that will even now help to uphold the legitimate diversity of traditions, strengthening and safeguarding them in fidelity to the Gospel. It will encourage the churches in their mission. This sort of primacy will already assist the Church on earth to be the authentic catholic *koinonia* in which unity does not curtail diversity, and diversity does not endanger but enhances unity. It will be an effective sign for all Christians as to how this gift of God builds up that unity for which Christ prayed.

61. Such a universal primate will exercise leadership in the world and also in both communions, addressing them in a prophetic way. He will promote the common good in ways that are not constrained by sectional interests, and offer a continuing and distinctive teaching ministry, particularly in addressing difficult theological and moral issues. A universal primacy of this style will welcome and protect theological enquiry and other forms of the search for truth, so that their results may enrich and strengthen both human wisdom and the Church's faith. Such a universal primacy might gather the churches in various ways for consultation and discussion.

62. An experience of universal primacy of this kind would confirm two particular conclusions we have reached:

   • that Anglicans be open to and desire a recovery and re-reception under certain clear conditions of the exercise of universal primacy by the Bishop of Rome;
   • that Roman Catholics be open to and desire a re-reception of the exercise of primacy by the Bishop of Rome and the offering of such a ministry to the whole Church of God.

63. When the real yet imperfect communion between us is made more visible, the web of unity which is woven from communion with God and reconciliation with each other is extended and strengthened. Thus the 'Amen' which Anglicans and Roman Catholics say to the one Lord comes closer to being an 'Amen' said together by the one holy people witnessing to God's salvation and reconciling love in a broken world.

Responses

Official Commentaries

The Statement has been widely discussed throughout the Christian world. In many places it was broadly welcomed, as it was seen to be addressing some of the most difficult issues in Anglican–Roman Catholic dialogue. The initial responses were the two official commentaries. The Anglican one, prepared by Dr Mary Tanner, introduces more than evaluates the Statement, with a view to encouraging readers to respond to the Commission's work, and to urge that 'concrete steps forward' are taken. She notes that 'The Report is not easy to summarise. Every sentence counts towards the building up of the whole.' Even so, it 'has gone a long way in examining those issues that were asked for by both Communions'. If there is a criticism, it is that in the challenges to both traditions (*Gift*, §58) '[i]t is unfortunate that the emphasis here is only on episcopal sharing, especially in a Report so keen to point to the inextricable relation between the ministry of oversight and the mind of the whole people of God'. Nevertheless, Tanner concludes: 'The Gift of Authority is itself a gift, an instrument to lead Anglican and Roman Catholics to respond to God's "Yes" with a single "Amen".'[1]

The official Roman Catholic Commentary, prepared by William Henn OFM Cap., is a substantial essay, analysing each Part of *Gift* in some detail.[2] Like Tanner, he focuses on how ARCIC II has dealt with the official responses made to *Authority I* and *II* in *The Final Report*, but from a Roman Catholic perspective. Henn's evaluation of *Gift* is overwhelmingly positive: it is 'credible not only to Anglicans and Roman Catholics, but to members of other communities as well'. Early on this Commentary notes 'That the notions of "authority" and "gift" go together ... would already provide a valuable service for Christian unity.' Further, the 'Yes/Amen' motif is a 'happy choice', a 'golden thread' woven throughout the document. Particularly significant is the way in which 'the mistake of opposing two realities or two values or two subjects which should not be opposed' is avoided. This is the 'genius' of the Statement, which is characterized by a rich 'catholicity' that is a 'serene and careful attempt to achieve a common understanding'. It gives it a 'synthetic power', seen in the interrelationships between Scripture and T/tradition, believer and community, and

---

[1] Mary Tanner, *A Commentary on* The Gift of Authority (London, 1999), 6.
[2] William Henn OFM Cap., *A Commentary on* The Gift of Authority *of the Anglican–Roman Catholic International Commission* (Rome: PCPCU, 1999), www.vatican.va/roman_curia/pontifical_councils/chrstuni/ angl-comm-docs/rc_pc_chrstuni_doc_19990512_commentary-fr-henn_en.html.

local congregation and whole Church. This synthetic quality 'characterized the writings of so many of the Fathers of the Church ... [*Gift*'s] authors rightly have chosen to employ a patristic way of thinking.' Henn sees §§32–33 as central to the Statement, not only numerically but theologically. They relate authority in the Church 'precisely to her nature as communion and mission' and are thus 'the doctrinal heart of the agreement'. He suggests that reference to these paragraphs should be included under 'new points of agreement' (*Gift*, §52), which is 'not only very impressive but may even be too modest'.

In terms of evaluation, Henn takes account of the official responses to ARCIC I, while giving most attention to Roman Catholic concerns. The section in Part II headed 'Reception and Re-Reception' (§§24–25) 'contains proposals which will be very agreeable to Catholics'. These are, first, 'that it is the *whole* apostolic Tradition which is received by the Church': picking and choosing as to which doctrines are 'central' misunderstands the organic relationships within the 'hierarchy of truths'. And secondly, 'the Church "as a whole" is presented as the only subject adequate to receive and pass on the living Tradition'. This correlates the 'ministry of memory', which bishops are called to exercise, with the *sensus fidelium* of the whole people of God, on 'the analogy of a symphony'. Henn questions the possible ambiguity around *sensus fidelium*, however: 'Could not the text be clearer as to the precise meaning of this expression?' He suggests that it is best related 'not to a subjective capacity, exercised either singly or in concert, but rather to the doctrinal content concerning matters of faith and morals which is actually believed by the faithful'.

The longest section of the Commentary concerns primacy and infallibility (4,500 of 12,500 words). After careful discussion of the way in which ARCIC II approaches how infallible teaching relates to its reception by believers—an issue unresolved by ARCIC I—he concludes: 'It seems that the text has addressed all of the issues mentioned in the official Anglican official response. What of the Roman Catholic reactions to ARCIC I's treatment of primacy?' Henn detects 'remarkable affinities' in *Gift* to the *relatio* made by Bishop Vincent Gasser at Vatican I about the distinctive ministry of the Bishop of Rome within, and not 'separate' from, the Church and its structures.[3] In the light of this analysis, Henn concludes that in

---

[3] Bishop Gasser was the spokesperson for the Deputation *de fide* of the Council, Henn notes, and his speech was made on 11 July 1870, and is cited in four footnotes to *Lumen Gentium*, §25. Though it did not appear in ARCIC texts, both ARCIC-I and ARCIC-II were cognizant of this important 'official' interpretation: see Jean-Marie Tillard, *The Bishop of Rome*, trans. John de Satgé (London: SPCK, 1983), 172–8.

Gift, as regards the primacy of the Bishop of Rome, 'ARCIC II seems to affirm substantially what the *Congregation* [for the Doctrine of the Faith] also affirms' (in its *Observations* on *The Final Report*,[4] re-affirmed in the official Vatican response).

In his 'Concluding Remarks', Henn writes, 'On the whole, *The Gift of Authority* seems reasonably successful in addressing the concerns' of 'the two official responses to ARCIC I's work on authority'. But he also indicates 'two areas in which . . . greater precision would render even more adequate the understanding of authority present in this text, and thereby also deepen the agreement between Anglicans and Roman Catholics'. One is the meaning of *sensus fidelium*, as noted above. The other is 'to identify more clearly the distinctive episcopal authority to teach as precisely a sharing by Christ of his own teaching authority'—a natural omission, he acknowledges, given that the laity were 'placed in special relief' in the text. An 'even more satisfying' reflection would be further development of 'the relationship between the ordained ministry and the proclamation of the Word of God'. The particular focus of the suggestion is 'additional attention to the sacramental foundation and significance of episcopal ordination', which 'could make even better what is already a remarkable agreement'.

Questions Raised in Responses

But not all responses to *Gift* were as positive as these official ones. The Statement also provoked a range of questions which it is difficult to sum up briefly: many of the concerns expressed are interwoven. Significant ones raised are gathered here under six headings:

> Universal primacy: a gift to be shared?
> Are new developments in Anglican and Roman Catholic ecclesial life taken with sufficient seriousness?
> Is synodality understood similarly in both communions?
> What does 'infallible teaching' mean?
> Is the view of the Church in *Gift* too ideal?
> Can reciprocal participation in ecclesial life really work?

Universal primacy: a gift to be shared?
Anglican responses raise concerns about the acceptance of the universal primacy as 'a gift to be shared'. These are complemented by Roman Catholic concerns about the actual exercise of authority by the universal primate.

---

[4] These *Observations* can be found in Christopher Hill and Edward Yarnold SJ (eds.), *Anglicans and Roman Catholics: The Search for Unity* (London: SPCK and CTS, 1994), 79–91.

Gift opens with an unqualified statement of the acceptance, in previous ARCIC Statements, of 'the need for a universal primacy exercised by the Bishop of Rome as a sign and safeguard of unity within a reunited Church' (§1). *Growing Together in Unity and Mission*, the synthesis of ARCIC's work made by the IARCCUM, is more cautious: 'Serious questions remain for Anglicans regarding the nature and jurisdictional consequences of universal primacy' (§23).[5]

The sharpest questions raised about the way *Gift* presents universal primacy come from evangelical Anglican sources, often not appreciating ARCIC II's call for its renewal. For example, it has been pointedly argued,

> If the Papacy is so valuable, why do other Christian bodies insist on doing without it? This is the question which ultimately has to be answered, and it must be said that the Commission has ducked the issue. In making the case for the reception of papal primacy it has not even tried to explain why Anglicans and other non-Roman Christians find it at best unnecessary and at worst unbiblical.[6]

In *Gift*, however, Anglicans are not being asked to accept the papal primacy as it now exists. Rather, it offers 'a vision of the future functioning of the Petrine Office, which is not yet fully realised'.[7]

Other Anglican responses express general concerns about the centralized nature of authority in the Roman Catholic Church, which is focused on the ministry of the universal primate. This is most clearly seen in the collation of nine provincial responses to *Gift* made by the IASCER, for the 2005 meeting of the Anglican Consultative Council (ACC).[8] These responses are critical of the Statement for its failure to critique the centralized exercise of authority in the Roman Catholic Church. They express

---

[5] IARCCUM, *Growing Together in Unity and Mission* (London: SPCK, 2007), www.vatican.va/roman_curia/pontifical_councils/chrstuni/angl-comm-docs/rc_pc_chrstuni_doc_20070914_growing-together_en.html.

[6] Gerald Bray, 'Article Review: *The Gift of Authority*', *The Churchman*, 113 (1999), http://churchsociety.org/churchman/page/churchman_vol_113_1999. Bishop Colin Buchanan is similarly critical of the Statement: 'The text is fully compatible with Roman Catholicism, and totally incompatible with anything that most Anglicans have known as Anglicanism': *Is Papal Authority a Gift to Us? A Critique of* The Gift of Authority (Cambridge: Grove Books, 2003), 33.

[7] Jean-Marie Tillard, cited in Adelbert Denaux, 'Authority in the Church: A Challenge to Both Anglicans and Roman Catholics', in *The Unity of Christians: The Vision of Paul Couturier* (*The Messenger*, October 2003), www.academia.edu/3184275/Authority_in_the_Church_A_Challenge_for_both_Anglicans_and_Roman_Catholics.

[8] IASCER, *Provincial Responses to the Work of the Second Anglican–Roman Catholic International Commission: An Interim Report* (London: ACC, 2005).

concern about 'the exercise of a juridical authority centralised in the Bishop of Rome' (Brazil), the 'magisterial' and 'jurisdictional' powers of the universal primate—'A universal primacy should be primarily pastoral' (Ireland); the exercise of immediate, ordinary, and universal jurisdiction by the universal primate (USA, England); and 'the place of laity in decision-making' (Canada).

Several provinces affirm the Anglican tradition of 'dispersed authority'. The Anglican Church in Aotearoa, New Zealand, and Polynesia comments, 'We do not see the model of a single spokesperson for the universal church as the only instrument of unity', adding, 'Our three Tikanga Church . . . enshrines a diversified model of unity and we affirm that plurality is as much a gift as a threat and should not be suppressed.' The Church of the Province of Southern Africa writes, 'Anglicans struggle with the issue of centralised authority in Roman Catholicism, which seemingly invalidates the integrity of diversity.'

The General Synod of the Church of England (February 2004) resolved, after debate,

> That this Synod . . . observing that *The Gift of Authority*'s treatment of the teaching authority of the Bishop of Rome is not sufficiently clear, request that ARCIC clarify in what sense this is a gift to be received by all the churches.

This IASCER collation covers a significant number of Anglican responses.

From a Roman Catholic perspective, the US Conference of Catholic Bishops (USCCB) acknowledged the difficulty with the exercise of authority by the universal primacy.[9] The Conference pointed out that 'Anglicans and Roman Catholics are still looking for the reformed understanding and practice of primacy that Pope John Paul II both acknowledges as needful and encourages' (para. 13). They feel that 'the rich Anglican tradition of lay participation in the deliberations of the church . . . is also an important gift to be shared' (para. 15).

The opportunities and questions around universal primacy continue to be discussed. On 17 September 2010, when Pope Benedict XVI visited Westminster Abbey for Evening Prayer, Rowan Williams, Archbishop of Canterbury, said:

---

[9] US Conference of Catholic Bishops (USCCB), 'Response to ARCIC's *The Gift of Authority*' (2003), www.usccb.org/beliefs-and-teachings/ecumenical-and-interreligious/ecumenical/anglican/response-gift-of-authority.cfm.

As Your Holiness's great predecessor reminded us all in his encyclical *Ut Unum Sint*, we must learn to reflect together on how the historic ministry of the Roman Church and its chief pastor may speak to the Church catholic—East and West, global north and global south—of the authority of Christ and his apostles to build up the Body in love; how it may be realised as a ministry of patience and reverence towards all, a ministry of creative love and self-giving that leads us all into the same path of seeking not our own comfort or profit but the good of the entire human community and the glory of God the creator and redeemer.

Are new developments in Anglican and Roman Catholic ecclesial life taken with sufficient seriousness?

The ordination of women as bishops has become widespread within the Anglican Communion, despite some disagreement within provinces where it is accepted. Pope John Paul II was firm in his teaching that the Church has no mandate for the ordination of women (*Ordinatio Sacerdotalis*, 1994).[10] Further, the ordination in 2003 of a non-celibate homosexual man as a bishop in the Episcopal Church of the USA raised questions for Roman Catholics and Anglicans alike in a number of areas. Prominent among these concerns were the understanding and practice of authority and ecclesiology as exercised across the provinces of the Anglican Communion, the mutual interdependence of churches, the role of episcopal and collegial authority in maintaining the unity of the communion, the processes of discernment in the communion of the Church, and the decisive role of Scripture and Tradition therein. These questions were addressed by the Inter-Anglican Theological and Doctrinal Commission in *The Virginia Report* (1997).[11]

The response of the Anglican Communion to these pressing questions about the responsibilities and demands of ecclesial communion was, at the initiative of the Archbishop of Canterbury, to set up a Commission, which produced *The Windsor Report* (2004).[12] This proposed a Covenant between provinces of the Anglican Communion which would 'make explicit and forceful the loyalty and bonds of affection which govern the relationships between the churches of the Communion' (§118). On the day of its

---

[10] See IARCCUM, *Growing Together in Unity and Mission*, §61.

[11] Inter-Anglican Theological and Doctrinal Commission, *The Virginia Report*, in James M. Rosenthal and Nicola Currie (eds.), *Being Anglican in the Third Millennium: The Official Report of the 10th Meeting of the Anglican Consultative Council* (Harrisburg: Morehouse, 1997), 211–81.

[12] The Lambeth Commission on Communion, *The Windsor Report* (London: ACC, 2004), www.anglicancommunion.org/media/68225/windsor2004full.pdf.

publication (18 October 2004), Archbishop Rowan Williams wrote to Cardinal Kasper, President of the PCPCU, asking for his informal reaction. Cardinal Kasper welcomed the Report, commenting that its proposals were 'in line with the general thrust of ARCIC's statements', since, 'As expressed in *The Gift of Authority* (1999), maintaining and strengthening the *koinonia* and a commitment to interdependence are constitutive aspects of the Church and vital for its unity.'[13] Cardinal Kasper concluded his letter by saying, 'For the continuation of our ecumenical dialogue, it is important for us to have a clear understanding of who our partner is.'[14]

Thus far Anglican developments have been in view. On the Roman Catholic side, the establishment of an Ordinariate structure for former Anglicans by the Apostolic Constitution *Anglicanorum Coetibus* (4 November 2009) is significant. Although set up as a 'pastoral response' by which Anglican congregations might be received into the Roman Catholic Church, it has been of concern to many Anglicans, as well as some Roman Catholics, who saw it as undermining ARCIC's work to deepen and strengthen the imperfect communion that we already share.

Is synodality understood similarly in both communions?
Considerable differences remain between Anglicans and Roman Catholics as regards the constitution of synodal structures and practices of consultation. There is relatively little consultation of the laity in the Roman Catholic Church, so that Anglican bodies asked ARCIC II to consider 'the role of laity in decision-making' (*Gift*, §3).[15] This is a major theme of the US Catholic bishops in their response to *Gift*:

> The document affirms the importance of 'synodality' in our two traditions (34), but does not sufficiently explore the difference in the two churches' history and present experience. In both traditions the full potential of synods has not been adequately realised. For example, in the Roman Catholic Church the present code of canon law limits the decision-making authority in diocesan synods to the bishop. In the Anglican Communion the unilateral actions of

---

[13] The drafting of the Covenant moved forward slowly: voting on it within the Anglican Communion was not complete when Dr Williams was succeeded by Bishop Justin Welby in 2013. At the time of writing it is effectively stalled.

[14] Cardinal Walter Kasper, 'Letter to his Grace Dr Rowan Williams, Archbishop of Canterbury', 17 December 2004, www.vatican.va/roman_curia/pontifical_councils/chrstuni/card-kasper-docs/rc_pc_chrstuni_doc_20041217_kasper-arch-canterbury_en.html.

[15] See Michael Root, '*The Gift of Authority*: An Observer's Report and Analysis', *The Ecumenical Review*, 52 (2000), 57–71, at pp. 63–4. Professor Root was the World Council of Churches observer on ARCIC II from 1995 to 1998, during which time *Gift* was prepared.

individual bishops, dioceses, and provinces undermine the reality of synodality. Such differences require further examination.[16]

Their concern is about not only what is said in *Gift* concerning bishops, but what is said concerning lay people:

> We find that the prominent role and theological understanding of the office of bishop in *The Gift of Authority* are at a remove from our actual experience, though for different reasons for Roman Catholics and Anglicans. On the side of Anglicans the document appears to exaggerate the independent role of the bishops and downplay the role of priests and laity. On the Roman Catholic side, the document seems not to take into account the exercise of Roman supervision that on occasion tends to limit the ability of bishops to serve in their role as the vicars of Christ in their own local churches.
>
> Furthermore, the role and participation of the laity, while affirmed, is not probed in depth, and what is affirmed does not fully reflect the experience of either of our churches. For example, *The Gift of Authority* 39 says that the decisions of an Anglican diocesan synod can stand only with the diocesan bishop's consent; this is not the case with regard to diocesan conventions and councils of the Episcopal Church. On the Roman Catholic side the document understates the relative lack of structures that would enable effective lay participation in decision-making (cf. *Gift* 54, 57).[17]

What does 'infallible teaching' mean?

Gift §42 explores what is meant 'when it is affirmed that the Church may teach *infallibly*', adding that 'Such infallible teaching is at the service of the Church's indefectibility.' The US Catholic bishops argue, however, that 'the theological understanding and ecclesial implications of the doctrine of infallibility and its relationship to indefectibility need to be further clarified'.[18] Some have seen in *Gift* a shift from the position of *Authority in the Church II* §29:

> To be a decisive discernment of the truth, the judgement of the Bishop of Rome must satisfy rigorous conditions. He must speak explicitly as the focus within the *koinonia*; without being under duress from external pressures; having sought to discover the mind of his fellow bishops and of the Church as a whole; and with a clear intention to issue a binding decision upon a matter of faith or morals. Some of these conditions were laid down by the

---

[16] USCCB, 'Response to ARCIC's *The Gift of Authority*', §12.
[17] Ibid., §§10, 11.
[18] Ibid., §14.

First Vatican Council. When it is plain that all these conditions have been fulfilled, Roman Catholics conclude that the judgement is preserved from error and the proposition true. If the definition proposed for assent were not manifestly a legitimate interpretation of biblical faith and in line with orthodox tradition, Anglicans would think it a duty to reserve the reception of the definition for study and discussion.

This last sentence was criticized by the Congregation for the Doctrine of the Faith (CDF), in its *Observations* on *The Final Report*, as inadequate to the teaching of Vatican I (*Pastor Aeternus* 4), where definitions promulgated as infallible are said to be irreformable '*ex sese, non autem ex consensu ecclesiae*' ('by themselves and not by reason of the agreement of the Church'). *Gift* §43 says only:

> Doctrinal definitions are received as authoritative in virtue of the divine truth they proclaim as well as because of the specific office of the person or persons who proclaim them within the *sensus fidei* of the whole people of God. When the people of God respond by faith and say 'Amen' to authoritative teaching it is because they recognise that this teaching expresses the apostolic faith and operates within the authority and truth of Christ, the Head of the Church.

The 'if' of *Authority in the Church II* has become 'when' in *Gift*: some have asked whether this represents a retreat from the conditions for reception expressed in *Authority in the Church II*.[19]

Is the view of the Church in The Gift of Authority *too ideal?*
Gift 'is an ideal statement, and in an ideal world the Church may be held to teach infallibly through the bishops', wrote Mary Tanner. 'But what about the messiness of history?'[20] Michael Root asks whether *Gift* recognizes

> the endemic character, not only of tension, but also of conflict within the life of the church—both conflict between authorities (as between Paul and Peter at Antioch) and conflict between those who exercise and those who are under authority (as between Paul and the church at Corinth)?[21]

---

[19] So Root, '*The Gift of Authority*', 64–8.
[20] Mary Tanner, 'Authority: Gift or Threat?', in Peter Fisher (ed.), *Unpacking the Gift* (London: Church House Publishing, 2002), 14–32.
[21] Root, '*The Gift of Authority*', 63. The way conflict in the Church is handled is closely related to the maintenance of communion: a significant Anglican resource is the third report of the Inter-Anglican Theological and Doctrinal Commission, *Communion, Conflict and Hope* (London: ACC, 2008), www.anglicancommunion.org/media/107645/IATDC-Inter-Anglican-Theological-and-Doctrinal-Commission.pdf.

Others have argued, in similar vein, that

> the report is insufficiently realistic about the history and present life of the Church. It does not deal with problems raised by the study of Church history for the theological claims it makes about the preservation of the Church from error and the unity of faith brought about by the exercise of the *sensus fidelium.*[22]

One response to this criticism has been that:

> *The Gift of Authority* is an agreed statement which offers a vision of the future, reunited Church, rather than a description of the two churches in their actual state. In this respect the text formulates an ideal, a vision of the Church which should inspire our two Communions.[23]

Can reciprocal participation in ecclesial life really work?
Encouraging divided churches to grow together is no easy matter, and some responses wonder whether what *Gift* proposes about steps forward is realistic.

An example is the suggestion that representatives of the Anglican bishops should be invited to the *ad limina* visits of Roman Catholic bishops to Rome (*Gift*, §59). This has already occurred in the case of the bishops of Papua New Guinea, where a Covenant between Anglicans and Roman Catholics was signed in 2003.[24] Some Roman Catholic leaders believe, however, that 'the proposal should not be encouraged until it has received an authoritative response from the sponsoring bodies'.[25] On the other hand, the US Catholic bishops suggest that Anglican participation in *ad limina* visits should occur.[26] They also recommend reciprocal non-voting participation of bishops in the Lambeth Conference, the ACC, the House of Bishops of The Episcopal Church, their own Conference, and similar non-voting

---

[22] Martin Davie, '"Yes" and "No"—a Response to *The Gift of Authority*', in Fisher (ed.), *Unpacking the Gift*, 33–59.

[23] Denaux, *The Unity of Christians*, 12.

[24] The text is available in James Rosenthal and Susan Erdey (eds.), *Living Communion: The Official Report of the 13th Anglican Consultative Council* (London: ACC, 2006), 151–4. The Covenant makes explicit reference to the work of ARCIC I. Cf. Theo Aerts and Peter Ramsden (eds.), *Studies and Statements on Romans and Anglicans in Papua New Guinea* (Port Moresby: SalPress, 1995). A key factor in the close relationship between Anglicans and Roman Catholics in Papua New Guinea is the martyrs of World War II from both traditions, commemorated on 2 September.

[25] So Abp Bernard Longley, '*Growing Together in Unity and Mission*—a Commentary', 20, https://iarccum.org/archive/IARCCUM_2000-2010/2007_iarccum_longley-bernard.pd.

[26] USCCB, 'Response to the Anglican–Roman Catholic International Commission's "The Gift of Authority"', §§21–28.

participation of clergy and laity at the Episcopal House of Deputies and Roman Catholic plenary Councils and Diocesan Synods, as suggested by *Growing Together in Unity and Mission* §109. This reciprocal participation in the life of the churches has begun to occur.

Directions for Further Work

The responses made to *Gift* are generally welcoming of the approach to authority and its exercise taken in the Statement. There are requests from several sources, however, for further work on the exercise of universal primacy by the Bishop of Rome. The resolution passed in February 2004 by the General Synod of the Church of England is representative of Anglican responses:

(e) Believing that any search for theological agreement on universal primacy requires that the contested claim of universal, ordinary and immediate jurisdiction for the Bishop of Rome be resolved, and noting that *The Gift of Authority* does not refer to this issue, [we] request that it again form part of the agenda of ARCIC.

(f) Observing that *The Gift of Authority's* treatment of the teaching authority of the Bishop of Rome is not sufficiently clear, [we] request that ARCIC clarify in what sense this is a gift to be received by all the churches.

Gift approaches the question of papal authority, and the possibility of infallible teaching being defined, by setting it in the context of a whole, dynamic ecclesiology for which the 'Yes'/'Amen' motif is central. In comparing *Gift* with *Church as Communion*, it is noteworthy that the latter says little about ecclesial structures, whereas *Gift* has a great deal to say about church structures and ministries, and how they interact in the service of *koinonia*. Some greater precision on *sensus fidelium* and episcopal ministry as expressing the teaching ministry of Christ would improve the text, as Henn suggests. But *Gift* does not address directly the question as to whether 'universal, ordinary and immediate' jurisdiction is necessary to fulfil the ministry of a universal primate. There is clearly more work to be done in this area.

Gift sketches a hermeneutic of papal authority and asks whether this hermeneutic can be accepted by both Anglicans and Roman Catholics. In effect, it asks readers, 'If the exercise of the universal primacy were to be seen like this . . . would it be acceptable to both Anglicans and Roman Catholics?' It is the conditionality—the hypothetical—which takes the discussion into the world of the 'ideal' or the 'transcendental', for which the Statement has been criticized. This is the move that leads many to say they do not recognize the church about which *Gift* speaks: it operates too smoothly and there is insufficient recognition of conflict. In effect, it asks readers, '*If* a reunited church operated in this way, could Anglicans and Catholics share communion within it?'

Cardinal Walter Kasper's response to Archbishop Rowan Williams's letter about *The Windsor Report* (December 2004) focuses the need for further work on ecclesiology:

> *The Windsor Report* has important ecumenical implications insofar as it would provide for a greater coherence within Anglicanism, allowing an enhancement of our understanding of the Anglican Communion precisely as a communion. For the continuation of our ecumenical dialogue, it is important for us to have a clear understanding of who our partner is. The text stands in line with our ARCIC documents, though there are other elements of ARCIC's work which we believe deserve further attention. Its recommendations address two underlying questions of broad ecumenical significance: the relationship between the universal Church and the local church; and a question which is becoming increasingly acute, namely, the tension between the Gospel, as reflected in the apostolic witness, and the approaches and trends of our post-modern societies.

This request is being taken up by ARCIC III, whose mandate is 'Church as communion, local and universal, and how in communion the local and universal Church come to discern right ethical teaching'.

Bibliography

Official Commentaries

Henn, William, OFM Cap., *A Commentary on* The Gift of Authority *of the Anglican–Roman Catholic International Commission* (Rome: PCPCU, 1999), www.vatican.va/roman_curia/pontifical_councils/chrstuni/angl-comm-docs/rc_pc_chrstuni_doc_19990512_commentary-fr-henn_en.html

Tanner, Mary, *A Commentary on* The Gift of Authority (London, 1999)

Ecclesial Responses

Australian Anglican–Roman Catholic Dialogue (AustARC), *The Challenge of Gospel Authority: An Agreed Statement of the Australian Anglican–Roman Catholic Dialogue* (Strathfield: St Paul, and Mulgrave: Broughton, 2004)

Church of England Council for Christian Unity, *The Gift of Authority: Report to the General Synod*, GS 1532. This provides background to the General Synod resolution on *The Gift of Authority* of 13 February 2004, www.churchofengland.org/media/1263087/gs1532.pdf

IASCER, *Provincial Responses to the Work of the Second Anglican–Roman Catholic International Commission: An Interim Report* (London: ACC, 2005). This summarizes official responses from the Church of Brazil, the Church of Canada, the Church of Ireland, The Episcopal Church of the USA, The Anglican Church of Australia, the Church of England, the Church in Wales, the Anglican Church in Aotearoa, New Zealand, and Polynesia, and the Church of the Province of Southern Africa, together with the correspondence of Canon Gregory Cameron, Director of Ecumenical Affairs for the Anglican Communion (2004–5)

USCCB, 'Response to the Anglican–Roman Catholic International Commission's "The Gift of Authority"' (2003), www.usccb.org/beliefs-and-teachings/ecumenical-and-interreligious/ecumenical/anglican/response-gift-of-authority.cfm

Significant Publications

Fisher, Peter (ed.), *Unpacking the Gift* (London: Church House Publishing, 2002). This includes the following chapters:

> Stephen Platten, 'The Context of *The Gift of Authority* in the History of Anglican–Roman Catholic Dialogue' (pp. 1–13)
>
> Mary Tanner, 'Authority: Gift or Threat?' (pp. 14–32)
>
> Martin Davie, '"Yes" and "No"—a Response to *The Gift of Authority*' (pp. 33–59)
>
> Christopher Hill, 'An Ecumenical Hermeneutic of Trust' (pp. 60–75)
>
> Martyn Percy, '*The Gift of Authority* in the Church of England: Sketching a Contextual Theology' (pp. 76–93)
>
> Flora Winfield, 'It's the Thought that Counts: Reflections from Local Contexts in Britain' (pp. 94–9)
>
> Peter Fisher, 'Conclusion' (pp. 100–7)

Baycroft, John, 'Understanding *The Gift of Authority*' (Wallington: Ecumenical Society of the Blessed Virgin Mary, 2000)

Bradshaw, Timothy, 'ARCIC III: *The Gift of Authority*', *Anvil*, 17 (2000), 201–11

Bray, Gerald, 'Article Review: *The Gift of Authority*', *The Churchman*, 113 (1999), http://churchsociety.org/churchman/page/churchman_vol_113_1999

Buchanan, Colin, *Is Papal Authority a Gift to Us? A Critique of* The Gift of Authority (Cambridge: Grove Books, 2003)

Butler, Sara, '*The Gift of Authority*: New Steps in Anglican–Roman Catholic Relations', *Ecumenical Trends*, 30 (2001), 81–5

Carey, Andrew, 'Anglicans are Urged to Say "Yes" to Pope', *Church of England Newspaper* (14 May 1999)

Denaux, Adelbert, '*Authority in the Church*: A Challenge to Both Anglicans and Roman Catholics', in *The Unity of Christians: The Vision of Paul Couturier* (*The Messenger*, October 2003), www.academia.edu/3184275/Authority_in_the_Church_A_Challenge_for_both_Anglicans_and_Roman_Catholics

Longley, Bernard, '*Growing Together in Unity and Mission*—a Commentary', https://

iarccum.org/archive/IARCCUM_2000-2010/2007_iarccum_longley-bernard.pdf

Meyers, R. A., '*The Gift of Authority*: New Steps in Anglican–Roman Catholic Relations. An Anglican Response', *Ecumenical Trends*, 30 (2001), 86–90

Nilson, J., '*The Gift of Authority*: An American Roman Catholic Appreciation', *One in Christ*, 36 (2000), 133–44

Root, Michael, '*The Gift of Authority*: An Observer's Report and Analysis', *The Ecumenical Review*, 52 (2000), 57–71

Ross, Alexander, 'To what Extent has the Process and Outcome of Provincial Reception across the Anglican Communion of the 1999 Agreed Statement of the Second ARCIC Commission, *The Gift of Authority*, Reflected the Wider *Wirkungsgeschichte* of the Document across World-Wide Anglicanism?', unpublished MTheol dissertation, University of Oxford, 2012

Sixtus, Bernd, 'How to Read *The Gift of Authority*', *International Journal for the Study of the Christian Church*, 4 (2004), 172–83

Tanner, Mary, 'The ARCIC Dialogue and the Perception of Authority', *Journal of Anglican Studies*, 1 (2003), 47–61

Relevant Ecclesial Documents

Benedict XIV, Apostolic Constitution, *Anglicanorum Coetibus* (Vatican City, 2009), http://w2.vatican.va/content/benedict-xvi/en/apost_constitutions/documents/hf_ben-xvi_apc_20091104_anglicanorum-coetibus.html

Francis I, Apostolic Exhortation, *Evangelii Gaudium* (Vatican City, 2013), http://w2.vatican.va/content/francesco/en/apost_exhortations/documents/papa-franc-esco_esortazione-ap_20131124_evangelii-gaudium.html

IARCCUM, *Growing Together in Unity and Mission* (London: SPCK, 2007), www.vatican.va/roman_curia/pontifical_councils/chrstuni/angl-comm-docs/rc_pc_chrstuni_doc_20070914_growing-together_en.html

Inter-Anglican Theological and Doctrinal Commission, *Communion, Conflict and Hope* (London: ACC, 2008), www.anglicancommunion.org/media/107645/IATDC-Inter-Anglican-Theological-and-Doctrinal-Commission.pdf

Inter-Anglican Theological and Doctrinal Commission, *The Virginia Report*, in James M. Rosenthal and Nicola Currie (eds.), *Being Anglican in the Third Millennium: The Official Report of the 10th Meeting of the Anglican Consultative Council* (Harrisburg: Morehouse, 1997), 211–81

International Theological Commission, '*Sensus Fidei* in the life of the Church' (Rome, 2014), www.vatican.va/roman_curia/congregations/cfaith/cti_documents/rc_cti_20140610_sensus-fidei_en.html

John Paul II, *Ut Unum Sint* (Vatican City: Libreria Editrice Vaticana, 1995), http://w2.vatican.va/content/john-paul-ii/en/encyclicals/documents/hf_jp-ii_enc_25051995_ut-unum-sint.html

Joint International Commission for the Theological Dialogue between the Roman Catholic Church and the Orthodox Church, *Ecclesiological and Canonical Consequences of the Sacramental Nature of the Church* (The Ravenna Document,

13 October 2007), www.vatican.va/roman_curia/pontifical_councils/chrstuni/ch_orthodox_docs/rc_pc_chrstuni_doc_20071013_documento-ravenna_en.html

Kasper, Cardinal Walter, Letter of His Eminence Cardinal Walter Kasper to His Grace Dr Rowan Williams, Archbishop of Canterbury (Vatican City: 2004), www.vatican.va/roman_curia/pontifical_councils/chrstuni/card-kasper-docs/rc_pc_chrstuni_doc_20041217_kasper-arch-canterbury_en.html

The Lambeth Commission on Communion, The Windsor Report (London: ACC, 2004), www.anglicancommunion.org/media/68225/windsor2004full.pdf

Williams, Rowan, 'Address at the Willebrands Symposium in Rome' (2009), http://rowanwilliams.archbishopofcanterbury.org/articles.php/766/archbishops-address-at-a-willebrands-symposium-in-rome

Williams, Rowan, 'Address at Westminster Abbey on the occasion of the visit of Pope Benedict XVI for Evening Prayer', http://rowanwilliams.archbishopofcanterbury.org/articles.php/945/the-visit-of-archbishop-rowan-williams-and-pope-benedict-xvi-to-westminster-abbey-for-evening-prayer

Chapter 5

Mary: Grace and Hope in Christ (2005)
The Seattle Statement

Introducing the Statement

ARCIC II took up 'a study of Mary in the life and doctrine of the Church' in response to a specific request from the 2001 Mississauga conference of Anglican and Roman Catholic bishops (*Mary: Grace and Hope in Christ*, §1).[1] The study involved issues which emerged after the breach between the Church of England and Rome in the sixteenth century. In the centuries since, Anglicans and Roman Catholics experienced different histories in relation to Mary, focused doctrinally in the papal definitions of her Immaculate Conception (1854) and Assumption (1950). The Commission did not attempt to write a 'Mariology', but the papal definitions could be rightly considered only in the setting of Christian faith regarding the Blessed Virgin Mary.

The Commission took over five years to produce *Mary*, a longer period of work than for previous ARCIC Statements.[2] This reflects the complexity of the issues involved, and the ongoing problem in Christian reflection on Mary of the separation of the doctrinal and spiritual dimensions of theology. ARCIC II endeavoured to offer a Statement which integrates theology and spirituality, pays close attention to reading Scripture together, reviews the history of Marian doctrines and devotion together, and seeks to respond together to the sharp questions before it. It follows the familiar order of ARCIC Statements: scriptural grounding, historical review, and reconsideration of documented differences towards agreement.

The whole text, starting from scriptural and patristic data, benefits from the eschatological—and thus doxological—focus set out in Section C, developed around Romans 8.29–30:

---

[1] ARCIC I addressed the authority of the two Marian definitions, but not so much their teaching: *Authority in the Church II* (1981), §30.

[2] Major papers from the Commission's work on Mary are published in Adelbert Denaux and Nicholas Sagovsky (eds.), *Studying Mary: Reflections on the Virgin Mary in Anglican and Roman Catholic Theology and Devotion. The ARCIC Working Papers* (London: T & T Clark, 2007).

175

Those who love God, who are called according to his purpose, God foreknew and predestined to be conformed to the image of his Son ... And those whom God predestined he also called; and those whom he called he also justified; and those whom he justified he also glorified.

This, the most distinctive aspect of the Statement, considers the place of Mary in primarily Pauline categories, using a 'from the future backwards' method (see Chapter 8). The title, *Mary: Grace and Hope in Christ*, invites reflection on the beginning and the fulfilment of the life of Mary within the communion of saints.

MARY: GRACE AND HOPE IN CHRIST

The Seattle Statement

The Anglican–Roman Catholic International
Commission: An Agreed Statement

CONTENTS

PREFACE

By the Co-Chairmen

In the continuing journey toward full communion, the Roman Catholic Church and the Churches of the Anglican Communion have for many years prayerfully considered a number of questions concerning the faith we share and the way we articulate it in the life and worship of our two households of faith. We have submitted Agreed Statements to the Holy See and to the Anglican Communion for comment, further clarification if necessary, and conjoint acceptance as congruent with the faith of Anglicans and Roman Catholics.

In framing this Agreed Statement, we have drawn on the Scriptures and the common tradition which predates the Reformation and the Counter Reformation. As in previous Anglican–Roman Catholic International Commission (ARCIC) documents, we have attempted to use language that reflects what we hold in common and transcends the controversies of the past. At the same time, in this statement we have had to face squarely dogmatic definitions which are integral to the faith of Roman Catholics but largely foreign to the faith of Anglicans. The members of ARCIC, over time, have sought to embrace one another's ways of doing theology and have considered together the historical context in which certain doctrines developed. In so doing, we have learned to receive anew our own traditions, illumined and deepened by the understanding of and appreciation for each other's tradition.

Our Agreed Statement concerning the Blessed Virgin Mary as pattern of grace and hope is a powerful reflection of our efforts to seek out what we hold in common and celebrates important aspects of our common heritage. Mary, the mother of our Lord Jesus Christ, stands before us as an exemplar of faithful obedience, and her 'Be it to me according to your word' is the grace-filled response each of us is called to make to God, both personally and communally, as the Church, the body of Christ. It is as figure of the Church, her arms uplifted in prayer and praise, her hands open in receptivity and availability to the outpouring of the Holy Spirit, that we are one with Mary as she magnifies the Lord. 'Surely,' Mary declares in her song recorded in the Gospel of Luke, 'from this day all generations will call me blessed.'

Our two traditions share many of the same feasts associated with Mary. From our experience we have found that it is in the realm of worship that we realise our deepest convergence as we give thanks to God for the Mother of the Lord who is one with us in that vast community of love and prayer we call the communion of saints.

+ Alexander J. Brunett
+ Peter F. Carnley

Seattle,
Feast of the Presentation,
February 2, 2004

THE STATUS OF THE DOCUMENT

The document published here is the work of the Anglican–Roman Catholic International Commission (ARCIC). It is a joint statement of the Commission. The authorities who appointed the Commission have allowed the statement to be published so that it may be widely discussed. It is not an authoritative declaration by the Roman Catholic Church or by the Anglican Communion, who will study and evaluate the document in due course.

Citations from Scripture are normally taken from the New Revised Standard Version. In some cases the Commission has offered its own translation.

MARY: GRACE AND HOPE IN CHRIST
The Seattle Statement

INTRODUCTION

1. In honouring Mary as Mother of the Lord, all generations of Anglicans and Roman Catholics have echoed the greeting of Elizabeth: 'Blessed are you among women, and blessed is the fruit of your womb' (Luke 1.42). The Anglican–Roman Catholic International Commission now offers this Agreed Statement on the place of Mary in the life and doctrine of the Church in the hope that it expresses our common faith about the one who, of all believers, is closest to our Lord and Saviour Jesus Christ. We do so at the request of our two Communions, in response to questions set before us. A special consultation of Anglican and Roman Catholic bishops, meeting under the leadership of the Archbishop of Canterbury, Dr George Carey, and Cardinal Edward I. Cassidy, President of the Pontifical Council for Promoting Christian Unity, at Mississauga, Canada in 2000, specifically asked ARCIC for 'a study of Mary in the life and doctrine of the Church.' This request recalls the observation of the Malta Report (1968) that 'real or apparent differences between us come to the surface in such matters as . . . the Mariological definitions' promulgated in 1854 and 1950. More recently, in *Ut Unum Sint* (1995), Pope John Paul II identified as one area in need of fuller study by all Christian traditions before a true consensus of faith can be achieved 'the Virgin Mary, as Mother of God and Icon of the Church, the spiritual Mother who intercedes for Christ's disciples and for all humanity' (para. 79).

2. ARCIC has addressed this topic once before. *Authority in the Church II* (1981) already records a significant degree of agreement:

    > We agree that there can be but one mediator between God and man, Jesus Christ, and reject any interpretation of the role of Mary which obscures this affirmation. We agree in recognising that Christian understanding of Mary is inseparably linked with the doctrines of Christ and the Church. We agree in recognising the grace and unique vocation of Mary, Mother of God Incarnate (*Theotókos*), in observing her festivals, and in according her honour in the communion of saints. We agree

that she was prepared by divine grace to be the mother of our Redeemer, by whom she herself was redeemed and received into glory. We further agree in recognising in Mary a model of holiness, obedience and faith for all Christians. We accept that it is possible to regard her as a prophetic figure of the Church of God before as well as after the Incarnation (para. 30).

The same document, however, points out remaining differences:

The dogmas of the Immaculate Conception and the Assumption raise a special problem for those Anglicans who do not consider that the precise definitions given by these dogmas are sufficiently supported by Scripture. For many Anglicans the teaching authority of the Bishop of Rome, independent of a council, is not recommended by the fact that through it these Marian doctrines were proclaimed as dogmas binding on all the faithful. Anglicans would also ask whether, in any future union between our two Churches, they would be required to subscribe to such dogmatic statements (para. 30).

These reservations in particular were noted in the official *Response of the Holy See to The Final Report* (1991, para. 13). Having taken these shared beliefs and these questions as the starting point for our reflection, we are now able to affirm further significant agreement on the place of Mary in the life and doctrine of the Church.

3. The present document proposes a fuller statement of our shared belief concerning the Blessed Virgin Mary and so provides the context for a common appreciation of the content of the Marian dogmas. We also take up differences of practice, including the explicit invocation of Mary. This new study of Mary has benefited from our previous study of reception in *The Gift of Authority* (1999). There we concluded that, when the Church receives and acknowledges what it recognises as a true expression of the Tradition once-for-all delivered to the Apostles, this reception is an act both of faithfulness and of freedom. The freedom to respond in fresh ways in the face of new challenges is what enables the Church to be faithful to the Tradition which it carries forward. At other times, some element of the apostolic Tradition may be forgotten, neglected or abused. In such situations, fresh recourse to Scripture and Tradition recalls God's revelation in Christ: we call this process *re-reception* (cf. *Gift* 24–25). Progress in ecumenical dialogue and understanding suggests that we now have an opportunity to re-receive together the tradition of Mary's place in God's revelation.

4. Since its inception ARCIC has sought to get behind opposed or entrenched positions to discover and develop our common inheritance of faith (cf. *Authority* I 25). Following *The Common Declaration* in 1966 of Pope Paul VI and the Archbishop of Canterbury, Dr Michael Ramsey, we have continued our 'serious dialogue . . . founded on the Gospels and on the ancient common traditions.' We have asked to what extent doctrine or devotion concerning Mary belongs to a legitimate 'reception' of the apostolic Tradition, in accordance with the Scriptures. This Tradition has at its core the proclamation of the trinitarian 'economy of salvation', grounding the life and faith of the Church in the divine communion of Father, Son and Spirit. We have sought to understand Mary's person and role in the history of salvation and the life of the Church in the light of a theology of divine grace and hope. Such a theology is deeply rooted in the enduring experience of Christian worship and devotion.

5. God's grace calls for and enables human response (cf. *Salvation and the Church* 9). This is seen in the Gospel account of the Annunciation, where the angel's message evokes the response of Mary. The Incarnation and all that it entailed, including the passion, death and resurrection of Christ and the birth of the Church, came about by way of Mary's freely uttered *fiat*—'let it be done to me according to your word' (Luke 1.38). We recognise in the event of the Incarnation God's gracious 'Yes' to humanity as a whole. This reminds us once more of the Apostle's words in 2 Corinthians 1.18–20 (*Gift* 8ff): all God's promises find their 'Yes' in the Son of God, Jesus Christ. In this context, Mary's *fiat* can be seen as the supreme instance of a believer's 'Amen' in response to the 'Yes' of God. Christian disciples respond to the same 'Yes' with their own 'Amen'. They thus know themselves to be children together of the one heavenly Father, born of the Spirit as brothers and sisters of Jesus Christ, drawn into the communion of love of the blessed Trinity. Mary epitomises such participation in the life of God. Her response was not made without profound questioning, and it issued in a life of joy intermingled with sorrow, taking her even to the foot of her son's cross. When Christians join in Mary's 'Amen' to the 'Yes' of God in Christ, they commit themselves to an obedient response to the Word of God, which leads to a life of prayer and service. Like Mary, they not only magnify the Lord with their lips: they commit themselves to serve God's justice with their lives (cf. Luke 1.46–55).

A. MARY ACCORDING TO THE SCRIPTURES

6. We remain convinced that the holy Scriptures, as the Word of God written, bear normative witness to God's plan of salvation, so it is to them that this statement first turns. Indeed, it is impossible to be faithful to Scripture and not to take Mary seriously. We recognise, however, that for some centuries Anglicans and Roman Catholics have interpreted the Scriptures while divided from one another. In reflecting together on the Scriptures' testimony concerning Mary, we have discovered more than just a few tantalizing glimpses into the life of a great saint. We have found ourselves meditating with wonder and gratitude on the whole sweep of salvation history: creation, election, the Incarnation, passion, and resurrection of Christ, the gift of the Spirit in the Church, and the final vision of eternal life for all God's people in the new creation.

7. In the following paragraphs, our use of Scripture seeks to draw upon the whole tradition of the Church, in which rich and varied readings have been employed. In the New Testament, the Old Testament is commonly interpreted typologically:[1] events and images are understood with specific reference to Christ. This approach is further developed by the Fathers and by medieval preachers and authors. The Reformers stressed the clarity and sufficiency of Scripture, and called for a return to the centrality of the Gospel message. Historical-critical approaches attempted to discern the meaning intended by the biblical authors, and to account for texts' origins. Each of these readings has its limitations, and may give rise to exaggerations or imbalances: typology can become extravagant, Reformation emphases reductionist, and critical methods overly historicist. More recent approaches to Scripture point to the range of possible readings of a text, notably its narrative, rhetorical and sociological dimensions. In this statement, we seek to integrate what is valuable from each of these approaches, as both correcting and contributing to our use of Scripture. Further, we recognise that no reading of a text is neutral, but each is shaped by the context and interest of its readers. Our reading has taken place within the context of our dialogue in

---

[1] By typology we mean a reading which accepts that certain things in Scripture (persons, places, and events) foreshadow or illuminate other things, or reflect patterns of faith in imaginative ways (e.g. Adam is a type of Christ: Romans 5.14; Isaiah 7.14 points towards the virgin birth of Jesus: Matthew 1.23). This typological sense was considered to be a meaning that goes beyond the literal sense. This approach assumes the unity and consistency of the divine revelation.

Christ, for the sake of that communion which is his will. It is thus an ecclesial and ecumenical reading, seeking to consider each passage about Mary in the context of the New Testament as a whole, against the background of the Old, and in the light of Tradition.

The Witness of Scripture: A Trajectory of Grace and Hope

8. The Old Testament bears witness to God's creation of men and women in the divine image, and God's loving call to covenant relationship with himself. Even when they disobeyed, God did not abandon human beings to sin and the power of death. Again and again God offered a covenant of grace. God made a covenant with Noah that never again would 'all flesh' be destroyed by the waters of a flood. The Lord made a covenant with Abraham that, through him, all the families of the earth might be blessed. Through Moses he made a covenant with Israel that, obedient to his word, they might be a holy nation and a priestly people. The prophets repeatedly summoned the people to turn back from disobedience to the gracious God of the covenant, to receive God's word and let it bear fruit in their lives. They looked forward to a renewal of the covenant in which there would be perfect obedience and perfect self-giving: 'This is the covenant which I will make with the house of Israel after those days, says the Lord: I will put my law within them, and I will write it upon their hearts; and I will be their God, and they shall be my people' (Jeremiah 31.33). In the prophecy of Ezekiel, this hope is spoken of not only in terms of washing and cleansing, but also of the gift of the Spirit (Ezekiel 36.25–28).

9. The covenant between the Lord and his people is several times described as a love affair between God and Israel, the virgin daughter of Zion, bride and mother: 'I gave you my solemn oath and entered into a covenant with you, declares the Sovereign Lord, and you became mine' (Ezekiel 16.8; cf. Isaiah 54.1 and Galatians 4.27). Even in punishing faithlessness, God remains forever faithful, promising to restore the covenant relationship and to draw together the scattered people (Hosea 1—2; Jeremiah 2.2, 31.3; Isaiah 62.4–5). Nuptial imagery is also used within the New Testament to describe the relationship between Christ and the Church (Ephesians 5.21–33; Revelation 21.9). In parallel to the prophetic image of Israel as the bride of the Lord, the Solomonic literature of the Old Testament characterises Holy Wisdom as the handmaid of the Lord (Proverbs 8.22f; cf. Wisdom 7.22–26) similarly emphasizing the theme of

responsiveness and creative activity. In the New Testament these prophetic and wisdom motifs are combined (Luke 11.49) and fulfilled in the coming of Christ.

10. The Scriptures also speak of the calling by God of particular persons, such as David, Elijah, Jeremiah and Isaiah, so that within the people of God certain special tasks may be performed. They bear witness to the gift of the Spirit or the presence of God enabling them to accomplish God's will and purpose. There are also profound reflections on what it is to be known and called by God from the very beginning of one's existence (Psalm 139.13–16; Jeremiah 1.4–5). This sense of wonder at the prevenient grace of God is similarly attested in the New Testament, especially in the writings of Paul, when he speaks of those who are 'called according to God's purpose,' affirming that those whom God 'foreknew, he also predestined to be conformed to the image of his Son . . . And those whom he predestined he also called; and those whom he called he also justified; and those whom he justified he also glorified' (Romans 8.28–30; cf. 2 Timothy 1.9). The preparation by God for a prophetic task is exemplified in the words spoken by the angel to Zechariah before the birth of John the Baptist: 'He will be filled with the Holy Spirit, even from his mother's womb' (Luke 1.15; cf. Judges 13.3–5).

11. Following through the trajectory of the grace of God and the hope for a perfect human response which we have traced in the preceding paragraphs, Christians have, in line with the New Testament writers, seen its culmination in the obedience of Christ. Within this Christological context, they have discerned a similar pattern in the one who would receive the Word in her heart and in her body, be overshadowed by the Spirit and give birth to the Son of God. The New Testament speaks not only of God's preparation for the birth of the Son, but also of God's election, calling and sanctification of a Jewish woman in the line of those holy women, such as Sarah and Hannah, whose sons fulfilled the purposes of God for his people. Paul speaks of the Son of God being born 'in the fullness of time' and 'born of a woman, born under the Law' (Galatians 4.4). The birth of Mary's son is the fulfilment of God's will for Israel, and Mary's part in that fulfilment is that of free and unqualified consent in utter self-giving and trust: 'Behold I am the handmaid of the Lord; let it be done to me according to your word' (Luke 1.38; cf. Psalm 123.2).

Mary in Matthew's Birth Narrative

12. While various parts of the New Testament refer to the birth of Christ, only two Gospels, Matthew and Luke, each from its own perspective, narrate the story of his birth and refer specifically to Mary. Matthew entitles his book 'the Genesis of Jesus Christ' (1.1) echoing the way the Bible begins (Genesis 1.1). In the genealogy (1.1–18) he traces the genesis of Jesus back through the Exile to David and ultimately to Abraham. He notes the unlikely role played in the providential ordering of Israel's salvation history by four women, each of whom stretches the boundaries of the Covenant. This emphasis on continuity with the old is counter-balanced in the following account of Jesus' birth by an emphasis on the new (cf. 9.17), a type of re-creation by the Holy Spirit, revealing new possibilities of salvation from sin (1.21) and of the presence of 'God with us' (1.23). Matthew stretches the boundaries further in holding together Jesus' Davidic descent through the legal fatherhood of Joseph, and his birth from the Virgin according to Isaiah's prophecy—'Behold a virgin shall conceive and bear a son' (Isaiah 7.14 LXX).

13. In Matthew's account, Mary is mentioned in conjunction with her son in such phrases as 'Mary his mother' or 'the child and his mother' (2.11, 13, 20, 21). Amid all the political intrigue, murder, and displacement of this tale, one quiet moment of reverence has captured the Christian imagination: the Magi, whose profession it is to know when the time has come, kneel in homage to the infant King with his royal mother (2.2, 11). Matthew emphasises the continuity of Jesus Christ with Israel's messianic expectation and the newness that comes with the birth of the Saviour. Descent from David by whatever route, and birth at the ancestral royal city, disclose the first. The virginal conception discloses the second.

Mary in Luke's Birth Narrative

14. In Luke's infancy narrative, Mary is prominent from the beginning. She is the link between John the Baptist and Jesus, whose miraculous births are laid out in deliberate parallel. She receives the angel's message and responds in humble obedience (1.38). She travels on her own from Galilee to Judaea to visit Elizabeth (1.40) and in her song proclaims the eschatological reversal which will be at the heart of her son's proclamation of the kingdom of God. Mary is the one who in recollection looks beneath the surface of events (2.19, 51) and represents the inwardness of faith and suffering (2.35). She

speaks on Joseph's behalf in the scene at the Temple and, although chided for her initial incomprehension, continues to grow in understanding (2.48–51).

15. Within the Lucan narrative, two particular scenes invite reflection on the place of Mary in the life of the Church: the Annunciation and the visit to Elizabeth. These passages emphasise that Mary is in a unique way the recipient of God's election and grace. The Annunciation story recapitulates several incidents in the Old Testament, notably the births of Isaac (Genesis 18.10–14), Samson (Judges 13.2–5) and Samuel (1 Samuel 1.1–20). The angel's greeting also evokes the passages in Isaiah (66.7–11), Zechariah (9.9) and Zephaniah (3.14–17) that call on the 'Daughter of Zion', i.e., Israel awaiting with joy the arrival of her Lord. The choice of 'overshadow' (*episkiasei*) to describe the action of the Holy Spirit in the virginal conception (Luke 1.35) echoes the cherubim overshadowing the Ark of the Covenant (Exodus 25.20), the presence of God overshadowing the Tabernacle (Exodus 40.35), and the brooding of the Spirit over the waters at the creation (Genesis 1.2). At the Visitation, Mary's song (*Magnificat*) mirrors the song of Hannah (1 Samuel 2.1–10), broadening its scope so that Mary becomes the one who speaks for all the poor and oppressed who long for God's reign of justice to be established. Just as in Elizabeth's salutation the mother receives a blessing of her own, distinct from that of her child (1.42), so also in the *Magnificat* Mary predicts that 'all generations will call me blessed' (1.48). This text provides the scriptural basis for an appropriate devotion to Mary, though never in separation from her role as mother of the Messiah.

16. In the Annunciation story, the angel calls Mary the Lord's 'favoured one' (Greek *kecharitomene*, a perfect participle meaning 'one who has been and remains endowed with grace') in a way that implies a prior sanctification by divine grace with a view to her calling. The angel's announcement connects Jesus' being 'holy' and 'Son of God' with his conception by the Holy Spirit (1.35). The virginal conception then points to the divine sonship of the Saviour who will be born of Mary. The infant not yet born is described by Elizabeth as the Lord: 'And why is this granted to me that the mother of my Lord should come to me?' (1.43). The trinitarian pattern of divine action in these scenes is striking: the Incarnation of the Son is initiated by the Father's election of the Blessed Virgin and is mediated by the Holy Spirit. Equally striking is Mary's *fiat*, her 'Amen' given in

faith and freedom to God's powerful Word communicated by the angel (1.38).

17. In Luke's account of the birth of Jesus, the praise offered to God by the shepherds parallels the Magi's adoration of the infant in Matthew's account. Again, this is the scene that constitutes the still centre at the heart of the birth story: 'They found Mary and Joseph and the baby lying in a manger' (Luke 2.16). In accordance with the Law of Moses, the baby is circumcised and presented in the Temple. On this occasion, Simeon has a special word of prophecy for the mother of the Christ-child, that 'a sword will pierce your own soul' (Luke 2.34–35). From this point on Mary's pilgrimage of faith leads to the foot of the cross.

The Virginal Conception

18. The divine initiative in human history is proclaimed in the good news of the virginal conception through the action of the Holy Spirit (Matthew 1.20–23; Luke 1.34–35). The virginal conception may appear in the first place as an absence, i.e., the absence of a human father. It is in reality, however, a sign of the presence and work of the Spirit. Belief in the virginal conception is an early Christian tradition adopted and developed independently by Matthew and Luke.[2] For Christian believers, it is an eloquent sign of the divine sonship of Christ and of new life through the Spirit. The virginal conception also points to the new birth of every Christian, as an adopted child of God. Each is 'born again (from above) by water and the Spirit' (John 3.3–5). Seen in this light, the virginal conception, far from being an isolated miracle, is a powerful expression of what the Church believes about her Lord, and about our salvation.

Mary and the True Family of Jesus

19. After these birth stories, it comes as something of a surprise to read the episode, narrated in all three Synoptic Gospels, which addresses the question of Jesus' true family. Mark tells us that Jesus'

---

[2] Given its strongly Jewish matrix in both Matthean and Lucan versions, an appeal to analogies with pagan mythology or to an exaltation of virginity over the married state to explain the origin of the tradition is implausible. Nor is the idea of virginal conception likely to derive from an over-literal reading of the Greek text of Isaiah 7.14 (LXX), for that is not the way the idea is introduced in the Lucan account. Moreover, the suggestion that it originated as an answer to the accusation of illegitimacy levelled at Jesus is unlikely, as that accusation could equally have arisen because it was known that there was something unusual about Jesus' birth (cf. Mark 6.3; John 8.41) and because of the Church's claim about his virginal conception.

'mother and his brothers' (Mark 3.31) come and stand outside, wanting to speak to him.[3] Jesus in response distances himself from his natural family: he speaks instead of those gathered around him, his 'eschatological family', that is to say, 'whoever does the will of God' (3.35). For Mark, Jesus' natural family, including his own mother, seems at this stage to lack understanding of the true nature of his mission. But that will be the case also with his disciples (e.g. 8.33–35, 9.30–33, 10.35–40). Mark indicates that growth in understanding is inevitably slow and painful, and that genuine faith in Christ is not reached until the encounter with the cross and the empty tomb.

20. In Luke, the stark contrast between the attitude towards Jesus of his natural and eschatological family is avoided (Luke 8.19–21). In a later scene (11.27–28) the woman in the crowd who utters a blessing on his mother, 'Blessed is the womb that bore you and the breasts that you sucked', is corrected: 'Blessed rather are those who hear the word of God and keep it'. But that form of blessing, as Luke sees it, definitely includes Mary who, from the beginning of his account, was ready to let everything in her life happen according to God's word (1.38).

21. In his second book, the Acts of the Apostles, Luke notes that between the ascension of the Risen Lord and the feast of Pentecost the apostles were gathered in Jerusalem 'together with the women and Mary the mother of Jesus, and with his brothers' (Acts 1.14). Mary, who was receptive to the working of God's Spirit at the birth of the Messiah (Luke 1.35–38), is here part of the community of disciples waiting in prayer for the outpouring of the Spirit at the birth of the Church.

Mary in John's Gospel

22. Mary is not mentioned explicitly in the Prologue of John's Gospel. However, something of the significance of her role in salvation history may be discerned by placing her in the context of the considered theological truths that the evangelist articulates in unfolding the good news of the Incarnation. The theological emphasis on the divine

---

[3] Although the word 'brother' usually denotes a blood brother, the Greek *adelphos*, like the Hebrew *'ah*, can have a broader meaning of kinsman, or relative (e.g. Genesis 29.12 LXX) or step-brother (e.g. Mark 6.17f). Relatives who are not siblings could be included in this use of the term at Mark 3:31. Mary did have an extended family: her sister is referred to at John 19.25 and her kinswoman Elizabeth at Luke 1.36. In the early Church different explanations of the references to the 'brothers' of Jesus were given, whether as step-brothers or cousins.

initiative, that in the narratives of Matthew and Luke is expressed in the story of Jesus' birth, is paralleled in the Prologue of John by an emphasis on the predestining will and grace of God by which all those who are brought to new birth are said to be born 'not of blood, nor of the will of the flesh, nor of the will of man, but of God' (1.13). These are words that could be applied to the birth of Jesus himself.

23. At two important moments of Jesus' public life, the beginning (the wedding at Cana) and the end (the Cross), John notes the presence of Jesus' mother. Each is an hour of need: the first on the surface rather trivial, but at a deeper level a symbolic anticipation of the second. John gives a prominent position in his Gospel to the wedding at Cana (2.1–12), calling it the beginning of the signs of Jesus. The account emphasises the new wine which Jesus brings, symbolizing the eschatological marriage feast of God with his people and the messianic banquet of the kingdom. The story primarily conveys a Christological message: Jesus reveals his messianic glory to his disciples and they believe in him (2.11).

24. The presence of the 'mother of Jesus' is mentioned at the beginning of the story: she has a distinctive role in the unfolding of the narrative. Mary seems to have been invited and be present in her own right, not with 'Jesus and his disciples' (2.1–2); Jesus is initially seen as present as part of his mother's family. In the dialogue between them when the wine runs out, Jesus seems at first to refuse Mary's implied request, but in the end he accedes to it. This reading of the narrative, however, leaves room for a deeper symbolic reading of the event. In Mary's words 'they have no wine', John ascribes to her the expression not so much of a deficiency in the wedding arrangements, as of the longing for salvation of the whole covenant people, who have water for purification but lack the joyful wine of the messianic kingdom. In his answer, Jesus begins by calling into question his former relationship with his mother ('What is there between you and me?'), implying that a change has to take place. He does not address Mary as 'mother', but as 'woman' (cf. John 19.26). Jesus no longer sees his relation to Mary as simply one of earthly kinship.

25. Mary's response, to instruct the servants to 'Do whatever he tells you' (2.5), is unexpected; she is not in charge of the feast (cf. 2.8). Her initial role as the mother of Jesus has radically changed. She herself is now seen as a believer within the messianic community. From this moment on, she commits herself totally to the Messiah and his word. A new relationship results, indicated by the change in

the order of the main characters at the end of the story: 'After this he went down to Capernaum, with his mother and his brothers and his disciples' (2.12). The Cana narrative opens by placing Jesus within the family of Mary, his mother; from now on, Mary is part of the 'company of Jesus', his disciple. Our reading of this passage reflects the Church's understanding of the role of Mary: to help the disciples come to her son, Jesus Christ, and to 'do whatever he tells you.'

26. John's second mention of the presence of Mary occurs at the decisive hour of Jesus' messianic mission, his crucifixion (19.25–27). Standing with other disciples at the cross, Mary shares in the suffering of Jesus, who in his last moments addresses a special word to her, 'Woman, behold your son', and to the beloved disciple, 'Behold your mother.' We cannot but be touched that, even in his dying moments, Jesus is concerned for the welfare of his mother, showing his filial affection. This surface reading again invites a symbolic and ecclesial reading of John's rich narrative. These last commands of Jesus before he dies reveal an understanding beyond their primary reference to Mary and 'the beloved disciple' as individuals. The reciprocal roles of the 'woman' and the 'disciple' are related to the identity of the Church. Elsewhere in John, the beloved disciple is presented as the model disciple of Jesus, the one closest to him who never deserted him, the object of Jesus' love, and the ever-faithful witness (13.25, 19.26, 20.1–10, 21.20–25). Understood in terms of discipleship, Jesus' dying words give Mary a motherly role in the Church and encourage the community of disciples to embrace her as a spiritual mother.

27. A corporate understanding of 'woman' also calls the Church constantly to behold Christ crucified, and calls each disciple to care for the Church as mother. Implicit here perhaps is a Mary-Eve typology: just as the first 'woman' was taken from Adam's 'rib' (Genesis 2.22, *pleura* LXX) and became the mother of all the living (Genesis 3.20), so the 'woman' Mary is, on a spiritual level, the mother of all who gain true life from the water and blood that flow from the side (Greek *pleura*, literally 'rib') of Christ (19.34) and from the Spirit that is breathed out from his triumphant sacrifice (19.30, 20.22, cf. 1 John 5.8). In such symbolic and corporate readings, images for the Church, Mary and discipleship interact with one another. Mary is seen as the personification of Israel, now giving birth to the Christian community (cf. Isaiah 54.1, 66.7–8), just as she had given birth earlier

to the Messiah (cf. Isaiah 7.14). When John's account of Mary at the beginning and end of Jesus' ministry is viewed in this light, it is difficult to speak of the Church without thinking of Mary, the Mother of the Lord, as its archetype and first realisation.

The Woman in Revelation 12

28. In highly symbolic language, full of scriptural imagery, the seer of Revelation describes the vision of a sign in heaven involving a woman, a dragon, and the woman's child. The narrative of Revelation 12 serves to assure the reader of the ultimate victory of God's faithful ones in times of persecution and eschatological struggle. In the course of history, the symbol of the woman has led to a variety of interpretations. Most scholars accept that the primary meaning of the woman is corporate: the people of God, whether Israel, the Church of Christ, or both. Moreover, the narrative style of the author suggests that the 'full picture' of the woman is attained only at the end of the book when the Church of Christ becomes the triumphant New Jerusalem (Revelation 21.1–3). The actual troubles of the author's community are placed in the frame of history as a whole, which is the scene of the ongoing struggle between the faithful and their enemies, between good and evil, between God and Satan. The imagery of the offspring reminds us of the struggle in Genesis 3.15 between the serpent and the woman, between the serpent's seed and the woman's seed.[4]

29. Given this primary ecclesial interpretation of Revelation 12, is it still possible to find in it a secondary reference to Mary? The text does not explicitly identify the woman with Mary. It refers to the woman as the mother of the 'male child who is to rule all the nations with a rod of iron', a citation from Psalm 2 elsewhere in the New Testament applied to the Messiah as well as to the faithful people of God (cf. Hebrews 1.5, 5.5, Acts 13.33 with Revelation 2.27). In view of

---

[4] The Hebrew text of Genesis 3.15 speaks about enmity between the serpent and the woman, and between the offspring of both. The personal pronoun (*hu'*) in the words addressed to the serpent, 'He will strike at your head,' is masculine. In the Greek translation used by the early Church (LXX), however, the personal pronoun *autos* (he) cannot refer to the offspring (neuter: *to sperma*), but must refer to a masculine individual who could then be the Messiah, born of a woman. The Vulgate (mis) translates the clause as *ipsa conteret caput tuum* ('she will strike at your head'). This feminine pronoun supported a reading of this passage as referring to Mary which has become traditional in the Latin Church. The Neo-Vulgate (1986), however, returns to the neuter *ipsum*, which refers to *semen illius*: '*Inimicitias ponam inter te et mulierem et semen tuum et semen illius; ipsum conteret caput tuum, et tu conteres calcaneum eius.*'

this, some patristic writers came to think of the mother of Jesus when reading this chapter.[5] Given the place of the book of Revelation within the canon of Scripture, in which the different biblical images intertwine, the possibility arose of a more explicit interpretation, both individual and corporate, of Revelation 12, illuminating the place of Mary and the Church in the eschatological victory of the Messiah.

Scriptural Reflection

30. The scriptural witness summons all believers in every generation to call Mary 'blessed'; this Jewish woman of humble status, this daughter of Israel living in hope of justice for the poor, whom God has graced and chosen to become the virgin mother of his Son through the overshadowing of the Holy Spirit. We are to bless her as the 'handmaid of the Lord' who gave her unqualified assent to the fulfilment of God's saving plan, as the mother who pondered all things in her heart, as the refugee seeking asylum in a foreign land, as the mother pierced by the innocent suffering of her own child, and as the woman to whom Jesus entrusted his friends. We are at one with her and the apostles, as they pray for the outpouring of the Spirit upon the nascent Church, the eschatological family of Christ. And we may even glimpse in her the final destiny of God's people to share in her son's victory over the powers of evil and death.

B. MARY IN THE CHRISTIAN TRADITION

Christ and Mary in the Ancient Common Tradition

31. In the early Church, reflection on Mary served to interpret and safeguard the apostolic Tradition centred on Jesus Christ. Patristic testimony to Mary as 'God-bearer' (*Theotókos*) emerged from reflection on Scripture and the celebration of Christian feasts, but its development was due chiefly to the early Christological controversies. In the crucible of these controversies of the first five centuries, and their resolution in successive Ecumenical Councils, reflection on Mary's role in the Incarnation was integral to the articulation of orthodox faith in Jesus Christ, true God and true man.

32. In defence of Christ's true humanity, and against Docetism, the early Church emphasised Jesus' birth from Mary. He did not just

---

[5] Cf. Epiphanius of Salamis (†402), *Panarion* 78.11; Quodvultdeus (†454), *Sermones de Symbolo* III, I.4–6; Oecumenius (†c.550), *Commentarius in Apocalypsin* 6.

'appear' to be human; he did not descend from heaven in a 'heavenly body', nor when he was born did he simply 'pass through' his mother. Rather, Mary gave birth to her son of her own substance. For Ignatius of Antioch (†c.110) and Tertullian (†c.225), Jesus is fully human, because 'truly born' of Mary. In the words of the Nicaeo-Constantinopolitan Creed (381), 'he was incarnate of the Holy Spirit and the Virgin Mary, and was made man.' The definition of Chalcedon (451), re-affirming this creed, attests that Christ is 'consubstantial with the Father according to the divinity and consubstantial with us according to the humanity.' The Athanasian Creed confesses yet more concretely that he is 'man, of the substance of his Mother.' This Anglicans and Roman Catholics together affirm.

33. In defence of his true divinity, the early Church emphasised Mary's virginal conception of Jesus Christ. According to the Fathers, his conception by the Holy Spirit testifies to Christ's divine origin and divine identity. The One born of Mary is the eternal Son of God. Eastern and Western Fathers—such as Justin (†c.150), Irenaeus (†c.202), Athanasius (†373), and Ambrose (†397)—expounded this New Testament teaching in terms of Genesis 3 (Mary is the antitype of 'virgin Eve') and Isaiah 7.14 (she fulfils the prophet's vision and gives birth to 'God with us'). They appealed to the virginal conception to defend both the Lord's divinity and Mary's honour. As the Apostles' Creed confesses: Jesus Christ was 'conceived by the Holy Spirit and born of the Virgin Mary.' This Anglicans and Roman Catholics together affirm.

34. Mary's title *Theotókos* was formally invoked to safeguard the orthodox doctrine of the unity of Christ's person. This title had been in use in churches under the influence of Alexandria at least from the time of the Arian controversy. Since Jesus Christ is 'true God from true God', as the Council of Nicaea (325) declared, these churches concluded that his mother, Mary, can rightly be called the 'Godbearer'. Churches under the influence of Antioch, however, conscious of the threat Apollinarianism posed to belief in the full humanity of Christ, did not immediately adopt this title. The debate between Cyril of Alexandria (†444) and Nestorius (†455), patriarch of Constantinople, who was formed in the Antiochene school, revealed that the real issue in the question of Mary's title was the unity of Christ's person. The ensuing Council of Ephesus (431) used *Theotókos* (literally 'Godbearer'; in Latin, *Deipara*) to affirm the oneness of Christ's person

by identifying Mary as the Mother of God the Word incarnate.[6] The rule of faith on this matter takes more precise expression in the definition of Chalcedon: 'One and the same Son . . . was begotten from the Father before the ages as to the divinity and in the latter days for us and our salvation was born as to the humanity from Mary the Virgin *Theotókos*.' In receiving the Council of Ephesus and the definition of Chalcedon, Anglicans and Roman Catholics together confess Mary as *Theotókos*.

The Celebration of Mary in the Ancient Common Traditions

35. In the early centuries, communion in Christ included a strong sense of the living presence of the saints as an integral part of the spiritual experience of the churches (Hebrews 12.1, 22–24; Revelation 6.9–11; 7; 8.3–4). Within the 'cloud of witnesses', the Lord's mother came to be seen to have a special place. Themes developed from Scripture and in devotional reflection reveal a deep awareness of Mary's role in the redemption of humanity. Such themes include Mary as Eve's counterpart and as a type of the Church. The response of Christian people, reflecting on these themes, found devotional expression in both private and public prayer.

36. Exegetes delighted in drawing feminine imagery from the Scriptures to contemplate the significance both of the Church and Mary. Fathers as early as Justin Martyr (†c.150) and Irenaeus (†c.202), reflecting on texts like Genesis 3 and Luke 1.26–38, developed, alongside the antithesis of Adam/New Adam, that of Eve/New Eve. Just as Eve is associated with Adam in bringing about our defeat, so Mary is associated with her Son in the conquest of the ancient enemy (cf. Genesis 3.15, *vide supra* footnote 4): 'virgin' Eve's disobedience results in death; the Virgin Mary's obedience opens the way to salvation. The New Eve shares in the New Adam's victory over sin and death.

37. The Fathers presented Mary the Virgin Mother as a model of holiness for consecrated virgins, and increasingly taught that she had remained 'Ever Virgin'.[7] In their reflection, virginity was understood not only as

---

[6] The Council solemnly approved the content of the Second Letter of Cyril to Nestorius: 'It was not that an ordinary man was born first of the holy Virgin, on whom afterwards the Word descended; what we say is that: being united with the flesh from the womb, the Word has undergone birth in the flesh . . . therefore the Holy Fathers had the courage to call the Holy Virgin *Theotókos*.' (DS 251)

[7] The Tome of Leo, which was decisive for the outcome of the Council of Chalcedon (451), states that Christ 'was conceived by the Holy Spirit in the womb of the Virgin Mother, who gave him birth without losing her virginity, as she conceived him without losing her virginity' (DS 291). Similarly Athanasius

physical integrity, but as an interior disposition of openness, obedience, and single-hearted fidelity to Christ which models Christian disciple-ship and issues in spiritual fruitfulness.

38. In this patristic understanding, Mary's virginity was closely related to her sanctity. Although some early exegetes thought that Mary was not wholly without sin,[8] Augustine (†430) witnessed to contemporary reluctance to speak of any sin in her.

> We must except the holy Virgin Mary, concerning whom I wish to raise no question when it touches the subject of sins, out of honour to the Lord; for from him we know what abundance of grace for overcoming sin in every particular was conferred on her who had the merit to conceive and bear him who undoubtedly had no sin.
>
> (*De natura et gratia* 36.42)

Other Fathers from West and East, appealing to the angelic saluta-tion (Luke 1.28) and Mary's response (Luke 1.38), support the view that Mary was filled with grace from her origin in anticipation of her unique vocation as Mother of the Lord. By the fifth century they hail her as a new creation: blameless, spotless, 'holy in body and soul' (Theodotus of Ancyra, *Homily* 6,11: †before 446). By the sixth century, the title *panaghia* ('all holy') can be found in the East.

39. Following the Christological debates at the councils of Ephesus and Chalcedon, devotion to Mary flourished. When the patriarch of Antioch refused Mary the title of *Theotókos*, Emperor Leo I (457–474) com-manded the patriarch of Constantinople to insert this title into the eucharistic prayer throughout the East. By the sixth century, com-memoration of Mary as 'God-bearer' had become universal in the eucharistic prayers of East and West (with the exception of the Assyrian Church of the East). Texts and images celebrating Mary's holiness were multiplied in liturgical poetry and songs, such as the *Akathist*, a hymn probably written soon after Chalcedon and still

---

speaks in *De Virginitate* (*Le Muséon* 42: 244.248) of "Mary, who . . . remained a virgin to the end [as a model for] all to come after her.' Cf. John Chrysostom (†407) *Homily on Matthew* 5,3. The first Ecumenical Council to use the term *Aeiparthenos* (*semper virgo*) was the Second Council of Constantinople (553). This designation is already implicit in the classical Western formulation of Mary's *virginitas* as *ante partum, in partu, post partum*. This tradition appears consistently in the western Church from Ambrose onward. As Augustine wrote, 'she conceived him as a virgin, she gave birth as a virgin, she remained a virgin' (*Sermo* 51.18; cf. *Sermo* 196.1).

[8] Thus Irenaeus criticises her for 'excessive haste' at Cana, 'seeking to push her son into performing a miracle before his hour had come' (*Adversus Haereses* III.16.7); Origen speaks of her wavering in faith at the cross, 'so she too would have some sin for which Christ died' (*Homilia in Lucam*, 17,6). Suggestions like these are found in the writings of Tertullian, Ambrose and John Chrysostom.

sung in the Eastern church. A tradition of praying with and praising Mary was thus gradually established. This has been associated since the fourth century, especially in the East, with asking for her protection.[9]

40. After the Council of Ephesus, churches began to be dedicated to Mary and feasts in her honour began to be celebrated on particular days in these churches. Prompted by popular piety and gradually adopted by local churches, feasts celebrating Mary's conception (December 8/9), birth (September 8), presentation (November 21), and dormition (August 15) mirrored the liturgical commemorations of events in the life of the Lord. They drew both on the canonical Scriptures and also on apocryphal accounts of Mary's early life and her 'falling asleep'. A feast of the conception of Mary can be dated in the East to the late seventh century, and was introduced into the Western church through southern England in the early eleventh century. It drew on popular devotion expressed in the second century *Protoevangelium of James*, and paralleled the dominical feast of the annunciation and the existing feast of the conception of John the Baptist. The feast of Mary's 'falling asleep' dates from the end of the sixth century, but was influenced by legendary narratives of the end of Mary's life already widely in circulation. In the West, the most influential of them are the *Transitus Mariae*. In the East the feast was known as the 'dormition', which implied her death but did not exclude her being taken into heaven. In the West the term used was 'assumption', which emphasised her being taken into heaven but did not exclude the possibility of her dying. Belief in her assumption was grounded in the promise of the resurrection of the dead and the recognition of Mary's dignity as *Theotókos* and 'Ever Virgin', coupled with the conviction that she who had borne Life should be associated to her Son's victory over death, and with the glorification of his Body, the Church.

---

[9] Witness the invocation of Mary in the early text known traditionally as *Sub tuum praesidium*: Ὑπὸ τὴν σὴν εὐσπλαγχνίαν, καταφεύγομεν, Θεοτόκε. Τὰς ἡμῶν ἰκεσίας, μὴ παρίδης ἐν περιστάσει, ἀλλ᾽ ἐκ κινδύνων ῥῦσαι λύτρωσαι ἡμᾶς, μόνη Ἁγνή, μόνη εὐλογημένη. (Cf. O. Stegemüller, *Sub tuum praesidium. Bemerkungen zur ältesten Überlieferung*, in: *ZKTh* 74 [1952], pp. 76–82 [77]). This text (with two changes) is used to this day in the Greek liturgical tradition; versions of this prayer also occur in the Ambrosian, Roman, Byzantine and Coptic liturgies. A familiar English version is: 'We fly to thy protection, O holy Mother of God; despise not our petitions in our necessities but deliver us from all dangers, O ever glorious and blessed Virgin.'

The Growth of Marian Doctrine and Devotion in the Middle Ages

41. The spread of these feasts of Mary gave rise to homilies in which preachers delved into the Scriptures, searching for types and motifs to illuminate the Virgin's place in the economy of salvation. During the High Middle Ages a growing emphasis on the humanity of Christ was matched by attention to the exemplary virtues of Mary. Bernard, for example, articulates this emphasis in his homilies. Meditation on the lives of both Christ and Mary became increasingly popular, and gave rise to the development of such devotional practices as the rosary. The paintings, sculptures and stained glass of the High and late Middle Ages lent to this devotion immediacy and colour.

42. During these centuries there were some major shifts of emphasis in theological reflection about Mary. Theologians of the High Middle Ages developed patristic reflection on Mary as a 'type' of the Church, and also as the New Eve, in a way that associated her ever more closely with Christ in the continuing work of redemption. The centre of attention of believers shifted from Mary as representing the faithful Church, and so also redeemed humanity, to Mary as dispensing Christ's graces to the faithful. Scholastic theologians in the West developed an increasingly elaborate body of doctrine about Mary in her own right. Much of this doctrine grew out of speculation about the holiness and sanctification of Mary. Questions about this were influenced not only by the scholastic theology of grace and original sin, but also by presuppositions concerning procreation and the relation between soul and body. For example, if she were sanctified in the womb of her mother, more perfectly even than John the Baptist and Jeremiah, some theologians thought that the precise moment of her sanctification had to be determined according to the current understanding of when the 'rational soul' was infused into the body. Theological developments in the Western doctrine of grace and sin raised other questions: how could Mary be free of all sin, including original sin, without jeopardising the role of Christ as universal Saviour? Speculative reflection led to intense discussions about how Christ's redeeming grace may have preserved Mary from original sin. The measured theology of Mary's sanctification found in the *Summa Theologiae* of Thomas Aquinas, and the subtle reasoning of Duns Scotus about Mary, were deployed in extended controversy over whether Mary was immaculate from the first moment of her conception.

43. In the Late Middle Ages, scholastic theology grew increasingly apart from spirituality. Less and less rooted in scriptural exegesis, theologians relied on logical probability to establish their positions, and Nominalists speculated on what could be done by the absolute power and will of God. Spirituality, no longer in creative tension with theology, emphasised affectivity and personal experience. In popular religion, Mary came widely to be viewed as an intermediary between God and humanity, and even as a worker of miracles with powers that verged on the divine. This popular piety in due course influenced the theological opinions of those who had grown up with it, and who subsequently elaborated a theological rationale for the florid Marian devotion of the Late Middle Ages.

From the Reformation to the Present Day

44. One powerful impulse for Reformation in the early sixteenth century was a widespread reaction against devotional practices which approached Mary as a mediatrix alongside Christ, or sometimes even in his place. Such exaggerated devotions, in part inspired by presentations of Christ as inaccessible Judge as well as Redeemer, were sharply criticised by Erasmus and Thomas More and decisively rejected by the Reformers. Together with a radical re-reception of Scripture as the fundamental touchstone of divine revelation, there was a re-reception by the Reformers of the belief that Jesus Christ is the only mediator between God and humanity. This entailed a rejection of real and perceived abuses surrounding devotion to Mary. It led also to the loss of some positive aspects of devotion and the diminution of her place in the life of the Church.

45. In this context, the English Reformers continued to receive the doctrine of the ancient Church concerning Mary. Their positive teaching about Mary concentrated on her role in the Incarnation: it is summed up in their acceptance of her as the *Theotókos*, because this was seen to be both scriptural and in accord with ancient common tradition. Following the traditions of the early Church and other Reformers like Martin Luther, the English Reformers such as Latimer (*Works*, 2.105), Cranmer (*Works*, 2.60; 2.88) and Jewel (*Works*, 3.440–441) accepted that Mary was 'Ever Virgin'. Following Augustine, they showed a reticence about affirming that Mary was a sinner. Their chief concern was to emphasise the unique sinlessness of Christ, and the need of all humankind, including Mary, for a Saviour (cf. Luke 1.47). Articles IX and XV affirmed the universality of human

sinfulness. They neither affirmed nor denied the possibility of Mary having been preserved by grace from participation in this general human condition. It is notable that the *Book of Common Prayer* in the Christmas collect and preface refers to Mary as 'a pure Virgin'.

46. From 1561, the calendar of the Church of England (which was reproduced in the 1662 *Book of Common Prayer*) contained five feasts associated with Mary: Conception of Mary, Nativity of Mary, Annunciation, Visitation, and Purification / Presentation. There was, however, no longer a feast of the Assumption (August 15): not only was it understood to lack scriptural warrant, but was also seen as exalting Mary at the expense of Christ. Anglican liturgy, as expressed in the successive *Books of Common Prayer* (1549, 1552, 1559, 1662) when it mentions Mary, gives prominence to her role as the 'pure Virgin' from whose 'substance' the Son took human nature (cf. Article II). In spite of the diminution of devotion to Mary in the sixteenth century, reverence for her endured in the continued use of the *Magnificat* in Evening Prayer, and the unchanged dedication of ancient churches and Lady Chapels. In the seventeenth century writers such as Lancelot Andrewes, Jeremy Taylor and Thomas Ken re-appropriated from patristic tradition a fuller appreciation of the place of Mary in the prayers of the believer and of the Church. For example, Andrewes in his *Preces Privatae* borrowed from Eastern liturgies when he showed a warmth of Marian devotion 'Commemorating the all holy, immaculate, more than blessed mother of God and ever virgin Mary.' This re-appropriation can be traced into the next century, and into the Oxford Movement of the nineteenth century.

47. In the Roman Catholic Church, the continued growth of Marian doctrine and devotion, while moderated by the reforming decrees of the Council of Trent (1545–63), also suffered the distorting influence of Protestant–Catholic polemics. To be Roman Catholic came to be identified by an emphasis on devotion to Mary. The depth and popularity of Marian spirituality in the nineteenth and the first half of the twentieth centuries contributed to the definitions of the dogmas of the Immaculate Conception (1854) and the Assumption (1950). On the other hand, the pervasiveness of this spirituality began to give rise to criticism both within and beyond the Roman Catholic Church and initiated a process of re-reception. This re-reception was evident in the Second Vatican Council which, consonant with

the contemporary biblical, patristic, and liturgical renewals, and with concern for ecumenical sensitivities, chose not to draft a separate document on Mary, but to integrate doctrine about her into the Constitution on the Church, *Lumen Gentium* (1964)—more specifically, into its final section describing the eschatological pilgrimage of the Church (Chapter VIII). The Council intended 'to explain carefully both the role of the Blessed Virgin in the mystery of the Word Incarnate and of the Mystical Body, as well as the duties of the redeemed human race towards the God-bearer, mother of Christ and mother of humanity, especially of the faithful' (art. 54). *Lumen Gentium* concludes by calling Mary a sign of hope and comfort for God's pilgrim people (art. 68–69). The Fathers of the Council consciously sought to resist exaggerations by returning to patristic emphases and placing Marian doctrine and devotion in its proper Christological and ecclesial context.

48. Soon after the Council, faced by an unanticipated decline in devotion to Mary, Pope Paul VI published an Apostolic Exhortation, *Marialis Cultus* (1974), to remove doubts about the Council's intentions and to foster appropriate Marian devotion. His review of the place of Mary in the revised Roman rite showed that she has not been 'demoted' by the liturgical renewal, but that devotion to her is properly located within the Christological focus of the Church's public prayer. He reflected on Mary as 'a model of the spiritual attitudes with which the Church celebrates and lives the divine mysteries' (art. 16). She is the model for the whole Church, but also a 'teacher of the spiritual life for individual Christians' (art. 21). According to Paul VI, the authentic renewal of Marian devotion must be integrated with the doctrines of God, Christ, and the Church. Devotion to Mary must be in accordance with the Scriptures and the liturgy of the Church; it must be sensitive to the concerns of other Christians and it must affirm the full dignity of women in public and private life. The Pope also issued cautions to those who err either by exaggeration or neglect. Finally, he commended the recitation of the *Angelus* and the Rosary as traditional devotions which are compatible with these norms. In 2002, Pope John Paul II reinforced the Christological focus of the Rosary by proposing five 'mysteries of Light' from the Gospels' account of Christ's public ministry between his Baptism and Passion. 'The Rosary,' he states, 'though clearly Marian in character, is at heart a Christocentric prayer' (*Rosarium Virginis Mariae* 1).

49. Mary has a new prominence in Anglican worship through the liturgical renewals of the twentieth century. In most Anglican prayer books, Mary is again mentioned by name in the eucharistic prayers. Further, August 15th has come to be widely celebrated as a principal feast in honour of Mary with Scripture readings, collect and proper preface. Other feasts associated with Mary have also been renewed, and liturgical resources offered for use on these festivals. Given the definitive role of authorised liturgical texts and practices in Anglican formularies, such developments are highly significant.

50. The above developments show that in recent decades a re-reception of the place of Mary in corporate worship has been taking place across the Anglican Communion. At the same time, in *Lumen Gentium* (Chapter VIII) and the Exhortation *Marialis Cultus* the Roman Catholic Church has attempted to set devotion to Mary within the context of the teaching of Scripture and the ancient common tradition. This constitutes, for the Roman Catholic Church, a re-reception of teaching about Mary. Revision of the calendars and lectionaries used in our Communions, especially the liturgical provision associated with feasts of Mary, gives evidence of a shared process of re-receiving the scriptural testimony to her place in the faith and life of the Church. Growing ecumenical exchange has contributed to the process of re-reception in both Communions.

51. The Scriptures lead us together to praise and bless Mary as the handmaid of the Lord, who was providentially prepared by divine grace to be the mother of our Redeemer. Her unqualified assent to the fulfilment of God's saving plan can be seen as the supreme instance of a believer's 'Amen' in response to the 'Yes' of God. She stands as a model of holiness, obedience and faith for all Christians. As one who received the Word in her heart and in her body, and brought it forth into the world, Mary belongs in the prophetic tradition. We are agreed in our belief in the Blessed Virgin Mary as *Theotókos*. Our two communions are both heirs to a rich tradition which recognises Mary as ever virgin, and sees her as the new Eve and as a type of the Church. We join in praying and praising with Mary whom all generations have called blessed, in observing her festivals and according her honour in the communion of the saints, and are agreed that Mary and the saints pray for the whole Church (see below in section D). In all of this, we see Mary as inseparably linked with Christ and the Church. Within this broad consideration of the role of Mary, we now focus on the theology of hope and grace.

C. MARY WITHIN THE PATTERN OF GRACE AND HOPE

52. Participation in the glory of God, through the mediation of the Son, in the power of the Spirit is the Gospel hope (cf. 2 Corinthians 3.18; 4.4–6). The Church already enjoys this hope and destiny through the Holy Spirit, who is the 'pledge' of our inheritance in Christ (Ephesians 1.14, 2 Corinthians 5.5). For Paul especially, what it means to be fully human can only be understood rightly when it is viewed in the light of what we are to become in Christ, the 'last Adam', as opposed to what we had become in the old Adam (1 Corinthians 15.42–49, cf. Romans 5.12–21). This eschatological perspective sees Christian life in terms of the vision of the exalted Christ leading believers to cast off sins that entangle (Hebrews 12.1–2) and to participate in his purity and love, made available through his atoning sacrifice (1 John 3.3; 4.10). We thus view the economy of grace from its fulfilment in Christ 'back' into history, rather than 'forward' from its beginning in fallen creation towards the future in Christ. This perspective offers fresh light in which to consider the place of Mary.

53. The hope of the Church is based upon the testimony it has received about the present glory of Christ. The Church proclaims that Christ was not only raised bodily from the tomb, but was exalted to the right hand of the Father, to share in the Father's glory (1 Timothy 3.16, 1 Peter 1.21). Insofar as believers are united with Christ in baptism and share in Christ's sufferings (Romans 6.1–6), they participate through the Spirit in his glory, and are raised up with him in anticipation of the final revelation (cf. Romans 8.17, Ephesians 2.6, Colossians 3.1). It is the destiny of the Church and of its members, the 'saints' chosen in Christ 'before the foundation of the world', to be 'holy and blameless' and to share in the glory of Christ (Ephesians 1.3–5, 5.27). Paul speaks as it were from the future retrospectively, when he says, 'those whom God predestined he also called; those whom he called he also justified; and those whom he justified he also glorified' (Romans 8.30). In the succeeding chapters of Romans, Paul explicates this many-faceted drama of God's election in Christ, keeping in view its end: the inclusion of the Gentiles, so that 'all Israel shall be saved' (Romans 11.26).

Mary in the Economy of Grace

54. Within this biblical framework we have considered afresh the distinctive place of the Virgin Mary in the economy of grace, as the one

who bore Christ, the elect of God. The word of God delivered by Gabriel addresses her as already 'graced', inviting her to respond in faith and freedom to God's call (Luke 1.28, 38, 45). The Spirit is operative within her in the conception of the Saviour, and this 'blessed among women' is inspired to sing 'all generations will call me blessed' (Luke 1.42, 48). Viewed eschatologically, Mary thus embodies the 'elect Israel' of whom Paul speaks—glorified, justified, called, predestined. This is the pattern of grace and hope which we see at work in the life of Mary, who holds a distinctive place in the common destiny of the Church as the one who bore in her own flesh 'the Lord of glory'. Mary is marked out from the beginning as the one chosen, called and graced by God through the Holy Spirit for the task that lay ahead of her.

55. The Scriptures tell us of barren women who were gifted by God with children—Rachel, Manoah's wife, Hannah (Genesis 30.1–24, Judges 13, 1 Samuel 1), and those past child-bearing—Sarah (Genesis 18.9–15, 21.1–7), and most notably Mary's cousin, Elizabeth (Luke 1.7, 24). These women highlight the singular role of Mary, who was neither barren nor past child-bearing age, but a fruitful virgin: in her womb the Spirit brought about the conception of Jesus. The Scriptures also speak of God's care for all human beings, even before their coming to birth (Psalm 139.13–18), and recount the action of God's grace preceding the specific calling of particular persons, even from their conception (cf. Jeremiah 1.4–5, Luke 1.15, Galatians 1.15). With the early Church, we see in Mary's acceptance of the divine will the fruit of her prior preparation, signified in Gabriel's affirmation of her as 'graced'. We can thus see that God was at work in Mary from her earliest beginnings, preparing her for the unique vocation of bearing in her own flesh the new Adam, in whom all things in heaven and earth hold together (cf. Colossians 1.16–17). Of Mary, both personally and as a representative figure, we can say she is 'God's workmanship, created in Christ Jesus for good works which God prepared beforehand' (Ephesians 2.10).

56. Mary, a pure virgin, bore God incarnate in her womb. Her bodily intimacy with her son was all of a piece with her faithful following of him, and her maternal participation in his victorious self-giving (Luke 2.35). All this is clearly testified in Scripture, as we have seen. There is no direct testimony in Scripture concerning the end of Mary's life. However, certain passages give instances of those who follow God's purposes faithfully being drawn into God's presence. Moreover, these

passages offer hints or partial analogies that may throw light on the mystery of Mary's entry into glory. For instance, the biblical pattern of anticipated eschatology appears in the account of Stephen, the first martyr (Acts 7.54–60). At the moment of his death, which conforms to that of his Lord, he sees 'the glory of God, and Jesus' the 'Son of Man' not seated in judgement, but 'standing at the right hand of God' to welcome his faithful servant. Similarly, the penitent thief who calls on the crucified Christ is accorded the special promise of being with Christ immediately in Paradise (Luke 23.43). God's faithful servant Elijah is taken up by a whirlwind into heaven (2 Kings 2.11), and of Enoch it is written, 'he was attested as having pleased God' as a man of faith, and was therefore 'taken up so that he should not see death; and he was not found because God had taken him' (Hebrews 11.5, cf. Genesis 5.24). Within such a pattern of anticipated eschatology, Mary can also be seen as the faithful disciple fully present with God in Christ. In this way, she is a sign of hope for all humanity.

57. The pattern of hope and grace already foreshadowed in Mary will be fulfilled in the new creation in Christ when all the redeemed will participate in the full glory of the Lord (cf. 2 Corinthians 3.18). Christian experience of communion with God in this present life is a sign and foretaste of divine grace and glory, a hope shared with the whole of creation (Romans 8.18–23). The individual believer and the Church find their consummation in the new Jerusalem, the holy bride of Christ (cf. Revelation 21.2, Ephesians 5.27). When Christians from East and West through the generations have pondered God's work in Mary, they have discerned in faith (cf. *Gift* 29) that it is fitting that the Lord gathered her wholly to himself: in Christ, she is already a new creation in whom 'the old has passed away and the new has come' (2 Corinthians 5.17). Viewed from such an eschatological perspective, Mary may be seen both as a type of the Church, and as a disciple with a special place in the economy of salvation.

The Papal Definitions

58. Thus far we have outlined our common faith concerning the place of Mary in the divine purpose. Roman Catholic Christians, however, are bound to believe the teaching defined by Pope Pius XII in 1950: 'that the Immaculate Mother of God, the ever Virgin Mary, having completed the course of her earthly life, was assumed body and soul into heavenly glory.' We note that the dogma does not adopt a

particular position as to how Mary's life ended,[10] nor does it use about her the language of death and resurrection, but celebrates the action of God in her. Thus, given the understanding we have reached concerning the place of Mary in the economy of hope and grace, we can affirm together the teaching that God has taken the Blessed Virgin Mary in the fullness of her person into his glory as consonant with Scripture and that it can, indeed, only be understood in the light of Scripture. Roman Catholics can recognise that this teaching about Mary is contained in the dogma. While the calling and destiny of all the redeemed is their glorification in Christ, Mary, as *Theotókos*, holds the pre-eminent place within the communion of saints and embodies the destiny of the Church.

59. Roman Catholics are also bound to believe that 'the most blessed Virgin Mary was, from the first moment of her conception, by a singular grace and privilege of almighty God and in view of the merits of Christ Jesus the Saviour of the human race, preserved immune from all stain of original sin' (Dogma of the Immaculate Conception of Mary, defined by Pope Pius IX, 1854).[11] The definition teaches that Mary, like all other human beings, has need of Christ as her Saviour and Redeemer (cf. *Lumen Gentium* 53; *Catechism of the Catholic Church* 491). The negative notion of 'sinlessness' runs the risk of obscuring the fullness of Christ's saving work. It is not so much that Mary lacks something which other human beings 'have', namely sin, but that the glorious grace of God filled her life from the beginning.[12] The holiness which is our end in Christ (cf. 1 John 3.2–3) was seen, by unmerited grace, in Mary, who is the prototype of the hope of grace for humankind as a whole. According to the

---

[10] The reference in the dogma to Mary being assumed 'body and soul' has caused difficulty for some, on historical and philosophical grounds. The dogma leaves open, however, the question as to what the absence of her mortal remains means in historical terms. Likewise, 'assumed body and soul' is not intended to privilege a particular anthropology. More positively, 'assumed body and soul' can be seen to have Christological and ecclesiological implications. Mary as 'God bearer' is intimately, indeed bodily, related to Christ: his own bodily glorification now embraces hers. And, since Mary bore his body of flesh, she is intimately related to the Church, Christ's body. In brief, the formulation of the dogma responds to theological rather than historical or philosophical questions in relation to Mary.

[11] The definition addressed an old controversy about the timing of the sanctification of Mary, in affirming that this took place at the very first moment of her conception.

[12] The assertion of Paul at Romans 3.23—'all have sinned and fall short of the glory of God'—might appear to allow for no exceptions, not even for Mary. However, it is important to note the rhetorical-apologetic context of the general argument of Romans 1–3, which is concerned to show the equal sinfulness of Jews and Gentiles (3.9). Romans 3.23 has a quite specific purpose in context which is unrelated to the issue of the 'sinlessness' or otherwise of Mary.

New Testament, being 'graced' has the connotation of being freed from sin through Christ's blood (Ephesians 1.6–7). The Scriptures point to the efficacy of Christ's atoning sacrifice even for those who preceded him in time (cf. 1 Peter 3.19, John 8.56, 1 Corinthians 10.4). Here again the eschatological perspective illuminates our understanding of Mary's person and calling. In view of her vocation to be the mother of the Holy One (Luke 1.35), we can affirm together that Christ's redeeming work reached 'back' in Mary to the depths of her being, and to her earliest beginnings. This is not contrary to the teaching of Scripture, and can only be understood in the light of Scripture. Roman Catholics can recognise in this what is affirmed by the dogma—namely 'preserved from all stain of original sin' and 'from the first moment of her conception.'

60. We have agreed together that the teaching about Mary in the two definitions of 1854 and 1950, understood within the biblical pattern of the economy of grace and hope outlined here, can be said to be consonant with the teaching of the Scriptures and the ancient common traditions. However, in Roman Catholic understanding as expressed in these two definitions, the proclamation of any teaching as dogma implies that the teaching in question is affirmed to be 'revealed by God' and therefore to be believed 'firmly and constantly' by all the faithful (i.e. it is *de fide*). The problem which the dogmas may present for Anglicans can be put in terms of Article VI:

> Holy Scripture containeth all things necessary to salvation: so that whatsoever is not read therein, nor may be proved thereby, is not to be required of any man, that it should be believed as an article of the Faith, or be thought requisite or necessary to salvation.

We agree that nothing can be required to be believed as an article of faith unless it is revealed by God. The question arises for Anglicans, however, as to whether these doctrines concerning Mary are revealed by God in a way which must be held by believers as a matter of faith.

61. The particular circumstances and precise formulations of the 1854 and 1950 definitions have created problems not only for Anglicans but also for other Christians. The formulations of these doctrines and some objections to them are situated within the thought-forms of their time. In particular, the phrases 'revealed by God' (1854) and 'divinely revealed' (1950) used in the dogmas reflect the theology of

revelation that was dominant in the Roman Catholic Church at the time that the definitions were made, and which found authoritative expression in the Constitution *Dei Filius* of the First Vatican Council. They have to be understood today in the light of the way this teaching was refined by the Second Vatican Council in its Constitution *Dei Verbum*, particularly in regard to the central role of Scripture in the reception and transmission of revelation. When the Roman Catholic Church affirms that a truth is 'revealed by God', there is no suggestion of new revelation. Rather, the definitions are understood to bear witness to what has been revealed from the beginning. The Scriptures bear normative witness to such revelation (cf. *Gift* 19). This revelation is received by the community of believers and transmitted in time and place through the Scriptures and through the preaching, liturgy, spirituality, life and teaching of the Church, that draw upon the Scriptures. In *The Gift of Authority* the Commission sought to explicate a method by which such authoritative teaching could arise, the key point being that it needs to be in conformity with Scripture, which remains a primary concern for Anglicans and Roman Catholics alike.

62. Anglicans have also questioned whether these doctrines must be held by believers as a matter of faith in view of the fact that the Bishop of Rome defined these doctrines 'independent of a Council' (cf. *Authority* II 30). In response, Roman Catholics have pointed to the *sensus fidelium*, the liturgical tradition throughout the local churches, and the active support of the Roman Catholic bishops (cf. *Gift* 29–30): these were the elements through which these doctrines were recognised as belonging to the faith of the Church, and therefore able to be defined (cf. *Gift* 47). For Roman Catholics, it belongs to the office of the Bishop of Rome that he should be able, under strictly limited conditions, to make such a definition (cf. *Pastor Aeternus* [1870], in *Denzinger-Schönmetzer, Enchiridion Symbolorum* [DS] 3069–3070). The definitions of 1854 and 1950 were not made in response to controversy, but gave voice to the consensus of faith among believers in communion with the Bishop of Rome. They were re-affirmed by the Second Vatican Council. For Anglicans, it would be the consent of an ecumenical council which, teaching according to the Scriptures, most securely demonstrates that the necessary conditions for a teaching to be *de fide* had been met. Where this is the case, as with the definition of the *Theotókos*, both Roman Catholics and Anglicans would agree that the witness of the Church

is firmly and constantly to be believed by all the faithful (cf. 1 John 1.1–3).

63. Anglicans have asked whether it would be a condition of the future restoration of full communion that they should be required to accept the definitions of 1854 and 1950. Roman Catholics find it hard to envisage a restoration of communion in which acceptance of certain doctrines would be requisite for some and not for others. In addressing these issues, we have been mindful that 'one consequence of our separation has been a tendency for Anglicans and Roman Catholics alike to exaggerate the importance of the Marian dogmas in themselves at the expense of the other truths more closely related to the foundation of the Christian faith' (*Authority* II 30). Anglicans and Roman Catholics agree that the doctrines of the Assumption and the Immaculate Conception of Mary must be understood in the light of the more central truth of her identity as *Theotókos*, which itself depends on faith in the Incarnation. We recognise that, following the Second Vatican Council and the teaching of recent Popes, the Christological and ecclesiological context for the Church's doctrine concerning Mary is being re-received within the Roman Catholic Church. We now suggest that the adoption of an eschatological perspective may deepen our shared understanding of the place of Mary in the economy of grace, and the tradition of the Church concerning Mary which both our communions receive. Our hope is that the Roman Catholic Church and the Anglican Communion will recognise a common faith in the agreement concerning Mary which we here offer. Such a re-reception would mean the Marian teaching and devotion within our respective communities, including differences of emphasis, would be seen to be authentic expressions of Christian belief.[13] Any such re-reception would have to take place within the context of a mutual re-reception of an effective teaching authority in the Church, such as that set out in *The Gift of Authority*.

---

[13] In such circumstances, the explicit acceptance of the precise wording of the definitions of 1854 and 1950 might not be required of believers who were not in communion with Rome when they were defined. Conversely, Anglicans would have to accept that the definitions are a legitimate expression of Catholic faith, and are to be respected as such, even if these formulations were not employed by them. There are instances in ecumenical agreement in which what one partner has defined as *de fide* can be expressed by another partner in a different way, as for example in the *Common Christological Declaration between the Catholic Church and the Assyrian Church of the East* (1994) or the *Joint Declaration on the Doctrine of Justification* between the Roman Catholic Church and the Lutheran World Federation (1999).

D MARY IN THE LIFE OF THE CHURCH

64. 'All the promises of God find their "Yes" in Christ: that is why we offer the "Amen" through him, to the glory of God' (2 Corinthians 1.20). God's 'Yes' in Christ takes a distinctive and demanding form as it is addressed to Mary. The profound mystery of 'Christ in you, the hope of glory' (Colossians 1.27) has a unique meaning for her. It enables her to speak the 'Amen' in which, through the Spirit's overshadowing, God's 'Yes' of new creation is inaugurated. As we have seen, this *fiat* of Mary was distinctive, in its openness to God's Word, and in the path to the foot of the cross and beyond on which the Spirit led her. The Scriptures portray Mary as growing in her relationship with Christ: his sharing of her natural family (Luke 2.39) was transcended in her sharing of his eschatological family, those upon whom the Spirit is poured out (Acts 1.14, 2.1–4). Mary's 'Amen' to God's 'Yes' in Christ to her is thus both unique and a model for every disciple and for the life of the Church.

65. One outcome of our study has been awareness of differences in the ways in which the example of Mary living out the grace of God has been appropriated into the devotional lives of our traditions. Whilst both traditions have recognised her special place in the communion of saints, different emphases have marked the way we have experienced her ministry. Anglicans have tended to begin from reflection on the scriptural example of Mary as an inspiration and model for discipleship. Roman Catholics have given prominence to the ongoing ministry of Mary in the economy of grace and the communion of saints. Mary points people to Christ, commending them to him and helping them to share his life. Neither of these general characterisations do full justice to the richness and diversity of either tradition, and the twentieth century witnessed a particular growth in convergence as many Anglicans were drawn into a more active devotion to Mary, and Roman Catholics discovered afresh the scriptural roots of such devotion. We together agree that in understanding Mary as the fullest human example of the life of grace, we are called to reflect on the lessons of her life recorded in Scripture and to join with her as one indeed not dead, but truly alive in Christ. In doing so we walk together as pilgrims in communion with Mary, Christ's foremost disciple, and all those whose participation in the new creation encourages us to be faithful to our calling (cf. 2 Corinthians 5.17, 19).

66. Aware of the distinctive place of Mary in the history of salvation, Christians have given her a special place in their liturgical and private prayer, praising God for what He has done in and through her. In singing the *Magnificat*, they praise God with her; in the Eucharist, they pray with her as they do with all God's people, integrating their prayers in the great communion of saints. They recognise Mary's place in 'the prayer of all the saints' that is being uttered before the throne of God in the heavenly liturgy (Revelation 8.3–4). All these ways of including Mary in praise and prayer belong to our common heritage, as does our acknowledgement of her unique status as *Theotókos*, which gives her a distinctive place within the communion of saints.

Intercession and Mediation in the Communion of Saints

67. The practice of believers asking Mary to intercede for them with her son grew rapidly following her being declared *Theotókos* at the Council of Ephesus. The most common form today of such intercession is the 'Hail Mary'. This form conflates the greetings of Gabriel and Elizabeth to her (Luke 1.28, 42). It was widely used from the fifth century, without the closing phrase, 'pray for us sinners now and at the hour of our death', which was first added in the 15th century, and included in the Roman Breviary by Pius V in 1568. The English Reformers criticised this invocation and similar forms of prayer, because they believed that it threatened the unique mediation of Jesus Christ. Confronted with exaggerated devotion, stemming from excessive exaltation of Mary's role and powers alongside Christ's, they rejected the 'Romish doctrine of . . . the Invocation of Saints' as 'grounded upon no warranty of Scripture, but rather repugnant to the Word of God' (Article XXII). The Council of Trent affirmed that seeking the saints' assistance to obtain favours from God is 'good and useful': such requests are made 'through his Son our Lord Jesus Christ, who is our sole Redeemer and Saviour' (DS 1821). The Second Vatican Council endorsed the continued practice of believers asking Mary to pray for them, emphasizing that 'Mary's maternal role towards the human race in no way obscures or diminishes the unique mediation of Christ, but rather shows its power . . . in no way does it hinder the direct union of believers with Christ, but rather fosters it' (*Lumen Gentium* 60). Therefore the Roman Catholic Church continues to promote devotion to Mary, while reproving those who either exaggerate or minimise Mary's role (*Marialis Cultus* 31). With this background

in mind, we seek a theologically grounded way to draw more closely together in the life of prayer in communion with Christ and his saints.

68. The Scriptures teach that 'there is one mediator between God and humankind, Christ Jesus, himself human, who gave himself as a ransom for all' (1 Timothy 2.5–6). As noted earlier, on the basis of this teaching 'we reject any interpretation of the role of Mary which obscures this affirmation' (*Authority* II 30). It is also true, however, that all ministries of the Church, especially those of Word and sacrament, mediate the grace of God through human beings. These ministries do not compete with the unique mediation of Christ, but rather serve it and have their source within it. In particular, the prayer of the Church does not stand alongside or in place of the intercession of Christ, but is made through him, our Advocate and Mediator (cf. Romans 8.34, Hebrews 7.25, 12.24, 1 John 2.1). It finds both its possibility and practice in and through the Holy Spirit, the other Advocate sent according to Christ's promise (cf. John 14.16–17). Hence asking our brothers and sisters, on earth and in heaven, to pray for us, does not contest the unique mediatory work of Christ, but is rather a means by which, in and through the Spirit, its power may be displayed.

69. In our praying as Christians we address our petitions to God our heavenly Father, in and through Jesus Christ, as the Holy Spirit moves and enables us. All such invocation takes place within the communion which is God's being and gift. In the life of prayer we invoke the name of Christ in solidarity with the whole Church, assisted by the prayers of brothers and sisters of every time and place. As ARCIC has expressed it previously, 'The believer's pilgrimage of faith is lived out with the mutual support of all the people of God. In Christ all the faithful, both living and departed, are bound together in a communion of prayer' (*Salvation and the Church* 22). In the experience of this communion of prayer believers are aware of their continued fellowship with their sisters and brothers who have 'fallen asleep,' the 'great cloud of witnesses' who surround us as we run the race of faith. For some, this intuition means sensing their friends' presence; for some it may mean pondering the issues of life with those who have gone before them in faith. Such intuitive experience affirms our solidarity in Christ with Christians of every time and place, not least with the woman through whom he became 'like us in all things except sin' (Hebrews 4.15).

70. The Scriptures invite Christians to ask their brothers and sisters to pray for them, in and through Christ (cf. James 5.13–15). Those

who are now 'with Christ', untrammelled by sin, share the unceasing prayer and praise which characterises the life of heaven (e.g. Revelation 5.9–14, 7.9–12, 8.3–4). In the light of these testimonies, many Christians have found that requests for assistance in prayer can rightly and effectively be made to those members of the communion of saints distinguished by their holy living (cf. James 5.16–18). It is in this sense that we affirm that asking the saints to pray for us is not to be excluded as unscriptural, though it is not directly taught by the Scriptures to be a required element of life in Christ. Further, we agree that the way such assistance is sought must not obscure believers' direct access to God our heavenly Father, who delights to give good gifts to his children (Matthew 7.11). When, in the Spirit and through Christ, believers address their prayers to God, they are assisted by the prayers of other believers, especially of those who are truly alive in Christ and freed from sin. We note that liturgical forms of prayer are addressed to God: they do not address prayer 'to' the saints, but rather ask them to 'pray for us'. However, in this and other instances, any concept of invocation which blurs the trinitarian economy of grace and hope is to be rejected, as not consonant with Scripture or the ancient common traditions.

The Distinctive Ministry of Mary

71. Among all the saints, Mary takes her place as *Theotókos*: alive in Christ, she abides with the one she bore, still 'highly favoured' in the communion of grace and hope, the exemplar of redeemed humanity, an icon of the Church. Consequently she is believed to exercise a distinctive ministry of assisting others through her active prayer. Many Christians reading the Cana account continue to hear Mary instruct them, 'Do whatever he tells you', and are confident that she draws the attention of her son to their needs: 'they have no wine' (John 2.1–12). Many experience a sense of empathy and solidarity with Mary, especially at key points when the account of her life echoes theirs, for example the acceptance of vocation, the scandal of her pregnancy, the improvised surroundings of her labour, giving birth, and fleeing as a refugee. Portrayals of Mary standing at the foot of the cross, and the traditional portrayal of her receiving the crucified body of Jesus (the *Pietà*), evoke the particular suffering of a mother at the death of her child. Anglicans and Roman Catholics alike are drawn to the mother of Christ, as a figure of tenderness and compassion.

72. The motherly role of Mary, first affirmed in the Gospel accounts of her relationship to Jesus, has been developed in a variety of ways. Christian believers acknowledge Mary to be the mother of God incarnate. As they ponder our Saviour's dying word to the beloved disciple, 'behold your mother' (John 19.27), they may hear an invitation to hold Mary dear as 'mother of the faithful': she will care for them as she cared for her son in his hour of need. Hearing Eve called 'the mother of all living' (Genesis 3.20), they may come to see Mary as mother of the new humanity, active in her ministry of pointing all people to Christ, seeking the welfare of all the living. We are agreed that, while caution is needed in the use of such imagery, it is fitting to apply it to Mary, as a way of honouring her distinctive relationship to her son, and the efficacy in her of his redeeming work.

73. Many Christians find that giving devotional expression to their appreciation for this ministry of Mary enriches their worship of God. Authentic popular devotion to Mary, which by its nature displays a wide individual, regional and cultural diversity, is to be respected. The crowds gathering at some places where Mary is believed to have appeared suggest that such apparitions are an important part of this devotion and provide spiritual comfort. There is need for careful discernment in assessing the spiritual value of any alleged apparition. This has been emphasised in a recent Roman Catholic commentary.

> Private revelation . . . can be a genuine help in understanding the Gospel and living it better at a particular moment in time; therefore it should not be disregarded. It is a help which is offered, but which one is not obliged to use . . . The criterion for the truth and value of a private revelation is therefore its orientation to Christ himself. When it leads us away from him, when it becomes independent of him or even presents itself as another and better plan of salvation, more important than the Gospel, then it certainly does not come from the Holy Spirit.
> (Congregation for the Doctrine of the Faith, *Theological Commentary on the Message of Fatima*, 26 June, 2000)

We are agreed that, within the constraints set down in this teaching to ensure that the honour paid to Christ remains pre-eminent, such private devotion is acceptable, though never required of believers.

74. When Mary was first acknowledged as mother of the Lord by Elizabeth, she responded by praising God and proclaiming his justice for the poor in her *Magnificat* (Luke 1.46–55). In Mary's response we can see an attitude of poverty towards God that reflects the divine commitment

and preference for the poor. In her powerlessness she is exalted by God's favour. Although the witness of her obedience and acceptance of God's will has sometimes been used to encourage passivity and impose servitude on women, it is rightly seen as a radical commitment to God who has mercy on his servant, lifts up the lowly and brings down the mighty. Issues of justice for women and the empowerment of the oppressed have arisen from daily reflection on Mary's remarkable song. Inspired by her words, communities of women and men in various cultures have committed themselves to work with the poor and the excluded. Only when joy is joined with justice and peace do we rightly share in the economy of hope and grace which Mary proclaims and embodies.

75. Affirming together unambiguously Christ's unique mediation, which bears fruit in the life of the Church, we do not consider the practice of asking Mary and the saints to pray for us as communion-dividing. Since obstacles of the past have been removed by clarification of doctrine, by liturgical reform and practical norms in keeping with it, we believe that there is no continuing theological reason for ecclesial division on these matters.

CONCLUSION

76. Our study, which opens with a careful ecclesial and ecumenical reading of the Scriptures, in the light of the ancient common traditions, has illuminated in a new way the place of Mary in the economy of hope and grace. We together re-affirm the agreements reached previously by ARCIC, in *Authority in the Church* II 30:

- that any interpretation of the role of Mary must not obscure the unique mediation of Christ;
- that any consideration of Mary must be linked with the doctrines of Christ and the Church;
- that we recognise the Blessed Virgin Mary as the *Theotókos*, the mother of God incarnate, and so observe her festivals and accord her honour among the saints;
- that Mary was prepared by grace to be the mother of our Redeemer, by whom she herself was redeemed and received into glory;
- that we recognise Mary as a model of holiness, faith and obedience for all Christians; and
- that Mary can be seen as a prophetic figure of the Church.

We believe that the present statement significantly deepens and extends these agreements, setting them within a comprehensive study of doctrine and devotion associated with Mary.

77. We are convinced that any attempt to come to a reconciled understanding of these matters must begin by listening to God's word in the Scriptures. Therefore our common statement commences with a careful exploration of the rich New Testament witness to Mary, in the light of overall themes and patterns in the Scriptures as a whole.

- This study has led us to the conclusion that it is impossible to be faithful to Scripture without giving due attention to the person of Mary (paragraphs 6–30).
- In recalling together the ancient common traditions, we have discerned afresh the central importance of the *Theotókos* in the Christological controversies, and the Fathers' use of biblical images to interpret and celebrate Mary's place in the plan of salvation (paragraphs 31–40).
- We have reviewed the growth of devotion to Mary in the medieval centuries, and the theological controversies associated with them. We have seen how some excesses in late medieval devotion, and reactions against them by the Reformers, contributed to the breach of communion between us, following which attitudes toward Mary took divergent paths (paragraphs 41–46).
- We have also noted evidence of subsequent developments in both our Communions, which opened the way for a re-reception of the place of Mary in the faith and life of the Church (paragraphs 47–51).
- This growing convergence has also allowed us to approach in a fresh way the questions about Mary which our two Communions have set before us. In doing so, we have framed our work within the pattern of grace and hope which we discover in Scripture—'predestined . . . called . . . justified . . . glorified' (Romans 8.30) (paragraphs 52–57).

Advances in Agreement

78. As a result of our study, the Commission offers the following agreements, which we believe significantly advance our consensus regarding Mary. We affirm together

- the teaching that God has taken the Blessed Virgin Mary in the fullness of her person into his glory as consonant with Scripture, and only to be understood in the light of Scripture (paragraph 58);

- that in view of her vocation to be the mother of the Holy One, Christ's redeeming work reached 'back' in Mary to the depths of her being and to her earliest beginnings (paragraph 59);
- that the teaching about Mary in the two definitions of the Assumption and the Immaculate Conception, understood within the biblical pattern of the economy of hope and grace, can be said to be consonant with the teaching of the Scriptures and the ancient common traditions (paragraph 60);
- that this agreement, when accepted by our two Communions, would place the questions about authority which arise from the two definitions of 1854 and 1950 in a new ecumenical context (paragraphs 61–63);
- that Mary has a continuing ministry which serves the ministry of Christ, our unique mediator, that Mary and the saints pray for the whole Church and that the practice of asking Mary and the saints to pray for us is not communion-dividing (paragraphs 64–75).

79. We agree that doctrines and devotions which are contrary to Scripture cannot be said to be revealed by God nor to be the teaching of the Church. We agree that doctrine and devotion which focuses on Mary, including claims to 'private revelations', must be moderated by carefully expressed norms which ensure the unique and central place of Jesus Christ in the life of the Church, and that Christ alone, together with the Father and the Holy Spirit, is to be worshipped in the Church.

80. Our statement has sought not to clear away all possible problems, but to deepen our common understanding to the point where remaining diversities of devotional practice may be received as the varied work of the Spirit amongst all the people of God. We believe that the agreement we have here outlined is itself the product of a re-reception by Anglicans and Roman Catholics of doctrine about Mary and that it points to the possibility of further reconciliation, in which issues concerning doctrine and devotion to Mary need no longer be seen as communion-dividing, or an obstacle in a new stage of our growth into visible *koinonia*. This agreed statement is now offered to our respective authorities. It may also in itself prove a valuable study of the teaching of the Scriptures and the ancient common traditions about the Blessed Virgin Mary, the Mother of God incarnate. Our hope is that, as we share in the one Spirit by which Mary was prepared and sanctified for her unique vocation, we may together participate with her and all the saints in the unending praise of God.

Responses

Of all the Statements issued by ARCIC II, the responses to *Mary: Grace and Hope in Christ* have been both the greatest in number, and the most varied in assessing its content.[1] The variety and number of responses indicate the complexities involved in the formation of doctrine as it develops. Since the Roman Catholic Church's distinctive teaching about Mary followed the sixteenth-century breach of communion, it is not surprising that ecclesial responses have come predominantly from the Anglican side, and from Evangelicals in particular. Academic analyses, however, have come from both Roman Catholic and Anglican scholars, in similar numbers: while raising concerns about points of detail, they are broadly positive.

Official Commentaries

The official Anglican and Roman Catholic commentaries, prepared by Timothy Bradshaw and Jared Wicks SJ respectively and issued at the same time as the Statement, are included in the *Study Guide* prepared by the Commission's co-secretaries.[2] They approach *Mary* in similar ways, setting the dialogue in its ecclesial contexts and then working through each part. Bradshaw raises questions for Anglicans readers to consider; Wicks offers additional material relevant to Roman Catholic audiences. Both assess the Statement against the Commission's mandate, as seen from the perspective of the Anglican and Roman Catholic traditions respectively. Both realize that the issues have to do with distinctively Roman Catholic belief and practice regarding Mary, so that the discussion is necessarily asymmetric.

Bradshaw's questions turn around how Anglicans relate to ARCIC's use of Scripture (where he sees 'much common ground', though querying the Commission's exegesis of the siblings of Jesus); assessment of historical developments; and the extent to which the language of the 1854 and 1950 dogmas is to be understood as 'literal' or 'symbolic'. More sharply, Bradshaw asks whether what the Statement calls the 'Distinctive Ministry of Mary'

---

[1] Publication details of responses are given in the Bibliography on pp. 237–41 below, which focuses on ecclesial and academic responses: it does not include the many media reports and popular commentaries.

[2] Timothy Bradshaw, 'The Anglican Commentary', and Jared Wicks SJ, 'The Roman Catholic Commentary', in Donald Bolen and Gregory Cameron (eds.), *Mary: Grace and Hope in Christ. The Text with commentaries and Study Guide* (London: Continuum, 2006), 133–65 and 167–203 respectively.

'seems to echo that of the Paraclete and Holy Spirit'.[3] The crucial theological issue is how Christians 'view the Church spanning earth and heaven ... and the legitimacy of contacting those heavenly disciples in glory for help and comfort here and now'.[4] Bradshaw concludes that 'ARCIC has been honest in producing a document in basically a Roman Catholic mode so that Anglicans can get the feel of what is being needed by Roman Catholics in any reunited Church'. He ends by writing that 'Mary herself, whatever her present role in heaven, must be saddened to know she is a focus of disagreement ... and will be rejoicing that efforts are being made to remedy this.'

In the Introduction to his Commentary, Wicks states that 'The Commission has responded admirably' to its mandate. He notes that 're-reception', as developed by the Commission in *The Gift of Authority*, is central to the method and conclusions of *Mary*.[5] As regards Mary in Scripture (Part A), he detects a perceived shift from 'narrative' (the Synoptic Gospels) to 'symbolic' readings (John—see further below). On Part B he offers explanatory comments on medieval developments in Marian devotion, and in Part C he pays attention to the precise wording of the Statement in relation to each dogma, and how in Part D it offers a 'reconciled diversity' regarding invocation of Mary. Overall, Wicks is warmly positive about *Mary*, with its 'luminous framework ... of a largely Pauline doctrine of our graced end and destiny' and its sensitivity to changing theological contexts in the Second Vatican Council and subsequent papal teaching. More, 'At least two characteristics of *Mary: Grace and Hope in Christ* make it unique among documents produced recently by bilateral ecumenical commissions.' First is the Commission's employing a biblical hermeneutic which seeks to integrate different methods: critical, grammatico-historical, and typological. Wicks sees this as not wholly successful, however, arguing that its symbolic aspect does not feed through fully into

---

[3] Bradshaw, 'The Anglican Commentary', 161; cf. 158.

[4] Ibid., 167. Bradshaw describes the method of Part C as 'that of reading back from fulfilment to inception' (ibid., 152), but discusses the conception and earthly end of Mary in that order, which the Statement deliberately reversed (*Mary*, §§58, 59). He also sees this method as 'strikingly reminiscent' of the 'paradoxical' Christology of Donald Baillie (*God was in Christ*, London: Faber & Faber, 1961, chapter 5). This 'has been found by critics to offer a picture of inspiration rather than full incarnation' (Bradshaw, 'The Anglican Commentary', 154). Applied to Mary, however, the distinction is apposite, and draws attention to the key role of the Holy Spirit in her end and origins.

[5] Wicks's extensive footnotes interact not only with earlier work by ARCIC, but other ecumenical dialogues and theological scholarship on Mary.

its conclusions.[6] The second characteristic, on the other hand, represents 'the great gain' of the Statement: 'prioritizing the perspective of the final destiny of graced human beings', its 'eschatological perspective'. This allows the Commission to

> deepen its understanding of Mary by placing her in a horizon of truths expressed in New Testament letters which make hardly any mention of her ... and, methodologically, to operate from a conviction of the unity of the diverse New Testament works.[7]

In short, the Commission has offered 'a lucid proposal' on Marian issues, offering possibilities for deepening the 'real but imperfect communion' which exists between Anglicans and Roman Catholics.

Bilateral Responses

Two national Anglican–Roman Catholic Consultations have considered the Statement—those in the USA (2007) and Canada (2009).[8] Both raise questions about 'acceptable diversity of belief in a reconciled church' (USA), but make essentially positive responses. They find that the Statement 'offers a significant contribution to our ecumenical dialogue' (USA) and 'represents a significant advance in our consensus regarding Mary'

---

[6] 'The Commission seems not to have fully appropriated the symbolic meanings found in John 2 and 19, since the resumés of the biblical section, in MGH [*Mary: Grace and Hope in Christ*] 20 and the first part of 51, make no mention of symbols and types but remain almost wholly within the sober gleanings from Luke. The Johannine paragraphs remain in the text, but the symbolic meanings found in them, have not contributed substantially to the central doctrinal outcome of this phase of dialogue' (Wicks, 'The Roman Catholic Commentary', 192). Several of Bradshaw's questions, however, arise from precisely the influence of 'symbolic meanings' in the Statement (notably Mary as 'New Eve': see 'The Anglican Commentary', 142, 144, 147, 161).

[7] 'The Roman Catholic Commentary', 194. Wicks 'recommends that readers of MGH 52–57 have the New Testament open before them for reading and pondering the many biblical passages to which these paragraphs refer as they weave their web of theological understanding concerning the economy of God's saving grace' (192–3). Wicks concludes his Commentary by suggesting 'Further Considerations of Sources and Doctrine for Dialogue on Mary'. The first suggestion is Roman Catholic liturgical prayers, notably the eleven collects from Marian feast days in the Roman Catholic calendar (195–7). The Commission did study these, and would agree that they 'serve well' as 'Catholic contributions on Mary in ecumenical dialogues': see Denaux and Sagovsky (eds.), *Studying Mary*, chapter 15. His second ('Thomistic') suggestion is fuller discussion of the mediation of Christ, which is 'like-making' and so 'participatory' in nature (an issue about which Bradshaw expresses hesitation: 'The Anglican Commentary', 149, 152). This issue was likewise given considerable attention by the Commission: see Denaux and Sagovsky (eds.), *Studying Mary*, chapters 8, 9, and 14.

[8] ARC Canada, 'A Response to *Mary: Grace and Hope in Christ*', *One in Christ*, 43/2 (2009), 167–82, http://iarccum.org/doc/?d=201; Anglican–Roman Catholic Dialogue in the USA (ARCUSA), 'Response to "Mary: Grace and Hope in Christ"' (October 2007), www.usccb.org/beliefs-and-teachings/ecumenical-and-interreligious/ecumenical/anglican/response-mary.cfm.

(Canada).[9] They encourage study of the Statement in local communities, as 'shared catechesis of our common faith concerning Mary' (Canada), in which participants 'share their experience of liturgical practice and devotion to Mary' (USA).

Before considering further responses made to the Statement, however, several issues relating to the Commission's mandate need to be clarified.

The Challenges of ARCIC II's Mandate

The Marian Definitions

One challenge derives from what ARCIC II was asked to do. Most Anglican responses struggle with what they perceive as the Statement's focus on the Marian definitions: it can feel as though *Mary* requires more movement from them than from Roman Catholics. It is important to note, however, that movement has taken place on both sides: as the Statement recognizes (*Mary*, §§48–50), Roman Catholic teaching in recent decades has sought to correct exaggerations in Marian devotion. Further, as the Co-Chairmen's Preface notes, the Commission 'had to face squarely dogmatic definitions which are integral to the faith of Roman Catholics but largely foreign to the faith of Anglicans'. Anglican and Roman Catholic experiences of the Marian doctrine and devotion involved are thus asymmetrical. Aware of this, rather than working from the papal definitions of 1854 and 1950, the Commission sought to study the place of Mary in God's economy of salvation in its own right. Yet the contents of the Marian definitions, the authority by which they were proclaimed, and their place in a reunited Church, were the presenting issues facing the Commission.[10]

Feminist Approaches to Mary

Some responses criticize *Mary* 'for its almost complete silence on the effect of Marian teachings on the lives of women, its failure to engage with feminist readings of Mary'.[11] The Commission's work was limited by its

---

[9] The ARC Canada response includes material on the seventeenth-century 'French school of spirituality', which 'deeply marked the life of the Catholic Church in Canada'. It also cites William Ullathorne (Catholic Archbishop of Birmingham, writing in 1855) and George Shea (writing in 1956) on the significance of the definitions for human well-being in the context of the mid-nineteenth and mid-twentieth centuries.

[10] The Second Vatican Council integrated its teaching on Mary into the Dogmatic Constitution on the Church, *Lumen Gentium*, chapter VIII (especially §63). ARCIC II members saw this as paralleling their exploration of the role of Mary in the economy of salvation as an aspect of ecclesiology, rather than developing a 'Mariology' standing by itself.

[11] Faith and Order Advisory Group of the Church of England (FOAG), General Synod Briefing Paper, 'Anglican–Roman Catholic International Commission Report: *Mary: Grace and Hope in Christ*', GS 1818, 6(c).

mandate to matters of documented disagreement, but it was aware of the significance of this critique.[12] Care was taken over language which has negative consequences for women: the combination of 'virgin' and 'mother' images applied to Mary, and abstract terms such as 'motherhood', were avoided.[13] The emphasis in the *Magnificat* on justice and empowerment was seen as giving an opportunity to take up some gender-related issues (*Mary*, §74).

A sensitive matter was the translation of *Theotókos*. The Commission chose not to use the traditional rendition, 'Mother of God', though this was retained in quotations (*Mary*, §§1, 46, 58). *Theotókos* was mostly left untranslated, or the literal rendition 'God-bearer' employed.[14] In citing ARCIC I (*Mary*, §2), and in the concluding paragraphs (*Mary*, §72, §76, §80) 'mother of God incarnate' is used, reflecting the term's precise theological meaning.

Our two traditions have to take feminist concerns seriously, whether such critique comes from a Christian perspective or from outside the churches. A generous and penitent ecumenical consideration of the use or misuse of Marian teaching and devotion remains to be developed.

The Use of Historical Evidence

Several responses comment on the use of historical evidence in *Mary*. Thus ARCUSA asked for 'fuller explanation of the process by which these dogmas were defined for the Roman Catholic Church' ('Response to "Mary: Grace and Hope in Christ"', §7). Some Anglican scholars see the Statement

---

[12] Charles Sherlock, 'The Journey: An Anglican Perspective', in Bolen and Cameron (eds.), *The Text with Commentaries and Study Guide*, 212–13, notes the discussion of feminist issues at the 1999 Commission meeting, and its ongoing concern about maternal language. Cf, ARCUSA, 'Images of God: Reflections on Christian Anthropology', used by the Commission: www.usccb.org/beliefs-and-teachings/ecumenical-and-interreligious/ecumenical/anglican/upload/arcusa-1983-statement.pdf; and Catharina Halkes, 'Mary and Women', in Hans Küng and Jürgen Moltmann (eds.), *Mary in the Churches*, Concilium, 168 (Edinburgh: T & T Clark, 1983), 66–73.

[13] As Harriet Harris perceptively notes, 'Perhaps cognizant of this mixed legacy, the Commission rarely speaks of Mary's femininity, or role as a natural mother, outside the doctrinal formulation of *Theotókos*': 'A Feminist Response to ARCIC's *Mary: Grace and Hope in Christ*', in *Mary: Grace and Hope in Christ: Essays of the Faith and Order Advisory Group of the Church of England*, GS Misc 872 (London: General Synod of the Church of England, 2008), 37–48, at p. 44.

[14] Contrast Harris, in *Essays of the FOAG*, who states that the Commission translates 'The appellation, *Theotókos* . . . as "Mother of God" rather than "God-bearer"' (38). She goes on to say, 'But in assuming the translation "Mother of God" rather than the more literal "God-bearer", it has missed an opportunity to allay fears, especially, but not only, from Reformed quarters' (39). On the other hand, Week 1 of the Study Guide is entitled 'The Mother of God' (92), and uses that term twice in the questions (95–6).

as offering a 'bland historical presentation' which 'virtually ignores the dynamic relationship between doctrine and context'.[15] Such responses touch on the method used by ARCIC from its beginning. In *The Malta Report* (§17) it is stated that

> we cannot escape the witness of our history; but we cannot resolve our differences by mere reconsideration of, and judgement upon, the past. We must press on in confident faith that new light will be given us to lead us to our goal.

In similar vein, the Preface to *The Final Report* states that the Commission

> determined, in accordance with our mandate, and in the spirit of Phil 3.13, 'forgetting what lies behind and straining forward to what lies ahead', to discover each other's faith as it is today, and to appeal to history only for enlightenment, not as a way of perpetuating past controversy.

Given the doctrinal importance of the historical development of the Marian definitions, ARCIC II examined closely the relevant periods: patristic, medieval, Reformation, Counter Reformation, nineteenth century, and modern.[16] Nevertheless, in accord with ARCIC's method, the outcome is a Statement in which historical data are cited only insofar as this was necessary to explain why agreement was reached. Whether further work related to historical developments needs to be done will depend on official responses from Roman Catholic and Anglican authorities.

Anglican Liturgical Practice

Some Anglican responses contest the claims made regarding the place of Mary in Anglican heritage and liturgical practice (*Mary*, §§46, 49), and some imply that the Commission did not examine the evidence.[17] Several responses from Evangelical Anglicans appear not to appreciate what the

---

[15] So Charlotte Methuen, 'Mary in Context: A Historical Methodological Reflection', in *Essays of the FOAG*, 15–23.

[16] See Denaux and Sagovsky (eds.), *Studying Mary*, especially the essays by Emmanuel Lanne, Rozanne Elder, Liam Walsh, Michael Nazir-Ali and Nicholas Sagovsky, and Sara Butler.

[17] For example those of the Church of Ireland and the Diocese of Sydney; see below. Close examination of the calendars and liturgical texts was carried out by Peter Cross (Roman Catholic) and Charles Sherlock (Anglican): see Denaux and Sagovsky (eds.), *Studying Mary*, chapter 15, which includes tables of feasts, readings and prayers. As regards Roman Catholic texts, in his official Commentary on *Mary: Grace and Hope in Christ*, Jared Wicks cites the eleven Collects from Marian feast-days in the calendar, which highlight 'God's initiative and the range of his work in the life and person of Mary . . . [which] can surely serve well in future Catholic contributions on Mary in ecumenical dialogues' ('The Roman Catholic Commentary', 195–9).

Anglican liturgical evidence discloses.[18] The Collect and Post-Communion prayer for 15 August in *Common Worship* include the following lines:

> ...grant that we who are redeemed by [Christ's] blood
> may share with [Mary] in the glory of your eternal kingdom ...
> ...strengthen us to walk with Mary the joyful path of obedience and so
> bring forth the fruits of holiness ...

These, and many similar prayers in use across the Anglican Communion, presume that Mary is not simply an historic figure, nor 'dead', but—in the language of the Statement—'truly alive' in the full presence of God (*Mary*, §65), active in ongoing obedience.[19]

Roman Catholic Responses

Responses from Roman Catholic scholars and media are in large part positive, not least the official Commentary noted above.[20] The most significant issue concerns the attempt in *Mary* to reformulate the Marian definitions in fresh language, without losing their essential content: 'God has taken the Blessed Virgin Mary in the fullness of her person into his glory' (*Mary*, §58—Assumption), and 'In view of her vocation to be the mother of the Holy One ... Christ's redeeming work reached "back" in Mary to the depths of her being, and to her earliest beginnings' (*Mary*, §59—Immaculate Conception).

It is for the Roman Catholic Church, through assessment by the Congregation for the Doctrine of the Faith (CDF), to discern whether it can recognize the richness of the doctrines defined in the papal formulations in the language used by ARCIC II to express them.

Anglican Responses

Anglican responses include some from ecclesial bodies, those penned by scholars, and reporting in the media. Much of the Statement is welcomed, but sharp criticisms are offered. In view of the nature of the Anglican Communion, the ecclesial responses are diverse, as this overview shows:

---

[18] So Martin Davie, '*Mary—Grace and Hope in Christ*: An Evangelical Anglican Response', *Anvil*, 23/1 (2006), also in *Essays of the FOAG*, 55. 15 August was included in the Church of England calendar from 2001, when *Common Worship* was authorized.

[19] An important learning for some Anglican members of ARCIC II was that Roman Catholic liturgical texts consistently place Mary in relation to Christ.

[20] Wicks, 'The Roman Catholic Commentary', 167–203. Some other Roman Catholic responses looked for more 'conservative' conclusions than ARCIC II offers: see the articles by Judith Marie Gentle and René Laurentin cited in the Bibliography on pp. 237–41 below.

- Fulcrum ('Renewing the Evangelical Centre in the Church of England') appreciates several aspects of the Statement, but 'awaits to be convinced that the [Marian definitions], or prayer addressed to Mary, are indeed consonant with Scripture'. Questions are raised about particular points, and the response looks for 'further discussion of the methodological principles underlying the dogmas of Mary'.
- The Faith and Order Advisory Group of the Church of England (FOAG) issued a set of eight essays from Anglican scholars of varied disciplines and approaches (GS Misc 872). It subsequently prepared a 'Briefing Paper' (GS 1818) for the February 2011 General Synod of the Church of England. Four areas of clarification are asked for on Marian issues, through 'further joint study at the international level': 'the relationship between doctrine and the reading of Scripture', the 'development of Marian theology and devotion', how these 'are perceived by, and impact on the lives of women', and their place 'within Anglicanism, taking the full range of Anglican perspectives into account'.

  The Synod, after significant discussion, moved that 'further joint study of the issues identified in GS 1818 be undertaken—in particular, the question of the authority and status of the Roman Catholic dogmas of the Immaculate Conception and the Assumption of the Blessed Virgin Mary for Anglicans'.
- The Church of Ireland's response found much of *Mary* to be 'helpful': 'the concept of a trajectory of grace and hope', the use of the Scriptures, the affirmation of the first four Councils, and of Mary's place in the communion of saints. The response locates Marian doctrine and spirituality in the Irish context, with extensive citations from Church of Ireland liturgical texts and hymns.[21]

  The Reservations listed are considerable, however, and expressed in strong terms.[22] The Agreed Statement neglects the place of art,[23] and underplays the role of the Holy Spirit; questions are raised about method,

---

[21] As well as the response itself, see Gillian Wharton, 'Mary in Celtic Spirituality', and Paddy Wallace, 'Mary, Mother of our Lord, as perceived by the Mothers' Union in Ireland', Essays 1 and 3 attached to Church of Ireland, Response to *Mary: Grace and Hope in Christ*, with eight supporting essays, http://ireland.anglican.org/cmsfiles/pdf/Information/Resources/CCU/arcic_mary.pdf.

[22] These Reservations, and the essays which support them, presume that ARCIC's work is to be assessed as to whether or not it accords with a Church's existing position, rather than being received as the fruit of dialogue and an invitation for exploration and reception.

[23] Bolen and Cameron (eds.), *The Text with Commentaries and Study Guide* includes a range of pictorial representations of Mary from Orthodox, Anglican, and Roman Catholic sources (between pp. 52 and 53).

especially the use of typology and the role of the Thirty-Nine Articles; ARCIC's re-phrasings of the Marian definitions are seen as 'highly ambiguous, if not tendentious', and their resting on infallible papal teachings seen as calling this further into question.

- The Synod of the Anglican Diocese of Sydney in 2005 'noted' *Mary*, stating 'that the Commission does not represent or speak on behalf of the Diocese' and requesting the Diocesan Doctrine Commission to prepare a report.[24] This is sharply polemical and somewhat idiosyncratic: its opening sections assert that 'One must already be strongly inclined towards a Catholic perspective, indeed be essentially in agreement with it, to find the ARCIC document believable' (§5).

The Sydney Report acknowledges that 'Evangelical Anglicans and Roman Catholics' in common 'confess that [Mary] is truly the Mother of God, *Theotokos*; that is, her son was God the Son and not merely Jesus the man' (§6). Most of the Report, however, concerns 'unresolved differences': 'Mary and communicating with the departed' (§§8–15), 'Mary as ever virgin' (§16), and the two papal definitions (§§17–20, of which ARCIC's position is admitted to be 'a possibility, perhaps').

These differing Anglican responses reflect the broad spectrum of belief and practice that continues to be held by committed Anglicans across the Communion.

Divine Grace and Human Response

Some negative responses are based on polemical misreadings of the Statement, notably the relationship of God's grace to Mary's response.[25] In particular, the Report of the Anglican Diocese of Sydney Doctrine Commission states the 'real danger in the Mary issue' as ARCIC's 'too easily wishing to emphasise Mary's cooperation with God in salvation . . . [seen in] Mary's "yes" to be Man cooperating with God in his salvation'.[26]

---

[24] Anglican Diocese of Sydney Doctrine Commission, 'Response to the Anglican and Roman Catholic International Commission (ARCIC) Report "Mary: Grace and Hope in Christ"', www.sds.asn.au/Site/103715.asp?a=a&ph=cl.

[25] Polemical assessments can readily be found in the religious media: see the response of the conservative Evangelical Church Society (http://churchsociety.org/issues_new/ecum/iss_ecum_arcic-mary.asp), or that of the liberal Anglican Modern Church Society (Nick Jowett, '*Mary: Grace and Hope in Christ*', *Signs of the Times*, 28 (January 2008), http://modernchurch.org.uk/signs-of-the-times/stpast/st2008/no-28-jan/mary-grace-and-hope-in-christ).

[26] Anglican Diocese of Sydney Doctrine Commission, 'Response', §§22–23. These sections conclude by affirming that 'Mary is a supreme example of "by faith alone", which looks outside of itself, trusting the word of God'—precisely the point made by the Statement, for example at §17.

Yet the Commission, well aware of this danger, never places 'yes' on Mary's lips. As articulated in *The Gift of Authority*, in the Scriptures it is God who pronounces 'Yes' towards creatures, in Christ: our place is to respond with 'Amen', itself the fruit of grace, the work of the Holy Spirit (see *The Gift of Authority*, §§8–10). Mary's 'Amen'—not 'yes'!—is 'given in faith and freedom to God's powerful Word communicated by the angel ([Luke] 1.38)' (*Mary*, §16; cf. §51).

Other Evangelical Anglicans, however, while making many criticisms of the Statement, welcome its 'clear emphasis on the prevenient grace of God'.[27] ARCUSA likewise 'appreciates the approach' of the Statement as considering Mary 'from the standpoint of a strong doctrine of God's prevenient grace' (§2). And ARC Canada states that 'The grace-hope pattern that pervades MGH is one in which God's grace is primary, the human response secondary.'

Further Work Sought

An overview of the responses made to *Mary* shows that requests for further work have mostly come from Anglican sources, in three main areas.

a. the use of a mix of methods in the interpretation of Scripture, and the consequent claim that the agreements reached are 'consonant with Scripture';
b. particular theological issues regarding Mary in the tradition: her holiness; the meaning of 'ever virgin'; the end of her earthly life in relation to resurrection; and invocation;
c. the authority by which the definitions were pronounced, and their status in a reconciled church (an issue also noted by some Roman Catholic commentators).

Mary and Scripture
Historical, Typological, and Critical Readings
Some Anglican commentators were amazed by how much there is in Scripture about Mary and her role in the economy of salvation. Appreciation was expressed for the challenge presented by the Statement for all readers to examine their own interpretive processes in its light. Other responses, however, ask whether the interpretive approach articulated, blending historical, typological, and critical elements, is adequate. Some

---

[27] Davie, 'An Evangelical Anglican Response', 52.

biblical scholars question the integrity of ARCIC II in seeming to harmonize 'the obdurate divergences of the texts' about Mary.[28]

How the Scriptures are read is affected by the confessional standpoint of their readers, including those taking an ecumenical stance. The Statement is the first ARCIC document to reflect explicitly on the use of Scripture, building on *The Gift of Authority*. It claims to offer 'an ecclesial and ecumenical reading, seeking to consider each passage about Mary in the context of the New Testament as a whole, against the background of the Old, and in the light of Tradition' (*Mary*, §7).

The question raised in some Anglican responses is whether the 1854 and 1950 definitions have guided the reading of Scripture in *Mary*, rather than Scripture being taken as normative for defining doctrine.[29] Conversely, other responses note that by consciously including typology, ARCIC II took up

> an 'exercise of the imagination' that embraces not only what the biblical text originally meant (that meaning which historical criticism sought) and what it means within the existing Christian traditions, but what it will mean when we are one in Christ.[30]

This recognizes the role given to 'eschatological' readings in the Statement, especially of Pauline texts, as well as the place of typology.

The work of ARCIC thus far has focused on what divides Anglicans and Roman Catholics. Issues concerning the best use of Scripture cut across both traditions. The 'ecclesial and ecumenical' biblical hermeneutic used in *Mary* thus merits further exploration as one which focuses on what unites.

The Marian Definitions: 'Consonant with Scripture'?

The larger Anglican concern has been the claim that 'the teaching about Mary in the two definitions of the Assumption and the Immaculate Con-

---

[28] So Paula Gooder and Peter Fisher, 'Mary: Mary in the New Testament Tradition', in *Essays of the FOAG*, 6–7. Michael Kennedy, 'Reflections on the Text', Essay 8 attached to the Church of Ireland, Response to *Mary: Grace and Hope in Christ*, questions ARCIC II's presumption of historical elements in Matthew and Luke's birth narratives.

[29] Notably section 6(a) of the FOAG Briefing Paper GS 1818.

[30] Feidhlimidh Magennis, 'The Use of Scripture in 'Mary, Grace and Hope in Christ'', a Joint Statement of the Anglican–Roman Catholic International Commission', (Irish Biblical Association Conference 2005, Union Theological College, Belfast), 2. Magennis attributes the phrase 'exercise in imagination' to John Muddiman, one of ARCIC II's biblical scholars. ARCIC II thus moved, he contends, beyond the work of the (US) National Lutheran–Roman Catholic Dialogue, whose work on Mary focused on historical criticism. He observes that 'historical-critical issues tend to be presented in footnotes rather than in the main text' of *Mary: Grace and Hope in Christ*, and later notes that 'The Commission may have been wiser to be more explicit about their dependence on and agreement with historical-critical approaches.'

ception, understood within the biblical pattern of the economy of hope and grace, can be said to be consonant with the teaching of the Scriptures and the ancient common traditions' (*Mary*, §78).

Anglican responses have requested further consideration of what 'consonant with' means in this context. Bill Croft offers three 'scenes' for the phrase:

> Scene 1: there is no contradiction of scripture;
> Scene 2: what is claimed goes with the general thrust of biblical witness;
> Scene 3: what is claimed, although working in particular areas where the scriptural witness is only indirect, or indeed where scripture is silent, can indubitably be supported by the wider scriptural witness.[31]

A fourth 'scene' would be teaching which is 'not consonant with' Scripture, but contrary to it. The concept is thus a multi-layered one. With regard to Mary, accepting her as *Theotókos* would be likely to be seen as coming under Scene 3, but also relates to Scene 2. The Commission rejected Scene 4 (*Mary*, §79), but all three types of meaning suggested by Croft are relevant to its approach.

The Roman Catholic Church holds that the definitions of 1854 and 1950 are part of a post-biblical tradition which is a legitimate development from the Scriptures, because they are closely linked to teaching found explicitly in them.[32] Many Anglicans, however, do not agree, some regarding them as contrary to Scripture. The issue is interwoven with the relationship of Scripture to T/tradition(s), agreement about which was reached by ARCIC II in *The Gift of Authority* (see §§14–23). In view of the disagreements about the way this agreement has been applied in *Mary*, it would seem that further study should be undertaken of the relationship between the formation of doctrine and the reading of Scripture, in particular as regards Mary.

Particular Theological Issues from the Christian Tradition

Anglican responses criticize several of the theological positions taken in *Mary*. Some are wary of calling Mary 'New Eve' (see *Mary*, §§36, 42, 51), though this is not unfamiliar in the Anglican tradition. The greatest concerns expressed, especially in Evangelical responses, focus on the holiness of Mary (notably in relation to Romans 3.23),[33] her continuing to be a

---

[31] Bill Croft, 'Consonant with Scripture?', in *Essays of the FOAG*, 9–14. He sees ARCIC II's position on the holiness of Mary as not fitting Scene 1; her being assumed 'body and soul' as not meeting Scene 2; and that the definitions are 'divinely revealed' as testing Scene 3.

[32] See Denaux and Sagovsky (eds.), *Studying Mary*, 24–35, especially 31–5.

[33] See ibid., 13–15, for the argument behind *Mary*, footnote 12.

virgin after the birth of Christ, and how her earthly life ended (particularly its relation to resurrection).

Mary's Holiness

The term 'sinlessness' is used in all Anglican responses which raise concerns around the holiness of Mary, including the official Commentary. Yet 'sinlessness' is employed only once in *Mary*, and then in quotation marks to indicate that, as a negative notion, it is not a helpful way of putting the issues involved (*Mary*, §59). Western approaches to sin, working from the past forwards, inevitably became entangled in insoluble debates such as those surrounding the 'maculist' controversies.[34] ARCIC II, in adopting a 'future backwards' method, sought to situate the theological issues around Mary in the light of the ultimate destiny of creation, as revealed in Christ.[35]

Only in the final stages of its discussion was the Eastern term used of Mary, *panaghia*, 'holy through and through'. It is mentioned in §38 but was omitted in §59, where its inclusion might have helped the Commission's approach to be better understood.

'Ever Virgin'

Related to Mary's holiness is the term 'ever virgin', a term which is problematic not least in view of changes in the understanding of human biology, as several responses indicate. There is unease about the implicit equation of sex with sinful behaviour in such language—an unease felt in the Commission. The notion of 'perpetual virginity', even when understood in ideal rather than literalist terms,[36] does not of itself make a connection between sin and sex, though it has been misused in that sense. While recognizing that Anglican and Roman Catholics are 'both heirs to a rich tradition which recognises Mary as ever virgin' (*Mary*, §51), what this means is left open, and the term does not form part of the Agreements in the Conclusion (§§77–79).

---

[34] See Denaux and Sagovsky (eds.), *Studying Mary*, 93–7. Methuen, 'Mary in Context', criticizes the Commission for neglecting patristic opinions regarding Mary and sin (notably Irenaeus and Origen). This is recognized in *Mary*, footnote 8; see Denaux and Sagovsky (eds.), *Studying Mary*, 40–4.

[35] This method also led to the order of discussion of the definitions, giving 'Assumption' first (*Mary*, §§56–58) and only then 'Immaculate Conception' (*Mary*, §59).

[36] See Denaux and Sagovsky (eds.), *Studying Mary*, 23: 'Since Mary functions as the Virgin Mother of the Messiah in the order of salvation history, she can be said to be "always a virgin" even if she had other children in the normal way. For salvation history, while related to ordinary history, nevertheless also transcends it.' Augustine taught that 'The whole Church is called Virgin . . . Which is this spiritual virginity? The perfect faith, the firm hope, the sincere love.' Augustine, *In Jo. Tr.* 13,12: J. P. Migne (ed.), *Patrologia Latina*, 35 (1845), 1499.

Some Anglican responses ask whether the mention of Jesus' brothers and sisters in Mark 6.3 is not a counter-indication against the belief that Mary remained a virgin after his birth. Footnote 3 of the Statement notes that *adelphos*, though it usually denotes a blood brother, can have a broader meaning of kinsman, or relative.[37] This claim is supported by scholars involved in the US Lutheran–Roman Catholic dialogue: 'It cannot be said that the NT identifies them [i.e. the brothers and sisters of Jesus] *without doubt* as blood brothers and sisters and hence as children of Mary. The solution favoured by scholars will in part depend on the authority they allot to later church insights.'[38] This raises again the question of the interpretation of the Scriptures in the process of tradition, and what 'consonant with Scripture' means.

The End of Mary's Earthly Life

Some responses, noting the tension in Scripture between the 'already' of God's saving work in Christ and the 'not yet' of new creation and resurrection, ask whether ARCIC II's eschatological approach resolves this tension too easily.[39] How does Mary, as a human being, become incorporated into Christ's resurrection? *Mary: Grace and Hope in Christ* is careful, as footnote 10 indicates (*Mary*, §58), not to enter into debates about the precise way in which Mary entered 'the glory of your eternal kingdom' (a phrase in Collects of several Anglican provinces). It speaks of Mary as 'truly alive' (§65), in a distinctive and ongoing relationship to her Son in view of her holiness and position as *Theotókos*.[40] The Commission came to the conclusion, however, that to say more was to run the risk of pinning down unduly the meaning of the mystery of God's saving work in Christ.

Invocation

Anglican responses concerning the practice of asking Mary to pray for others largely reflect the 'churchmanship' of their authors. Those who

---

[37] Denaux and Sagovsky (eds.), *Studying Mary*, 21–3, offers a fuller rationale for this footnote.

[38] Raymond E. Brown et al. (eds.), *Mary in the New Testament: A Collaborative Assessment by Protestant and Roman Catholic Scholars* (London: Chapman, 1978), index topic 'Brothers (and sisters) of Jesus' (p. 321).

[39] Davie, 'An Evangelical Anglican Response', 57.

[40] The Anglican Diocese of Sydney Doctrine Commission, 'Response', under the heading 'Mary and Communicating with the Departed', claims that 'At the Reformation of the Church of England there was a decisive rejection of communication between the living and the dead' (§11). The Book of Common Prayer, however, includes assurances of the communion between the Church militant and triumphant. Further, in the New Testament no believer is said to be 'dead', but to have 'fallen asleep' in Christ.

identify as Catholic welcome this aspect of *Mary: Grace and Hope in Christ*,[41] while most responses from Evangelicals reject it,[42] and Liberal sources question it.[43] Given this diversity, it is difficult to know what work beyond what ARCIC has already done might ease the situation. As noted earlier, it is important for Anglicans to recognize that, while asking Mary (or other saints) to pray for us forms a significant element in the spiritual life of Roman Catholics, it is not required of their personal devotional life.

A terminological clarification which may assist some Anglicans is the distinction made by Roman Catholics between 'worship' (*latreia*, offered only to God) and 'devotion, reverence or veneration' (*dulia*).[44] Mary is never 'worshipped', but revered or venerated for her holiness, and for her distinctive relationship with her Son, and thus may be asked to pray for believers. This is also the position of the Orthodox, and many other Christians. Archbishop Michael Ramsey in 1967 pointed out to Cardinal Suenens that the seventeenth-century Church of England theologian Bishop John Pearson said of Mary and Christ: 'Let her be honoured and esteemed, let him be worshipped and adored.'[45] Ramsey said that this was his position and that 'much modern practical Mariology seemed to transgress that distinction'. Authentic 'Marian devotion' involves acknowledging Mary's unique place in the communion of saints, especially her closeness to the risen and exalted Lord Jesus, and typically includes asking her to pray for suppliants, especially when in danger or near death.

Beyond this clarification, it is difficult to say what further work should be undertaken by ARCIC in these areas. The responses indicate that much is to be gained by Anglicans and Roman Catholics reflecting together on *Mary: Grace and Hope in Christ* at local levels. In this process *Studying Mary* and the *Study Guide* offer significant resources.

The Question of Authority

Underlying many responses from Anglican sources are concerns about the implications of the Commission's work for Christian authority and its exercise. The authority of Scripture is seen as coming under question,

[41] Thomas Seville, '*Mary: Grace and Hope in Christ*', *New Directions* (January 2008), 6–7.
[42] Anglican Diocese of Sydney Doctrine Commission, 'Response', and Church of Ireland, Response.
[43] Jowett, '*Mary: Grace and Hope in Christ*'.
[44] The Second Vatican Council's Constitution on the Church, *Lumen Gentium*, §63, while, teaching that Mary holds a unique and distinctive place in the people of God, did not continue the older distinction between *dulia*, offered to saints in general, and *hyperdulia*, offered to Mary.
[45] Peter Webster, *Archbishop Ramsey* (London: Ashgate, 2015), 193–4.

along with concerns over the different ecclesial processes by which Anglicans and Roman Catholics discern divine revelation, and the extent to which consequent doctrinal determinations are discerned and can be enforced. The 2001 General Synod of the Church of England debate about *Mary* focused its resolution on this area, requesting that

> further joint study of the issues identified in GS 1818 be undertaken—in particular, the question of the authority and status of the Roman Catholic dogmas of the Immaculate Conception and the Assumption of the Blessed Virgin Mary for Anglicans.[46]

The issues involved have been addressed by ARCIC in several Agreed Statements, the first two being part of *The Final Report: Authority in the Church I* (1976) and *II* (1981, together with an *Elucidation*). In *The Gift of Authority: Authority in the Church III*, ARCIC II brought this work to the point where full agreement was reached.

It is only against this background that the Conclusion of *Mary* can be properly understood. The Commission expresses the hope 'that this agreement, when accepted by our two Communions, would place the questions about authority which arise from the two definitions of 1854 and 1950 in a new ecumenical context'. In doing so, it is recognized that 'Any such re-reception would have to take place within the context of a mutual re-reception of an effective teaching authority in the Church, such as that set out in *The Gift of Authority*' (*Mary*, §63). Understanding the cross-pollination of these two Agreed Statements of ARCIC II is essential to appreciating the Commission's proposals in both. On the one hand, in the context of agreement on the interrelationship of the Scriptures, Tradition(s), and the exercise of authority, *The Gift of Authority* proposes a way forward regarding the distinctive ministry of the Bishop of Rome in solemnly defining doctrines (*The Gift of Authority*, §47), without considering the occasions on which this has been exercised, the definitions of 1854 and 1950. On the other hand, *Mary* considers their content and how they might be re-received in a Church no longer divided.

Conclusion

Mary has stirred fresh interest regarding the journey towards reconciliation between the Anglican Communion and the Roman Catholic Church, especially among Anglican Evangelicals. The further work most needed for

---

[46] Church of England General Synod, February 2011, Motion 18.

this journey to continue is not directly related to Mary, but concerns the use of Scripture, and the exercise of authority.

More particularly:

- As regards Scripture, the 'ecclesial and ecumenical' biblical hermeneutic used in *Mary* merits further exploration.
- As regards Mary herself, should the Commission return to consider her ministry in a future report, attention would have to be given to those critical responses to *Mary* which highlighted feminist concerns about the Marian definitions and devotion.
- As regards the relationship between Marian teaching and authority, further study is needed of the relationship between the formation of doctrine and the reading of Scripture. Areas identified in responses as insufficiently resolved are the historical development of Marian doctrine and devotion; her holiness; transition to God's glory; and invocation.

While recognizing that progress is hindered when barriers remain, the way forward would seem to be best approached through what unites: ARCIC I and II were asked to focus on what divides. The need is more for deep reflection on the issues at local and regional levels, with a humble openness to conversion of heart and mind on all sides.

As to what further work on Mary should be undertaken by ARCIC III, this will depend on official responses from Roman Catholic and Anglican authorities. The more urgent task is for Anglicans and Roman Catholics to reflect together on *Mary*. In this process *Studying Mary* and the *Study Guide* offer significant resources. As the opening paragraphs of *Mary* conclude,

> When Christians join in Mary's 'Amen' to the 'Yes' of God in Christ, they commit themselves to an obedient response to the Word of God, which leads to a life of prayer and service. Like Mary, they not only magnify the Lord with their lips: they commit themselves to serve God's justice with their lives (cf. Luke 1.46–55).　　　　　　　　　　　　　　(*Mary*, §5)

Bibliography

Official Commentaries

Bradshaw, Timothy, 'The Anglican Commentary', in Donald Bolen and Gregory Cameron (eds.), *Mary: Grace and Hope in Christ: The Text with Commentaries and Study Guide* (London: Continuum, 2006), 133–65, www.anglicancommunion.org/relationships/ecumenical-dialogues/roman-catholic/arcic.aspx, under the January 2004 meeting

Wicks, Jared, 'The Roman Catholic Commentary', in Donald Bolen and Gregory Cameron (eds.), *Mary: Grace and Hope in Christ: The Text with Commentaries and Study Guide* (London: Continuum, 2006), 167–203, www.vatican.va/roman_curia/pontifical_councils/chrstuni/angl-comm-docs/rc_pc_chrstuni_doc_20050516_commentary-wicks_en.html

Documentation from ARCIC II

Bolen, Donald, and Gregory Cameron (eds.), *Mary, Grace and Hope in Christ: The Text with Commentaries and Study Guide* (London: Continuum, 2006). As well as the official commentaries (listed above), this includes:

> The Seattle Statement (text) (pp. 7–88)
> Study Guide (over six sessions) (pp. 89–131)
> Charles Sherlock, 'The Journey: An Anglican Perspective' (pp. 204–31)
> Sara Butler, 'The Mary Statement: A Roman Catholic Perspective' (pp. 232–56)

Denaux, Adelbert, and Nicholas Sagovsky (eds.), *Studying Mary: Reflections on the Virgin Mary in Anglican and Roman Catholic Theology and Devotion. The ARCIC Working Papers* (London: T & T Clark, 2007). This includes fifteen essays by members of the Commission, and a 'redactional history' of the Commission's work on the Statement by Adelbert Denaux.

Ecclesial Responses

Anglican Communion Office, 'An Introduction to the Mary Document' (February 2006), www.anglicancommunion.org/resources/document-library.aspx?author=Ecumenical+Dialogues&tag=ARCIC

Anglican Diocese of Sydney Doctrine Commission, 'Response to the Anglican and Roman Catholic International Commission (ARCIC) Report "Mary: Grace and Hope in Christ"', www.sds.asn.au/Site/103715.asp?a=a&ph=cl

ARC Canada, 'A Response to Mary: Grace and Hope in Christ', *One in Christ* 43/2 (2009), 167–82, http://iarccum.org/doc/?d=201

ARCUSA, 'Response to "Mary: Grace and Hope in Christ"' (October 2007), www.usccb.org/beliefs-and-teachings/ecumenical-and-interreligious/ecumenical/anglican/response-mary.cfm

FOAG, *Mary: Grace and Hope in Christ: Essays*, GS Misc 872 (London: General Synod of the Church of England, 2008), www.churchofengland.org/media/1166644/gs%20misc%20872.pdf. This includes:

> Paula Gooder and Peter Fisher, 'Mary: Mary in the New Testament Tradition' (pp. 1–8)
> Bill Croft, 'Consonant with Scripture' (pp. 9–14)
> Charlotte Methuen, 'Mary in Context: A Historical Methodological Reflection' (pp. 15–23)
> Thomas Seville, 'The Place of the Blessed Virgin Mary in the Context of the Doctrine of the Incarnation' (pp. 24–36)

Harriet Harris, 'A Feminist Response to ARCIC's *Mary: Grace and Hope in Christ*' (pp. 37–48)

Martin Davie, '*Mary, Grace and Hope in Christ*—An Evangelical Anglican Response' (pp. 49–65)

Thomas Seville, 'Scripture and Authority in the Roman Catholic Church—with Reference to the Two Marian Teachings Regarded as Dogma' (pp. 66–83)

David Hilborn, 'Scripture, Authority and the Marian Dogmas: An Evangelical Perspective' (pp. 84–90)

Church of Ireland, Response to *Mary: Grace and Hope in Christ*, with eight supporting essays, http://ireland.anglican.org/cmsfiles/pdf/Information/Resources/CCU/arcic_mary.pdf

FOAG, General Synod Briefing Paper GS 1818, 'Anglican–Roman Catholic International Commission Report: *Mary: Grace and Hope in Christ*', GS 1818, Motion 18, www.churchofengland.org/media/1165099/gs%201818.pdf

Kings, Graham, '*Fulcrum* Response to the Anglican–Roman Catholic International Commission Agreed Statement, Mary: Grace and Hope in Christ', www.fulcrum-anglican.org.uk/articles/mary-grace-and-hope-in-christ-fulcrum-response-to-the-anglican-roman-catholic-international-commission-agreed-statement/

Significant Publications

Bhaldraithe, E. de, 'The Challenge of the ARCIC Agreement on Mary', *Doctrine and Life*, 60/1 (2010), 21–36

Borsch, F. H., 'Mary and Scripture: A Response to "Mary: Grace and Hope in Christ: An Agreed Statement of the Anglican–Roman Catholic International Commission"', *Anglican Theological Review*, 89/3 (2007), 375–99

Bruni, G., 'Dialogo Chiesa cattolica romana—Communione anglicana: Maria: grazia e esperanza in Christo', in G. Bruni, *Mariologia ecumenica: approcci, documenti, prospettive* (Bologna: EDB, 2009), 243–96

Carter, David, 'Mary: Grace and Hope in Christ: Some Reflections', *One in Christ*, 41/2 (2006), 66–82; *Ecumenical Trends*, 35/3 (2006), 8–15.

Chapman, M. E., 'The Virgin Mary, Luther, and the Church: A Doctrinal Interpretation from a Lutheran Perspective', *Ecumenical Trends*, 36/9 (2007), 10–15

Chapman, M. E., *The Fantasy of Reunion: Anglicans, Catholics, and Ecumenism, 1833–1882* (Oxford: Oxford University Press, 2014), chapter 4

Farrell, Marie, '"Mary: Grace and Hope in Christ"—Some Observations and Comments', *The Australasian Catholic Record*, 84 (2007), 259–66

Flanagan, Donald, 'An Ecumenical Breakthrough—Mary: Grace and Hope in Christ', *Doctrine and Life*, 55/8 (2005), 20–7

Gentle, Judith Marie, 'Reclaiming England for Our Lady: The Concept of Redemption in the Caroline Divines and in the Anglo-Catholic Theologians', in *Mary at the Foot of the Cross—VIII: Coredemption as Key to a Correct Understanding of Redemption, and Recent Attempts to Redefine Redemption*

Contrary to the Belief of the Church, Acts of the Eighth International Symposium on Marian Coredemption (New Bedford, USA: Franciscans of the Immaculate, 2008)

Halkes, Catharina, 'Mary and Women', in Hans Küng and Jürgen Moltmann (eds.), *Mary in the Churches, Concilium* 168 (Edinburgh: T & T Clark, 1983), 66–73

Harris, Alana, and Harris, Harriet, 'A Marian Pilgrimage: Reflections and Questions about ARCIC's *Mary: Grace and Hope in Christ*', *Ecclesiology*, 2/3 (2006), 339–56

Hintzen, G., 'Das anglikanisch-katholische Dialogdokument "Maria: Gnade und Hoffnung in Christus": Eine Evaluation aus katholischer Sicht', *Catholica*, 59/3 (2005), 167–88

Jeske, Richard L., '*Mary: Grace and Hope in Christ*: A Review from a Lutheran Perspective', *Ecumenical Trends*, 36/6 (2007), 6–15

Jowett, Nick, '*Mary: Grace and Hope in Christ*', *Signs of the Times*, 28 (January 2008), http://modernchurch.org.uk/signs-of-the-times/stpast/st2008/no-28-jan/mary-grace-and-hope-in-christ

Laurentin, René, '"It is impossible to be faithful to Scripture and not to take Mary seriously": A Comment on the Joint Declaration of the Anglican–Roman Catholic International Commission on *Mary: Grace and Hope in Christ*', www.30giorni.it/articoli_id_9991_l3.htm

Leahy, Brendan, 'The Achievements and Challenges of *Mary, Grace and Hope in Christ*', *Louvain Studies*, 33 (2008), 117–35

Leahy, Brendan, 'What are they Saying about *Mary, Grace and Hope in Christ?*', *Irish Theological Quarterly*, 75/1 (2010), 45–55

Magennis, Feidhlimidh, 'The Use of Scripture in "Mary, Grace and Hope in Christ", a Joint Statement of the Anglican–Roman Catholic International Commission' (Irish Biblical Association Conference 2005, Union Theological College, Belfast)

Maltby, Judith, 'Anglicanism, the Reformation and the Anglican–Roman Catholic International Commission's Agreed Statement *Mary: Grace and Hope in Christ*', *Theology*, 110 (2007), 171–9

Marsden, John, '*Mary: Grace and Hope in Christ*—An Anglican View', *Milltown Studies*, 56 (2005), 105–13

McLoughlin, William M., and Pinnock, Jill (eds.), *Mary for Time and Eternity* (Leominster: Gracewing, 2007)

Miller, Desmond, '*Mary: Grace and Hope in Christ*—The ARCIC Statement', in William M. McLoughlin and Jill Pinnock (eds.), *Mary for Time and Eternity* (Leominster: Gracewing, 2007), 15–21

O'Donnell, Christopher, 'Ecumenical Progress on the Blessed Virgin: ARCIC 2005: Context and Content', *Milltown Studies*, 56 (2005), 87–104

Painter, John, 'ARCIC on Mary: An Historical Consideration of the Use of Early Church Evidence in the Seattle Statement', *Journal of Anglican Studies*, 4/1 (2006), 59–80

Ruddock, Bruce, 'Ecumenical Reflections *on Mary, Grace and Hope in Christ*', *The Pastoral Review*, 3/1 (2007), 42–6

Sagovsky, Nicholas, 'Marie: Divisions oecuméniques et unité', *Istina*, 50/3 (2005), 250–60

Sagovsky, Nicholas, 'Mary and Christian Hope: Background to the ARCIC Statement', in William M. McLoughlin and Jill Pinnock (eds.), *Mary for Time and Eternity* (Leominster: Gracewing, 2007), 3–14

Seville, Thomas, '*Mary: Grace and Hope in Christ*', *New Directions* (January 2008), 6–7

Soosai Rethinam, Raja, '*Mary: Grace and Hope in Christ* against the Background of Recent Mariological Research', STD dissertation, KU University, Leuven, 2010

Unterseher, C. C., 'Mary in Contemporary Protestant Theological Discourse', *Worship*, 81/3 (2007), 194–212

Warner, Martin, '*Mary, Grace and Hope in Christ*: A New Understanding of Scripture and Tradition?', *International Journal for the Study of the Christian Church*, 5/3 (2005), 265–71

Wicks, J., 'Tra la Scrittura e la prospettiva escatologica', in G. Cereri and J. F. Puglisi (eds.), *Enchiridion oecumenicum: Documenti del dialogo teologico interconfessionale (7): dialoghi internazionali 1995–2005* (Bologna: Dahoniane, 2006), 157–80

Chapter 6

From ARCIC II to ARCIC III:
Pointers for Further Work

The mandate given to ARCIC II in 1982 by Pope John Paul II and the Archbishop of Canterbury, Robert Runcie, was

> to continue the work already begun: to examine ... the outstanding doctrinal differences which still separate us, with a view to their eventual resolution; to study all that hinders the mutual recognition of the ministries of our Communions, and to recommend what practical steps will be necessary when, on the basis of our unity in faith, we are able to proceed to the restoration of full communion.

The request relating to 'practical steps' was, with ARCIC II's warm support, passed in 2001 to the International Anglican–Roman Catholic Communion on Unity and Mission (IARCCUM), whose synthesis of ARCIC's work, *Growing Together in Unity and Mission*, is the firstfruit.

What Further Work by ARCIC III is Needed?

The analyses of the Agreed Statements of ARCIC II made in this volume suggest, first, that overall the greatest need is for a shift in focus towards what unites Anglicans and Roman Catholics, as well as what divides them. The mandate for ARCIC II focused on 'the outstanding doctrinal differences which still separate us', thus restricting its work, since it was unable to highlight areas of significant agreement between Anglicans and Roman Catholics. Thus significant common teaching on social issues, though recognized in principle, was left aside in *Life in Christ*, while in *Mary: Grace and Hope in Christ*, Mary's role as a woman embodying justice could be given only brief attention. The analyses made here of the responses to the work of ARCIC II point to the need for the Commission to be allowed to consider not only what divides, but what unites.

The mandate given to ARCIC III, to explore 'Church as Communion, local and universal, and how in communion the local and universal Church come to discern right ethical teaching', is open to such an approach, supported by the Commission's intention to employ 'receptive ecumenism' in its work. As part of this mandate, ARCIC III may be in a position to consider work needed or suggested as useful in the analyses of responses to each Agreed Statement, which are summarized below in turn.

Salvation and the Church (1987)

The 1999 Lutheran–Roman Catholic *Joint Declaration on the Doctrine of Justification* sets this Statement in a new context. It has effectively been received officially by the Roman Catholic Church as well as by the Anglican Communion, though some exploration of Roman Catholic teaching on penance, purgatory, and indulgences may be helpful.

The larger need is for this fundamental agreement on the core concerns of the Reformation to become effective in local churches across both traditions.

Church as Communion (1991)

The 'communion ecclesiology' set out in this Statement is well integrated into the life of both traditions, including the recognition of some 'constitutive elements', such as shared lectionaries, and common teaching by bishops on social issues. Care is needed, however, to avoid misunderstandings, were *koinonia* to be taken in isolation from other scriptural images of the Church.

Positively, promoting the practice of ecclesial communion is an ongoing challenge for each local church, not least in congregational life. It is hindered by our ongoing divisions, most visible in our disparate relationships at local and universal levels, the reconciliation of which remains the ultimate goal of ARCIC, and relates closely to the mandate of ARCIC III.

Life in Christ: Morals, Communion and the Church (1994)

The differentiated agreements on sexuality made in this Statement have now to be reconsidered in the light of new contexts in both the Anglican Communion and the Roman Catholic Church. More particularly, further consideration is needed as regards how moral norms and conscience are understood, along with clarification as to the sacramentality of marriage and how the two traditions respond to changing understandings of marriage.

All these matters, and the need to explore areas of agreement, not least in social ethics, relate to the second part of ARCIC III's mandate, 'how in communion the local and universal Church come to discern right ethical teaching'.

The Gift of Authority: Authority in the Church III (1999)

The challenges raised in the responses to this Agreed Statement are well summarized by Cardinal Kasper: 'the relationship between the universal Church and the local church',[1] which relates closely to the first part of ARCIC III's mandate, 'Church as communion, local and universal'.

A particular aspect of this topic is the exercise of papal authority (the 'universal' level). The question as to how authority is exercised for the sake of communion and mission at local and intermediate levels, together with that of the participation and the engagement of the faithful, complements this.

Mary: Grace and Hope in Christ (2005)

The major area in which further work is needed does not concern Mary herself, so much as how the formation of doctrine is integrated with the reading of Scripture, *sensus fidei,* the historical development of doctrine and the teaching authority of the magisterium—areas considered in *The Gift of Authority* which (as noted above) are closely related to the first part of ARCIC III's mandate.

Requests have been made by some Anglicans for work on the holiness of Mary, her transition to God's glory, and the practice of invocation. Perhaps more significant have been those calls for serious engagement with feminist concerns surrounding Marian teaching and devotion. However, both tasks lie outside the Commission's current mandate.

Into the Future: How?

The way ARCIC works is evolving, as outlined in these stages of its doctrinal method, which indicate ways forward for the third phase of Anglican–Roman Catholic dialogue.

Overcoming Doctrinal Division by Going to our Origins

ARCIC's original mandate named it as 'a serious dialogue which, founded on the Gospels and on the ancient common traditions, may lead to that unity in truth, for which Christ prayed.' The Commission made significant progress by walking this way, and, as time went on, developing the theology of *koinonia,* a 'communion ecclesiology'. Fresh language was used to get

---

[1] Cardinal Walter Kasper, 'Letter to his Grace Dr Rowan Williams, Archbishop of Canterbury', 17 December 2004, www.vatican.va/roman_curia/pontifical_councils/chrstuni/card-kasper-docs/rc_pc_chrstuni_doc_20041217_kasper-arch-canterbury_en.html.

behind the controversial language of the past, while sustaining a 'real yet imperfect communion'.

This approach was fruitful for issues arising from Reformation divisions, and offered new perspectives for church authorities to consider on eucharist, ministry, and salvation. Yet it was impotent to resolve issues arising since the sixteenth-century breach of communion: fresh disputes over papal authority and divergences over morals.

Employing a Complementary Eschatological Method

ARCIC II deepened its method by seeking to work from the future back-wards, as well as from the past forwards. In taking in an eschatological perspective, the Commission recognized that reconciliation can come about only as an act of hope and faith, a 'pro-visional' expression of divine *koinonia*. In doing so, it was recognized that all we do in this age, while shaped and inspired by our shared vision of God's kingdom, is partial. Our actions in the service of full, visible unity in Christ are therefore to be marked by mutual openness, deep humility, and hope.

Taking Seriously our Divided Practice

ARCIC III is asked to consider 'Church as Communion, local and universal, and how in communion the local and universal Church come to discern right ethical teaching'. This takes the Commission into considering how ecclesial communion is lived in practice: the self-understanding, structures, and processes of decision-making in each tradition. It means facing up to their shortcomings, and frank acknowledgement of where our ecclesial manner of life gets in the way of the mission of God: in short, it is a call for ecclesial repentance.

Engaging in Receptive Learning

To work 'pro-visionally' towards the goal of full communion demands not only repentance, but being open to the gifts we can each receive from the other that may contribute to resolve our shortcomings and divisions. It involves reflecting on what unites us, and the many ways in which Anglicans and Roman Catholics share already in 'real but imperfect com-munion': use of the Scriptures, prayer in common, theological education, joint witness through caring, and advocacy on social issues for example.

This dynamic of receiving and giving thus embraces dialogue on both what unites and what divides, and of re-receiving elements of the apostolic Tradition which may have been obscured or forgotten in the course of our wounded history (see *The Gift of Authority*, §§24–25).

Conclusion: Walking Together

The encouragements and challenges which the Agreed Statements of ARCIC II present to both Anglicans and Roman Catholics are profound. Looking back over the analysis of responses made to the five Agreed Statements of ARCIC II, it can be seen that the mandate given to ARCIC III relates closely to much of the further work sought. For ARCIC's work to be received, there is need, at all levels of each tradition, for delight that we share so much, and a humble openness to conversion of heart and mind. Without these, the ecumenical journey will come to nothing.

In walking together in the interwoven tasks of dialogue and action, Anglicans and Roman Catholics commit themselves not only to work towards a Church fully reconciled, but to know more deeply what full communion in Christ means, and that for the sake of the whole creation. In so doing, we are enabled, by God's grace, to respond to the challenge which is 'increasingly acute':

> the tension between the Gospel, as reflected in the apostolic witness, and the approaches and trends of our post-modern societies. Both questions are faced by all Churches; though in different ways, we are confronted by many of the same problems and the same challenges. Therefore we should seek to undertake to address these issues in dialogue, so that we can give witness together to a world which has a pressing need for the common witness of the Church.[2]

---

[2] Ibid.

PART B

THE SCOPE AND METHOD
OF ARCIC II'S WORK

Chapter 7

The Use of Scripture in the Agreed Statements of ARCIC

Adelbert Denaux

In their Common Declaration of 1966, Pope Paul VI and the Archbishop of Canterbury, Dr Michael Ramsey, expressed their intention 'to inaugurate between the Roman Catholic Church and the Anglican Communion a serious dialogue which, founded on the Gospels and on the ancient common traditions, may lead to that unity in truth, for which Christ prayed'. *The Malta Report* (1968) explicitly noted the need of this foundation for the future dialogue (§2), while the members of ARCIC I summarized their work in saying: 'We have taken seriously the issues that have divided us, and have sought solutions by re-examining our common inheritance, particularly the Scriptures' (*The Final Report*, Introduction, §3).

Neither the *Malta Report* nor ARCIC I did clarify, however, how the constituent parts of the formula 'the Gospels and the ancient common traditions', and the relationship between them, are to be understood. Why this focus on 'the Gospels' and not on 'the Scriptures' as a whole? What is exactly meant by the 'ancient common traditions' (plural)? What are they (are the early creeds included and how many so-called ecumenical councils)? How far do they reach in space and time? How do these 'ancient common traditions' relate to the apostolic Tradition? Does the addition of 'ancient common traditions' in the formula imply that the dialogue should not be based on Scripture alone (*sola scriptura*) but that the Scriptures should be understood in the light of the ancient traditions or that the latter are seen as a legitimate development and interpretation of the Scriptures?

Scripture and the 'Ancient Common Traditions'

ARCIC I did not directly or systematically address the historical issue of the relation between Scripture and Tradition, but ARCIC II has certainly paid attention to it. It states that 'Within Tradition the Scriptures occupy a unique and normative place and belong to what has been given once-for-all' (*The Gift of Authority*, §19), and speaks of 'the dynamic interdependence of Scripture and apostolic Tradition and the normative place of Scripture within Tradition' (*The Gift of Authority*, §52). And further:

> To safeguard the authenticity of its memory the Church was led to acknowledge the canon of Scripture as both test and norm. But the quickening of its memory requires more than the repetition of the words of Scripture. It is achieved under the guidance of the Holy Spirit by the unfolding of revealed truth as it is in Jesus Christ. . . . To keep alive the memory of Christ means to remain faithful to all that we know of him through the apostolic community. (*Church as Communion*, §26)

The relation between the canon of Scripture and the living apostolic Tradition, as expressed in the creeds and in the life of the Church, is aptly described in *Church as Communion* §31:

> This memory, realised and freshly expressed in every age and culture, constitutes the apostolic tradition of the Church. In recognizing the canon of Scripture as the normative record of the revelation of God, the Church sealed as authoritative its acceptance of the transmitted memory of the apostolic community. This is summarised and embodied in the creeds. The Holy Spirit makes this tradition a living reality which is perpetually celebrated and proclaimed by word and sacrament, pre-eminently in the eucharistic memorial of the once-for-all sacrifice of Christ, in which the Scriptures have always been read. Thus the apostolic tradition is fundamental to the Church's communion which spans time and space, linking the present to past and future generations of Christians.

It is even described more explicitly in §50 of the same document, citing the Common Declaration of Pope John Paul II and Archbishop Robert Runcie (2 October 1989), where it is said that the

> certain yet imperfect communion we already share . . . is grounded in faith in God our Father, in our Lord Jesus Christ, and in the Holy Spirit; our common baptism into Christ; our sharing of the Holy Scriptures, of the Apostles' and Nicene Creeds; the Chalcedonian definition and the teaching of the Fathers; our common Christian inheritance for many centuries.[1]

The Gift of Authority §§19–23 describes the dynamic interdependence of Scripture and apostolic Tradition, and the normative place of Scripture within Tradition.

---

[1] See Appendix B4 below.

How Does ARCIC II Use Scripture Directly?

When one reads the five Statements of ARCIC II, one may say that its authors, among whom are two biblical scholars (one Anglican and one Roman Catholic), have tried to go beyond the polemical language of the past controversies and to use a language that is nearer to our common biblical and patristic heritage. Indeed, 'since its inception ARCIC has sought to get behind opposed or entrenched positions to discover and develop our common inheritance of faith' (*Mary: Grace and Hope in Christ*, §4). The Scriptures influence not only the language used in the documents, but also the themes developed (such as Church, salvation, moral life, authority), the way of thinking, and the arguments used.

The way Scripture is used is varied in shape and form. One can distinguish the following usages of Scripture in the ARCIC II papers:

a) Citation

First of all, there is a striking number of references to biblical texts, mainly from the New Testament, in all ARCIC II Statements. Sometimes biblical texts are quoted, taking into account their context:

> *Salvation and the Church*, §17 (Eph 2.6), §23 (Rom 2.6; Lk 17.10)
>
> *Church as Communion*, §17 (Rom 12.5; Eph 1.23; 3.4), §23 (Rev 7.9–10), §38 (Eph 1.9, 10)
>
> *Life in Christ: Morals, Communion and the Church*, §9 (Jn 17.4), §21 (Acts 2.42; 4.32), §22 (Phil 2.1–5), §23 (Mt 5.43; Jn 13.34), §27 (Eph 4.15; Phil 2.12–13)
>
> *The Gift of Authority*, §8 (2 Cor 1.18–20), §21 (2 Cor 10.8), §32 (1 Thess 1.5), §33 (Jn 17.23), §48 (2 Cor 4.1, 7; Lk 22.31–32)
>
> *Mary: Grace and Hope in Christ*, §1 (Lk 1.42), §5 (Lk 1.38), §8 (Jer 31.33), §9 (Ezek 16.8), §10 (Rom 8.28–30; Lk 1.15), §11 (Gal 4.4; Lk 1.38), §17 (Lk 2.16; 2.34–35), §18 (John 3.3–5), §20 (Lk 11.27–28), §21 (Acts 1.14), §22 (Jn 1.13), §25 (Jn 2.5–12), §26 (Jn 19.26), §29 (Rev 12.5), §55 (Col 1.16–17; Eph 2.10), §56 (Gen 5.24; Heb 11.5), §57 (2 Cor 5.17), §64 (2 Cor 1.20; Col 1.27), §68 (1 Tim 2.5–6), §69 (Heb 4.15), §71 (Jn 2.1–12, §72 (Jn 19.27; Gen 3.20), §77 (Rom 8.30)

The references and quotations are not to be seen as an attempt to find scriptural proof texts for certain positions already taken. They rather show that Scripture was the main source from which the members of ARCIC II tried to come to a common mind and language in overcoming the divisions of the past. Moreover, where in the past some biblical texts led to different interpretations due to confessional oppositions, ARCIC II made a permanent attempt to arrive at a common interpretation of controversial biblical texts.

In *The Gift of Authority*, a specific biblical text is used to explain a larger notion. The 'Yes' of God and the 'Amen' of the Church, mentioned by the Apostle Paul in 2 Corinthians 1.18–20, is used as a key concept to understand the reality of 'Authority in the Church' (§§7–31).

b) Scriptural Exegesis

In comparison with the other documents of ARCIC II, the Agreed Statement *Mary: Grace and Hope in Christ* has explored new ways of reading Scripture. This may have to do with the theme of the document: the two Marian dogmas and Marian devotion (notably the invocation of Mary). The drafters of the document were aware that in some circles the role of Mary has been minimized, in reaction to perceived exaggerations of Roman Catholic Marian devotion in some circles. More particularly, they knew the objection heard in many non-Roman churches that the two dogmas are not in accordance with Scripture. In the light of this we can point to two specific uses of Scripture in *Mary: Grace and Hope in Christ*, and an explicit hermeneutic awareness.

- *Exegetical work.* The members of ARCIC II felt the need of an extensive exegetical study of all texts concerning the biblical figure of Mary (*Mary*, §§12–30). This study led the Commission to the conviction that 'it is impossible to be faithful to Scripture and not to take Mary seriously' (§6). The scriptural evidence that Mary plays a specific role in salvation history is a challenge to those who claim to take the Bible very seriously and at the same time minimize the role of Mary in their personal life and in the life of the Church.
- *Biblical patterns.* The members of ARCIC II were fully aware that the New Testament text does not speak about the 'immaculate conception' and the 'assumption into heaven' of Mary, the Mother of God. But they found that the essence of these two doctrines could be well understood in the light of the biblical pattern of God's prevenient grace, and of the anticipation of the eschatological fulfilment (*Mary*, §§52–63: Mary in the biblical pattern of grace and hope). In the latter sense, the two doctrines might be said to be in 'accordance with Scripture', a multi-level concept which has to be qualified.

Biblical Themes in ARCIC II's Work

There are synthetic presentations in ARCIC II's work of the biblical or New Testament theology of central themes such as salvation (see *Salvation and the Church*, §§12–13) and *koinonia*/communion (see *Church as Communion*, §§6–13: 'Communion Unfolded in Scripture'). Two particular themes, however, stand out.

a) *Koinonia* and Ecclesiology

The biblical notion of *koinonia* is the central concept to describe the reality of the Church. ARCIC I already stated: 'Fundamental to all our Statements is the concept of *koinonia* (communion) . . . Although "*koinonia*" is never equated with "Church" in the New Testament, it is the term that most aptly expresses the mystery underlying the various New Testament images of the Church' (*Final Report*, Introduction, §5).

ARCIC II has taken up this conviction in devoting a full Agreed Statement to *Church as Communion*. Its first part outlines how 'communion' is unfolded in Scripture (§§6–15). It looks at:

- its Old Testament roots: 'God wants his people to be in communion with him and with each other' (§7);
- its fulfilment in the New Testament (§§8–11);
- the occurrence of the term in the New Testament (§12);
- the many ways it is there conveyed: 'This communion is participation in the life of God through Christ in the Holy Spirit, making Christians one with each other' (§13); and
- the different dimensions of *koinonia* (§15).

In sum: 'This fellowship in one body, sustained through Word and Sacrament, is in the New Testament called *koinonia* (communion). "*Koinonia* with one another is entailed by our *koinonia* with God in Christ. This is the mystery of the Church"' (*Salvation and the Church*, §1, quoting *The Final Report*, Introduction, §5).

b) Anthropology

Life in Christ in its opening paragraph makes this affirmation: 'Anglicans and Roman Catholics derive from the Scriptures and Tradition the same controlling vision of the nature and destiny of humanity and share the same fundamental moral values'. Later it states, 'Both our traditions draw their vision from the Scriptures. To the Scriptures, therefore, we now turn, to discover the origins of our common heritage in the Gospel of Jesus Christ and the faithful response of the Christian community' (§16).

In *Life in Christ* §§17–35, this biblical description is given of our common heritage in matters of Christian moral life. More particularly, the members of ARCIC II who prepared this Statement were convinced that their common vision of human sexuality and on Christian marriage is based on Scripture:

- 'Both our traditions affirm with Scripture that human sexuality is part of God's good creation (cf. Gen 1.27; see further Gen 24; Ruth 4; the Song of Songs; Eph 5.21–32; etc.)' (§55);
- 'The New Testament is unequivocal in its witness that the right ordering and use of sexual energy is an essential aspect of life in Christ (cf. Mk 10.9; Jn 8.11; 1 Cor 7; 1 Pt 3.1–7; Heb 13:4)' (§57);
- 'Both [traditions] affirm that a faithful and lifelong marriage between a man and a woman provides the normative context for a fully sexual relationship. Both appeal to Scripture and the natural order as the sources of their teaching on this issue' (§87).

Reading Scripture from an Ecumenical Perspective

In *Mary: Grace and Hope in Christ* §7, for the first time ARCIC explored in any kind of detail its method of interpreting Scripture, and tried to define what it calls an 'ecumenical reading' of Scripture. This paragraph gives a synthetic survey of the various methods employed in 'the whole tradition of the Church':

- typological reading (the New Testament, patristic and medieval periods);
- the clarity and sufficiency of Scripture (the Reformers);
- historical-critical approaches (eighteenth century to twentieth century); and
- more recent approaches (narrative, rhetorical, and sociological reading).

The different methods arose in reaction to others, and in assimilating valuable insights from the surrounding culture. The Reformation is a reaction to typological interpretation; the historical-critical method is a legacy of the more 'rational' approach of the Enlightenment which was first accepted by Protestant scholars and which then spilled over into Roman Catholic and Orthodox scholarship; and the more post-modern readings are a reaction to historical-critical scholarship. ARCIC II recognized that each of these methods has its strengths and weaknesses. This is also true of post-modern readings, although it is not stated explicitly.

ARCIC II was aware that within the different confessional traditions some methods are more acceptable and more widely used than others. But it sought to overcome these confessional reductions or preferences for one specific method. It expressed its conviction that a truly ecumenical reading of Scripture seeks 'to draw upon the whole tradition of the Church' and 'to integrate what is valuable from each of these approaches, as both correcting and contributing to our use of Scripture' (*Mary*, §7).

ARCIC II further recognized 'that no reading of a text is neutral, but each is shaped by the context and interest of its readers'. This is true for the different readings employed in the course of history as well as for confessional readings. *Mary: Grace and Hope in Christ* §7 thus seeks to formulate what it understands to be an 'ecumenical reading', which is to be distinguished from the different methods employed in the past until now, and in the different confessions. The context and interest of an ecumenical reading are clearly and honestly stated: 'Our reading has taken place within the context of our dialogue in Christ, for the sake of that communion which is his will' (see Jn 17).

An ecumenical reading might be compared with some of the more modern 'contextual approaches' such as liberationist, feminist, ecological readings, and so on, which take a particular perspective in reading the text of the Bible. Applied to the interpretation of texts about Mary in the New Testament, an ecumenical reading is described as follows: 'It is thus an ecclesial and ecumenical reading, seeking to consider each passage about Mary in the context of the New Testament as a whole, against the background of the Old, and in the light of Tradition' (*Mary*, §7).

- It is an 'ecumenical' reading because of its attempt both to take a wholistic approach, and also to read 'beyond the borders'.
- It is an 'ecclesial' reading because it reads the Bible in the light of the apostolic Tradition as it is developed in the Church of Jesus Christ (which is not simply to be identified with one of the Christian confessions, even when Roman Catholics believe that the Church of Christ 'subsists' in the Roman Catholic Church).
- It is a 'canonical' reading because it reads each individual passage of the Bible 'in the context of the New Testament as a whole, against the background of the Old'.
- It is a 'traditional' reading because it reads the Bible 'in the light of the Tradition' (with capital T, hence pointing to the 'apostolic Tradition', which cannot be simply equated with the various regional or confessional 'traditions': see *The Gift of Authority*, §§14–17 and footnote 1). It accepts that this ongoing Tradition, which embodies intrinsically the 'catholicity' of the Church of Christ, has integrated and will integrate all that is valuable from each of these approaches.

ARCIC II believes there is a truly ecumenical method of interpreting Scripture, which is not the same as any one confessional reading of Scripture. An ecumenical reading of Scripture can be helpful to overcome what is reductionist in confessional readings. The ecumenical movement at large invites the churches to conversion and reform. One aspect of the latter is the challenge for each church to convert from an exclusivist confessional reading to an inclusive ecclesial and ecumenical reading of Scripture. This does not mean that any church has to give up its confessional reading, but that each church or ecclesial communion has to discern what is of remaining value in its confessional reading and how it can purify its reading in order to enlarge it by receiving what is valuable in the readings of other Christian churches and so to come to a truly 'catholic' and 'apostolic' reading of Scripture.

Chapter 8

The Doctrinal Methods of ARCIC II

Charles Sherlock and Nicholas Sagovsky

ARCIC's Characteristic Method:
Origins, Fresh Language, *Koinonia*

In its first phase, ARCIC employed a method in which the Anglican and Roman Catholic members, grounding their work on the original sources of 'the Gospels and the ancient common traditions' (1966 Common Declaration), re-examined controverted questions as partners.[1] This led them repeatedly to the discovery of a common faith which could be expressed in doctrinal agreements, using language which avoided the traditional terms of controversy. These agreements were reached by and expressed in 'our avoidance of the emotive language of past polemics and our seeking to pursue *together* that restatement of doctrine which new times and conditions are, as we both recognise, regularly calling for' (*The Final Report*, Preface).

This approach also undergirds *Salvation and the Church*, the first Agreed Statement from ARCIC II. In this, questions of language were necessarily to the fore, given its focus on the Reformation controversies surrounding justification and sanctification. But this method has not always been appreciated by church authorities. On the Anglican side, the Evangelical Fellowship in the Anglican Communion sent an Open Letter to the bishops gathering for the 1988 Lambeth Conference, objecting to the language used about the eucharist and justification in ARCIC's texts. On the Roman Catholic side, the *Observations* of the Congregation for the Doctrine of the Faith (CDF) on *The Final Report* (1982) and on *Salvation and the Church* (1988) assess these documents critically because, it is argued, the language employed by ARCIC did not correspond to Catholic doctrinal

---

[1] The 'ancient common traditions' include the theological decisions of the Councils of Nicea (325), Constantinople (381), Ephesus (431), and Chalcedon (451). The writings of the Fathers East and West of these times were seen as common ground with Rome by the Reformers.

terminology.[2] Nevertheless, ARCIC's linguistic method was commended by John Paul II at a 1980 audience for the Commission. The Pope observed that the method of ARCIC is 'to go behind the habit of thought and expression born and nourished in enmity and controversy, to clothe it in a language at once traditional and expressive of the insights of an age which no longer glories in strife'.

This language-oriented approach is not the whole story. This characteristic ARCIC method engages language and tradition with a theology of *koinonia,* which continued to deepen as ARCIC's work progressed (see further Chapters 9 and 10 below). At the heart of the testimony of 'the Gospels and the ancient common traditions' to the revelation of God in Christ is the Church's confession of God as Trinity. Here the concept of *koinonia*—communion/fellowship/participation—is central: communion in the Church is grounded in our communion in Christ and the Spirit, and thus with one another, participating in the divine communion of the Holy Trinity. A theology grounded in *koinonia*— a 'communion ecclesiology'—naturally draws out what Christians have 'in common' before identifying what is distinctive about particular traditions, churches or communions.

ARCIC I thus employed a communion ecclesiology to get behind controversial language to explore the faith which Anglicans and Roman Catholics (and other Christians) share, in such a way that differences may be seen in new ways. This approach can be seen to grow in strength and be used with increasing confidence in the documents of ARCIC I, as the Introduction to the *The Final Report* makes clear:

> Fundamental to all our Statements is the concept of *koinonia* (communion). In the early Christian tradition, reflection on the experience of *koinonia* opened the way to the understanding of the mystery of the Church ... Union with God in Christ Jesus through the Spirit is the heart of Christian *koinonia* ... *Koinonia* with one another is entailed by our *koinonia* with God in Christ. This is the mystery of the Church.[3]

This motif is also the systematic key to *Church as Communion* (1991), which varied ARCIC's approach in two main ways. On the one hand, given *The Final Report* and *Baptism, Eucharist and Ministry* from the World

---

[2] A similar approach is found in the official Vatican response (1991) to *The Final Report*: ARCIC II responded to this in *Clarifications of Certain Aspects of the Agreed Statements on Eucharist and Ministry of the First Anglican–Roman Catholic International Commission* (London: Church House and CTS, 1994).

[3] *The Final Report*, §§4, 5.

Council of Churches (WCC) Faith and Order Commission, *koinonia* did not now need exposition, and was not controverted. So the language-oriented, 'getting behind' approach was less relevant, though still significant. On the other hand, the opportunity was taken to harvest the insights gained from *The Final Report* and *Baptism, Eucharist and Ministry*, and from wider ecumenical dialogues, in understanding 'church' in terms of communion, an approach that proved especially valuable because of its Trinitarian background and echoes.

Differences Arising since Separation: Reception and Re-Reception

In the Statements considered thus far, the Commission was dealing with issues in which there was a long shared heritage, before the Reformation breach. The resolving of differences through a fresh reading of contro-verted issues which employs a linguistic method and theology of *koinonia* is possible for such concerns. But what sort of method is helpful in approach-ing areas of division arising since the sixteenth-century separation?

One approach taken by ARCIC II was to develop the concepts of 'recep-tion' and 're-reception': these became increasingly significant in its work. In earlier ecumenical understanding, reception 'represents the process by which the local churches accept the decision of a Council and thereby recognize its authority', as the 1971 Louvain meeting of Faith and Order stated.[4] In *The Gift of Authority* (1999), ARCIC II took a wider perspective, arguing that reception entails 'the constant and perpetual reception and communication of the revealed Word of God in many varied circum-stances and continually changing times' (*Gift*, §16). It is closely related to the normal process of passing on the apostolic Tradition, the ongoing transmission of the Gospel of Jesus' death and resurrection. As Paul explained to the church of Corinth, he 'traditioned' to them the Gospel which he himself had first 'received' and which they in turn 'received' (1 Cor 15.1–2). The reception of conciliar definitions by a local church is the solemn and formal realization of this broader process of reception.

But reception does not always take place smoothly. ARCIC II thus recognized that

---

[4] Günther Gassmann (ed.), *Documentary History of Faith and Order*, Faith and Order Paper 159 (Geneva: WCC, 1993). It also noted that 'Even after the formal conclusion of such a process and the canonical reception of a Council's doctrinal formula . . . the process of reception continues in some way or other as long as the churches are involved in self-examination.'

> Within the Church the memory of the people of God may be affected or even distorted by human finitude and sin. Even though promised the assistance of the Holy Spirit, the churches from time to time lose sight of aspects of the apostolic Tradition, failing to discern the full vision of the kingdom of God in the light of which we seek to follow Christ.   (*Gift*, §25)

In situations such as these,

> Fresh recourse to Tradition in a new situation is the means by which God's revelation in Christ is recalled ... there may be a rediscovery of elements that were neglected and a fresh remembrance of the promises of God ... a sifting of what has been received because some of the formulations of the Tradition are seen to be inadequate or even misleading in a new context. This whole process may be termed *re-reception*.   (*Gift*, §25)

Understood in this way, 're-reception' implies that reception is not a linear, but a never ending process, a continuing dynamism in the life of churches. It needs constant renewal because of the changes of time and culture, and because of human finitude and sin. Where partial or defective reception of the apostolic Tradition has led to divisions between Christian churches or traditions, re-reception becomes a means of ending processes of divided reception and turning backwards to full communion. It is particularly relevant in addressing questions which have arisen after a breach of communion—which for Anglicans and Roman Catholics focus in particular on moral issues and the ministry of the Bishop of Rome as universal primate.

In *Life in Christ: Morals, Communion and the Church* (1994), ARCIC II continued to use its characteristic method, but found it necessary to write at greater length and in more detail, owing to the development in separation of different approaches to new questions. This more descriptive approach also led to the Statement speaking not so much of *koinonia* as of a 'shared vision' of Christ and of humanity. Further, the conclusions reached are expressed in 'double negative' terms, rather than the positive claims of earlier Statements: it is argued that, were the approach taken in *Life in Christ* adopted, remaining differences on moral issues would not of themselves constitute reasons to stay apart, but would be open for 're-reception' in the context of a Church fully reconciled.

An Eschatological Method

Even so, *Life in Christ* shows that ARCIC's characteristic doctrinal method was revealing its limits. In particular, it came to be realized that this approach orients discussion to the past, appeal to which can produce only limited outcomes. The Co-Chairmen of the original Commission, in their Preface to *The Final Report*, recognised the limits of an approach through history alone as insufficient to breach the gap between the two traditions. ARCIC I therefore

> Determined, in accordance with our mandate, and in the spirit of Philippians 3.13, 'forgetting what lies behind and straining forward to what lies ahead', to discover each other's faith as it is today and to appeal to history only for enlightenment, not as a way of perpetuating past controversy.

The Philippians text highlights the need for an eschatological method to complement ARCIC's now familiar method, taking a future-oriented as well as a past-oriented perspective into account. This is largely absent in *The Final Report*, *Church as Communion*, and *Salvation and the Church*—ARCIC's work on Reformation-focused divisions. In these texts *koinonia* is understood as communion in the divine life into which God is drawing us in Christ. Yet in these Statements 'Church' overwhelmingly concerns the people of God of this *present* age. Occasional references to the goal of a 'transformed creation' appear (so *Church as Communion*, §16), but not in relation to the Church. When a 'pilgrimage' perspective is offered (*Church as Communion*, §48) it refers to the life of the earthly Church.[5]

Two long sections in *Life in Christ* (1994) focus on the past: 'Common Heritage' (§§12–35) and 'Paths Diverge' (§§36–53). But the Statement opens with 'Shared Vision' (§§4–11), with its key question, 'What are persons called to be, as individuals and as members one of another in the human family?' Significantly, the 'Common Heritage' section is dominated by the motif of the 'patterning power of the kingdom', viewing moral formation in Christ from the perspective of the reign of God which Jesus proclaimed, embodied, and promised—the dimension of hope. (It is noticeably absent from the concluding section, 'Communion and the Church', however: §§96–102). *Life in Christ* thus marks a transition in ARCIC's method, bringing eschatological as well as historical perspectives into play, while sustaining the key motif of *koinonia*.

The gradual shift towards an 'eschatological' focus is more evident in *The Gift of Authority* (1999), which forms a 'bridging' document in terms of ARCIC's method. The topics considered include those amenable to

---

[5] *Salvation and the Church*, §22 makes a similar 'pilgrimage' reference, but the point is to turn the edge of possible issues surrounding indulgences and penitential practice, rather than bring an eschatological perspective.

ARCIC's characteristic approach, notably the relationship between the Scriptures and T/tradition (see *Gift*, §§14–23). But others involve differences which have arisen since the sixteenth-century breach of communion, most notably surrounding the ministry of the Bishop of Rome. Not only is this ministry experienced asymmetrically by Anglicans and Roman Catholics, but official teaching about the papal office has developed in the post-Reformation centuries, as have reactions to it.

To what extent can there be a doctrinal method explicating defined teachings which can satisfy both Roman Catholics and Anglicans, in the knowledge that what satisfies one tradition will be seen as far from perfect by the other? In a Church fully reconciled, Anglicans would have to be able to live with the fact that Roman Catholics take teaching about the papal ministry in a certain way (or range of ways); Roman Catholics would have to be content that Anglicans take it in ways that may differ, sometimes inconsistently, from Roman Catholic teaching. Reaching agreement only on what we agree on is inadequate: earthed reflection about the acceptable limits to doctrinal diversity in a reconciled church requires the exploration and possible re-reception of diversities with which both traditions can live.

In *Life in Christ* it was recognized that reconciliation concerning decisions taken in isolation calls for a shift in method. Yet when it comes to questions of authority and its exercise in a reconciled visible *koinonia*, the shifts needed are of kind rather than degree. So ARCIC's characteristic method was adapted by the inclusion of an eschatological element, in order to take the dialogue 'ahead of' as well as 'behind' opposed or entrenched positions, into an envisioned future unity. This approach asks what practical steps and re-receptions are necessary to move into this new territory, and how acceptable they may be to both Anglicans and Roman Catholics. This brave step forward, however, has led to considerable misunderstanding of the work of the Commission.

In *The Gift of Authority*, this shift can be seen in the way that the 'Yes/ Amen' motif, from which its major conclusions emerge, acts as a kind of counterpoint to an ecclesiology of *koinonia*. Our 'Amen' to God's 'Yes' in Christ leads believers to the affirmation that the 'Amen' which we utter now in communion is 'at the heart of the great liturgy of heaven' (§13). Eschatology is also present in the recognition that 'the full vision of the kingdom of God' functions as a 'future' criterion for discerning the apostolic Tradition (§25). Again, synodality is about believers, 'like their predecessors', together following 'Jesus on the Way . . . until he comes again' (§34). And the importance given to 're-reception' in the Statement reflects a future-oriented perspective, especially as it is applied in the final paragraphs to the distinctive ministry offered by the Bishop of Rome (§§60–62).

The most significant examples of papal teaching ministry since the Reformation are the 1854 definition of the immaculate nature of the conception of the Blessed Virgin Mary, and the proclamation in 1950 of her bodily assumption. When the Commission came to considering these, ARCIC's method of reflecting on the testimony to Mary in the Scriptures and ancient common traditions produced agreement.[6] But it did not enable the Commission to resolve current differences over Marian dogmas, nor could it connect adequately with patristic understanding of Mary as a corporate, typological figure (e.g. of the Church). It was noted, however, that Paul and other New Testament writers understand humanity in fundamentally corporate and future-oriented terms (so Rom 5; 1 Cor 15; Heb 12.1–2; 1 Jn 3.2–3). These texts witness to the vision of redeemed humanity in Christ, in which we participate now by faith, in the light of doing so 'face to face' in the new creation. Taking a similarly 'future backwards' approach to Mary led to a breakthrough. As *Theotókos*, Mary remains in a unique relation to the One she bore in her own flesh: in view of Christ's resurrection and ascension, she can thus be understood as the fulfilment in human terms of the hope believers have in Christ, a hope which reached 'backwards' from this future into her own life to the fullest extent (*Mary*, §§52–57).

This way of re-expressing theological teaching on the end and beginning of Mary's life may appear forced or fanciful, especially since the Marian dogmas are so tightly linked in the West to an Augustinian theology of sin and grace. But it bears significant witness to what it means to be human in today's world, to the ways in which believers participate actively in the divine work of recreation, and to the hope which lies before us—of which Mary is a unique paradigm. This approach also represents a significant development of the 'Yes/Amen' motif in *Gift*: its paradigmatic expression is the Annunciation narrative (Lk 1.26–38), with its profound theology of grace (see *Gift*, §16). Situating Mary in a 'Pauline' eschatological framework may bring surprises (see the citation of Eph 2.10 in *Mary*, §55), but affords an illuminating re-orientation of the Christian tradition to the future as well as the past.

Mary: Grace and Hope in Christ is set out structurally on characteristic ARCIC lines, with the canonical Scriptures considered first, then historical

[6] Such agreement can be seen already in *Authority in the Church II*, §30 (1981).

issues taken up (the 'past to present' method). But, as with *Life in Christ* and *The Gift of Authority*, these paragraphs are the fruit of a significant 'future to present' re-reading of the Scriptures and the ancient common traditions. When it comes to the theological content of the Church's teaching on Mary, the 'future backwards' method comes to full flower. In the process, Reformation and Enlightenment concerns about accessible and critical exegesis are respectively taken into account, and typological insights from the Western medieval and Eastern Christian traditions sensitively harvested. Even so, the Statement recognizes that in a church fully reconciled, the status of the two Roman Catholic dogmas about Mary, and the authority of the Bishop of Rome which undergirds them, can be resolved only when these and similar matters are re-received in the light of the future to which God calls us and all creation.

The 'future backwards' approach also illuminates a further dimension of the work of ARCIC. It comes to see Mary as not only a particular woman viewed through the lens of historical research (i.e. viewed 'by sight') but more deeply, in terms of our corporate (redeemed) humanity (i.e. viewed 'by faith') as a type of the people of God. *Mary: Grace and Hope in Christ* thus seeks not so much to reconcile 'liberal/Enlightenment' perspectives with 'traditional/dogmatic' ones as to fold them together, just as a communion ecclesiology views the Church through the eyes both of 'faith' (as confessed in the creeds) and of 'sight' (the lived reality of church which we experience in this age).

This approach also constitutes a further invitation and motivation towards a Church fully reconciled, a reconciliation which becomes possible only as theology is approached not so much as scholastic propositions but as Christian spirituality. The Commission's experience of living in varied houses of prayer, its common life of prayer, its joint reflection on the Scriptures, and its sharing of the Ministry of the Word in the eucharist—but not yet in holy communion—played major roles in its work regarding Mary, from the elegant reflection on the Scriptures in the early paragraphs to the illuminating discussion of the invocation of the saints in the final sections.

Conclusion: A 'Pro-Visional' Hermeneutic

In sum, the doctrinal method of ARCIC has passed through two major stages. In the first, characteristic phase, the Commission made significant progress by working together from the Scriptures and ancient common traditions, which ultimately led to the development of the theology of *koinonia*, a communion ecclesiology. This employed fresh language to get behind the controversial language of the past and allow the two traditions to continue in a 'real yet imperfect communion'. Such an approach produced much fruit in relation to issues arising from Reformation divisions, and offered new perspectives for church authorities to consider. Yet it was impotent to resolve issues arising since the breach of communion.

The doctrinal method of ARCIC II, as reflected in its later Agreed Statements, deepened the Commission's method by introducing the concept of 're-reception', and orienting it to working from the future backwards, as well as from the past forwards. This can be seen in the 'patterning power of the kingdom' theme of *Life in Christ*, the 'Yes/Amen' and re-reception motifs in *The Gift of Authority*, and especially the 'reversal' of Romans 8.30 in *Mary: Grace and Hope in Christ*. In taking into its method an eschatological perspective, ARCIC II recognized that reconciliation can come about only as an act of hope and faith, as a graced response to the divine initiative. Above all, its call for mutual re-receptions of treasured traditions entails a 'pro-visional' expression of divine *koinonia*, accepting the partial yet authentic nature of our present participation in the new creation in Christ.

This doctrinal hermeneutic means that our actions in the service of full, visible unity in Christ are called to be inseparable from mutual openness and deep humility. Anglicans and Roman Catholics—and other Christian traditions—who follow this path will, by the grace and *koinonia* of the Holy Spirit, be enabled to walk together on the Way of Christ into the future to which God calls us.

Chapter 9

Theological Themes in the Agreed Statements of ARCIC II

Charles Sherlock

Each Agreed Statement issued by ARCIC II takes up a particular topic, as set out in successive mandates agreed by Anglican and Roman Catholic authorities. Rather than engaging in an unfolding dialogue, the Commission thus worked on a series of distinct issues, assisted by consultants skilled in the area concerned.

As regards method, the doctrinal hermeneutic of ARCIC II developed with each Statement (see Chapter 8 above). As regards the content of its Agreed Statements, on the other hand, the process of reaching agreement turned on the Commission identifying and exploring a motif which could allow it to 'get behind' polemical positions and open up new insights. In *The Final Report* this can be seen most clearly in relation to the eucharist, where the concept of *anamnesis*, understood in the light of biblical perspectives on the Passover, enabled ARCIC I to issue an Agreed Statement, and then an Elucidation, followed by ARCIC II's *Clarifications*.

This chapter seeks to elucidate major theological themes across the work of ARCIC II. First, however, a sketch is given of the motif–the 'engine-room'–of each of its five Agreed Statements, to clarify the particularity of each topic addressed.

The 'Engine-Room' of Each Agreed Statement

Salvation and the Church faces foundational theological issues of the English Reformation which undergirded the presenting twentieth-century issues of eucharist, ministry, and authority. Rather than focusing on the capacity of the will, the place of reason, or the effects of sin, which revolve around human experience, the Commission chose to focus its work on the unmerited grace of God in Christ, activated by the Holy Spirit. This theo-centric approach enabled it to reach an agreement which took into account the official teaching of both traditions, while placing them in a newly-discerned context of grace.

Church as Communion is the only ARCIC Statement not focused on Anglican–Roman Catholic differences. Rather, it aimed to set out agreement on the foundations of the ecclesiology of *koinonia*, the scriptural motif of increasing prominence in the work of ARCIC I. Communion thus forms a clear 'engine-room' for this Agreed Statement: significantly, as expounded more fully below, this helped the Commission move beyond the explicit biblical data to a strongly Trinitarian understanding of *koinonia*.

Life in Christ: Morals, Communion and the Church, on the other hand, considers a specific area of dialogue, differences around moral questions and ethical teaching. A significant phrase is the 'patterning power of the kingdom', reflecting the emerging significance of eschatology in the Commission's work. This image is grounded in a sustained emphasis not on 'What ought we to do?', but on 'What kind of persons are we called to become?' (§6). *Life in Christ* was issued in 1994: as explored in Chapter 3 above, significant differences have since emerged among Anglicans and Roman Catholics over same-sex sexual acts. Even so, the formative influence of what the kingdom of God calls us to become continues to be sustained in both traditions.

The Gift of Authority is subtitled *Authority in the Church III*, since it builds on ARCIC I's two partial agreements in this area in *The Final Report*. The mandate for ARCIC II asked that it consider Anglican concerns about the authority of Scripture and the place of the laity in decision-making, and Roman Catholic teaching on the place of tradition and the ministry of the Bishop of Rome. In this third consideration of authority, the Commission worked from the particular and the local to the universal, seeing authority as God's gift of 'authoring' life, salvation, and new life in Christ. In analysing how the believer's initial response to the Gospel unfolds, it adopted Paul's motif of God's life-transforming 'Yes' in Christ, which elicits our 'Amen'. By employing this 'engine-room', ARCIC II was able both to reach agreement on each area of its mandate, and also to ask for a 're-reception' of the ministry of the Bishop of Rome, while raising questions about the way authority is exercised in each tradition.

Mary: Grace and Hope in Christ drew ARCIC II into a different style of working. The place of Mary in the economy of salvation calls not only for scriptural and historical analysis, but also for engagement with diverse patterns of Marian devotion, while paying close attention to the papally defined dogmas about her conception and destiny. The common agreement between Anglicans and Roman Catholics on Mary as *Theotókos* enabled the Commission to affirm that she holds a distinctive place among the people of God, having the closest relationship to her risen son. In view of this, the Statement uses a 'reversal' of Romans 8.30 as its 'engine-room', opening up common understanding of the ministry of Mary from the 'future backwards' rather than just from the past forwards.

Theological Themes in ARCIC II

This chapter now turns to overall theological themes in the work of the Commission. It does not claim to present a definitive view, nor to do justice to the rich tapestry of insights drawn from the Scriptures and the Christian tradition.

It is important to recognize that, since the Anglican and Roman Catholic traditions have much in common, and since the mandates which governed ARCIC's work were specific, significant areas of Christian belief remain implicit in Agreed Statements. Thus none deals directly with Christology, because Anglicans and Roman Catholics alike confess the Apostles', Nicene, and Athanasian Creeds, and affirm the Chalcedonian Definition (see *The Malta Report*, §3). Agreement is sometimes reached on the ground of accepted teaching, and may indeed illuminate it: for example, the place of Mary in the development of orthodox belief in the full humanity, deity, and unity of the person of Christ (*Mary*, §§31–33). But a number of theological themes characterize ARCIC's work.

a) The *Koinonia* of the Triune God: Father, Son, and Spirit

'Fundamental to all our Statements is the concept of *koinonia* (communion)', states the Introduction to *The Final Report* (§4). It is seen as 'the term that most aptly expresses the mystery underlying the various New Testament images of the Church'. In sum, '*Koinonia* with one another is entailed by our *koinonia* with God in Christ. This is the mystery of the Church' (§5). Further, 'Throughout the work of ARCIC, work which continues, *koinonia* or communion has been a key concept. *Church as Communion* is probably the best short presentation of an ecumenical ecclesiology of communion', Nicholas Sagovsky concludes.[1]

In the work of ARCIC I, however, *koinonia* was used in reference to relationships within the Church, or our relationship with God.[2] This is its

---

[1] Nicholas Sagovsky, *Ecumenism, Christian Origins and the Practice of Communion* (Cambridge: Cambridge University Press, 2000), especially chapters 2 and 9. His exposition notes the origins of the social concept in Plato and Aristotle, while seeing its Christian grounding in both the Augustinian (chapter 8) and Cappadocian (chapter 7) theological traditions. See further Chapter 10 below.

[2] *The Malta Report* only uses 'Communion' as a term to refer to the Anglican Communion or Roman Catholic Church, as well as references to 'inter-communion' in the sense of eucharistic sharing.

primary use in the New Testament, the initial reference coming in Acts 2: the Spirit-endowed community 'devoted themselves to the apostles' teaching and *koinonia*, to the breaking of bread and the prayers' (Acts 2.42), given practical expression in the sharing of goods. This apostolic *koinonia* was deeper and richer than human fellow-feeling or cooperation: it was 'the fellowship/communion (*koinonia*) of the Holy Spirit' (2 Cor 13.13), to participate in which both called for and enabled the overcoming of all human divisions. What ARCIC II added to *The Final Report* is grounding *koinonia* not so much *ecclesio*logically as *theo*logically; not the mystery of the Church so much as the mystery of the *koinonia* of the Holy Trinity, reading the testimony of Acts in 'vertical' as well as 'horizontal' terms. So *Church as Communion* states early on,

> Communion embraces both the visible gathering of God's people and its divine life-giving source. We are thus directed to the life of God, Father, Son and Holy Spirit, the life God wills to share with all people. There is held before us the vision of God's reign over the whole of creation. (§3)

And later,

> At the centre of this communion is life with the Father, through Christ, in the Spirit. Through the sending of his Son the living God has revealed that love is at the heart of the divine life. (§15)

ARCIC II, in identifying *koinonia* as at the root of the Church's identity and nature, thus situates it in the life of the Holy Trinity, into whose communion all creatures are being drawn through God's saving and reconciling work. This emphasis is present across the work of ARCIC II. *Salvation and the Church* begins with 'The will of God, Father, Son and Holy Spirit', before going on to cite *The Final Report* on *koinonia*. *Life in Christ*, while focused on ethical issues, presupposes a Trinitarian perspective, since human beings are made in the image of the triune God: 'In speaking of God as Trinity in Unity, Father, Son and Holy Spirit, we are affirming that the Being of God is a unity of self-communicating and interdependent relationships' (§7), the divine life of true freedom into which human beings are called. In *Gift*, the nature of authority ('gift') and its exercise (responding to God's 'Yes') are explored in terms of the will of God the Father revealed in the living Word and the guidance of the Holy Spirit. And *Mary* cannot be understood without its affirmation of classical Christology (§§32–34), the work of the Spirit in Mary, and the enduring relationship of Son and Father. Believers 'know themselves to be children together of the one heavenly Father, born of the Spirit as brothers and sisters of Jesus Christ, drawn into the communion of love of the blessed Trinity. Mary epitom-ises such participation in the life of God' (*Mary*, §5).

In short, the major theological theme which threads its way through each Agreed Statement of ARCIC II is a Trinitarian understanding of *koinonia*. It denotes more than the earthly life of the people of God, 'fellowship' as a human experience. Rather, *koinonia* in the work of ARCIC II expresses a deeper, eschatological view of humankind and creation, drawn into the divine communion of Father, Son, and Spirit, into which, by grace, they will grow until 'God will be all in all' (1 Cor 15.28).

b) The Priority of Divine Grace

Differences over grace are commonly perceived as lying at the heart of Reformation disputes. Not a few Protestants still believe that Roman Catholics hope to be 'saved by works'; conversely, emphasis on 'by faith' can in practice be an 'easy work' that avoids discipline. More subtle are debates about human 'cooperation' with God (synergism), with Mary as the definitive example.

Against this background—still present in some popular circles—the consistent emphasis in the work of ARCIC II on the priority of God's grace, the divine initiative of costly love, is striking. The issue was unavoid-able in *Salvation and the Church*, given the Commission's mandate to work on the issues surrounding justification. But it is threaded through *Church as Communion*, with its emphasis on *koinonia* as *God's* work in Christ, through the Spirit. The emphasis in *Life in Christ* on what we are called to become, rather than what we ought to do, reflects a similar emphasis: right ethical behaviour is grounded in the enabling call of God, not human action independent of divine. Similarly, the insight that true authority is understood in terms of 'gift'—a *divine* gift—in *Gift* is founded on sustained agreement on the priority of God's work. Our 'Amen' to God, and to the will of God, is possible only because of God's 'Yes' in Christ.

This emphasis on grace in ARCIC II's work is seen most clearly in *Mary*, especially its exegesis of the Annunciation narrative (§§5, 15–16). It is not uncommon to hear a writer or preacher affirm that, just as Mary said 'Yes' to God, so should we. Of itself this is innocent enough: but if her response is seen as being necessary to allow God's saving work to proceed, we are on dangerous ground. Luke's account is beautifully nuanced, as ARCIC II's exegesis shows: Mary is already 'graced' (as the perfect participle *keka-ritomene* expresses), excluding ideas of 'human work'. She does not say 'Yes', acting out of her own strength, but 'Let it be to me according to your word'. Traditional artistic representations of the Annunciation show rays of light coming from above, or words on a scroll proceeding from Gabriel's lips to Mary's womb: the living Word of God already enabling her response. And as it is a graced, and so truly free human response, there is no suggestion of her being forced into submission, 'spiritual rape'. The Annunciation is a work of Trinitarian grace: as *Mary* states (§16),

> The trinitarian pattern of divine action in these scenes is striking: the Incarnation of the Son is initiated by the Father's election of the Blessed Virgin and is mediated by the Holy Spirit. Equally striking is Mary's *fiat* ['let it be'], her 'Amen' given in faith and freedom to God's powerful Word communicated by the angel. ([Luke] 1.38)

c) The Word of God: Written, Traditioned, and Living

Anglicans and Roman Catholics alike receive the canonical Scriptures of the Old and New Testament as the divinely inspired 'word of God written'. In the past, however, they were experienced quite differently: Anglican congregations encountered them in every service, while many Roman Catholics had little direct exposure to them. Anglicans were delighted by the Second Vatican Council's enthusiasm for the Bible, and many provinces took up the 'Three-Year Lectionary', one of the Council's outcomes. Anglican scholars welcomed the dynamic understanding of 'Sacred Tradition' in the Divine Constitution on Revelation, *Dei Verbum*, though others continued to question the extent to which Rome accepts biblical authority. For its part, Rome questioned whether the Reformation motif *sola scriptura* isolates the Bible from the life of the Church, and fails to coordinate it with the Christian tradition.[3] These issues about the relationship of Scripture and Tradition thread through the work of ARCIC I, notably regarding authority, where the Commission acknowledged that it had reached 'partial' agreements.

Both *Salvation and the Church* and *Church as Communion* make extensive use of Scripture, repeatedly citing it as carrying ultimate weight. *Life in Christ*, given its subject-matter, gives considerable space to historical and ethical analysis, yet grounds its 'Shared Vision' (§§4–11) and 'Common Heritage' (especially §§12–30) in biblical exegesis. This is also crucial to the agreements reached about the two Marian dogmas in *Mary* (§§52–57). As Adelbert Denaux shows in Chapter 7, the citation and careful employment

---

[3] Though affirmed by some Anglicans, *sola scriptura* is not found in Anglican formularies. Further, the phrase is in the ablative, not nominative case (cf. *sola fide*): i.e. it means '*by* Scripture alone', not 'Scripture only'.

of Scripture is a feature of every ARCIC II Statement. But the 1988 Lambeth Conference asked ARCIC II to explore the matter further, as did the 1991 official response of the Holy See to *The Final Report*. *Gift* is the outcome of ARCIC's renewed and specific work in this area. Christ, the living Word, it argues, is the revelatory source of both the people of God and the written Scriptures. God's 'revelation has been entrusted to a community', in which 'the faith of the community precedes the faith of the individual', whose 'Amen' is bound up with that of the people of God. Thus, as *Gift* concludes, 'Word of God and Church of God cannot be put asunder' (§23).

As regards 'tradition', *Gift* argues that it is a dynamic process, 'far more than the transmission of true propositions concerning salvation' (§14; compare *Dei Verbum*). Further, the Commission accepted the 1963 Montreal Faith and Order Conference's use of English capitals and plurals to distinguish its different aspects. This sees 'Tradition' as 'the Gospel itself, transmitted from generation to generation in and by the Church', the 'apostolic Tradition' of Christ crucified and raised (see 1 Cor 15.1–3). Used without a capital, 'tradition' refers to 'the traditionary processes', the ways by which the once-for-all Tradition continues to be passed on, while the plural 'traditions' refers to the particular forms this takes.[4] This approach situates the Scriptures as the central 'thread' and norm in the ongoing life of the Church. As *Gift* §19 concludes,

> Within Tradition the Scriptures occupy a unique and normative place and belong to what has been given once-for-all. As the written witness to God's 'Yes' they require the Church constantly to measure its teaching, preaching and action against them.

Gift goes on to develop the concepts of 'reception'—the regular, usual process of believers encountering Christ through the Scriptures and means of grace—and 're-reception' (§§24–25). The latter involves 'fresh recourse to Tradition', which is needed when human sin has obscured or forgotten an aspect of the Gospel, or when a new situation calls for 'rediscovery of elements that were neglected and a fresh remembrance of the promises of God', or even a 'sifting of what has been received because some formulations of the Tradition are seen to be inadequate or even misleading in a new context'. In both reception and re-reception, insights are sought from 'biblical scholars and theologians and the wisdom of holy persons',

---

[4] *Gift*, footnote 1. This lists 'liturgy, theology, canonical and ecclesiastical life in the various cultures and faith communities' as typical 'peculiar features' of traditions.

and the *sensus fidei* with which every Christian is endowed. In this way 'there is an exchange, a mutual give-and-take, in which bishops, clergy and lay people receive from as well as give to others within the whole body' (§28).

Articulated most fully in *Gift*, such an understanding of revelation as engaging believers with the Word of God living and written, acting through the whole Church as guided by the Spirit, runs as a thread throughout each Agreed Statement of ARCIC II.

d) 'Pro-Visional', Multi-Dimensioned Hope

One critique of ARCIC's work has been that the view of the Church presented is too ideal. In response, Commission members would argue that, especially in *Gift*, the institutional life of God's people is addressed, and that implementing ARCIC's agreements is the purpose for which the IARCCUM was set up. More directly, however, practical reconciliation remains out of reach without agreement about ecclesial ideals. A strong motif of hope runs through ARCIC II's work, undergirding recommenda-tions affecting life in this non-ideal age. This hope is 'pro-visional': it shapes the present towards the vision of God who 'through Christ has reconciled all things to himself, whether on earth or in the heavenlies, making peace by the blood of his cross' (Col 1.20). It is also experienced now as less than complete, hope known by faith rather than sight (see Rom 8.24; 1 Cor 13.1–10). God's people are always *in via*, on the Way.

This theme of 'pro-visional' hope is present in the unfolding method of ARCIC II. As traced in Chapter 8, an 'eschatological method' emerged gradually in its work—doing theology 'from the future backwards' rather than just the past forwards. As noted there, the roots of this 'turn' can be already found in the Co-Chairs' Preface to *The Final Report*, which cites Philippians 3.13, 'forgetting what lies behind and straining forward to what lies ahead', complementing the characteristic ARCIC method of 'getting behind past polemics'. This analysis in terms of method, however, does not do full justice to the thread of hope woven throughout the work of ARCIC II. The ecumenical project, in whatever way it is understood, responds to Christ's prayer for 'those who *will* believe in me through their word, *ut unum sint*—that they may be one' (Jn 17.20–21). Hope is thus part of the *raison d'être* of ARCIC, but its work goes beyond this minimum. The Agreed Statements of ARCIC II are increasingly shaped towards a 'pro-visional' understanding of the people of God, of humankind, and of the whole created order, drawn towards the new creation, the 'new heaven and earth'—partially, provisionally, walking by faith, not sight.

Salvation and the Church, as noted earlier, orients discussion towards Reformation disputes. Yet its discussion of 'Salvation and Justification' opens with the affirmation that the Scriptures 'speak of our entry *with all the saints* into our eternal inheritance, of our vision of God face to face, and of our participation in the joy of the final resurrection' (§12, emphasis added). Likewise, sanctification—another Reformation area of debate— is seen as involving 'the restoring *and perfecting* in humanity of the likeness of God marred by sin. We grow into conformity with Christ, the perfect image of God, *until he appears and we shall be like him*' (§17, emphasis added). Practical Christian life is the outcome of God's bringing into being

> a renewed humanity, the humanity of Jesus Christ himself, the 'last Adam' or 'second man' (cf. 1 Cor 15.45, 47). He is the firstborn of all creation, the prototype and source of our new humanity. Salvation involves participating in this humanity, so as to live the human life now as God has refashioned it in Christ (cf. Col 3.10). (§19)

We have thus been 'created in Christ Jesus for good works, which God prepared beforehand to be our way of life' (Eph 2.10): they are, as it were, 'waiting ahead' for us to take up in our pilgrimage to the new creation.

These agreements in *Salvation and the Church* arose from concerns over difference regarding justification by faith, understood as the personal level of salvation. But, as the title indicates, salvation in Christ is a communal reality, seen in the corporate life of the people of God. The Church 'is thus a sign and foretaste of God's Kingdom' (§26), and, even though its life is marred by sin in this age, it is 'called to be, and by the power of the Spirit actually is, a sign, steward and instrument of God's design' (§29). The motifs of 'sign and foretaste', taken up in *Church as Communion*, are thus marks of hope at the ecclesial level—and more, as anticipations of the kingdom of God. In *Life in Christ* this is stated explicitly: 'Life in Christ is the gift and promise of new creation (cf. 2 Cor 5.17), the ground of community, and the pattern of social relations' (§4). How this plays out in the moral life of disciples is articulated in terms akin to the approach of *Salvation and the Church* to 'good works'. 'The fundamental moral question, therefore, is not 'What ought we to do?', but *'What kind of persons are we called to become?'* For children of God, moral obedience is nourished by *the hope of becoming like God* (cf. 1 Jn 3.1–3)' (§6, emphasis added).

These interwoven dimensions of living in hope come together in *Gift* in terms of 'Amen', the graced response of creatures to God's 'Yes' in Christ. The personal 'Amen' of the believer, evoked by the Spirit, is drawn into the 'Amen' of the local church, which in *koinonia* with the whole Church is offered in the eucharistic thanksgiving (§§11–14). This 'Amen' has echoes deeper and wider than those of a particular time and place: it is a sign and foretaste of creation's response to God's reconciling work in Christ. This is clearly seen in the Statement's conclusion:

> We have come to a shared understanding of authority by seeing it, in faith, as a manifestation of God's 'Yes' to his creation, calling forth the 'Amen' of his creatures . . . In a broken world, and to a divided Church, God's 'Yes' in Jesus Christ brings the reality of reconciliation, the call to discipleship, and a *foretaste of humanity's final goal* when through the Spirit all in Christ utter their 'Amen' to the glory of God . . . When the churches, through their exercise of authority, display the healing and reconciling power of the Gospel, then the wider world is offered a vision of what God intends for all creation.
>
> (*Gift*, §50, emphasis added)

'Hope' is most clearly seen as a theme in the work of ARCIC II in *Mary*: 'hope' is paired with 'grace' in its title. She holds a distinctive place in the people of God as the mother of the Lord Jesus, *Theotókos*, 'mother of God incarnate', not only as a historic individual, but as participating already in the 'end' of all humanity and creation. Mary may thus be confessed as 'mother of the faithful' and 'mother of the new humanity' (§72). Mary embodies hope in Christ, hope entered into as she, in graced freedom, put her trust in the Word of God: 'let it be to me according to God's will'. This hope was lived out in her costly vocation, through misunderstandings and the pain of seeing her son die, to the new hope of the 'third day' and the day of Pentecost. Her life patterns the 'pro-visional' hope of every disciple, called to walk with Christ, bear his cross, and through the Spirit share his risen life until he comes in glory.

Salvation and the Church concludes its argument (§31) with this affirmation of practical, 'pro-visional' hope, a theme which threads a deepening path across the work of ARCIC II:

> The source of the Church's hope for the world is God, who has never abandoned the created order and has never ceased to work within it. It is called, empowered, and sent by God to proclaim this hope and to communicate to the world the conviction on which this hope is founded. Thus the Church participates in Christ's mission to the world through the proclamation of the Gospel of salvation by its words and deeds. It is called to affirm the sacredness and dignity of the person, the value of natural and political communities and the divine purpose for the human race as a whole; to witness against the structures of sin in society, addressing humanity with the Gospel of repentance and forgiveness and making intercession for the world. It is called to be an agent of justice and compassion, challenging and

assisting society's attempts to achieve just judgement, never forgetting that in the light of God's justice all human solutions are provisional. While the Church pursues its mission and pilgrimage in the world, it looks forward to 'the end, when Christ delivers the kingdom to God the Father after destroying every rule and every authority and power' (1 Cor 15.24).

Conclusion

This overview of themes in the work of ARCIC II shows that, while each Agreed Statement revolves around a particular presenting issue, the foundations on which the conclusions and recommendations rest—Trinitarian faith, divine grace, the Word of God, and the hope of creation reconciled to God—are classic. In view of the shared Western theological inheritance of Anglicans and Roman Catholics, this similarity of emphases is not unsurprising, and sustains the hope of full communion.

In short, the Second Anglican–Roman Catholic International Commission—as sign, instrument and foretaste of *koinonia*—has in its work made common confession of the Catholick Faith, 'that we worship One God in Trinity, and Trinity in Unity'.

Chapter 10

The *Koinonia* Ecclesiology of ARCIC I and II

Nicholas Sagovsky

The work of ARCIC I and II has been to address communion-dividing issues. Not all the issues that divide our two Communions are ecclesiological. There are doctrinal issues, like those concerning the doctrine of Mary, and there are ethical issues, like those concerning human interventions at the beginning and end of life, but many of the issues that divide the two Communions are ecclesiological.

The Final Report of ARCIC I (1981) contains joint Agreed Statements on eucharist, ministry, and authority—all of them ecclesiological issues. The work of ARCIC II has also been largely in the field of ecclesiology. The ARCIC II Statement on justification is called *Salvation and the Church*, and the Statement on ethics *Life in Christ: Morals, Communion and the Church*. The ARCIC II Statement on the exercise of authority in the Church, *The Gift of Authority*, is explicitly an essay in ecclesiology, and the approach to the doctrine of Mary and the invocation of the saints in *Mary: Grace and Hope in Christ* is again explicitly ecclesiological. Undergirding all this work is the one ARCIC Statement that does not address a communion-dividing issue: *Church as Communion*. This was written to lay 'a necessary foundation for further work', so that the undergirding ecclesiology of ARCIC's work could be made explicit. It gives us a fine, brief statement of an ecclesiology of communion: the ecclesiology (or type of ecclesiology) on which the work of ARCIC and many other ecumenical dialogues rest.

The Church Visible and Invisible

From the beginning, the Christian churches have understood themselves as expressing realities both visible and invisible. The relation between the invisible and the visible Church—the people of God seen through the eyes of faith and sight respectively—is perhaps the central question in ecclesiology. Before the Reformation, where critique of the visible Church was sporadic and sometimes brutally suppressed, it was easy, in both East and West, to insist that the visible Church, with all its structures and functioning, was to be identified with the earthly kingdom of God. This was the ideology that supported the Church's deployment of power, especially through the sacraments and the priesthood. The visible Church, by the will and command of Christ, represented the invisible and eternal kingdom, which was also to be identified with the invisible Church, the Bride of Christ, purified and glorified. A closer reading of Augustine, and especially of the *City of God*, would have sounded a warning note against too easy an identification of the Church *in via*, the pilgrim Church on earth, with the heavenly Jerusalem, the City of God. For Augustine, the earthly Church was indeed the sacrament of the heavenly, but it was imperfect, constantly in need of repentance and renewal.

The Reformation turned on the perceived need for such repentance and renewal. The European religious movement of the sixteenth century, using the criterion of the newly appropriated teaching of Scripture, judged the earthly Church of Rome in the light of the early Church and of the eschatological, heavenly Church, and on both counts found it wanting. Article XIX, attached to the Book of Common Prayer, begins: 'The visible Church of Christ is a congregation of faithful men [*sic*] . . .'. In so doing, it presupposes the existence of an invisible, heavenly Church of Christ about which there is little doctrinal controversy (though there was much controversy about purgatory and the Last Judgement). By and large, there was and is continuing agreement about the life of the Church invisible: the communion of all the redeemed in Christ. In our, later, era of ecumenism, the question has been how far that agreement can be pushed into our understanding of the life of the Church visible: the church(es) visible seen as 'sacrament' of (pledge of and participation in) the Church invisible.

Key Twentieth-Century Theological Developments

A number of theological developments in the twentieth century made possible the work of ARCIC and other similar ecumenical dialogues. One was the flourishing of patristic studies after the closing down of much biblical scholarship in the Roman Catholic Church in the reaction against Modernism (1907). The exodus of Orthodox scholars after the Russian Revolution (1917) brought a much richer appreciation in the West of Orthodoxy as a living tradition, and with that an appreciation of a eucharistic ecclesiology that had not been through the mill of scholasticism.[1] In the West, the work of scholars like Yves Congar and Henri de Lubac developed an understanding of Catholicism that went behind the nineteenth-century ultramontane reaction to the perils of the papacy and the Church in Western Europe.

A second development, related to the first, was the revival in the understanding of God as Trinity. The work of the major theologians of the twentieth century, theologians like Karl Barth, Karl Rahner, and Hans Urs von Balthasar, is from start to finish Trinitarian. It accords with the approach in a classic statement of patristic Orthodoxy such as Vladimir Lossky's *The Mystical Theology of the Eastern Church* (1957).[2] Lossky's is not a text in ecclesiology, but it shows how all Christian theology is to be seen as Trinitarian, participatory, a means of mystical ascent within the life of the Church. The Church itself, in its inner reality, is nothing less than a participation in the life of the Trinity.

A third development was the revival of scriptural studies in the Roman Catholic Church, and within that the cautious acceptance of critical method. Scripture scholars began to go behind the ahistorical accounts of the life and structure of the Church which had been developed in the Middle Ages, and which had increasingly been deployed in triumphalist mode, to an understanding of the Church—following Newman—as having *developed* and *changed*, while always remaining the same: the Church as willed by Christ. There was a new openness to the New Testament witness to diversity in the life of the churches, to the Church as incomplete, *in via*, a pilgrim church, to the variety of metaphors used in Scripture to describe the shared life of the people of God. This was the immediate backdrop to the ecclesiological freshness of *Lumen Gentium* and other documents from the Second Vatican Council (1962–5).

A fourth development, closely related to the second and the third, was a renewed understanding of the eucharist, a shift away from the individualism which could ultimately be traced back to the Middle Ages, and towards a re-appropriation of the eucharist as a common participation by the people of God in the life of Christ, and with that, a participation in the life of the Trinity. Anglican scholarship contributed greatly to this: for example, through Gregory Dix's *The Shape of the Liturgy* (1945), the contribution of E. C. Ratcliff to the liturgy of the Church

---

[1] The work of John Zizioulas, *Being as Communion: Studies in Personhood and the Church* (Yonkers, NY: St Vladimir's Seminary Press, 1985), has been very important here.

[2] Vladimir Lossky, *The Mystical Theology of the Eastern Church* (Yonkers, NY: St Vladimir's Seminary Press, 1957).

of South India (1948), and L. S. Thornton's New Testament study, *The Common Life in the Body of Christ* (1950).[3] Dix's argument that there was a fourfold *action* to the eucharist was immensely influential in the development of a more dynamic (and pneumatic) understanding of the eucharist: one which enabled eucharistic authenticity to be discerned across ecumenical divides.

A fifth development was that of the ecumenical movement itself. The formation of the World Council of Churches (1948) from the twin movements of Faith and Order and Life and Work gave an immense boost to ecumenical rapprochement. The Roman Catholic Church kept its distance but the presence of ecumenical observers played an increasingly significant role at Vatican II.

The Second Vatican Council

Out of the *aggorniamento* of the Council there came a new openness to participation in the ecumenical movement, the charter of which is *Unitatis Redintegratio*, the Decree on Ecumenism (1964).[4] This firmly bases its approach to ecumenism on an ecclesiology of communion. It refers several times to Christians of other traditions as 'separated brethren',[5] acknowledging that

> Men [sic] who believe in Christ and have been truly baptised are in communion with the Catholic Church even though this communion is imperfect

and that

> all who have been justified by faith in Baptism are members of Christ's body, and have a right to be called Christian, and so are correctly accepted as brothers by the children of the Catholic Church.   (§3)

This paragraph goes on to grant that

> Some and even very many of the significant elements and endowments which together go to build up and give life to the Church itself, can exist outside the visible boundaries of the Catholic Church: the written word of God; the life of grace; faith, hope and charity, with the other interior gifts

---

[3] Gregory Dix, *The Shape of the Liturgy* (London: Dacre, 1945); L. S. Thornton, *The Common Life in the Body of Christ* (London: Dacre, 1950).

[4] www.vatican.va/archive/hist_councils/ii_vatican_council/documents/vat-ii_decree_19641121_unitatis-redintegratio_en.html.

[5] Among those Christian communions in which 'Catholic traditions and institutions in part continue to exist', the Anglican Communion is said to have 'a special place' (§3).

of the Holy Spirit, and visible elements too. All of these, which come from Christ and lead back to Christ, belong by right to the one Church of Christ. (§3)

The way was prepared for the kind of dialogue at which ARCIC has worked for more than thirty years, but even more for the outworking of practical ecumenical projects of the type sketched by IARCCUM. As *Unitatis Redintegratio* continues,

> The term 'ecumenical movement' indicates the initiatives and activities planned and undertaken, according to the various needs of the Church and as opportunities offer, to promote Christian unity. These are: first, every effort to avoid expressions, judgements and actions which do not represent the condition of our separated brethren with truth and fairness and so make mutual relations with them more difficult; then, 'dialogue' between competent experts from different Churches and Communities. (§4)

At this point, the key word 'subsists' is introduced for the relation between 'the one and only Church' and the Roman Catholic Church. It is clear that the word is used in the Decree on Ecumenism to facilitate an open rather than a closed, an inclusive rather than an exclusive, approach:

> When such actions are undertaken prudently and patiently by the Catholic faithful, with the attentive guidance of their bishops, they promote justice and truth, concord and collaboration, as well as the spirit of brotherly love and unity. This is the way that, when the obstacles to perfect ecclesiastical communion have been gradually overcome, all Christians will at last, in a common celebration of the Eucharist, be gathered into the one and only Church in that unity which Christ bestowed on His Church from the beginning. We believe that this unity subsists in the Catholic Church as something she can never lose, and we hope that it will continue to increase until the end of time. (§4)

This inclusiveness is clearly built on a theology of the Trinity as an open and inclusive communion, and the life of the Church as a sharing, a participation in that communion which is not to be identified *tout court* with the life of the Roman Catholic Church.

ARCIC and the Church as Communion

It is not clear that the members of ARCIC I had from the beginning a strong hold on the ecclesiology of communion. This was new territory, and their approach developed over time. What is clear is that 'relationship' is at the centre of their understanding of the eucharist:

By his word God calls us into a new relationship with himself as our Father and with one another as his children—a relationship inaugurated by baptism into Christ through the Holy Spirit, nurtured and deepened through the eucharist, and expressed in a confession of one faith and a common life of loving service. (*Eucharist*, §2)

It is communion with Christ that sets the direction for the understanding of Christ's presence in the eucharist: 'Communion with Christ in the eucharist presupposes his true presence, effectually signified by the bread and wine which, in this mystery, become his body and blood' (*Eucharist*, §6).

It is in the Statement on ministry and ordination that the term *koinonia* first appears:

The life and self-offering of Christ perfectly expresses what it is to serve both God and man. All Christian ministry, whose purpose is always to build up the community (*koinonia*), flows from and takes its shape from this source and model. The communion of men with God (and with each other) requires their reconciliation. (*Ministry and Ordination*, §3)

This is how the context for the Church's need for ministry, and its practice of ordination, is set.

It is in the first Statement on authority that the use of *koinonia* becomes central. It begins:

The confession of Christ as Lord is the heart of the Christian faith. To him God has given all authority in heaven and on earth. As Lord of the Church he bestows the Holy Spirit to create a communion of men with God and with one another. To bring this *koinonia* to perfection is God's eternal purpose. (*Authority in the Church I*, §1)

In the succeeding paragraphs the term *koinonia* (as an equivalent of 'communion') is used six times, most notably at §23:

If God's will for the unity in love and truth of the whole Christian community is to be fulfilled, this general pattern of the complementary primatial and conciliar aspects of *episcope* serving the *koinonia* of the churches needs to be realised at the universal level.

This is further developed in the second Statement on authority, in the discussion of *jus divinum*:

[The universal primate] is to be the sign of the visible *koinonia* God wills for the Church and an instrument through which unity in diversity is realised. It is to a universal primate thus envisaged within the collegiality of the bishops and the *koinonia* of the whole Church that the qualification *jure divino* can be applied. (*Authority in the Church II*, §11)

This line of thinking is much more fully developed in *The Gift of Authority*.

The importance of the use of *koinonia* for the whole *of The Final Report* is made very clear in the Introduction: 'This theme of *koinonia* runs through our Statements. In them we present the eucharist as the effectual sign of *koinonia*, *episcope* as serving the *koinonia*, and primacy as a visible link and focus of *koinonia*' (Introduction, §6). Various key points about an ecclesiology of communion are stressed: 'Union with God in Christ Jesus through the Spirit is the heart of the Christian *koinonia* ... *Koinonia* with one another is entailed by our *koinonia* with God in Christ. This is the mystery of the Church' (Introduction, §5). The link is made with another key ecclesiological theme when it is said that 'The Church as *koinonia* requires visible expression because it is intended to be the "sacrament" of God's saving work' (Introduction, §7). Within the ecclesiology of communion, 'the one Church is a communion of local churches' (Introduction, §6).

Church as Communion uses 'communion' systematically to provide an understanding of the Church. For the first time ARCIC defines its usage of *koinonia*, here with respect to the New Testament:

> In the New Testament the word *koinonia* (often translated 'communion' or 'fellowship') ties together a number of basic concepts such as unity, life together, sharing and partaking. The basic verbal form means 'to share', 'to participate', 'to have part in', 'to have something in common' or 'to act together'. The noun can signify fellowship or community. It usually signifies a relationship based on participation in a shared reality (e.g. 1 Cor 10.16). This usage is most explicit in the Johannine writings: 'We proclaim to you what we have seen and heard, so that you also may have fellowship with us. And our fellowship is with the Father and with his Son, Jesus Christ' (1 Jn 1.3; cf. 1 Jn 1.7). (*Church as Communion*, §12)

Later in the document, the meaning of communion as it applies to the life of the Church is summed up:

> In the light of all that we have said about communion it is now possible to describe what constitutes ecclesial communion. It is rooted in the confession of the one apostolic faith, revealed in the Scriptures, and set forth in the Creeds. It is founded upon one baptism. The one celebration of the eucharist is its pre-eminent expression and focus. It necessarily finds expression in shared commitment to the mission entrusted by Christ to his Church. It is a life of shared concern for one another in mutual forbearance, submission, gentleness and love; in the placing of the interests of others above the interests of self; in making room for each other in the body of Christ; in solidarity with the poor and the powerless; and in the sharing of gifts both

material and spiritual (cf. Acts 2.44). Also constitutive of life in communion is acceptance of the same basic moral values, the sharing of the same vision of humanity created in the image of God and recreated in Christ and the common confession of the one hope in the final consummation of the Kingdom of God. (*Church as Communion*, §45)

The inclusion of 'the same basic moral values' points forward to *Life in Christ* (where 'vision' is a keyword). The later reference to the 'Communion of Saints' (*Church as Communion*, §48), whereby the Church 'declares its conviction that the eucharistic community on earth is itself a participation in a larger communion which includes the martyrs and confessors and all who have fallen asleep in Christ throughout the ages' points forward to *Mary: Grace and Hope in Christ*.

In *The Gift of Authority* this sketch of an ecclesiology of communion is related to the exercise of authority in the Church. Significantly, it begins from the exercise of authority in the local church before moving to episcopacy, conciliarity, synodality, and, only then, primacy. New themes relating to communion are now introduced: the importance of faithful transmission of tradition to ensure the diachronic unity of the communion of churches; the importance of memory and of bishops as exercising a 'ministry of memory'; the *sensus fidelium*; reception and re-reception; the ministry of the universal primate; the 'Amen' of the people of God. All of these play their part in a rich description of the way authority is exercised within the Church understood as a communion of churches. It is against this background that *Mary: Grace and Hope in Christ* can be seen as giving a critical account of the way in which doctrines relating to Mary have developed within the Roman Catholic tradition and the form in which they might be received by Anglicans.

Communion Ecclesiology: Critique

A theology of communion cannot resolve every issue of ecclesiology: no one image is adequate to encompass the mystery of the Church of God. The *koinonia* ecclesiology of ARCIC I and II has borne rich fruits, but it leaves some important questions to be addressed.

1. An ecclesiology of communion is well placed to set up the problem of the universal church and the local churches. If it is approached 'from below'—from the life of the local church (as in *The Gift of Authority*) in communion with other churches to make up the One, Holy, Catholic, Apostolic Church, the question then becomes, 'What

is that holds the churches together?' or 'How do churches in communion together respond to new questions and practices within the local churches?' If it is approached 'from above' the question becomes, 'How is the communion of the Trinity in which the Church participates promoted, discerned and protected within the life of the local churches?' Both of these approaches—which are, broadly speaking, 'Aristotelian' and 'Platonic' respectively—are possible within an ecclesiology of communion. Each produces a markedly different approach to questions of ecumenism. The questions here are vital not only for Anglicans but also for Roman Catholics.

2. To what extent does the notion of *koinonia* presuppose unity, and to what extent can it embrace conflict? Clearly, when *koinonia* is used to describe the shared life of the Trinity ('from above') there is no suggestion that it is being used to transcend conflict. However, when it is used to describe the life of a human community, such as a city or a monastery ('from below'), it must be used to suggest 'sharing' or 'participation' through conflict, and therefore issues of power, or it will not be true to human experience. '*Koinonia* and the limits to diversity' (especially in moral teaching) is an important area for discussion in thinking about 'a church fully reconciled'.

3. An ecclesiology of *koinonia* firmly places discussion of the life of the Church in the right area—the personal and the relational—rather than the juridical, but the visible Church is also a human institution and wholesale adoption of a communion-centred approach to the life of the Church can all too easily lead to the bypassing of juridical categories and juridical exploration. Yet if the work of ARCIC is to be of practical use (rather than a visionary aspiration), it is going to have to be translated into the world of the Church as institution and therefore of canon law. An ecclesiology of *koinonia* needs to be related to an understanding of the structures and practices by which it is sustained.

4. Within both traditions there are real problems with the practice of an ecclesiology of communion. Anglicans are seeking to find more coordination and to identify limits to diversity by means of the proposed Covenant. Roman Catholics are often critical of the workings of the Curia and the way in which the authority of Rome is deployed within the local church. Neither tradition is currently at ease with the relation between the central authorities of the Church, such as they are, as representative of the Church universal and the local churches in communion with each other.

5. A central issue within an ecclesiology of *koinonia* is that of consensus and authority. If the life of the churches consists in *koinonia*, who, within the *koinonia*, has the responsibility for identifying the consensus within the *koinonia*? Must it always be the clergy? Can the laity sometimes operate critically over against the clergy, as Newman proposed in *On Consulting the Laity in Matters of Doctrine*? How is the synodality of the Church to be articulated, and what is the responsibility of a universal primate within that process? These questions are identified but not resolved in *The Gift of Authority*.

Conclusion

An ecclesiology of communion must always be deployed against an eschatological horizon. The full expression of *koinonia* within church structures can only be an eschatological ideal. In the ordinary processes of history, *koinonia* will always fall short, as churches jostle for position and power within communion. The danger of accepting this as an unavoidable reality, however, is that we shall be content with that degree of communion which we currently enjoy, and not press on in hope of visible unity.

The very exercise of pressing on towards that goal together generates a deeper *koinonia* within and beyond the work of ARCIC. An ecclesiology of communion could lead us to rest content with the 'reconciled diversity' we currently enjoy between the churches. The ecclesiology of communion which has been developed in ARCIC I and ARCIC II is a work in progress. Its current incompletion can itself act as a dynamic for further ecumenical exploration.

PART C

THE ARCIC II STORY

Charles Sherlock

Introduction

Brief accounts of the thirteen meetings of ARCIC I can be found in the printed edition of *The Final Report*, pages 102–5. These gave a human face to the Commission, and allowed readers to gain an understanding of how it went about its work.

As noted in the Introduction to this volume, ARCIC III was asked as part of its mandate to 'promote the reception of [the Commission's] previous work' and 'present the work of ARCIC as a corpus, with appropriate introduction'; the three members who served on ARCIC II were assigned editorial responsibility for this task. It soon became clear that a similar account to that provided in *The Final Report* was desirable, not least since ARCIC II ran for twice as long as ARCIC I, and did its work in times of growing stress in ecumenical relationships. This story of ARCIC II's work has been drawn up by the Revd Dr Charles Sherlock, a member of ARCIC II from 1991.

The accounts of meetings until 1990 are taken from the 'Relations entre les Communions' sections in each issue of *Irénikon*, the journal issuing from the community of Chevetogne, a place of some significance in the ARCIC story. Of particular importance are the lively series of articles 'Anglicans et autres chrétiens', almost certainly penned by Fr Jean-Marie Tillard OP, a member of ARCIC (and other ecumenical dialogues) from its beginnings until his death in 2001. These reports are attributed to 'correspondance particulière': Adelbert Denaux comments that 'It seems to us that the style and ideas of this "correspondance particulière" are those of Jean-Marie Tillard'.[1]

---

[1] Adelbert Denaux and John Dick (eds.), *From Malines to ARCIC* (Leuven: Leuven University Press, 1997), 122, note 25.

The accounts of meetings from 1991 to 2004 are based in part on reports that Dr Sherlock made each year to the Primate of the Anglican Church of Australia. For the 1999–2004 meetings, these are supported by Adelbert Denaux, 'The Redactional History of the ARCIC Document on Mary', an Appendix to *Studying Mary*, and by essays in the Study Guide to *Mary: Grace and Hope in Christ* by two of that Statement's drafters, Charles Sherlock (Anglican) and Sara Butler (Roman Catholic).[2]

Dr Sherlock wishes to particularly thank the staff of the Veech Library of the Catholic Institute of Sydney, and of the Mannix Library of Catholic Theological College, Melbourne, for assistance with access to *Irénikon*. He also acknowledges the detailed comments made by Bishop Christopher Hill, Co-Secretary of ARCIC (1974–81) and ARCIC II (1982–9, member 1990) and now a member of ARCIC III.

All this said, responsibility for these chapters, their documentation, and the interpretations made of the work of ARCIC is taken wholly by the author.

Full lists of members of ARCIC II at each stage of its work can be found in Appendix A.

---

[2] Adelbert Denaux and Nicholas Sagovsky (eds.), *Studying Mary: Reflections on the Virgin Mary in Anglican and Roman Catholic Theology and Devotion. The ARCIC Working Papers* (London: T & T Clark, 2007); Donald Bolen and Gregory Cameron (eds.), *Mary, Grace and Hope in Christ: The Text with Commentaries and Study Guide* (London: Continuum, 2006), 204–31, 232–6.

Chapter 11

A New Commission: First Agreed Statement

Beginnings: Hope and Realism

1982 was a high point in ecumenical endeavour. Three foundational documents were published:

> *Baptism, Eucharist and Ministry* (the 'Lima' document) from the World
>   Council of Churches (WCC) Faith and Order Commission (January);
> *The Final Report* from ARCIC (March); and
> *The Mystery of the Church and the Eucharist in the Light of the Trinity*,
>   from the Joint International Commission for the Theological Dialogue
>   between the Roman Catholic Church and the Orthodox Church (July).[1]

These and other documents reflected and focused a growing ecumenical spirit across the churches. This ranged from local study groups to national and international bilateral dialogues (many initiated by the Vatican's Pontifical Council for Promoting Christian Unity) and the ongoing work of the Groupe des Dombes and the WCC Faith and Order Commission. In England, Belgium, Canada, New Zealand, South Africa, and the USA, local Anglican–Roman Catholic dialogue groups (ARCs) worked vigorously on Anglican–Roman Catholic relations, especially responding to and promoting the study of *The Final Report*. The Anglican Communion took the process of responding to ARCIC I very seriously, with responses sought (and obtained) from every province as to whether the agreements reached in *The Final Report* were 'congruent' with Anglican teaching.[2]

---

[1] The January 1982 plenary meeting of the Secretariat for Promoting Christian Unity (SPCU) heard all three documents analysed positively by its President, Cardinal Willebrands, who also noted that a second ARCIC was in the process of formation: *Irénikon*, 56 (1983), 85–7.

[2] The 1991 meeting of the Anglican Consultative Council (ACC-5) supported the request of ARCIC's Co-Chairmen that all Anglican provinces be asked to respond to identical questions on *The Final Report*, so that it could be considered carefully at the Lambeth Conference of 1988, and so one Anglican Communion response be formulated. Further, it asked that Anglican Ecumenical Officers meet to gather these responses: they did so in January 1987, resulting in *The Emmaus Report* (London: ACC, 1987). This includes the responses of nineteen provinces, and reports on all ecumenical matters relating to the Anglican Communion, notably *Baptism, Eucharist and Ministry*. This document came to ACC-7 (Singapore, 1987), which drafted the Resolutions on *The Final Report* adopted at Lambeth 1988 (see further below).

Third Common Declaration

It was in this hopeful context that on 29 May 1982 the Archbishop of Canterbury, Robert Runcie, and Pope John Paul II met in Canterbury and issued the Common Declaration which established ARCIC II.[3] The positive atmosphere was dampened by the publication of the largely negative *Observations* on *The Final Report* by the Vatican's Congregation for the Doctrine of the Faith (CDF),[4] nuanced critique from the Evangelical Fellowship in the Anglican Communion,[5] and sharper criticism from the Church of England's conservative evangelical Church Society. Further, the spreading practice in the Anglican Communion of ordaining women as priests was increasingly seen as raising serious obstacles. Issues and events such as these continued to interact with the work of the Commission.

Recognizing the need for wider representation, the number of Commission members was increased from eight to twelve from each tradition. ARCIC I personnel had come from the UK (8), US (4), Italy (2), Australia, and Canada: in addition to these countries, Barbados, Ghana, and Kenya were represented on ARCIC II in 1983; one woman from each tradition was a member. Three Anglicans (and their Co-Secretary) and three Roman Catholics continued from ARCIC I, while Dr Günther Gassmann (Germany, Lutheran) continued as the Observer from the WCC Faith and Order Commission. The new Co-Chairmen were both from England: Bishop Mark Santer (Anglican) and Bishop Cormac Murphy-O'Connor (Roman Catholic).

The new Commission was mandated to consider outstanding doctrinal differences and the mutual recognition of ministries, and to recommend practical steps needed to restore full communion. Anglican responses to *The Final Report* had pointed up the need to consider the underlying Reformation question of 'justification by faith'. The 1981 Anglican Consultative

---

[3] A second phase of ARCIC had the support not only of the (then) SPCU, but also of the ACC, which met in Newcastle, UK, immediately following ARCIC's final meeting at Windsor in 1981: see *Report of the Fifth Meeting of ACC* (London: ACC, 1982), 39–40. ACC-6 (1984), looking back on the setting up of ARCIC II, noted that 'the Archbishop of Canterbury was able to do this on behalf of the Communion as a result of the careful discussion of the matter at ACC-5': *Bonds of Affection: Proceedings of ACC-6, Badagry, Nigeria* (London: ACC, 1984), 95.

[4] Christopher Hill and Edward Yarnold SJ (eds.), *Anglicans and Roman Catholics: The Search for Unity* (London: SPCK and CTS, 1994), 79–91. The *Observations* were concluded on 29 March 1982, but issued in the wake of a letter of 30 October 1982 from the CDF Prefect, Cardinal Ratzinger, to the ARCIC Co-Chairmen (see Hill and Yarnold (eds.), *The Search for Unity*, 92–3).

[5] Hill and Yarnold (eds.), *The Search for Unity*, 283–97.

Council (ACC) meeting, as well as setting in train processes for the Anglican Communion to respond to *The Final Report*, requested that ARCIC take up this question, since

> it is an issue which for some may put the ARCIC agreements in question. We believe the issue should be taken up in the light of the extensive agreement on justification already achieved, internationally and regionally, in Lutheran–Roman Catholic discussions.[6]

Conversely, Roman Catholic responses, and the Roman Catholic–Orthodox report on *The Mystery of the Church*, drew attention to the need to take further the underlying concept of Church as *koinonia* in *The Final Report*.

1983   Casa Cardinale Piazza, Venice, Italy

ARCIC II's initial meeting, from 30 August to 6 September 1983, focused on the theme of 'The Church, Grace and Salvation'. Papers were presented on justification (Donald Cameron and John Thornhill), the reconciliation of ministries (Henry Chadwick, Edward Yarnold), and the relationship between salvation and the Church. The situation in England, where the Church of England and the English Free Churches, notably the Methodist Church, were in the final stages of negotiating the first part of a two-part Covenant towards possible re-union, were also reported to the meeting. It was agreed that local ARCs should report to ARCIC about such local developments.

A working group—the Co-Chairmen and Co-Secretaries together with Chadwick and Julian Charley (Anglicans) and Jean-Marie Tillard and Edward Yarnold (Roman Catholics)—was requested to draft material on 'justification by faith' for the 1984 meeting. The group met at St Albans in June 1984 and noted the significant point that, in contrast to Roman Catholic–Lutheran differences, no formal divergence existed between Anglicans and Roman Catholics on the issue: the differences lay more in how justification is to be lived out (compare the pastoral emphases of Articles XI–XIV and the Homilies listed in Article XXX). The group therefore recommended that the issues be approached from the perspective of the human response of faith to divine grace, and in relation to the role of the Church in salvation.

---

[6] *Report of the Fifth Meeting of ACC*, 40.

1984   St John's College, University of Durham, England

The contexts in which ARCIC meets inevitably affect the ethos of dis-cussion. In 1984, ARCIC met at Durham, where the presence of retired Archbishop Michael Ramsey was deeply appreciated. New Commission members were coming to terms with the nature of their work in the footsteps of ARCIC I. Those from non-European backgrounds questioned the attention being given to sixteenth-century debates, seeking an approach shaped more by the praxis of living amid non-Christians. There was also opportunity for engagement with theologians from the University of Durham, the Church of England Bishop of Durham, Dr David Jenkins, and a meeting with members of the English ARC. At these, the challenges of the 'new contexts' of ecumenical hope and post-Christendom societies were before the Commission.

The theme for the 1984 meeting was 'The Church, Salvation and the Doctrine of Justification'. Papers were presented on justification from ecumenical perspectives (John Pobee), the Council of Trent's response to Luther (Henry Chadwick), and the sacramentality of the Church (Jean-Marie Tillard). Several members questioned the working group's approach, arguing that attention to Roman Catholic–Lutheran issues (e.g. 'formal cause') was needed. The meeting was able to reach consensus on the overall shape of an Agreed Statement, and asked the working group to draft a text for the next meeting which took into account the diversity of material considered. This group met at Pleshey, England, and drafted a text for the 1985 Commission meeting.

1985   Friars of the Atonement, Graymoor, New York, USA

In the months leading up to the 1985 ARCIC meeting, *The Final Report* was discussed by the General Synod of the Church of England, and the Catholic Bishops' Conference of England and Wales issued its response. Both were generally positive, but also raised questions. Ecumenical covenants were signed in Liverpool and Scotland, where the presence of Prince Charles and Princess Diana at a papal Mass had caused con-troversy. The tenth Jesuit Conference on Ecumenism took the Report as its main study, including a round table with ARCIC members. A thirty-minute video was produced in England: this showed the worship of two Anglican and Roman Catholic parishes, and the Commission member Julian Charley outlined the main points of *The Final Report*. ARCIC's work was becoming known.

This—along with the issue of the ordination of women (see below) was the context in which the Commission met at the Friars of the Atonement centre, Graymoor. Its founder, Fr Paul Watson (a former Episcopalian/ Anglican priest), had in 1908 initiated the Week of Prayer for Christian Unity. This developed, under the influence of Abbé Paul Couturier, into the Octave between the Confession of Peter to the Conversion of Paul (18–25 January).[7]

In discussion of the Pleshey text, 'The Church and Justification', some members wanted a stronger emphasis on the Church's role in salvation, and ecclesiology as the context for considering justification. Others wanted to concentrate on justification in itself, and looked for comment on distinctive Roman Catholic practices such as indulgences, masses for the dead, and purgatory.

The text was sent to the Sub-Commission for revision during the meeting, while other members discussed the reconciliation of ministries, and the idea of 'stages towards unity'. When the Sub-Commission reported, however, the consensus reached previously was tested by questions from members for whom the text was new. The task of drafting a definitive Statement was passed back to the Sub-Commission, which was asked to take up the relation between justification and sanctification, and the sacramentality of the Church.

The Ordination of Women: Ecumenical Correspondence

1985 saw significant exchanges of letters between Anglican and Roman Catholic leaders. On 13 July, Cardinal Willebrands, President of the PCPCU, wrote to ARCIC's Co-Chairmen regarding the reconciliation of ministries, one of the specific tasks assigned to ARCIC II. Given the revision of the Ordinals of both traditions taking place, and the progress shown in *The Final Report*, the Cardinal affirmed its claim that a 'new context' exists for considering the judgement on Anglican orders in *Apostolicae Curae*. Were agreement in faith regarding the eucharist and ministry able to reached, the way might be found to surmount the difficulties which have presented an obstacle to a 'mutual recognition of ministries'. This long letter concentrates in some detail on the 1896 papal decision, and alludes to the ordination of women as priests only as another issue which ARCIC

---

[7] These are the northern hemisphere dates. In the southern hemisphere mid-January is the height of summer holidays: from 1946 the Week came to be observed from the Sunday after Ascension Day to Pentecost.

II must face, though 'it is well known that the Roman Catholic judgement on the validity of Anglican orders is felt as more fundamental and more profound'.

The ordination of women as priests had come more into public view a fortnight earlier, when—in the lead-up to the General Synod of the Church of England—the *Church Times* published an exchange of letters between Archbishop Runcie and John Paul II on the issue. The Pope recalled a similar exchange in 1975–6 between Archbishop Donald Coggan and Paul VI (who knew the Church of England well), and the CDF document *Inter Insigniores* of October 1976, as noted at Lambeth 1978 by Cardinal Willebrands.

The Co-Chairmen, Bishops Murphy-O'Connor and Santer, tabled the letter of Cardinal Willebrands for discussion at ARCIC's meeting. The ordination of women had been under discussion several times in ARCIC I, and was addressed in the *Elucidations on Ministry and Ordination*, §5. In view of the exchanges between the Archbishop of Canterbury, John Paul II, and the Cardinal, however, ARCIC II discussed the topic for the first time in a 'truly serious way and adequate time' at Graymoor, though no conclusions were reached.[8] At a press conference after the meeting, the Anglican Co-Secretary, Canon Christopher Hill, noted that 'It is the beginning of discussion, as far as ARCIC is concerned.'[9]

The Co-Chairmen made a positive response to Cardinal Willebrands on 14 January 1986. In this they affirmed warmly the approach suggested by the Cardinal, and noted the possibility of a further *Elucidation* on the reconciliation of ministries, with the possibility that 'the problem at the heart of *Apostolicae Curae* . . . would be resolved'. No such *Elucidation* eventuated, however: as the letter stated, the ordination of women has created 'a new and grave obstacle to the reconciliation of ministries'.[10]

The topic was to gain higher prominence in 1986, following a resolution in September 1985 of the House of Bishops of the Episcopal Church in the USA (ECUSA), which indicated its intention to open the episcopate to women, and referred the question to the Archbishop of Canterbury. On 9 February 1986 Archbishop Runcie and Pope John Paul II met for a brief conversation and prayer in Bombay, at which this subject was raised. Later in his Indian visit, Archbishop Runcie acknowledged that the resolution had created a 'serious obstacle to the reconciliation of ministries',

---

[8] *Irénikon*, 58 (1985), 507.
[9] *Church Times*, 13 September 1985, as cited in *Irénikon*, 58 (1985), 507.
[10] See ARCIC II's *Clarifications of . . . Eucharist and Ministry*, considered in Chapter 13 below.

and had been referred to ARCIC II. A month later, the (triennial) Anglican Primates' Meeting took place in Toronto, where facing the issue was regarded as urgent.

On 17 June 1986, Cardinal Willebrands replied at some length to a letter of 22 November 1985 from Archbishop Runcie, in which the theological arguments related to the ordination of women are opened up in detail.[11] They agree that the issue must be taken up by ARCIC II, but the Cardinal concludes that 'The practice of ordaining men only to the priesthood is an integral and essential aspect of the reality of the Church.'

1986 St Michael's College, Llandaff, Wales, United Kingdom: *Salvation and the Church*

The Sub-Commission on the justification Statement met at Storrington in January 1986, and worked on this and also a plan for future work: the outcomes were sent to Commission members in preparation for its 1986 meeting at Llandaff, Wales (26 August – 4 September).

After detailed discussion, and some minor amendments, the full Commission adopted unanimously its first Agreed Statement, *Salvation and the Church* (see Chapter 1 above). After the authorities of both Communions had approved its publication, it was issued in January 1987.

The Llandaff meeting also considered the future work of the Commission. Given the exchanges of the previous year, the ordination of women (as bishops as well as priests) called for further discussion. The Storrington Sub-Commission had proposed that this be considered in the wider context of its possible impact on ecclesial communion, a view supported by most Commission members, though some sought a study of the issue in its own right. The precise nature of the Commission's next work remained unclear, however—but, as *Irénikon*'s correspondent noted, 'The Llandaff meeting marked an important transition for ARCIC II. After three years of marking time, the Commission seems to have found its appropriate ethos and cohesion.'[12]

The Anglican Primates had met in Toronto in March 1986, and set out a 'double process' in relation to exploring the possible consecration of women as bishops. ECUSA and the other Anglican provinces were asked

---

[11] The text of both letters—an impressive exchange—is given in *Irénikon*, 59 (1986), 352–65 in French, and in English as *Women Priests: Obstacle to Unity? Documents and Correspondence, Rome and Canterbury 1975–1986* (London: CTS, 1986).
[12] *Irénikon*, 59 (1986), 385.

to address separately eight carefully framed points, and to report to one another in time for the bishops to come to Lambeth 1988 well prepared.[13] ACC met in Singapore a month later, and—also looking to Lambeth 1988—focused mainly on the exercise of authority in the Anglican Communion, the underlying issue regarding acceptance of women as bishops. The Council passed a resolution expressing the hope that, as with the ordination of women as deacons and priests, provinces would respect one another's decisions.

The November 1986 meeting of the General Synod of the Church of England spent some time considering *The Final Report.* The questions proposed by ARCIC's Co-Chairmen in 1981 were voted on, with strongly positive responses made. The Synod asked, however, that ARCIC II consider further 'the place of the laity in decision-making, the Marian dogmas, and universal primacy in its relationship to the Bishop of Rome'. These issues would continue to shape the Commission's work for two decades.

---

[13] These points—perceptive ones—are listed in *Irénikon*, 59 (1986), 387. The issue led to inter-province divisions, notably the decision of the Bishop of London, Dr Graham Leonard, to 'adopt' a dissident ECUSA parish in Tulsa, USA, a decision rejected by both the English and US Houses of Bishops, but prescient of later developments.

Chapter 12

Koinonia Articulated:
Second Agreed Statement

1987   Palazzola, Rome, Italy

For the first time no Sub-Commission undertook work between ARCIC meetings. The Commission thus met in early September 1987 with a relatively open agenda, albeit one with the motif of *koinonia* to the fore, at Villa Palazzola, near Rome.

Palazzola has a long and diverse history going back to Roman times: at one stage it was a Cistercian monastery. For some time it has been the holiday/retreat house of the English College in Rome, across the lake from Castel Gandolfo, the papal summer residence, from where John Paul II visited the Commission on its second day. The Pope recalled the Common Declaration of 1982, and warmly encouraged members in their work towards 'the unity for which Christ prayed for his disciples'.[1]

This papal visit, near the commencement of the meeting, marked a significant beginning to a new project, 'Growing in Communion'. The Commission set itself to reflect on the Church as *koinonia*, utilizing the work of ARCIC I, the World Council of Churches (WCC) Faith and Order Commission's Lima Statement *Baptism, Eucharist and Ministry*, and other resources. This topic would serve as the wider context for considering 'the reconciliation of ministries, the ordination of women, moral questions and the stages towards full communion', the formal mandate of ARCIC II.[2]

The Lambeth Conference 1988

July 1988 saw Anglican bishops from around the globe gather in London for the Lambeth Conference.[3] Extensive preparations had been made,

---

[1] A large plaque on a wall in the courtyard of Villa Palazzola commemorates this visit, which was of considerable significance for the resident community.

[2] From the *Communiqué* of the 1987 meeting.

[3] See *The Truth Shall Make You Free: The Lambeth Conference 1988. The Reports, Resolutions & Pastoral Letters from the Bishops* (London: Church House, 1988).

especially as regards ecumenical relationships, and there were high expectations of a positive reception of *The Final Report*.[4] Bishops from united churches were members for the first time, and ARCIC's Roman Catholic Co-Chairman (Bishop Cormac Murphy-O'Connor) and Co-Secretary (Monsignor Kevin McDonald) were present as ecumenical observers. The Archbishop of Canterbury, Robert Runcie, chose as the topic for his opening address 'The Nature of the Unity We Seek'. He placed emphasis on its ultimate expression in the 'new creation', so that the widest context for all ecumenical endeavour must be 'the unity of all creation'. In arguing this, he recalled warmly the World Day of Prayer at Assisi in the preceding year, where he 'saw the vision of a new style of Petrine ministry—an ARCIC primacy rather than a papal monarchy'.[5]

Significantly, the four responses to this address were given by non-Anglicans: Dr Emilio Castro (WCC General Secretary), Fr Pierre Duprey (Secretariat for Promoting Christian Unity, and a member of ARCIC I and II), Metropolitan John Zizioulas (Orthodox), and Mrs Elizabeth Templeton (Church of Scotland).[6] Each drew attention to the nature of the Church and the exercise of authority as key issues before the Conference. While Castro and Templeton focused on practical matters, Duprey and Zizioulas offered important biblical and theological reflections, in particular the significance of eschatology and *koinonia* for ecclesiology.

Section 3 of the Conference was devoted to ecumenical relations, and its report draws heavily on these opening addresses. 'The Church in the World on the Way to the Kingdom' (a subheading) describes this Church as called to be sign, instrument, firstfruits, and provisional embodiment of the kingdom. *The Final Report* (along with other Anglican dialogue reports) is cited several times in the following discussion, which concludes with an extended analysis of *koinonia* largely based on ARCIC's work.[7] Both ARCIC II Co-Chairmen and five other members were engaged in Section 3: it would seem that these discussions contributed significantly to the Commission's work.

---

[4] *The Emmaus Report* (London: ACC, 1987), 42–77, whose work led to the resolutions prepared by ACC-7 (Singapore) for Lambeth.

[5] *The Lambeth Conference 1988*, 21. On 27 October 1986 John Paul II had called the first inter-faith 'World Day of Prayer for Peace' at Assisi, which served to place the search for Christian unity against the background of inter-faith understanding and cooperation in the service of peace.

[6] All four addresses are included in the Appendices to *The Lambeth Conference 1988*, 273–92. Jean-Marie Tillard, 'La leçon oecuménique de Lambeth 88', *Irénikon*, 61 (1988), 530–5 offers a lively and perceptive analysis of the Conference's decisions from the perspective of a member of ARCIC I and II.

[7] *The Lambeth Conference 1988*, 144–8.

The first Resolution of the Conference was on women in the episcopate, the pressing issue with the Anglican Communion at the time. It asked the Archbishop of Canterbury, in consultation with the Primates, to set up a Commission to explore consequential internal Anglican relationships (the 'Eames Commission', named after its Chair, the Archbishop of Dublin). Ecumenical relationships (in alphabetical order) form the next block of sixteen resolutions. Resolution 8 concerns ARCIC, and given its significance is quoted in full:

This Conference:

1. Recognises the Agreed Statements of ARCIC I on 'Eucharistic Doctrine, Ministry and Ordination,' and their *Elucidations*, as consonant in substance with the faith of Anglicans and believes that this agreement offers a sufficient basis for taking the next step forward towards the reconciliation of our Churches grounded in agreement in faith.

2. Welcomes the assurance that, within an understanding of the Church as communion, ARCIC II is to explore further the particular issues of the reconciliation of ministries; the ordination of women; moral questions; and continuing questions of authority, including the relation of Scripture to the Church's developing tradition and the role of the laity in decision-making within the Church.

3. Welcomes *Authority in the Church* (I and II), together with the *Elucidation*, as a firm basis for the direction and agenda of the continuing dialogue on authority and wishes to encourage ARCIC II to continue to explore the basis in Scripture and tradition of the concept of a universal primacy, in conjunction with collegiality, as an instrument of unity, the character of such a primacy in practice, and to draw upon the experience of other Christian Churches in exercising primacy, collegiality and conciliarity.

4. In welcoming the fact that the ordination of women is to form part of the agenda of ARCIC II, recognises the serious responsibility this places upon us to weigh the possible implications of action on this matter for the unity of the Anglican Communion and for the universal Church.

5. Warmly welcomes the first Report of ARCIC II, *Salvation and the Church* (1987), as a timely and significant contribution to the understanding of the Churches' doctrine of salvation and commends this Agreed Statement about the heart of Christian faith to the provinces for study and reflection.[8]

The above Resolution was passed overwhelmingly, but not without debate: an opposition Resolution was proposed by the (conservative evangelical,

---

[8] Ibid., 210–11, and www.lambethconference.org/resolutions/1988/1988-8.cfm.

English) Church Society and the Archbishop of Sydney, Australia. The decisive vote for Resolution 8 was thus particularly significant. It sets out a highly positive response to the parts of *The Final Report* relating to eucharist and ministry, sufficient to warrant taking practical steps towards reconciliation between the Anglican and Roman Catholic traditions (§8.1). The Resolution is more guarded about the Statements on authority (§8.3), however, reflecting the concerns noted in *The Emmaus Report* and expressed by Archbishop Runcie in his opening address.

Thus, while the Resolution re-affirms the original mandate given to ARCIC II, which centres on the reconciliation of ministries and moral issues, work is also asked for on the relationship of Scripture and Tradition, the role of the laity in decision-making (§8.2), and the concept of universal primacy (§8.3): tasks taken up later in *The Gift of Authority*). The ordination of women is recognized as raising issues for the Anglican Communion (§8.4) and is now specified for discussion by ARCIC. These issues would come to shape the later work of ARCIC II, and also serve to situate the reconciliation of *ministries* within the reconciliation of *churches*.

1988   Edinburgh, Scotland, United Kingdom

ARCIC II met in early September 1988, only weeks after Lambeth. It received a draft on the nature of *koinonia* prepared by a Sub-Commission which worked in pairs (John Baycroft and John Thornhill, Julian Charley and Jean-Marie Tillard) and had met in Birmingham between Easter and Lambeth. The resulting draft was based on a broad sweep of Scripture and the early Fathers. However, after a brief discussion, many members of the Commission asked that it be revised, and a working group was assigned this task. By the meeting's end an outline had been sketched, which was referred to the Sub-Commission. As it happened, its work would be influenced by a series of publications. In summarizing these, it is necessary to understand the complex web of communications, arising from Lambeth 1988 Resolutions 1 and 8, which would contribute to ARCIC II's work on *koinonia*.

But first it is necessary to note the issue of women in the episcopate. This was discussed at some length by the full Commission in Edinburgh, and then referred to a second working group. As the focal point for reflecting on its mandate to explore the reconciliation of ministries, Cardinal Willebrands's detailed correspondence with the Co-Chairmen in 1985 on *Apostolicae Curae* was considered, but now less hopefully. Some Roman

Catholic members asked whether women as bishops put at risk the commitment of the Anglican Communion to 'the historic episcopate', as expressed in the Lambeth Quadrilateral. In its Communiqué, the Commission saw this issue as 'a major problem in the reconciliation of ministries between our two Communions'.

On 6 August 1988 (Transfiguration) Archbishop Runcie had written to Pope John Paul II to express thanks for the presence of Roman Catholic Observers at the Lambeth Conference, and for the greetings from the Pope read by Fr Pierre Duprey. The letter noted that while the Conference had before it the issue of the ordination of women, its Resolutions about ARCIC's work 'represent a very strong affirmation by the Anglican Communion about the results of our dialogue'. The Pope responded on 8 December (the Conception of the Blessed Virgin Mary), expressing his concern about 'the new and perplexing situation for the members of ARCIC II', and noting that were the Church of England to ordain women as priests then the position of the Archbishop of Canterbury in the Anglican Communion would be 'delicate'. Even so, the papal letter opened by seeing the Archbishop's letter as 'a further indication of . . . the strong bond of communion by which we are already united'.[9]

On 11 February 1989, the Revd Barbara Harris was consecrated as Bishop Suffragan of the Episcopal Diocese of Massachusetts: the issue of women in the episcopate was no longer a matter of theory. A few weeks later, the first *Report of the Archbishop of Canterbury's Commission on Communion and Women in the Episcopate* was published. The Commission's title, 'Communion and . . .' is significant, and shapes the four headings in the Report, each of which commences '*Koinonia* and . . .'. The Report lays down foundations and 'pastoral guidelines', and in an Appendix, 'Ecumenical Evidence'.

Soon after the Commission's Edinburgh meeting, the Congregation for the Doctrine of the Faith (CDF) issued *Observations on Salvation and the Church of ARCIC II*.[10] This was sent to the Co-Chairmen by

---

[9] The letters were not published until the Primates' Meeting in April 1989, and made public in *The Times* of 28 April. They were included as an Appendix to *Report of the Archbishop of Canterbury's Commission on Communion and Women in the Episcopate* (London: ACC, 1989); see The Eames Commission, *The Official Reports of the Archbishop of Canterbury's Commission on Communion and Women in the Episcopate* (Toronto: Anglican Book Centre, 1994), for all three Reports by the Commission. Of its seven members, one (Dr Mary Tanner) was on ARCIC II, and its Co-Secretary (Canon Christopher Hill) was Anglican Co-Secretary of ARCIC II. The other Co-Secretary, Bishop Michael Nazir-Ali, would join ARCIC II in 1991.

[10] *Observations on Salvation and the Church of ARCIC II* (London: CTS, 1988). The *Observations* (two pages) are accompanied by a Commentary (twelve pages), the letter from Cardinal Willebrands, and the Co-Chairs' response.

Cardinal Willebrands, who noted two points: that the CDF saw the Statement as 'substantially positive', and that the Commission should engage in 'a deeper ecclesiological study' (as he was aware was taking place). The reply from the Co-Chairmen accepts this, noting that the *Observations* 'will help the Commission to give greater specificity to this study, particularly with reference to the sacramental character of the Church and its concrete realisation in the life of the Christian community'.

The Sub-Commission on *koinonia*, which met in January 1989, took all these exchanges into account, along with the addresses on ecumenical relations and the Report of Section 3 from the Lambeth Conference. Its work was sent to members in preparation for the 1989 meeting of the full Commission. Alongside this work on the reconciliation of ministries and on ecclesiology, another working group (Oliver O'Donovan, Brendan Soane, Kevin McDonald) commenced work on moral questions, the part of its mandate that the Commission had not yet taken up.

1989   Casa Cardinale Piazza, Venice, Italy

When the Commission met in Venice (28 August–6 September 1989) it had two fewer Roman Catholic members, Fr Abraham Adappur SJ and Bishop Bernard Wallace having resigned.

The draft of the Sub-Commission on *koinonia* followed the schema agreed in Edinburgh, had received comments from Commission members and some specialists, and seemed 'indeed ripe', ready for acceptance after discussion. But this did not eventuate: some members, both Anglican and Roman Catholic, attacked its terminology as too close to that of *The Final Report*, described as 'ecumenical jargon'. Language was looked for that was 'more exciting, less aristocratic, more piercing, nearer the speech of ordinary Christians'.[11] This led to a new Introduction being drafted, and some changes made by a subcommittee: agreement was able to be reached on what would become most of *Church as Communion*, but the work on catholicity was contested, and time ran out before this could be resolved,

The morals group had outlined an approach focused on the explicit reasons for differences between the two traditions: this was received positively, and the group was asked to continue.

---

[11] *Irénikon*, 62 (1989), 361; see also *Irénikon*, 63 (1990), 371–2.

Fourth Common Declaration

Less than a month after the Commission's meeting concluded, Archbishop Runcie made a four-day visit to Rome (announced several months previously).[12] On 2 October 1989 he and Pope John Paul II issued a further Common Declaration, in which they recognized the progress made by ARCIC on eucharist and ministry, while recognizing that the latter was in question in relation to the ordination of women. The Declaration speaks of the 'real yet imperfect communion' between Anglicans and Roman Catholics. Archbishop Runcie, addressing the General Synod of the Church of England a little later, recalled John Paul II's words as they parted: 'The collegiality we have is *affective*—let us make it *effective*.'[13]

In late April 1990, the Anglican Primates met in Larnaca, Cyprus, and the meeting was followed in July by the eighth ACC meeting in Cardiff: the key issues were Anglican identity and the exercise of authority. A second Report from the Eames Commission was received, which focused on the question of the extent to which different provinces (or churches) are in communion when there is disagreement about matters regarded as essential by some. The Report cites the words of the 1989 Common Declaration about 'real yet imperfect communion', and welcomes ARCIC II's working on *koinonia*.

Meanwhile, in June 1990 the Revd Dr Penelope Jamieson was consecrated Bishop of Dunedin, New Zealand, having been elected in late 1989. This had the effect of 'normalizing' the reality of Anglican women in the episcopate, rather than it being seen as a North American phenomenon.

1990   Gort Muire Carmelite Centre, Dublin, Ireland: *Church as Communion*

When the Commission met in Dublin (28 August–6 September 1990) it had two fewer Anglican members, Bishop David Gitari (Kenya) and Professor Henry Chadwick having resigned: Chadwick had been a member of ARCIC I and was sorely missed. Canon Christopher Hill moved from

---

[12] Archbishop Runcie was accompanied by the Anglican Co-Chair of ARCIC II, Bishop Mark Santer, and the Co-Secretary Canon Christopher Hill. The Roman Catholic Co-Chair, Bishop Cormac Murphy-O'Connor, was able to take part in several events during the visit. As noted above, Hill was also Co-Secretary of the Eames Commission, ensuring reliable communication between the two bodies. *Irénikon*, 62 (1989), 533–41, and the *Church Times*, 6 October 1989, give full accounts of the visit.

[13] *Church of England Newspaper*, 17 November 1989.

Anglican Co-Secretary to Commission member, with Canon Stephen Platten joining as Co-Secretary.

After minimal redaction, unanimous approval was given to the second Agreed Statement of ARCIC II, *Church as Communion* (see Chapter 2 above).[14] Compared with the struggles of previous meetings, this was a fruitful one: not only was a Statement referred to church authorities for publication, but ample time was able to be given to the outline on morals prepared by the subgroup, which was asked to bring a first draft to the next full meeting.

The Commission was further encouraged by the sermon preached in St Patrick's Cathedral by Archbishop Henry McAdoo, an ARCIC pioneer, which countered the 'lingering gloom' around ecumenical endeavour: 'it is no mere fashion, nor a luxury, but an obligation'.[15]

---

[14] *Church as Communion*, completed in 1990, was published in January 1991, during the (northern) Week of Prayer for Christian Unity.
[15] Archbishop McAdoo was a member of the Joint Preparatory Commission which produced the *Malta Report*, and Anglican Co-Chair of ARCIC I.

Chapter 13

A Reformed Commission:
Third Agreed Statement

1991   Paris, France: A Reformed Commission

In April 1991 Dr George Carey was enthroned as Archbishop of Canterbury, and with *Church as Communion* finished, opportunity was taken to review ARCIC II. From 1991 eight rather than twelve members were appointed from each tradition; since the Commission's immediate mandate was to address ethical questions, two morals consultants from each tradition were included, including the former Commission member the Revd Professor Oliver O'Donovan. The Co-Chairs and Co-Secretaries from the pre-1991 Commission continued, along with two Roman Catholic members (Bishop Pierre Duprey and Fr Jean-Marie Tillard), one Anglican (Bishop John Baycroft), and the World Council of Churches observer (Dr Günther Gassmann). Eleven new members joined, two of whom were unable to be present until 1992 and one until 1993. Commission members now came from Australia, Belgium, Brazil, Canada, England, France, Germany, Ireland, Italy, Pakistan, and the USA, and included two women.[1]

The revised Commission met at a girls' boarding school in Paris from 27 August to 5 September 1991. An initial task was for members to meet one another and become familiar with ARCIC's mode of working. Given the new Commission's mandate to work on moral life, the meeting began by members from each tradition being asked to indicate how they saw moral formation taking place in the other. Anglican members noted the confessional as influential for Roman Catholics, who saw the use of the Ten Commandments at each eucharist as significant for Anglicans—which led to a few chuckles, and the realization that our perceptions of one another were dated and that each tradition faces similar new challenges. Further, it was realized that each Commission member brought different life-experiences of moral formation, practice, and lifestyle to the meeting: the Anglican members were all married (and one divorced), while all the

---

[1] Details of members are given in Appendix A below.

Roman Catholic members were ordained or religious, and so celibate. Conversations outside formal meetings—notably during an afternoon off to visit Chartres Cathedral by train—opened up reflections which would be infelicitous in the group as a whole.

The outline on morals prepared in Dublin had been filled out by a sub-Commission meeting in Oxford. The Commission, however, questioned the adequacy of its theological foundation, and a new structure emerged in discussion, with significant input from the morals consultants. Responses to the Oxford and Dublin drafts revolved around two main issues:

1. A firmer theological grounding was sought, based in a Trinitarian understanding of the *imago Dei* paired with a 'new creation' perspective: this drew debate on how 'natural law' was to be included. This ethos would come to shape the ethos of the document, epitomized in Peter Baelz's phrase, 'the patterning power of the Kingdom'.
2. Several Anglican members insisted on the need to recognize that contraception and divorce must be seen as wider than personal issues. They have strong social consequences in 'third world' contexts, and the social dimension of sin must not be forgotten.

Considerable time was spent on seeking to understand in depth the responses of each tradition to divorce and remarriage (and to a lesser extent, contraception). It became evident that seeking to respond to such issues *in separation* had shaped divergent approaches, notably the historical and socio-political circumstances of English history. Conversely, the sense of coherence which Roman Catholic members found in the symbol of global communion offered by the Bishop of Rome, alongside the varied approaches to moral theological method in the Roman Catholic tradition, impressed Anglican members. It was recognized that, since the documented differences between the two traditions were contraception and divorce, concentrating only on these would further the perception that the Christian tradition is fixated on sexuality. For an Agreed Statement to have real usefulness, a wider perspective needed to be brought, including the changes in moral theology of the past half-century, although the Commission's mandate limited the possibilities.

Agreement was able to be reached on an outline in which scriptural perspectives, our common heritage, and our shared vision would set the context for considering the documented differences in moral practice, about which a good deal of ground was cleared. In sum, what would become Section C of *Life in Christ* was sketched, Sections D and E commenced, and the ideas in Sections A and F affirmed. The work was passed to a Sub-Commission, with Professor Peter Baelz, one of the Anglican morals consultants, undertaking the drafting: the elegant readability of the final Statement owes much to his skills.

The Commission also had before it the official response of the Holy See to *The Final Report*, released publicly on 5 December 1990. This was worked through in detail—somewhat of a baptism of fire for new members. Its closeness to the Congregation for the Doctrine of the Faith's *Observations* of 1982 was noted, and questions were raised about the continued lack of understanding of ARCIC's method. It was left to the Co-Chairs to consider a way forward.

Alongside these two pieces of work, the Commission considered how best to approach the other aspects of its mandate referred to it by Lambeth 1988 and by Roman Catholic authorities. These included the relationships between Scripture and Tradition, the exercise of authority, and the nature of primacy. It was agreed to do so within the framework of 'reception', and two papers on this were commissioned. As regards the ordination of women, two Statements by local ARCs were discussed: 'The Experience of Women in Ministry' (Anglican–Roman Catholic Dialogue in Canada), and 'The Image of God' (Anglican–Roman Catholic Dialogue in the USA). These bear not only on questions of ministry, but also on the place of Mary in Christian understanding.

1992   St George's House, Windsor, England

St George's House, Windsor, the location for the 1992 meeting, is another place of significance to ARCIC. It was there that the first Agreed Statement was concluded, in 1971, and *The Final Report* was brought together, in 1981. The Co-Chairs arranged for a re-union of present and former members during the 1992 meeting, to ascertain how best to approach the Holy See's response to *The Final Report*. Difficult though this latter task was, the Commission was encouraged by its work having been endorsed in a joint Statement from Pope John Paul II and Archbishop George Carey during a visit of the latter to Rome in May.

A new draft of the morals text had been circulated prior to the Windsor meeting. This integrated moral theology and practice with the motif of 'communion', and introduced the phrase 'the patterning power of the Kingdom'. The Commission worked in groups on particular sections, which were taken up by the morals consultants into successive drafts—a process enabled by computers being available for the first time. By the meeting's end an Introduction, Section B, 'Shared Vision' (theological), and Section

C, 'Common Heritage' (historical), had been drafted, with outlines made of 'Divergence and Convergence', 'Agreements and Disagreements', and a final chapter on common witness. A feature of the discussion was clarifying misconceptions each tradition had of the other regarding responding to marriage breakdown, and the way arguments on contraception had developed since *Humanae Vitae* in 1968.

ARCIC's wider mandate to consider the interaction of Scripture, tradition, and the exercise of authority was taken up through the papers on 'reception' commissioned in 1991.[2] There was no immediate outcome from this, but seeds were sown which would bear fruit later. Related to this, and in view of the pending ordination of women as priests in England and Australia, an informal evening discussion took place focused on the experience of the ministry of women. It was agreed that the issue was best approached through the larger lens of ARCIC's mandate, and papers were commissioned along these lines.

1993   Casa Cardinale Piazza, Venice, Italy: *Life in Christ: Morals, Communion and the Church*; *Clarifications*

The focus of the September 1993 meeting was on bringing the morals text to completion: *Life in Christ: Morals, Communion and the Church* (see Chapter 3 above). By far the longest ARCIC Statement yet, it is notable for its focus on 'what kind of persons we are called to become' and its analysis of the effects of divided traditions making decisions separately when faced by new issues. It comes to a 'double negative' conclusion, questioning whether the limited disagreement which remains 'is itself sufficient to justify a continued breach of communion'—a shift in ARCIC's method (§1; see Chapter 8 above). *Life in Christ*, the first ecumenical agreement on ethics, was concluded in September 1993 but published in 1994, preceded by the papal encyclical *Veritatis Splendor* on moral life of November 1993, on which no ARCIC members had worked, though there are similarities of approach.

The Commission also had before it the draft of a 'Response to the Response' of the Holy See to *The Final Report*, prepared by four participants in ARCIC I,[3] taking note of the Commission's discussion at Windsor:

---

[2] Charles Sherlock, 'Scripture, Tradition and Teaching Authority: "Reception" as a Way Forward', and Jean-Marie Tillard OP, 'Tradition and Reception', later published in *One in Christ*, 28 (1992), 307–22.
[3] The Revd Julian Charley and Bishop Christopher Hill (Anglicans); Bishop Pierre Duprey and Fr Jean-Marie Tillard (Roman Catholics).

Clarifications of . . . Eucharist and Ministry.[4] In just one session's discussion, after several amendments proposed by Bishop Duprey which assisted some Anglican members considerably, this was approved for publication. That it was directed only to Roman Catholic authorities drew unfavourable responses from some Anglican sources. It was published with a positive letter from Cardinal Cassidy, PCPCU President, who noted that *Clarifications* had been 'examined by the appropriate dicasteries of the Holy See', and that 'The agreement reached on Eucharist and Ministry by ARCIC I is thus greatly strengthened and no further study would seem to be required at this stage.' Study of the third part of *The Final Report*, 'Authority in the Church', however, 'would seem urgent', he wrote.

Reflection on authority began with discussion of a seminal paper on 'Scripture, Tradition and Memory' by Jean-Marie Tillard and John Baycroft. The Commission agreed to work further in 1994 on authority, and commissioned papers on the Scriptures, tradition, and the exercise of authority. In doing so, the Anglican members in particular realized that this new task for the Commission focused on issues which had arisen—at least in formal terms—following the breach between Rome and the Church of England. ARCIC was thus beginning to walk on new ground, which was likely to test its familiar method of working from the Scriptures and ancient common traditions.

---

[4] *Clarifications of Certain Aspects of the Agreed Statements on Eucharist and Ministry of the First Anglican–Roman Catholic International Commission* (London: Church House and CTS, 1994), www.prounione.urbe.it/dia-int/arcic/doc/e_arcic_classifications.html. Cardinal Cassidy's letter can also be found in *Information Service*, 87/4 (1994), 237. ACC-9, meeting in Cape Town in January 1993, had asked ARCIC II to 'proceed as a matter of priority with its mandate to give attention to the official responses of both Churches': see www.anglicancommunion.org/communion/acc/meetings/acc9/resolutions.cfm#s3.

Chapter 14

From 1896* to 1998:
Fourth Agreed Statement

1994   St George's College, Jerusalem, Israel

ARCIC's meeting in Jerusalem provided a catalyst for meetings of church leaders in the Holy Land. It also gave Commission members opportunities to explore briefly together this city of Jewish and Christian beginnings, and to visit Jericho and Haram El-Sharif. However, since its Venice meeting several events had occurred which affected the life of the Commission.

- The Jerusalem meeting was the last for Dr Günther Gassmann, the World Council of Churches (WCC) Faith and Order observer, who had participated in every ARCIC meeting and kept the Commission abreast of the wider ecumenical movement, not least other dialogues. On the Roman Catholic side, Monsignor William Steele, Ecumenical Officer for the Roman Catholic Church in England, joined the Commission. At the personal level, Henrietta Santer, to whom Bishop Mark Santer was married, had died. Bishop Mark handed over his role as Anglican Co-Chair to Bishop John Baycroft, but continued as a member.
- On 28 June 1992, the Congregation for the Doctrine of the Faith (CDF) had issued a Letter to the Bishops of the Catholic Church on 'Some Aspects of the Church Understood as Communion',[1] which later became public. Given its stress on the necessity of the Petrine ministry being 'interior' to every particular church (§13), it was read by many as anti-ecumenical, even as a counter to *Church as Communion*. While the Eastern Orthodox are acknowledged as 'particular churches', though

---

* 1896 is the date of Leo XIII's papal Bull *Apostolicae Curae* in which ordinations carried out according to the Anglican rite were declared to be 'absoloutely null and utterly void'.

[1] CDF, Letter to the Bishops of the Catholic Church on 'Some Aspects of the Church Understood as Communion' (1992), www.vatican.va/roman_curia/congregations/cfaith/documents/rc_con_cfaith_doc_28051992_communionis-notio_en.html. The address by Cardinal Ratzinger 'The Ecclesiology of the Constitution on the Church, Vatican II, "Lumen Gentium"', published in *L'Osservatore Romano* (English edition), 19 September 2001, p. 5, explains the origin and purpose of the Letter.

wounded by lack of the Petrine ministry, others are spoken as 'ecclesial communities which have not retained the apostolic succession and a valid Eucharist' (§17), a comment offensive to Anglicans and others. Members of the Commission from the Pontifical Council for Promoting Christian Unity (PCPCU) noted that the Letter is an internal document, issued to correct false emphases within the Roman Catholic Church, and that it concludes, 'This situation seriously calls for ecumenical commitment on the part of everyone' in exploring and becoming open to Petrine ministry.

- On 25 March 1993, the PCPCU issued the *Directory for the Application of Principles and Norms on Ecumenism*. Commission members were introduced to this by PCPCU staff, with particular focus on the updated provisions in Section IVB for sharing in worship and sacramental life, and the norms in Section V for ecumenical dialogue.[2]
- Following the 1992 decision of the General Synod of the Church of England, women had been ordained in 1994 as priests, the Archbishop of Canterbury participating.[3] Pope John Paul II wrote to Archbishop Carey affirming strongly the opposition of the Roman Catholic Church: this action of the Church of England, which involved the leader of the Anglican Communion, was seen as signalling a change in the position of the Communion as a whole.

The Commission began its meeting by reviewing these events, before working through the papers prepared for the meeting. The first, by Sr Sara Butler, examined the historical data to see if a definitive decision against ordaining women had been made in the past: it concluded that no direct decision could be found. In the process, Butler recognized that the 'in principle' decision by Lambeth 1968 to allow Anglican provinces to proceed predated the commencement of ARCIC, as did the first canonically acknowledged ordinations, in Hong Kong in 1971.[4] This affirmed the claim in the *Elucidations on Ministry and Ordination* in *The Final Report* that

---

[2] *Directory for the Application of Principles and Norms on Ecumenism* was issued over the signatures of the PCPCU President, Cardinal Cassidy, and PCPCU Secretary, Bishop Pierre Duprey, a member of ARCIC I and II: see www.vatican.va/roman_curia/pontifical_councils/chrstuni/general-docs/rc_pc_chrstuni_doc_19930325_directory_en.html.

[3] In 1992 women had been ordained as priests in the Anglican Church of Australia, after two decades of debate shaped by the strong opposition of its first and largest diocese, Sydney, focused primarily on 'headship' and scriptural interpretation, rather than issues of concern to the Roman Catholic Church.

[4] Sr Sara Butler, 'The Ordination of Women: A New Obstacle to the Recognition of Anglican Orders', *Anglican Theological Review*, 78/1 (Winter 1996), 96–115.

the agreements reached in it on ministry are not affected by the ordination of women, though this remains a major obstacle to the reconciliation of ministries.

The second paper, by the Australian members Peter Cross and Charles Sherlock, responded to the 1993 paper by Jean-Marie Tillard and John Baycroft, 'Scripture, Tradition and Memory', using the ordination of women as a case study. It explored authority as involving 'anticipation of the future' as well as receiving from the past: how is Christ's rule as Lord understood 'pro-visionally', in ways that receive the apostolic Tradition in a manner open to change? This led into consideration of the Sub-Commission's outline paper on 'Authority in the Church III', in small groups. A plenary session was able to bring these together around the idea of authority as creative 'authoring', a gift in which is entailed a 'double Yes' in Christ (see 2 Corinthians 1.17–20), from God and from people of faith: concepts developed by a Sub-Commission (John Baycroft, Peter Cross, Nicholas Sagovsky, Jean-Marie Tillard) in preparation for the 1995 meeting.

1995   Casa Cardinale Piazza, Venice, Italy

The Commission met in early September 1995, strongly encouraged by the encyclical *Ut Unum Sint* issued by Pope John Paul II in May 1995, especially as it sought to grapple with the issues surrounding primacy and the ministry of the Bishop of Rome. Professor Michael Root was the new observer from the WCC, while Dr Donald Anderson was the Anglican Co-Secretary for this meeting.

The meeting was largely taken up by detailed work on the draft of 'Authority III' prepared by the Sub-Commission in Birmingham, which looked at authority in relation to the Scriptures, Tradition, and the exercise of teaching authority. Significant progress was made, largely through the gradual accumulation of insights building on *Authority in the Church I* and *II* of *The Final Report*, focused on the positive approaches of authority as 'gift', and the 'double Yes' motif from the Jerusalem ARCIC meeting. Progress was made in coming to understand the meaning of primacy, but further work was needed on the actual exercise of authority. The draft was again referred to the Sub-Commission, in the hope that it might be concluded in the following year.

Alongside work on authority, formal discussion took place on the ordination of women. A subgroup formulated a statement based on the Jerusalem papers, which (after discussion and amendment) was approved in plenary: 'The Ordination of Women and Ecclesial Communion'.[5] In this, agreement was reached on a wide range of matters touching the roles and ministries of men and women generally, but not on the ordination of women. The consecration of women as bishops, especially as diocesans, was seen as placing deeper strains on ecumenical relationships than ordaining women as priests, since it raises issues about the apostolic college around Christ, as well as what it means for a eucharistic president to act *in persona Christi*. The main conclusion was that the ordination of women does not set back the agreements reached in *The Final Report* and *Clarifications*. However, it was agreed that the draft not be issued as an Agreed Statement, but could be published in the name of the drafters (which did not eventuate).

1996   Mechelen (Malines), Belgium

For its 1996 meeting, ARCIC was invited by Cardinal Daneels, Archbishop of Mechelen, to meet in that city in association with a commemoration of the seventy-fifth anniversary of the Malines Conversations held there from 1921 to 1925. Bishop Patrick Kelly replaced Monsignor William Steele as a Roman Catholic member, while Canon David Hamid became the Anglican Co-Secretary. Canon Richard Marsh, the Archbishop of Canterbury's Secretary for Ecumenical Affairs, joined the Commission as the Archbishop's observer.

Celebrating the Malines Conversations, Seventy-Five Years On

St Rombout's Cathedral, Mechelen, contains the tomb of Cardinal Mercier, through whose auspices the Malines Conversations had taken place: the chapel where his body rests is dedicated to the cause of Christian unity. Though 1996 was the centenary of *Apostolicae Curae*, it was into the Malines celebration that energy was poured: a significant sign from the Roman Catholic Church of its commitment to ecumenical reconciliation, not least through the work of ARCIC.

On Saturday 31 August 1996 the Commission joined in a full day of public lectures, concluded with a prayer service in the Cathedral.[6] The Archbishop of Canterbury, together with Cardinals Daneels, Cassidy, and

---

[5] In 1975 an Anglican–Roman Catholic Consultation on the Ordination of Women to the Priesthood had been held at Versailles: members included Fr Pierre Duprey and Fr Yves Congar OP (Roman Catholic) and Bishop Donald Cameron and Canon Christopher Hill (Anglican). Its Statement, which refers to the ministry section in *The Final Report*, was circulated to the bishops at the 1978 Lambeth Conference, but never published.

[6] The lectures and addresses, together with summaries of ARCIC's meetings and a bibliography, are included in Adelbert Denaux and John Dick (eds.), *From Malines to ARCIC* (Leuven: Leuven University Press, 1997).

Willebrands (current and former PCPCU Presidents), dozens of bishops, and hundreds of other Anglican and Roman Catholic leaders, participated. Pope John Paul II sent a fulsome greeting, which was read by Cardinal Cassidy, while Archbishop Carey in his address stated unequivocally the Anglican Communion's ongoing commitment to the ecumenical process.[7]

The optimism inspired by this occasion was dampened by the Commission's considering a CDF *Responsum ad Propositum Dubium* (response to a doubt expressed on some teaching) regarding the exercise of universal and general magisterium.[8] It argues that *Ordinatio Sacerdotalis*, John Paul II's encyclical on the ordination of women as priests, is an example of such teaching, and so is given 'infallibly'. PCPCU members of the Commission explained that the *Responsum* does not refer to the Pope teaching infallibly, but that the universal tradition of male-only clergy constitutes an example of 'general' magisterial teaching being given infallibly.

The main part of the meeting, however, continued the work on authority. The 'double Yes' motif (see 2 Cor 1.17–20) had been explored by the Commission's Scripture scholars, whose work showed that this pairing is not symmetrical biblically. It is better expressed in terms of God's 'Yes' and our human responsive 'Amen'; indeed, in the Scriptures, strictly speaking only God is recorded as making an unqualified 'Yes' to creation. Human responses to revelation are partial and qualified unless drawn by the Spirit into Christ, whose untrammelled 'Amen' embraces them. With this in mind, the sections on Scripture and T/tradition were settled, and work progressed on collegiality and synodality. The 'Yes/Amen' motif and the draft's title, *The Gift of Authority: Authority in the Church III*, would remain through to the completion of the Statement in 1998. The work was passed once more to the Sub-Commission.

Fifth Common Declaration

Later in 1996 Pope John Paul II received Archbishop Carey in Rome, and on 5 December they issued a further Common Declaration.[9] This affirmed the work of ARCIC II, but noted the 'new situation . . . [given] the ordination of women as priests and bishops in some Provinces of the

---

[7] Archbishop Carey left Mechelen that evening to travel to Trondheim, Norway, for the signing of the Anglican–Lutheran Porvoo Agreement, an event which drew comment from some presenters.

[8] CDF, *Responsum ad Propositum Dubium Concerning the Teaching Contained in 'Ordinatio Sacerdotalis'*, issued on 28 October 1998, www.vatican.va/roman_curia/congregations/cfaith/documents/rc_con_cfaith_doc_19951028_dubium-ordinatio-sac_en.html.

[9] See Appendix B5 below.

Anglican Communion' and suggested that it might be necessary 'to consult further about how the relationship between the Anglican Communion and the Catholic Church is to progress'.

Nevertheless, the Declaration encouraged Christians to make full use of the opportunities open to them, noting the publication of the 1993 *Directory for the Application of Principles and Norms on Ecumenism*, and looked forward to the year 2000 as an opportunity for 'common witness to the Word made flesh'.

1997   Virginia Theological Seminary, Alexandria, Virginia, USA

The full Commission met at this attractive seminary in early September 1997. It undertook significant work on what was now called *The Gift of Authority*, based on further drafting work by the Sub-Commission. By the meeting's end, agreement had been reached on the interrelationship of Scripture and T/tradition(s), grounded in the 'Yes/Amen' motif, the processes of reception and re-reception, and with 'Exercise of Authority' at an advanced stage. But further work remained to be done on primacy, especially the ministry of the Bishop of Rome: an 'Anglicans say this, Roman Catholics hold that' approach remained in these paragraphs, which the Commission was seeking to minimize as far as possible.

As well as this work, the Commission considered the near-final version of *The Virginia Report*, prepared by the Inter-Anglican Theological and Doctrinal Commission for Lambeth 1998. Within a theology of *koinonia*, this addressed developing structures of authority within the Anglican Communion. Several amendments suggested by ARCIC were incorporated into the final version of the Report.[10]

Local ARCs continued to engage with ARCIC's work, as well as their own dialogues. In 1995, Sr Mary McKillop was beatified during a visit to Sydney by Pope John Paul II: she would later become Australia's first canonized saint. Given the long-standing Catholic–Protestant sectarianism in that nation's past, the Australian Anglican–Roman Catholic Dialogue worked towards an Agreed Statement, 'The Saints and Christian Prayer', issued in November 1997.[11] Much of this would later be incorporated into *Mary: Grace and Hope in Christ*, Section D.

---

[10] Inter-Anglican Theological and Doctrinal Commission, *The Virginia Report*, in James M. Rosenthal and Nicola Currie (eds.), *Being Anglican in the Third Millennium: The Official Report of the 10th Meeting of the Anglican Consultative Council* (Harrisburg: Morehouse, 1997), 211–81.

[11] www.cam.org.au/Portals/66/Resources/Documents/AnglicanChurch/AustARCC_TheSaintsand-ChristianPrayer_1997.pdf.

The 1998 Lambeth Conference

The Lambeth Conference in 1998 is remembered for the sharp disagreements among the bishops over issues related to homosexuality.[12] Resolution 1.10 on this matter came to be read by some as a decision calling for assent by Anglicans, but by others as advisory. However the Resolution was received, the issue led to divisions within the Anglican Communion, which would affect the reception by Rome of *Life in Christ* (which was itself 'welcomed' in Resolution IV.5a, 'Ecclesiology and Ethics').

The Conference also voted to 'accept and endorse' the final Eames Report, effectively meaning that differences over women in all three orders of ministry had become a matter of pastoral care between and within provinces and dioceses. This had the effect of rendering ARCIC's challenging task of working towards the reconciliation of ministries more difficult.

On the ecumenical front, the Conference re-affirmed its 'commitment to full, visible unity' while recognizing that 'some anomalies may be bearable when there is an agreed goal of visible unity' (Resolution IV.1). To ensure cohesion between the various dialogues in which Anglicans are involved, the Conference established the Inter-Anglican Standing Commission on Ecumenical Relations (IASCER: Resolution IV.3).[13]

As regards ARCIC, Lambeth 1998 took four significant actions:

> First, the Conference 'continues to be grateful' for its achievements, 'strongly encourages its continuation', and 'encourages the referral to Provinces' of the three completed ARCIC II documents (*Salvation and the Church*, *Church as Communion*, and the about-to-be-released *Life in Christ: Morals, Communion and the Church*).
>
> Secondly, the Conference 'recognises the special status' of the eucharist and ministry agreements accepted at Lambeth 1988, and asked that 'new Provincial liturgical texts and practices be consonant with accepted ecumenical agreements . . . for example BEM [*Baptism, Eucharist and Ministry*] and ARCIC' (Resolutions IV.23b and IV.12).

---

[12] See *Transformation and Renewal: The Official Report of the Lambeth Conference 1998* (Harrisburg, PA: Morehouse, 1999). The Resolutions are available at www.lambethconference.org/resolutions/1998.

[13] IASCER was also charged with considering 'continuing Anglican churches', an issue which would later lead to the Vatican setting up an Ordinariate for former Anglican groups. The progress in Anglican–Moravian (the Fetter Lane Agreement) and Anglican–Lutheran relations in Europe (the Meissen and Porvoo Agreements), Canada (the Waterloo Declaration), and the USA was welcomed and affirmed: the need for consistency between these, and with ARCIC's work, would seem to have prompted the setting-up of IASCER. Resolutions were also passed regarding relations with the Assyrian, Baptist, Methodist, Moravian, Oriental Orthodox, Orthodox, Pentecostal, and Reformed traditions, and the work of the WCC.

Thirdly, it 'welcomes the proposal for a high-level consultation to review Anglican–Roman Catholic relationships', as implied in the 1996 Common Declaration, suggesting 2000 as an appropriate date.

Fourthly, it 'welcomes warmly the invitation of Pope John Paul II in his Encyclical Letter *Ut Unum Sint* (1995) to consider the ministry of unity of the Bishop of Rome in the service of the unity of the Universal Church', asking IASCER to receive provincial responses.[14]

1998　Palazzola, Rome, Italy: *The Gift of Authority*

When the Commission met at Villa Palazzola in late August, it was evident that the attention given to moral issues at Lambeth 1998 had made a significant impression on the Roman Catholic members. Further, they noted the various ways in which the ministry of Anglican women as bishops—eleven of whom were members of the Conference—was being received. On the other hand, Cardinal Ratzinger's recent commentary on the apostolic letter *Ad Tuendam Fidem*, in which *Apostolicae Curae* was used as an example of a historical judgement to be held definitively, brought out Anglican concerns.[15] ARCIC's PCPCU members were able to set this in context, while noting the Commission's discussion.

At the meeting's beginning, Bishop Mark Santer, Anglican Co-Chair, indicated his intention to retire from the Commission, and that he would be replaced by Bishop Frank Griswold (Presiding Bishop of the Episcopal Church in the USA, who was able to be present at Palazzola for the last two days). With the work on authority near completion, one evening was spent considering future work. A priority was seen to be the 'high-level consultation' between Anglican and Roman Catholic bishops proposed at Lambeth 1998 for 2000: a Sub-Commission was set up to prepare for this, along with PCPCU and Anglican Consultative Council officials. It was also recognized that ARCIC had not responded to earlier requests for more work on the Marian dogmas.

But bringing *The Gift of Authority* to completion was the major focus of the meeting, with Section III ('The Exercise of Authority in the Church') requiring the most attention. The subgroup which worked on this (Nicholas Sagovsky and Charles Sherlock (Anglicans); Jean-Marie Tillard and Liam

---

[14] *Transformation and Renewal*, 256.
[15] Congregation for the Doctrine of the Faith, 'Doctrinal Commentary on the Concluding Formula of the *Professio Fidei*' (1998), www.vatican.va/roman_curia/congregations/cfaith/documents/rc_con_ cfaith_doc_1998_ professio-fidei_en.html.

Walsh (Roman Catholics)) was able to agree surprisingly quickly on the need for a mutual 're-reception of the ministry of a universal primacy by the Bishop of Rome'. This entailed a significant shift in ARCIC's method (see Chapter 8 above), since the issues around papal authority had been formalized long after the breach between Rome and the Church of England.

The subgroup's work was endorsed by the full Commission in the morning session prior to ARCIC's planned audience with Pope John Paul II. As members, in a variety of ecclesiastical dress, entered Castel Gandolfo, the heavens opened, rain bucketed down, thunder roared, and lightning flashed. What sort of divine verdict was this on our agreement on the critical issue of papal authority? (Similar heavenly signals had apparently accompanied the approval of *Pastor Aeternus* in 1871 . . .) The audience was formal, and carried considerable meaning, albeit with different resonances for Commission members: a few had had regular meetings with the Pope, while for most (including Roman Catholics) this was a new experience of significant spiritual significance. Each member was presented with a medal commemorating John Paul II's twentieth anniversary.

The new agreement in Section III meant that Section IV ('Agreement in the Exercise of Authority: Steps Towards Visible Unity') needed to be re-drafted, which required two full days of work. The former 'Anglicans say this, Roman Catholics hold that' approach was able to be reduced to just one item of asymmetry between the traditions: the distinctive ministry of the Bishop of Rome. The Commission came to recognize more clearly how the different experiences of this ministry affected the presuppositions brought to the issue by Anglicans and Roman Catholics. Further, opportunity was taken to frame as sharply as possible the questions about authority and its exercise which both traditions need to face. With this work done, the full text of *The Gift of Authority: Authority in the Church III* was able to be read through and voted on paragraph by paragraph, with less than thirty minutes remaining in the meeting.[16]

---

[16] The Statement was referred to church authorities and published in 1999: *The Gift of Authority: Authority in the Church III* (London: Church Publishing and CTC; Toronto: Anglican Book Centre, 1999).

Chapter 15

Widening the Dialogue: IARCCUM, Fifth Agreed Statement

1999   The Queen of Apostles Renewal Centre, Mississauga, Toronto, Canada

ARCIC II met in September 1999 with a new Anglican Co-Chair, Bishop Frank Griswold, a new member from the Pontifical Council for Promoting Christian Unity (PCPCU), Bishop Walter Kasper, and new tasks. Its early days were taken up with discussing responses and reactions to *The Gift of Authority*. The Mississauga centre had been chosen for the meeting in order to assess its suitability as a location for the high-level consultation planned for 2000, whose members would be pairs of bishops from places around the globe where Anglicans and Roman Catholics live alongside one another. The Commission considered these plans, and drafted a document summarizing the work and approach of ARCIC for the consultation.

The main work undertaken, however, was considering how best to approach the issues surrounding the Blessed Virgin Mary. Anglican members soon realized, even more sharply than with the earlier work on authority, that the issues involved concerned differences which had largely developed since the sixteenth-century breach of communion. Conversely, Roman Catholic members appreciated the significant developments which had taken place at Vatican II in relation to the place of Mary in theology and devotional life. The Commission determined early in its discussion to seek to offer a Statement which integrated theology and spirituality, and in the interpretation of the Scriptures to utilize approaches from the heritage of both traditions.

Fr Jean-Marie Tillard OP had been asked by the Co-Chairs to prepare a paper for initial discussion: this advocated approaching the dogmas as expressions of revealed truth using the category of 'myth'.[1] Consensus

---

[1] Jean-Marie Tillard OP, 'The Marian Issues', in Adelbert Denaux and Nicholas Sagovsky (eds.), *Studying Mary: Reflections on the Virgin Mary in Anglican and Roman Catholic Theology and Devotion. The ARCIC Working Papers* (London: T & T Clark, 2007), 4–11.

emerged in discussion, however, that such an approach was unhelpful in addressing the communion-dividing issues. Several articles were considered, including one from Rowan Williams, then Bishop of Monmouth, and from the members Adelbert Denaux and John Muddiman, who would work closely together on the scriptural material. Two presentations were made to the Commission, from Dr Anna Williams (Yale University, on Mary in the Anglican tradition), and Dr Harry McSorley (University of Toronto, on ecumenical resources for the study).

In the light of this significant input, ten topics were identified for specific work: papers were commissioned from members, and a draft schema was drawn up. Though differing from the eventual Statement, a significant note states that 'the main emphasis will be on Mary in relation to Christ and the Church, but issues of Christian anthropology may be included, with sensitivity, at certain appropriate points'. This way of putting priorities followed discussion of how feminist insights might assist the work, assisted by the Statement of the Anglican–Roman Catholic Dialogue in the USA (ARCUSA) 'Images of God: Reflections on Christian Anthropology'. The Commission concluded, however, that since these topics, and the emphases in the *Magnificat* on justice and empowerment, were not matters of division between us, they did not properly fall within ARCIC II's mandate. As matters turned out, this decision left a significant lacuna in the Agreed Statement, and would lead to it being misunderstood in some circles. Care was taken with women's experience and 'mother' language: this included avoidance of the term 'Mother of God' (as the translation of *Theotókos*), which many English-speaking Anglicans hear as 'Mother of the Creator' (see Chapter 5 above).

Mississauga 2000: Anglican and Roman Catholic Bishops' Meeting

The year 2000 was an eventful one as regards ARCIC's work. It commenced with Pope John Paul II inviting the Ecumenical Patriarch and the Archbishop of Canterbury to join him in opening the Jubilee Door of St Paul Outside the Walls, Rome, at the beginning of the (northern) Week of Prayer for Christian Unity, a highly significant ecumenical gesture.

In May, thirteen pairs of Anglican and Roman Catholic bishops from each continent met, by invitation of the Archbishop of Canterbury and the PCPCU President, in Mississauga for ten days, beginning with several days of retreat. While most 'pairs' knew each other, some were barely aware of the existence of the other tradition, but all who took part were most enthusiastic about the experience. The consultation, assisted by consultants from ARCIC II, drew up the Statement 'Communion in Mission', with its accompanying 'Action Plan' that established the International Anglican–Roman Catholic Communion on Unity and Mission (IARCCUM). The bishops also stated, 'We believe that now is the appropriate time for the authorities of our two Communions to recognise and endorse this new stage through the signing of a Joint Declaration of Agreement.'[2]

2000   Les Filles du Coeur de Marie, Montmartre, Paris, France

Against the background of this encouraging progress, the Commission met from 26 August to 3 September 2000 in the convent of a Benedictine order of women, Les Filles du Coeur de Marie, adjacent to Sacré-Coeur, Paris. The Archbishop of Seattle, Alexander Brunett, replaced Bishop Murphy-O'Connor as Roman Catholic Co-Chair, but Fr Jean-Marie Tillard OP was unable to attend because of illness. Dom Emmanuel Lanne OSB (from Chevetogne, Belgium) participated in the Commission from 2000 as a consultant regarding matters relating to the Eastern churches.

The main part of the meeting was consideration of the papers prepared by members, several of which are included in *Studying Mary*. These covered the biblical data (Adelbert Denaux, John Muddiman); developments in the patristic (Emmanuel Lanne) and medieval periods (Rozanne Elder), the Anglican tradition (especially the Reformation: Michael Nazir-Ali and Nicholas Sagovsky) and Vatican II (Sara Butler, noting the placement of Mary in *Lumen Gentium* rather than in a separate Constitution); original sin (Liam Walsh); the two dogmas (John Baycroft and Jean-Marie Tillard); Mary and the saints (Peter Cross and Charles Sherlock, building on the 1997 Statement of the Australian Anglican–Roman Catholic Dialogue (AustARC), 'The Saints and Christian Prayer'); and Mary in Brazilian popular devotion (Jaci Maraschin). During the meeting Denaux and Muddiman wrote brief papers on Ephesians 2.3, Romans 3.23, and Mary's family (see footnotes 1, 3, and 12 in *Mary: Grace and Hope in Christ*).

The prepared papers offered some surprises, notably the English Reformers' affirmation of Mary as 'ever virgin', and (following Augustine) their reticence about her being a sinner. We learnt that England's eastern counties were the fountain-head of extreme Marian devotion in the fourteenth century, and consequent iconoclasm in the sixteenth: Mariolatry was not

---

[2] 'Communion in Mission', §§4–6, *Information Service*, 104/3 (2000), 138–9.

just a 'continental' importation to England! Another surprise was Elder's finding that the petition 'pray for us now and at the hour of our death' does not appear in 'Ave Maria' prior to the Black Death of the mid-fourteenth century.

Several papers underscored the need to ground the discussion in a strong understanding of grace, focused on Romans 8.30. This, together with the emphasis on eschatology from Cross and Sherlock's papers, saw an 'Emerging Shape of the ARCIC Study on Mary' drafted. It recommended 'a document with a doxological/liturgical tone', and notes that 'an organising motif might be the Romans 8.30 scheme: calling, justifying, sanctifying, glorifying'. An outline for a biblical section was included, leading into the 'common tradition' and noting themes such as 'perpetual virginity, sinlessness of Mary, *panaghia*, dormition', and one considering 'Mary in the liturgical life of contemporary Anglicans and Catholics'. This outline concludes with the question, 'What do we want to say about the dogmatic definitions in the light of the above?', revealing the inconclusive nature of discussion of the dogmas thus far.

With this 'Emerging Shape' in mind, four further papers were sought: exegesis of the two Marian dogmas and the context for their promulgation (Butler and Walsh); the English Reformation revisited (Sagovsky and Nazir-Ali); contemporary liturgical provisions (Cross and Sherlock); and the patristic period viewed from Eastern and Western perspectives (Lanne). It was becoming clear that a focus to bring the work together was needed, and that a Pauline approach might be that focus.

Alongside this work, the Commission spent some time considering the document *Dominus Jesus*, issued by the Congregation for the Doctrine of the Faith (CDF) on 6 August 2000,[3] and the 'Note on the Expression "Sister Churches"' sent to Catholic bishops by Cardinal Ratzinger (CDF President) around the same time.[4] The former gave robust teaching on the 'unicity' of the Church, but spoke of 'ecclesial communities' (including Anglican) as 'not Churches in the proper sense' and implied that Christian unity means return to Rome. The 'Note', though addressed primarily to the Orthodox, denied the term 'sister' to any relationship between the Roman Catholic Church and the Anglican Communion, although Paul VI, at the canonization of the Forty Martyrs of England and Wales in 1970, looked forward to the day 'when the Roman Catholic Church . . . is able to embrace

---

[3] www.vatican.va/roman_curia/congregations/cfaith/documents/rc_con_cfaith_doc_20000806_dominus-iesus_en.html.
[4] http://natcath.org/NCR_Online/documents/sisterchurches.htm.

her ever-beloved sister in the one authentic communion of the family of Christ'. Cardinal Walter Kasper (PCPCU President) assisted the Commission in understanding the context and intention of these documents.

2001   Church of Ireland College of Education, Dublin, Ireland

Fr Jean-Marie Tillard OP, a foundation member of ARCIC, had died during the year. His absence was felt profoundly: Commission members 'recalled, with deep appreciation and affection, by informal conversation and litur-gical commemoration', his immense and distinctive contribution to ARCIC, and to ecumenical endeavours more widely.[5] Fr Tillard was replaced by Bishop Malcolm McMahon OP; Bishop Marc Ouellet (new PCPCU Secretary) replaced Cardinal Kasper; and Canon Donald Bolen took over the Co-Secretary's work from Monsignor Galligan.

The 2001 meeting commenced with the commissioned papers, whose precision gave clarity to the issues of the patristic period and the text of the dogmas. Close attention was then paid to 'Mary in the Scriptures', as drafted by Adelbert Denaux and John Muddiman, including the issue of typology, and to revision of the schema. Agreement was reached on the scriptural data on Mary, her significance as *Theotókos*, and members being open to 're-receiving' the dogmas. Other sections were but sketches, how-ever, and the Commission struggled to move forward. A crucial realization was that whereas Anglicans tend to see Mary as a wonderful example from the past, Roman Catholics experience her as a living presence. Do we sing *Magnificat* because Mary sang it once, or sing it with her now? The Commission came to appreciate anew that her incontrovertible status as *Theotókos* is a present as well as a past reality, since she is indeed 'truly alive'.

Against this background, a drafting group was established to develop the Romans 8.30 approach, and bring a fresh draft to the 2002 meeting in Vienna: Sara Butler and Adelbert Denaux (Roman Catholics), Nicholas Sagovsky and Charles Sherlock (Anglicans). They met in January 2002 at the Benedictine monastery of Chevetogne in Belgium, the community of which Emmanuel Lanne was a member. These days proved to be the decisive 'moment' in the work: the 'reversal' of Romans 8.30—glorified, justified, called, predestined—set Mary within a 'Pauline' framework. Texts such as Colossians 1.27 and Ephesians 2.8–10 were read in a new light, such that Mary is acknowledged in the first place as a corporate rather than individual figure. This 'eschatological' approach enabled agreement to be

---

[5] Denaux and Sagovsky (eds.), *Studying Mary*, 248.

323

reached on Mary's place in the 'economy of hope and grace' (the order being significant), and gave hope that both traditions could 're-receive' the dogmas. Traditional approaches to Mary grounded in election, the Annunciation, or history moved from the 'past forwards', which was unavoidably in thrall to sin: where might an approach from the 'future backwards' lead us?

By week's end, the Sub-Commission had prepared a full draft of Sections A–C for consideration by the full Commission. The drafters were increasingly aware that the Marian dogmas, and the authority by which they were defined, concern differences which have arisen since the breach between Canterbury and Rome. Earlier Agreed Statements dealt with areas in which their shared heritage was sundered in the sixteenth century—eucharist, ministry, grace—or different moral responses made to new situations. Since the Marian dogmas were not going to be 'un-defined', it was recognized that if Anglicans and Roman Catholics are to be reconciled, then a way needed to be found of understanding them which both traditions can affirm and live with. The 'Pauline' and eschatological approach employed sought to offer ARCIC a methodology which effectively faced this new situation in dialogue.

2002 Am Spiegeln Focolare Centre, Vienna, Austria

The Commission met at the Focolare Centre, Vienna, in early September 2002, with Fr Charles Morerod OP joining as a Roman Catholic member, while Canon Jonathan Gough became the Archbishop of Canterbury's observer. The initial two days were spent in strong discussion of the Chevetogne draft, paragraph by paragraph. The text was warmly affirmed, and its methodology accepted: the modifications suggested revolved around how the Marian dogmas could be approached.

The Commission then worked in pairs on each section of the drafted material, one drafter accompanying each pair. The newest material concerned invocation and mediation, where the AustARC 1997 Statement, 'The Saints and Christian Prayer', was taken up. The overall outcome was a tighter draft in the scriptural area, in which typological and patristic, historic-grammatical, Reformation and academic, and critical readings were woven together. The historical and theological section was reshaped, with close discussion given to *Sub tuum praesidium,* the earliest known 'Marian' prayer (see *Mary,* footnote 9). General approval was given to the work on invocation/mediation: the 'ministry of Mary'. The eschatological motif was broadly sustained, but it remained to be seen how this would work out in relation to the content of the dogmas, and their authority.

A few weeks later, ACC-12 met in Hong Kong and passed this 'Resolution on Anglican–Roman Catholic Relations':

This Anglican Consultative Council:

1. welcomes the statement 'Communion in Mission' and the accompanying Action Plan resulting from the international meeting of Roman Catholic and Anglican bishops in May 2000 in Mississauga Canada;
2. welcomes also the establishment of the International Anglican–Roman Catholic Commission for Unity and Mission which will oversee the preparation of a Common Statement and which will take other steps to further growth towards unity in mission;
3. expresses its gratitude to the Archbishop of Canterbury and Cardinal Edward Cassidy for their efforts in bringing about this new development in Anglican–Roman Catholic relations, and encourages member churches to give support to this new stage on the journey to full visible unity between the Roman Catholic Church and the Anglican Communion.[6]

The drafting group met again in Chevetogne in November. The history paragraphs were brought together as one section, and the 're-receptions' of the place of Mary in both traditions clarified. The main progress, however, was reading the papal definitions through the eschatological motif, following the 'reversal' of Romans 8.30. This is emphasized in the Statement by consideration of the doctrine of the Assumption being placed first, affirming that 'God has taken the Blessed Virgin Mary in the fullness of her person into his glory' (*Mary*, §58). The Commission's understanding of Mary's conception follows, with the affirmation that 'Christ's redeeming work reached "back" in Mary to the depths of her being, and to her earliest beginnings' (*Mary*, §59). Both the Anglican and Roman Catholic drafters were convinced that this reading expressed the profound scriptural truth that God's grace not only 'goes before' in salvation, but 'reaches back' to transform this old creation into the new, and that Mary is rightly seen as embodying this hope.

2003   ECUSA Conference Centre, West Palm Beach, Florida, USA

The full Commission met in July 2003 in Florida. Bishop Brian Farrell (new PCPCU Secretary) replaced Bishop Ouellet as a Roman Catholic member, while Canon Gregory Cameron took over the reins as Anglican Co-Secretary from (now Bishop) David Hamid.

---

[6] www.anglicancommunion.org/communion/acc/meetings/acc12/resolutions.cfm#s28.

Solid work was done on the draft text regarding the content of the dogmas. The Statement was close to completion, and with work having been in progress for five years, there was pressure to finish. But the issues around the dogmas having binding authority remained, and no definitive title had been decided. Further, members (especially those of the drafting group) did not want to short-circuit ARCIC's tradition of a paragraph-by-paragraph reading and vote on a Statement.

The Co-Chairs therefore agreed to have a 'half-meeting' in Seattle in late January 2004, timed to precede the scheduled meeting of IARCCUM, and to enable the Commission to hand over its work on the Feast of the Presentation of Christ in the Temple, 2 February. Events turned out quite differently from these plans, however.

2004   Palisades Retreat Center, Seattle, Washington, USA

In the months following the Florida meeting, the General Convention of the Episcopal Church in the USA (ECUSA) had voted to confirm the consecration as bishop of a priest living in a same-sex relationship, which took place in 2003. Bishop Frank Griswold, Anglican Co-Chair of ARCIC II since 1999, who participated in the consecration, stood down as ARCIC Co-Chair, and IARCCUM was suspended. Bishop Griswold was replaced by the Anglican Co-Chair of IARCCUM, Archbishop Peter Carnley, Primate of the Anglican Church of Australia.

The opening days of the meeting were dominated by a different matter. Prior to the Florida meeting, potential 'commentaries' had been sought from selected readers by the Co-Secretaries. On the Anglican side, the near-final Florida draft had been referred to the Bishop of Durham, Dr Tom Wright, whose response (quite unexpectedly) attacked the text with some vehemence. Given the academic, ecclesial, and spiritual respect in which he was held, working through his critique was extremely painful for the two Anglican drafters. Nevertheless, this commentary led to a thorough review of the Statement: the outcome was the correction of some small errors and some minor improvements, but the Commission decided to stand firm on the shape, method, and content of the document.

Over five full days of work—the meeting was planned to be shorter than usual—the Statement was brought to a conclusion. On the question of subscription to the dogmas in a reunited Church, precedents from the dialogue between the Assyrian Church of the East and Rome were employed, as well as reference made to *The Gift of Authority*. The last twist of this final meeting of ARCIC II, however, was finding a title for the Statement.

Over the years several had been suggested, with agreement that 'Mary' should be the first word, and that 'Christ' must appear prominently. 'Grace' and 'hope' had become increasingly prominent in the work, but only in the last minutes available was *Mary: Grace and Hope in Christ* proposed, and immediately accepted.

ARCIC II concluded its work with a memorable Vespers for the Feast of Presentation—a good way to end, even if the Commission was unable to hand over its work formally to IARCCUM, since this latter body had been suspended by the Vatican in view of ECUSA's actions in 2003. These events had seen the Archbishop of Canterbury, Rowan Williams, set up a Commission to report on how the Anglican Communion should respond. The Archbishop also sought formal counsel from the Roman Catholic Church, who offered it through a small Sub-Commission of IARCCUM instead of PCPCU alone. This group met immediately following ARCIC's Seattle meeting: its findings were a significant resource for *The Windsor Report* of 2004, in view of which PCPCU lifted the suspension of IARCCUM, which resumed work in 2005.[7]

Mary: Grace and Hope in Christ was launched publicly on 17 May 2005.[8]

Postscript

ACC-13 met in Nottingham a month after the publication of *Mary: Grace and Hope in Christ*, and passed this 'Resolution on Anglican–Roman Catholic Relations':

The Anglican Consultative Council:
a. welcomes the publication of the Agreed Statement of the Anglican–Roman Catholic International Commission (ARCIC), *Mary, Grace and Hope in Christ*, and the completion of the second phase of the Commission's work;
b. expresses its gratitude to all the members of ARCIC over the last thirty-five years for their outstanding contribution to Anglican–Roman Catholic dialogue;
c. offers its thanks for the ongoing work of the members of the International Anglican–Roman Catholic Commission on Unity and Mission (IARCCUM),

---

[7] The report of the IARCCUM and PCPCU Sub-Commission, 'Ecclesiological Reflections on the Current Situation in the Anglican Communion in the Light of ARCIC' (2004), is available at https://iarccum.org/archive/IARCCUM_2000-2010/2004_iarccum_ecclesiological_reflections.pdf and in *Information Service*, 119/3 (2005), 102–15. The members included both ARCIC II Co-Secretaries.
[8] *The Text with Commentaries and Study Guide*, edited by the Co-Secretaries, was published soon afterwards (London: Continuum, 2006): this includes the full text of the Agreed Statement, the two official Commentaries, essays from each of the Anglican and Roman Catholic drafters, and group discussion outlines. See the Bibliography in Chapter 5 above, pp. 237–41.

and encourages them to proceed with the work of drafting a Common Statement of Faith (which can represent the 'harvesting' of the convergence in faith discerned in the work of ARCIC) and with the other initiatives of common witness being developed by IARCCUM;

d.   asks the Director of Ecumenical Studies to ensure that Provinces are invited to undertake a process of study of all the Agreed Statements of the second phase of ARCIC, and, in particular, that they have the opportunity to evaluate the way in which any Common Statement of Faith produced by IARCCUM might represent an appropriate manner in which to recognise the convergence of Christian Faith between the Anglican Communion and the Roman Catholic Church expressed in the work of ARCIC;

e.   respectfully requests His Holiness the Pope and His Grace the Archbishop of Canterbury to proceed to the commissioning of a third phase of ARCIC and of theological dialogue between the Anglican Communion and the Roman Catholic Church in pursuit of the full visible unity of Christ's Body here on earth, which is the stated goal for the ecumenical quest in both traditions.[9]

IARCCUM's *Growing Together in Unity and Mission* (2007) fulfilled the request for a Common Statement of Faith, and in May 2011 a third stage of the dialogue opened when ARCIC III commenced work.

---

[9]   www.anglicancommunion.org/communion/acc/meetings/acc13/resolutions.cfm#s15.

Appendix A

ARCIC II Participants

Members' titles and positions are listed as at the time of their appointment and membership.

Co-Chairmen

Anglican

The Rt Revd Mark Santer, Bishop of Birmingham, UK, 1982–99

The Most Revd Frank Griswold, Presiding Bishop, The Episcopal Church in the USA, 1999–2003

The Most Revd Peter Carnley, Archbishop of Perth, Primate of the Anglican Church in Australia, 2004

Roman Catholic

The Rt Revd Cormac Murphy-O'Connor, Bishop of Arundel and Brighton, UK, 1982–99

The Most Revd Alexander J. Brunett, Archbishop of Seattle, USA, 1999–2004

Co-Secretaries

Anglican

The Revd Canon Christopher Hill, Canon Residentiary, St Paul's Cathedral, London, UK, (1983–9; ARCIC II, 1990; now ARCIC III) (previously Co-Secretary for ARCIC I, 1974–81)

The Revd Canon Stephen Platten, Archbishop of Canterbury's Secretary for Ecumenical Affairs, London, UK, 1990–4

The Revd Dr Donald Anderson, Archbishop of Canterbury's Director of Ecumenical Relations and Studies, London, UK, 1995–6

The Revd Canon David Hamid, Director of Ecumenical Affairs and Relations, Anglican Communion Office, London, UK, 1996–2002

The Revd Canon Gregory Cameron, Director of Ecumenical Affairs and Studies, Anglican Communion Office, London, UK, 2002–4

Roman Catholic

The Very Revd Monsignor Richard L. Stewart, Staff Member, Secretariat for Promoting Christian Unity, The Vatican, 1983–5

The Very Revd Monsignor Kevin McDonald, Staff Member, Pontifical Council for Promoting Christian Unity, The Vatican, 1985–93

The Very Revd Monsignor Timothy Galligan, Staff Member, Pontifical Council for Promoting Christian Unity, The Vatican, 1993–2001

The Revd Canon Donald Bolen, Staff Member, Pontifical Council for Promoting Christian Unity, The Vatican, 2001–4

Members

In chronological order of appointment, then alphabetical:

Anglican

The Revd Professor Henry Chadwick, Regius Professor Emeritus of Divinity, University of Cambridge, UK, 1983–9 (also ARCIC I, 1969–81)

The Revd Julian Charley, Rector, St Peter's, Everton, and Warden of Shrewsbury House, Liverpool, UK, 1983–90 (also ARCIC I, 1969–81)

The Revd Canon Christopher Hill, Canon Residentiary, St Paul's Cathedral, London, UK, 1990 (previously Co-Secretary, 1983–9; ARCIC II, 1990; now ARCIC III)

The Rt Revd Arthur A. Vogel, Bishop of West Missouri, USA, 1983–90 (also ARCIC I, 1969–81)

The Rt Revd John Baycroft, Suffragan Bishop of Ottawa, Canada, 1983–2004

The Rt Revd E. Donald Cameron, Assistant Bishop, Diocese of Sydney, Australia, 1983–90

The Revd Dr Kortright Davis, Associate Professor of Theology, Howard University Divinity School, Washington, DC, USA; formerly Vice-Principal, Codrington College, Barbados, 1983–90

The Rt Revd Dr David M. Gitari, Bishop of Mount Kenya East, Kenya, 1983–9

The Revd Professor Oliver O'Donovan, Regius Professor of Moral and Pastoral Theology, University of Oxford, UK, 1983–90

Professor John Pobee, Programme on Theological Education, World Council of Churches, Geneva, Switzerland; formerly Professor of Religious Studies, University of Ghana, 1983–90

Dr Mary Tanner, Theological Secretary, Board for Mission and Unity, General Synod of the Church of England, London, UK, 1983–90

The Revd Professor Robert J. Wright, Professor of Church History, General Theological Seminary, New York, USA, 1983–90

Dr E. Rozanne Elder, Professor of History, Western Michigan University, USA, 1991–2004

The Revd Professor Jaci Maraschin, Professor of Theology, Ecumenical Institute, São Paulo, Brazil, 1991–2004

Rt Revd Dr Michael Nazir-Ali, Bishop of Rochester, UK, 1991–2003

The Revd Canon Dr Charles Sherlock, Senior Lecturer, Trinity College Theological School; formerly Senior Lecturer, Ridley College, Melbourne, Australia; 1991–2004 (now ARCIC III)

The Revd Canon Dr Nicholas Sagovsky, Canon Theologian, Westminster Abbey, London, UK, 1992–2004 (now ARCIC III)

The Revd Dr John Muddiman, University Lecturer in New Testament, University of Oxford, Mansfield College, Oxford, UK, 1993–2004

Roman Catholic

The Revd Fr Jean-Marie R. Tillard OP, Professor of Dogmatic Theology, Dominican Faculty of Theology, Ottawa, Canada, 1983–2000 (also ARCIC I, 1969–81)

The Rt Revd Pierre Duprey, Titular Bishop of Thibare, Secretary, Pontifical Council for Promoting Christian Unity, The Vatican, 1983–99 (also ARCIC I, 1969–81)

The Revd Dr Edward Yarnold SJ, Tutor in Theology, Campion Hall, Oxford, UK, 1983–90 (also ARCIC I, 1969–81)

The Revd Fr Abraham Adappur SJ, Staff Member, Lumen Institute, Cochin, India, 1983–8

The Revd Fr Peter Damian Akpunonu, Rector, Bigard Memorial Seminary, Enugu, Nigeria, 1983–90

The Rt Revd Brian Ashby, Bishop of Christchurch, New Zealand, 1983–4

Sister Dr Mary Cecily Boulding OP, Lecturer in Systematic Theology, Ushaw College, Durham, UK, 1983–90

The Most Revd Peter Butelezi OMI, Archbishop of Bloemfontein, South Africa, 1983–90

The Rt Revd Raymond W. Lessard, Bishop of Savannah, USA, 1983–90

The Revd Brendan Soane, Spiritual Director, Pontificio Collegio Beda, Rome, Italy, 1983–90

The Revd Fr John Thornhill SM, Lecturer in Systematic Theology, Catholic Theological Union, Hunters Hill, Australia, 1983–90

The Most Revd Bernard J. Wallace, Bishop of Rockhampton, Australia, 1986–8

Sister Sara Butler MSBT, Professor of Dogmatic Theology, St Joseph's Seminary, Yonkers, New York, USA, 1991–2004

The Revd Dr Peter Cross, Lecturer in Systematic Theology, Catholic Theological College, Clayton, Australia, 1991–2004

The Revd Brian V. Johnstone CSSR, Professor, Accademia Alphonsonia, Rome, Italy, 1991–3

The Revd Professor Liam Walsh OP, Professor Emeritus, Faculty of Theology, University of Fribourg, Switzerland, 1991–2004

The Revd Dr Adelbert Denaux, Professor, Faculty of Theology, Catholic University, Leuven, Belgium, 1993–2004 (now ARCIC III)

The Rt Revd Monsignor William Steele, Episcopal Vicar for Mission and Unity, Diocese of Leeds, UK, 1994–5

The Most Revd Patrick A. Kelly, Archbishop of Liverpool, UK, 1996–2000

Cardinal Walter Kasper, Secretary, Pontifical Council for Promoting Christian Unity, The Vatican, 1999–2000

The Rt Revd Marc Ouellet PSS, Secretary, Pontifical Council for Promoting Christian Unity, The Vatican, 2001–2

The Rt Revd Malcolm McMahon OP, Bishop of Nottingham, UK, 2001–4

The Revd Professor Charles Morerod OP, Dean of the Faculty of Philosophy, Pontificia Università San Tommaso d'Aquino, Rome, Italy, 2002–4

The Rt Revd Brian Farrell LC, Secretary, Pontifical Council for Promoting Christian Unity, The Vatican, 2003–4

Consultants

Morals

The Very Revd Peter Baelz, retired Dean of Durham and formerly Professor of Moral and Pastoral Theology, University of Oxford, UK, 1990–3

The Revd Professor Enda McDonough, Professor of Moral Theology, St Patrick's College, Maynooth, Ireland, 1990–1

The Revd Professor Oliver O'Donovan, Professor of Moral and Pastoral Theology, University of Oxford, UK, 1991–2

The Revd Bruce Williams OP, Professor of Moral Theology, Pontifical University of St Thomas Aquinas, Rome, Italy, 1990–1

Mary

Dom Emmanuel Lanne OSB, Monastery of Chevetogne, Belgium, 2001–4

Observers

Ecumenical

The Revd Dr Günther Gassmann, Director, Faith and Order Commission, World Council of Churches, Geneva, Switzerland, 1969–94

Professor Michael Root, Professor, Trinity Lutheran Seminary, Columbus, Ohio, USA, 1995–8

The Revd Dr Michael Kinnamon, Dean, Lexington Theological Seminary, Kentucky, USA, 2001–3

For the Archbishop of Canterbury

The Revd Dr Donald Anderson, Anglican Consultative Council, London, UK, 1993–4

The Revd Canon Richard Marsh, Archbishop of Canterbury's Secretary for Ecumenical Affairs, London, UK, 1996–9

The Revd Dr Herman Browne, Archbishop of Canterbury's Assistant Secretary for Ecumenical and Anglican Communion Affairs, London, UK, 2000–1

The Revd Canon Jonathan Gough, Archbishop of Canterbury's Secretary for Ecumenism, London, UK, 2002–4

Administrative Staff

Mrs Christine Codner, Anglican Communion Office, London, UK

Ms Giovanna Ramon, Pontifical Council for Promoting Christian Unity, The Vatican

Appendix B

Common Declarations by the Pope and the Archbishop of Canterbury

History

In 1960, an informal meeting took place when Archbishop Geoffrey Fisher was received in the Vatican by Pope John XXIII—the first meeting between a Pope and Archbishop of Canterbury since the Reformation. Following the Second Vatican Council, a formal visit was made by Archbishop Michael Ramsey to Pope Paul VI in 1966. At the time of that visit, and on the five occasions when Popes and Archbishops of Canterbury have met formally since then, they have issued a Declaration.

The texts of these Common Declarations are set out below. Archbishops and Popes have met more informally on fairly frequent occasions, such as the visit of Archbishop Rowan Williams to meet Pope John Paul II shortly after Dr Williams was enthroned in 2003, and again when the Archbishop attended the Inauguration of the Ministry of Pope Benedict XVI in 2005.

1. Common Declaration of 24 March 1966

The Common Declaration by Pope Paul VI and the Archbishop of Canterbury Dr Michael Ramsey, made in Rome, Saint Paul Outside the Walls, 24 March 1966

In this city of Rome, from which Saint Augustine was sent by Saint Gregory to England and there founded the cathedral see of Canterbury, towards which the eyes of all Anglicans now turn as the centre of their Christian Communion, His Holiness Pope Paul VI and His Grace Michael Ramsey, Archbishop of Canterbury, representing the Anglican Communion, have met to exchange fraternal greetings.

At the conclusion of their meeting they give thanks to Almighty God Who by the action of the Holy Spirit has in these latter years created a new atmosphere of Christian fellowship between the Roman Catholic Church and the Churches of the Anglican Communion. This encounter of the 23 March 1966 marks a new stage in the development of fraternal relations, based upon Christian charity, and of sincere efforts to remove the causes of conflict and to re-establish unity.

In willing obedience to the command of Christ who bade His disciples love one another, they declare that, with His help, they wish to leave in the hands of the God of mercy all that in the past has been opposed to this precept of charity, and that they make their own the mind of the Apostle which he expressed in these words: 'Forgetting those things which are behind, and reaching forth unto those things which are before, I press towards the mark for the prize of the high calling of God in Christ Jesus' (Phil 3.13–14).

They affirm their desire that all those Christians who belong to these two Communions may be animated by these same sentiments of respect, esteem and fraternal love, and in order to help these develop to the full, they intend to inaugurate between the Roman Catholic Church and the Anglican Communion a serious dialogue which, founded on the Gospels and on the ancient common traditions, may lead to that unity in truth, for which Christ prayed. The dialogue should include not only theological matters such as Scripture, Tradition and Liturgy, but also matters of practical difficulty felt on either side.

His Holiness the Pope and His Grace the Archbishop of Canterbury are, indeed, aware that serious obstacles stand in the way of a restoration of complete communion of faith and sacramental life; nevertheless, they are of one mind in their determination to promote responsible contacts between their Communions in all those spheres of Church life where collaboration is likely to lead to a greater understanding and a deeper charity, and to strive in common to find solutions for all the great problems that face those who believe in Christ in the world of today.

Through such collaboration, by the Grace of God the Father and in the light of the Holy Spirit, may the prayer of Our Lord Jesus Christ for unity among His disciples be brought nearer to fulfilment, and with progress towards unity may there be a strengthening of peace in the world, the peace that only He can grant who give 'the peace that passeth all understanding', together with the blessing of Almighty God, Father, Son and Holy Spirit, that it may abide with all men for ever.

+ Michael Cantuariensis
Paulus PP. VI

2. Common Declaration of 29 April 1977

The Common Declaration by Pope Paul VI and the Archbishop of Canterbury Dr Donald Coggan. The Vatican, 29 April 1977

1. After four hundred years of estrangement, it is now the third time in seventeen years that an Archbishop of Canterbury and the Pope embrace in Christian friendship in the city of Rome. Since the visit of Archbishop Ramsey eleven years have passed, and much has happened in that time to fulfil the hopes then expressed and to cause us to thank God.

2. As the Roman Catholic Church and the constituent Churches of the Anglican Communion have sought to grow in mutual understanding and Christian love, they have come to recognise, to value and to give thanks for a common faith in God our Father, in our Lord Jesus Christ, and in the Holy Spirit; our common baptism into Christ; our sharing of the Holy Scriptures, of the Apostles' and Nicene Creeds, the Chalcedonian definition, and the teaching of the Fathers; our common Christian inheritance for many centuries with its living traditions of liturgy, theology, spirituality and mission.

3. At the same time in fulfilment of the pledge of eleven years ago to 'a serious dialogue which, founded on the Gospels and on the ancient common traditions, may lead to that unity in truth, for which Christ prayed' (Common Declaration, 1966) Anglican and Roman Catholic theologians have faced calmly and objectively the historical and doctrinal differences which have divided us. Without compromising their respective allegiances, they have addressed these problems together, and in the process they have discovered theological convergences often as unexpected as they were happy.

4. The Anglican--Roman Catholic International Commission has produced three documents: on the Eucharist, on Ministry and Ordination and on Church and Authority. We now recommend that the work it has begun be pursued, through the procedures appropriate to our respective Communions, so that both of them may be led along the path towards unity. The moment will shortly come when the respective Authorities must evaluate the conclusions.

5. The response of both Communions to the work and fruits of theological dialogue will be measured by the practical response of the faithful to the task of restoring unity, which as the Second Vatican Council says 'involves the whole Church, faithful and clergy alike' and 'extends to everyone according to the talents of each' (*Unitatis*

Redintegratio, para. 5). We rejoice that this practical response has manifested itself in so many forms of pastoral cooperation in many parts of the world; in meetings of bishops, clergy and faithful.

6. In mixed marriages between Anglicans and Roman Catholics, where the tragedy of our separation at the sacrament of union is seen most starkly, cooperation in pastoral care (*Matrimonia Mixta*, para. 14) in many places has borne fruit in increased understanding. Serious dialogue has cleared away many misconceptions and shown that we still share much that is deep-rooted in the Christian tradition and ideal of marriage, though important differences persist, particularly regarding remarriage after divorce. We are following attentively the work thus far accomplished in this dialogue by the Joint Commission on the Theology of Marriage and its Application to Mixed Marriages. It has stressed the need for fidelity and witness to the ideal of marriage, set forth in the New Testament and constantly taught in Christian tradition. We have a common duty to defend this tradition and ideal and the moral values which derive from it.

7. All such cooperation, which must continue to grow and spread, is the true setting for continued dialogue and for the general extension and appreciation of its fruits, and so for progress towards that goal which is Christ's will—the restoration of complete communion in faith and sacramental life.

8. Our call to this is one with the sublime Christian vocation itself, which is a call to communion; as St. John says, 'that which we have seen and heard we proclaim also to you, so that you may have fellowship with us; and our fellowship is with the Father and His Son Jesus Christ' (1 John 1:3). If we are to maintain progress in doctrinal convergence and move forward resolutely to the communion of mind and heart for which Christ prayed we must ponder still further his intentions in founding the Church and face courageously their requirements.

9. It is their communion with God in Christ through faith and through baptism and self-giving to Him that stands at the centre of our witness to the world, even while between us communion remains imperfect. Our divisions hinder this witness, hinder the work of Christ (*Evangelii Nuntiandi*, para. 77) but they do not close all roads we may travel together. In a spirit of prayer and of submission to God's will we must collaborate more earnestly in a 'greater common witness to Christ before the world in the very work of evangelisation' (*Evangelii Nuntiandi*, ibid.). It is our desire that the means of this collaboration be sought: the increasing spiritual hunger in all parts of God's world

invites us to such a common pilgrimage. This collaboration, pursued to the limit allowed by truth and loyalty, will create the climate in which dialogue and doctrinal convergence can bear fruit. While this fruit is ripening, serious obstacles remain both of the past and of recent origin. Many in both communions are asking themselves whether they have a common faith sufficient to be translated into communion of life, worship and mission. Only the communions themselves through their pastoral authorities can give that answer. When the moment comes to do so, may the answer shine through in spirit and in truth, not obscured by the enmities, the prejudices and the suspicions of the past.

10. To this we are bound to look forward and to spare no effort to bring it closer: to be baptized into Christ is to be baptized into hope—and 'hope does not disappoint us because God's love has been poured into our hearts through the Holy Spirit which has been given us' (Rom 5.5).

11. Christian hope manifests itself in prayer and action—in prudence but also in courage. We pledge ourselves and exhort the faithful of the Roman Catholic Church and of the Anglican Communion to live and work courageously in this hope of reconciliation and unity in our common Lord.

Donald Cantuar
Paulus PP. VI

3. Common Declaration of 29 May 1982

Common Declaration of Pope John Paul II and the Archbishop of Canterbury Dr Robert Runcie. May 29th 1982

1. In the Cathedral Church of Christ at Canterbury the Pope and the Archbishop of Canterbury have met on the eve of Pentecost to offer thanks to God for the progress that has been made in the work of reconciliation between our communions. Together with leaders of other Christian Churches and Communities we have listened to the Word of God; together we have recalled our one baptism and renewed the promises then made; together we have acknowledged the witness given by those whose faith has led them to surrender the precious gift of life itself in the service of others, both in the past and in modern times.

2. The bond of our common baptism into Christ led our predecessors to inaugurate a serious dialogue between our Churches, a dialogue founded on the Gospels and the ancient common traditions, a dialogue which has as its goal the unity for which Christ prayed to his Father 'so that the world may know that thou hast sent me and has loved them even as thou hast loved me' (Jn 17.23). In 1966, our predecessors Pope Paul VI and Archbishop Michael Ramsey made a Common Declaration announcing their intention to inaugurate a serious dialogue between the Roman Catholic Church and the Anglican Communion which would 'include not only theological matters such as Scripture, Tradition and Liturgy, but also matters of practical difficulty felt on either side' (Common Declaration, par. 6). After this dialogue had already produced three statements on Eucharist, Ministry and Ordination, and Authority in the Church, Pope Paul VI and Archbishop Donald Coggan, in their Common Declaration in 1977, took the occasion to encourage the completion of the dialogue on these three important questions so that the Commission's conclusions might be evaluated by the respective Authorities through procedures appropriate to each Communion. The Anglican–Roman Catholic International Commission has now completed the task assigned to it with the publication of its Final Report, and as our two Communions proceed with the necessary evaluation, we join in thanking the members of the Commission for their dedication, scholarship and integrity in a long and demanding task undertaken for love of Christ and for the unity of his Church.

3. The completion of this Commission's work bids us look to the next stage of our common pilgrimage in faith and hope towards the unity for which we long. We are agreed that it is now time to set up a new

international Commission. Its task will be to continue the work already begun: to examine, especially in the light of our respective judgements on *The Final Report,* the outstanding doctrinal differences which still separate us, with a view towards their eventual resolution; to study all that hinders the mutual recognition of the ministries of our Communions; and to recommend what practical steps will be necessary when, on the basis of our unity in faith, we are able to proceed to the restoration of full communion. We are well aware that this new Commission's task will not be easy, but we are encouraged by our reliance on the grace of God and by all that we have seen of the power of that grace in the ecumenical movement of our time.

4. While this necessary work of theological clarification continues, it must be accompanied by the zealous work and fervent prayer of Roman Catholics and Anglicans throughout the world as they seek to grow in mutual understanding, fraternal love and common witness to the Gospel. Once more, then, we call on the bishops, clergy and faithful people of both our Communions in every country, diocese and parish in which our faithful live side by side. We urge them all to pray for this work and to adopt every possible means of furthering it through their collaboration in deepening their allegiance to Christ and in witnessing to him before the world. Only by such collaboration and prayer can the memory of the past enmities be healed and our past antagonisms overcome.

5. Our aim is not limited to the union of our two Communions alone, to the exclusion of other Christians, but rather extends to the fulfilment of God's will for the visible unity of all his people. Both in our present dialogue, and in those engaged in by other Christians among themselves and with us, we recognise in the agreements we are able to reach, as well as in the difficulties which we encounter, a renewed challenge to abandon ourselves completely to the truth of the Gospel. Hence we are happy to make this Declaration today in the welcome presence of so many fellow Christians whose Churches and Communities are already partners with us in prayer and work for the unity of all.

6. With them we wish to serve the cause of peace, of human freedom and human dignity, so that God may indeed be glorified in all his creatures. With them we greet in the name of God all men of good will, both those who believe in him and those who are still searching for him.

7. This holy place reminds us of the vision of Pope Gregory in sending St Augustine as an apostle to England, full of zeal for the preaching of the Gospel and the shepherding of the flock. On this eve of Pentecost,

we turn again in prayer to Jesus, the Good Shepherd, who promised to ask the Father to give us another Advocate to be with us for ever, the Spirit of truth (cf. Jn 14.16), to lead us to the full unity to which he calls us. Confident in the power of this same Holy Spirit, we commit ourselves anew to the task of working for unity with firm faith, renewed hope and ever deeper love.

ROBERT CANTUAR
JOHN PAUL II

4. Common Declaration of 2 October 1989

The Common Declaration by Pope John Paul II and the Archbishop of Canterbury Dr Robert Runcie. October 2, 1989

After worshipping together in the Basilica of Saint Peter and in the Church of Saint Gregory, from where Saint Augustine of Canterbury was sent by Saint Gregory the Great to England, Pope John Paul II, Bishop of Rome, and His Grace Robert Runcie, Archbishop of Canterbury, now meet again to pray together in order to give fresh impetus to the reconciling mission of God's people in a divided and broken world, and to review the obstacles which still impede closer communion between the Catholic Church and the Anglican Communion.

Our joint pilgrimage to the Church of Saint Gregory, with its historic association with Saint Augustine's mission to England, reminds us that the purpose of the Church is nothing other than the evangelisation of all peoples, nations and cultures, We give thanks together for the readiness and openness to receive the Gospel that is especially evident in the developing world, where young Christian communities joyfully embrace the faith of Jesus Christ and vigorously express a costly witness to the Gospel of the Kingdom in sacrificial living. The word of God is received, 'not as the word of man, but as what it really is, the word of God' (1 Thess 2.13). As we enter the last decade of the second millennium of the birth of Jesus Christ, we pray together for a new evangelisation throughout the world, not least in the continent of Saint Gregory and Saint Augustine where the progressive secularisation of society erodes the language of faith and where materialism demeans the spiritual nature of humankind.

It is in such a perspective that the urgent quest for Christian unity must be viewed, for the Lord Jesus Christ prayed for the unity of his disciples 'so that the world may believe' (Jn 17.21). Moreover Christian disunity has itself contributed to the tragedy of human division throughout the world. We pray for peace and justice, especially where religious differences are exploited for the increase of strife between communities of faith.

Against the background of human disunity the arduous journey to Christian unity must be pursued with determination and vigour, whatever obstacles are perceived to block the path. We here solemnly re-commit ourselves and those we represent to the restoration of visible unity and full ecclesial communion in the confidence that to seek anything less would be to betray our Lord's intention for the unity of his people.

This is by no means to be unrealistic about the difficulties facing our dialogue at the present time. When we established the Second

Anglican-Roman Catholic International Commission in Canterbury in 1982, we were well aware that the Commission's task would be far from easy. The convergences achieved within the report of the First Anglican-Roman Catholic International Commission have happily now been accepted by the Lambeth Conference of the bishops of the Anglican Communion. This report is currently also being studied by the Catholic Church with a view to responding to it. On the other hand, the question and practice of the admission of women to the ministerial priesthood in some Provinces of the Anglican Communion prevents reconciliation between us even where there is otherwise progress towards agreement in faith on the meaning of the Eucharist and the ordained ministry. These differences in faith reflect important ecclesiological differences and we urge the members of the Anglican-Roman Catholic International Commission and all others engaged in prayer and work for visible unity not to minimise these differences. At the same time we also urge them not to abandon either their hope or work for unity. At the beginning of the dialogue established here in Rome in 1966 by our beloved predecessors Pope Paul VI and Archbishop Michael Ramsey, no one saw clearly how long-inherited divisions would be overcome and how unity in faith might be achieved. No pilgrim knows in advance all the steps along the path. Saint Augustine of Canterbury set out from Rome with his band of monks for what was then a distant corner of the world. Yet Pope Gregory was soon to write of the baptism of the English and of 'such great miracles ... that they seemed to imitate the powers of the apostles' (Letter of Gregory the Great to Eulogius of Alexandria). While we ourselves do not see a solution to this obstacle, we are confident that through our engagement with this matter our conversations will in fact help to deepen and enlarge our understanding. We have this confidence because Christ promised that the Holy Spirit, who is the Spirit of Truth, will remain with us forever (cf. Jn 14.16–17).

We also urge our clergy and faithful not to neglect or undervalue that certain yet imperfect communion we already share. This communion already shared is grounded in faith in God our Father, in our Lord Jesus Christ, and in the Holy Spirit; our common baptism into Christ; our sharing of the Holy Scriptures, of the Apostles' and Nicene Creeds; the Chalcedonian definition and the teaching of the Fathers; our common Christian inheritance for many centuries. This communion should be cherished and guarded as we seek to grow into the fuller communion Christ wills. Even in the years of our separation we have been able to recognise gifts of the Spirit in each other. The ecumenical journey is not only about the removal of obstacles but also about the sharing of gifts.

As we meet together today we have also in our hearts those other Churches and Ecclesial Communities with whom we are in dialogue. As we have said once before in Canterbury, our aim extends to the fulfilment of God's will for the visible unity of all his people.

Nor is God's will for unity limited exclusively to Christians alone. Christian unity is demanded so that the Church can be a more effective sign of God's Kingdom of love and justice for all humanity. In fact, the Church is the sign and sacrament of the communion in Christ which God wills for the whole of his creation.

Such a vision elicits hope and patient determination, not despair or cynicism. And because such hope is a gift of the Holy Spirit we shall not be disappointed; for 'the power at work within us is able to do far more abundantly than all we ask or think. To him be glory in the Church and in Christ Jesus to all generations, for ever and ever. Amen' (Eph 3.20–21).

ROBERT CANTUAR
JOHN PAUL II

5. Common Declaration of 5 December 1996

The Common Declaration by Pope John Paul II and the Archbishop of Canterbury Dr George Carey December 5, 1996

Once again in the city of Rome an Archbishop of Canterbury, His Grace George Carey representing the Anglican Communion, and the Bishop of Rome, His Holiness Pope John Paul II have met together and joined in prayer.

Conscious that the second Christian millennium, now in its closing years, has seen division, even open hostility and strife between Christians, our fervent prayer has been for the grace of reconciliation. We have prayed earnestly for conversion—conversion to Christ and to one another in Christ. We have asked that Catholics and Anglicans may be granted the wisdom to know, and the strength to carry out, the Father's will. This will enable progress towards that full visible unity which is God's gift and our calling.

We have given thanks that in many parts of the world Anglicans and Catholics, joined in one baptism, recognise one another as brothers and sisters in Christ and give expression to this through joint prayer, common action and joint witness. This is a testimony to the communion we know we already share by God's mercy and demonstrates our intention that it should come to the fullness willed by Christ. We have given particular thanks for the spirit of faith in God's promises, persevering hope and mutual love which has inspired all who have worked for unity between the Anglican Communion and the Catholic Church since our predecessors Archbishop Michael Ramsey and Pope Paul VI met and prayed together. In the Church of Saint Gregory on the Celian Hill, we have remembered with gratitude the common heritage of Anglicans and Catholics rooted in the mission to the English people which Pope Gregory the Great entrusted to Saint Augustine of Canterbury.

For over twenty-five years a steady and painstaking international theological dialogue has been undertaken by the *Anglican–Roman Catholic International Commission* (ARCIC). We affirm the signs of progress provided in the statements of ARCIC I on the Eucharist and on the understanding of ministry and ordination, which have received an authoritative response from both partners of the dialogue. ARCIC II has produced further statements on salvation and the Church, the understanding of the Church as communion, and on the kind of life and fidelity to Christ we seek to share. These statements deserve to be more widely known. They require analysis, reflection and response. At present the International

346

Commission is seeking to further the convergence on authority in the Church. Without agreement in this area we shall not reach the full visible unity to which we are both committed. The obstacle to reconciliation caused by the ordination of women as priests and bishops in some provinces of the Anglican Communion has also become increasingly evident, creating a new situation. In view of this, it may be opportune at this stage in our journey to consult further about how the relationship between the Anglican Communion and the Catholic Church is to progress. At the same time, we encourage ARCIC to continue and deepen our theological dialogue, not only over issues connected with our present difficulties but also in all areas where full agreement has still to be reached.

We are called to preach the Gospel, urging it 'in season and out of season' (2 Tim 4.2). In many parts of the world Anglicans and Catholics attempt to witness together in the face of growing secularism, religious apathy and moral confusion. Whenever they are able to give united witness to the Gospel they must do so, for our divisions obscure the Gospel message of reconciliation and hope. We urge our people to make full use of the possibilities already available to them, for example in the Catholic Church's *Directory for the Application of Principles and Norms on Ecumenism* (1993). We call on them to repent of the past, to pray for the grace of unity and to open themselves to God's transforming power, and to cooperate in all appropriate ways at local, national and provincial levels. We pray that the spirit of dialogue may prevail which will contribute to reconciliation and prevent new difficulties from emerging. Whenever actions take place which show signs of an attitude of proselytism they prevent our common witness and must be eliminated.

We look forward to the celebration of 2000 years since the Word become flesh and dwelt among us (cf. Jn 1.14). This is an opportunity to proclaim afresh our common faith in God who loved the world so much that he sent his Son, not to condemn the world but so that the world might be saved through him (cf. Jn 3.16–17). We encourage Anglicans and Catholics, with all their Christian brothers and sisters, to pray, celebrate and witness together in the year 2000. We make this call in a spirit of humility, recognising that credible witness will only be fully given when Anglicans and Catholics, with all their Christian brothers and sisters, have achieved that full, visible unity that corresponds to Christ's prayer 'that they may all be one' so that the world may believe' (Jn 17.21).

GEORGE CANTUAR
JOHN PAUL II

6. Common Declaration of 23 November 2006

Common Declaration of the Archbishop of Canterbury Rowan Williams and Pope Benedict XVI. The Vatican, 23 November 2006

Forty years ago, our predecessors, Pope Paul VI and Archbishop Michael Ramsey, met together in this city sanctified by the ministry and the blood of the Apostles Peter and Paul. They began a new journey of reconciliation based on the Gospels and the ancient common traditions. Centuries of estrangement between Anglicans and Catholics were replaced by a new desire for partnership and cooperation, as the real but incomplete communion we share was rediscovered and affirmed. Pope Paul VI and Archbishop Ramsey undertook at that time to establish a dialogue in which matters which had been divisive in the past might be addressed from a fresh perspective with truth and love.

Since that meeting, the Roman Catholic Church and the Anglican Communion have entered into a process of fruitful dialogue, which has been marked by the discovery of significant elements of shared faith and a desire to give expression, through joint prayer, witness and service, to that which we hold in common. Over thirty-five years, the *Anglican–Roman Catholic International Commission* (ARCIC) has produced a number of important documents which seek to articulate the faith we share. In the ten years since the most recent Common Declaration was signed by the Pope and the Archbishop of Canterbury, the second phase of ARCIC has completed its mandate, with the publication of the documents *The Gift of Authority* (1999) and *Mary: Grace and Hope in Christ* (2005). We are grateful to the theologians who have prayed and worked together in the preparation of these texts, which await further study and reflection.

True ecumenism goes beyond theological dialogue; it touches our spiritual lives and our common witness. As our dialogue has developed, many Catholics and Anglicans have found in each other a love for Christ which invites us into practical cooperation and service. This fellowship in the service of Christ, experienced by many of our communities around the world, adds a further impetus to our relationship. The *International Anglican–Roman Catholic Commission for Unity and Mission* (IARCCUM) has been engaged in an exploration of the appropriate ways in which our shared mission to proclaim new life in Christ to the world can be advanced and nurtured. Their report, which sets out both a summary of the central conclusions of ARCIC and makes proposals for growing together in mission and witness, has recently been completed and submitted for review to the Anglican Communion Office and the Pontifical Council for Promoting Christian Unity, and we express our gratitude for their work.

In this fraternal visit, we celebrate the good which has come from these four decades of dialogue. We are grateful to God for the gifts of grace which have accompanied them. At the same time, our long journey together makes it necessary to acknowledge publicly the challenge represented by new developments which, besides being divisive for Anglicans, present serious obstacles to our ecumenical progress. It is a matter of urgency, therefore, that in renewing our commitment to pursue the path towards full visible communion in the truth and love of Christ, we also commit ourselves in our continuing dialogue to address the important issues involved in the emerging ecclesiological and ethical factors making that journey more difficult and arduous.

As Christian leaders facing the challenges of the new millennium, we affirm again our public commitment to the revelation of divine life uniquely set forth by God in the divinity and humanity of Our Lord Jesus Christ. We believe that it is through Christ and the means of salvation found in him that healing and reconciliation are offered to us and to the world.

There are many areas of witness and service in which we can stand together, and which indeed call for closer cooperation between us: the pursuit of peace in the Holy Land and in other parts of the world marred by conflict and the threat of terrorism; promoting respect for life from conception until natural death; protecting the sanctity of marriage and the well-being of children in the context of healthy family life; outreach to the poor, oppressed and the most vulnerable, especially those who are persecuted for their faith; addressing the negative effects of materialism; and care for creation and for our environment. We also commit ourselves to inter-religious dialogue through which we can jointly reach out to our non-Christian brothers and sisters.

Mindful of our forty years of dialogue, and of the witness of the holy men and women common to our traditions, including Mary the *Theotókos*, Saints Peter and Paul, Benedict, Gregory the Great, and Augustine of Canterbury, we pledge ourselves to more fervent prayer and a more dedicated endeavour to welcome and live by that truth into which the Spirit of the Lord wishes to lead his disciples (cf. Jn 16.13).

Confident of the apostolic hope 'that he who has begun this good work in you will bring it to completion' (cf. Phil 1:6), we believe that if we can together be God's instruments in calling all Christians to a deeper obedience to our Lord, we will also draw closer to each other, finding in his will the fullness of unity and common life to which he invites us.

Rowan Cantuar
Benedict XVI